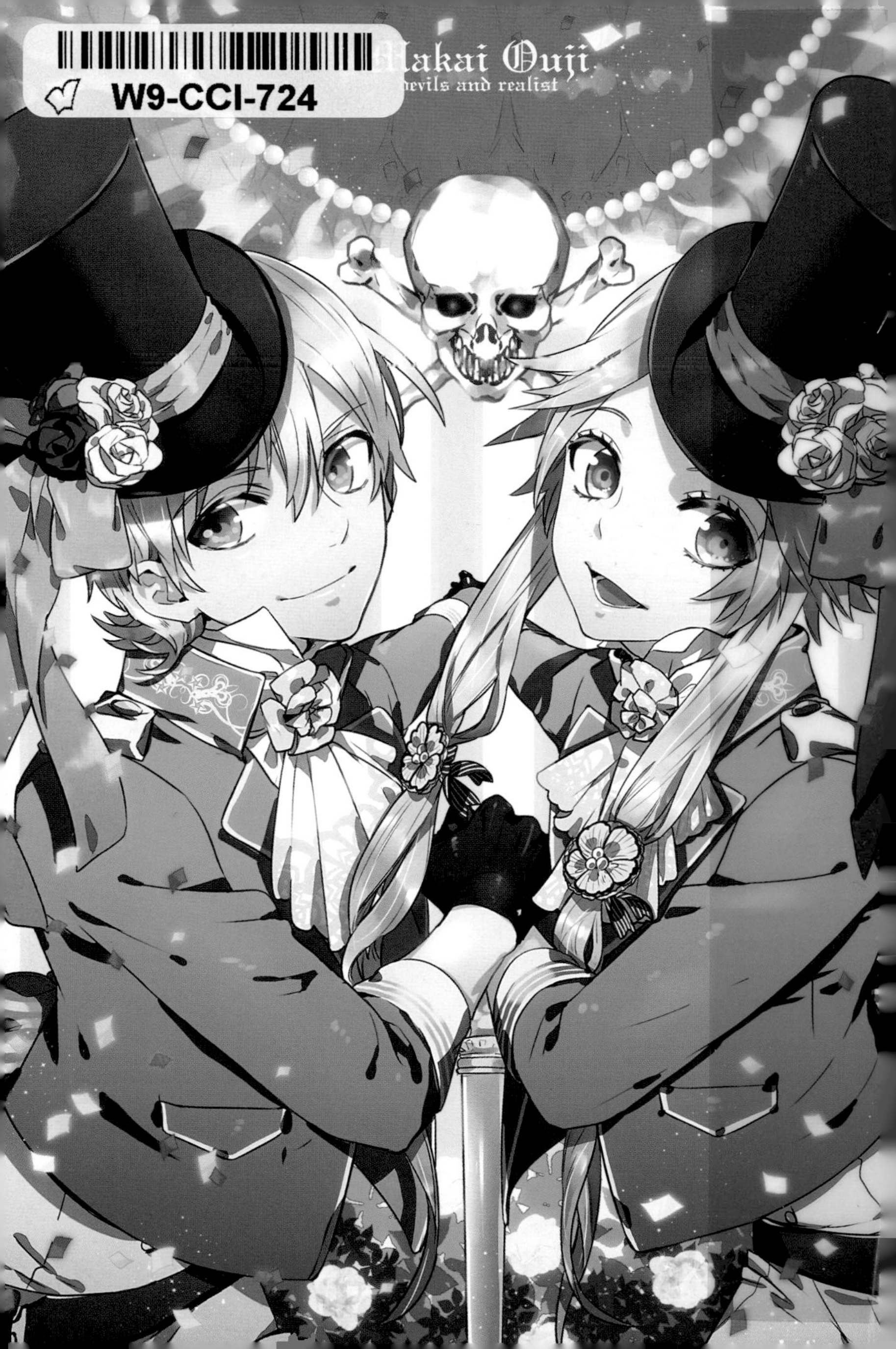
akai Ouji
devils and realist

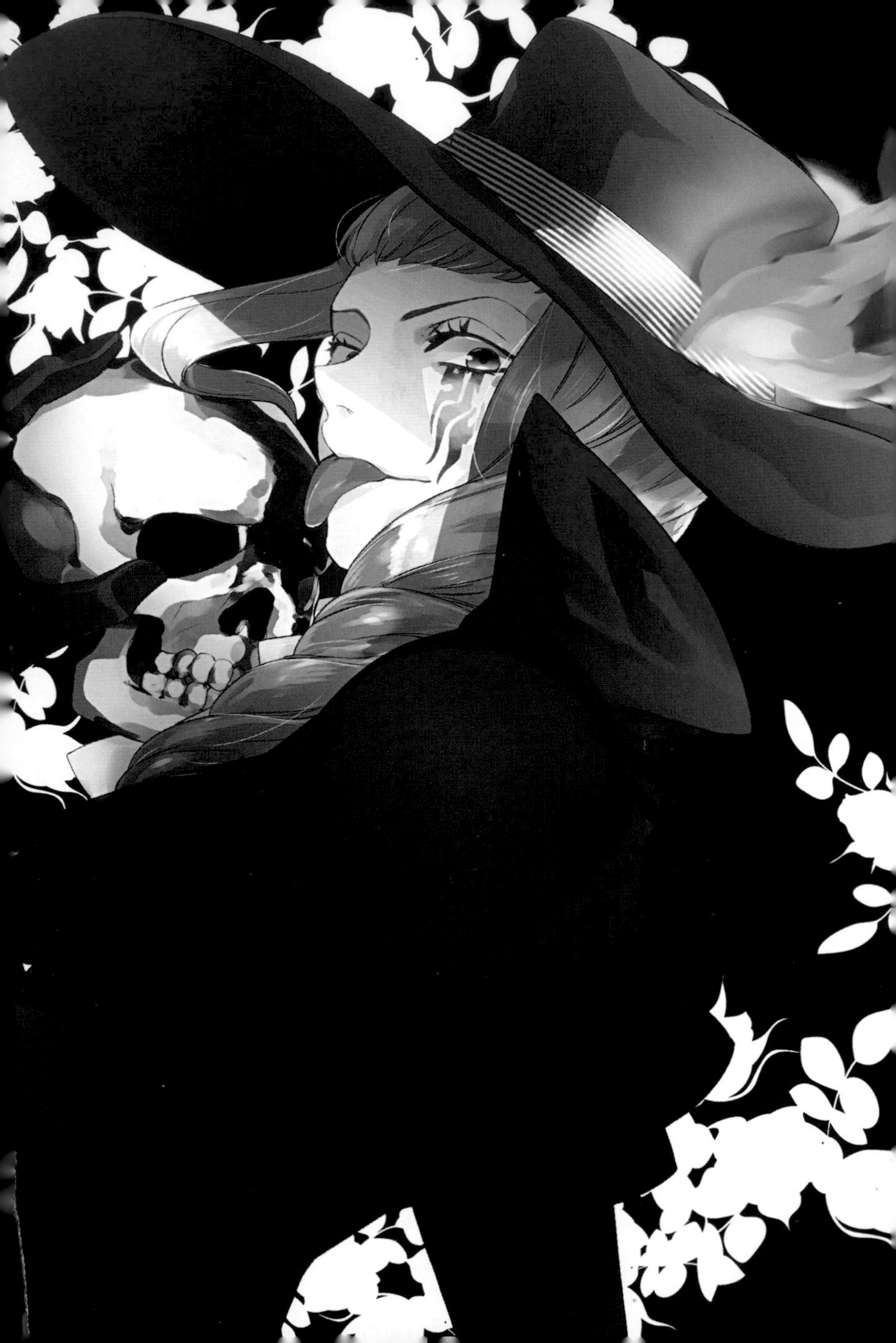

Devils and Realist
vol. 8

story by Madoka Takadono
art by Utako Yukihiro

Cast of Characters

Camio

A candidate for representative king, Camio is Solomon's 53rd pillar and a Great President of Hell. He is an excellent student at school and serves as class representative.

William

A brilliant realist from a famous noble family. As the descendant of King Solomon, he is the Elector with the authority to choose the representative of the king of Hell. He is slowly beginning to accept this role.

Kevin

William's capable yet gambling-addicted butler, who is also the pastor at the academy. In truth, he is the angel Uriel, who has been dispatched from Heaven.

Sytry

A candidate for representative king, Camio is Solomon's 53rd pillar and a Great President of Hell. He is an excellent student at school and serves as class representative.

Dantalion

Seventy-first Pillar of Hell who commands its leading 36 armies. He is Grand Duke of the Underworld and a candidate to represent the king. At school, students rely on him during sporting events.

Metatron

An angel with enormous power. He encourages Uriel to join him in a heavenly conspiracy to convince Michael to go to sleep.

The Story So Far

Demons Dantalion and Sytry appear suddenly before impoverished noble William Twining to tell him that he is the Elector who will determine the representative king of Hell. The two of them masquerade as students, and William lives a life more and more entangled with the doings of Hell. While all this is going on, the War of the Roses begins at school, and Isaac challenges William to a magic duel. When Dantalion is summoned by Isaac, Sytry presses him about the secret of King Solomon's death in the past. Eventually, the War of the Roses ends in defeat for William's side. In the shadows, a movement starts that will lay bare Kevin's true identity...

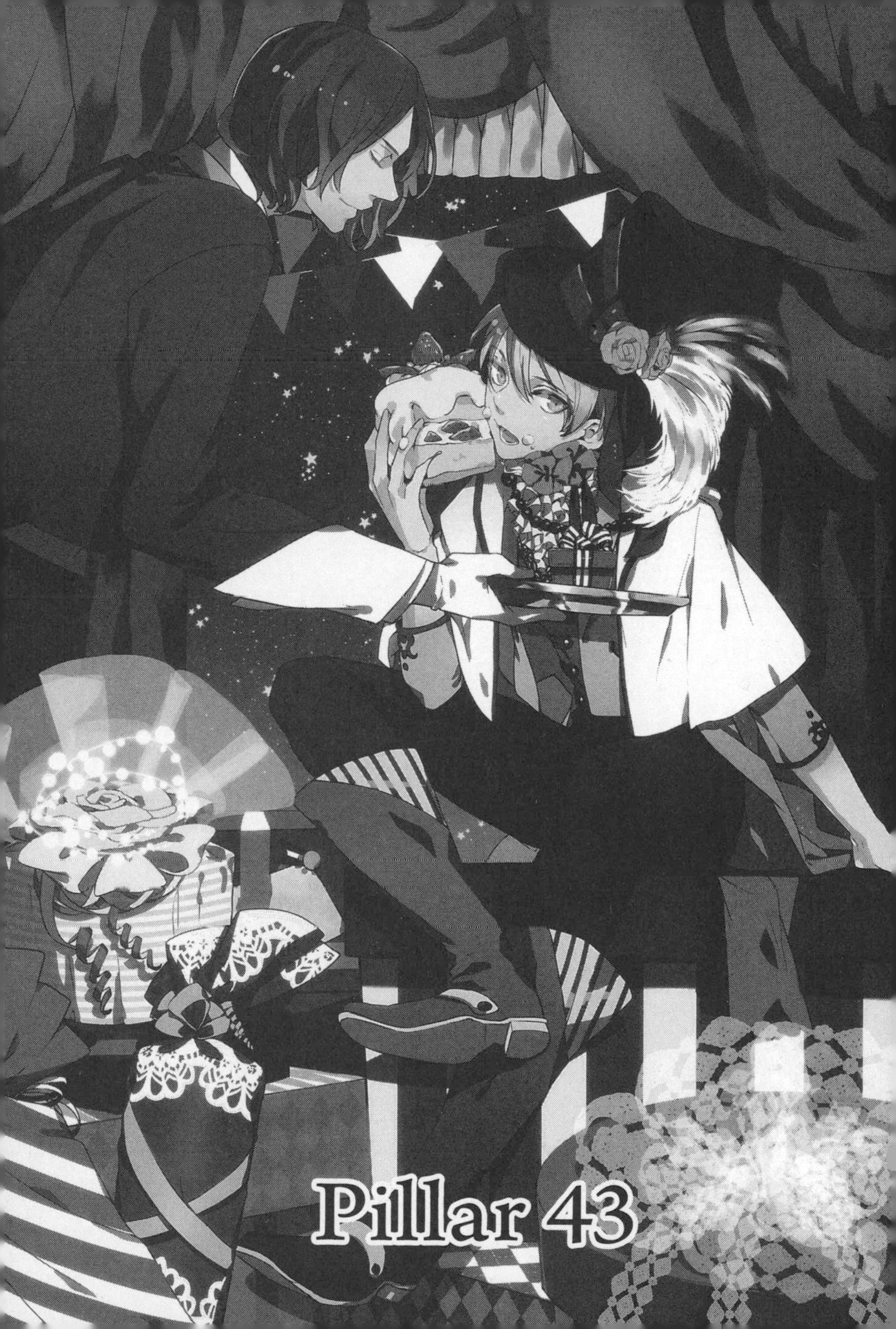
Pillar 43

I'M THE ONE TAKING THE REINS IN THIS WORLD!

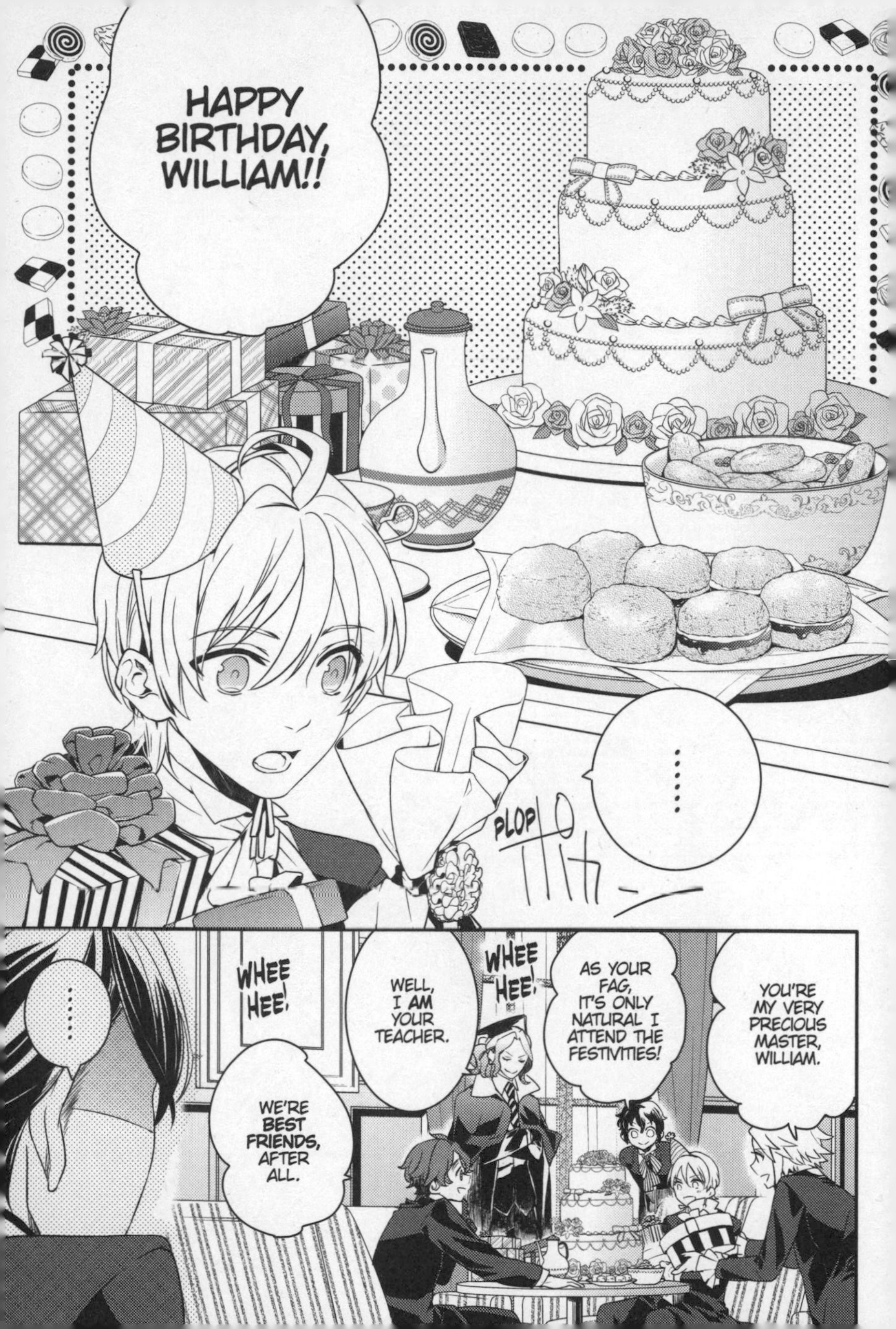
HAPPY BIRTHDAY, WILLIAM!!
......
PLOP
YOU'RE MY VERY PRECIOUS MASTER, WILLIAM.
AS YOUR FAG, IT'S ONLY NATURAL I ATTEND THE FESTIVITIES!
WHEE HEE!
WELL, I AM YOUR TEACHER.
WHEE HEE!
WE'RE BEST FRIENDS, AFTER ALL.
......

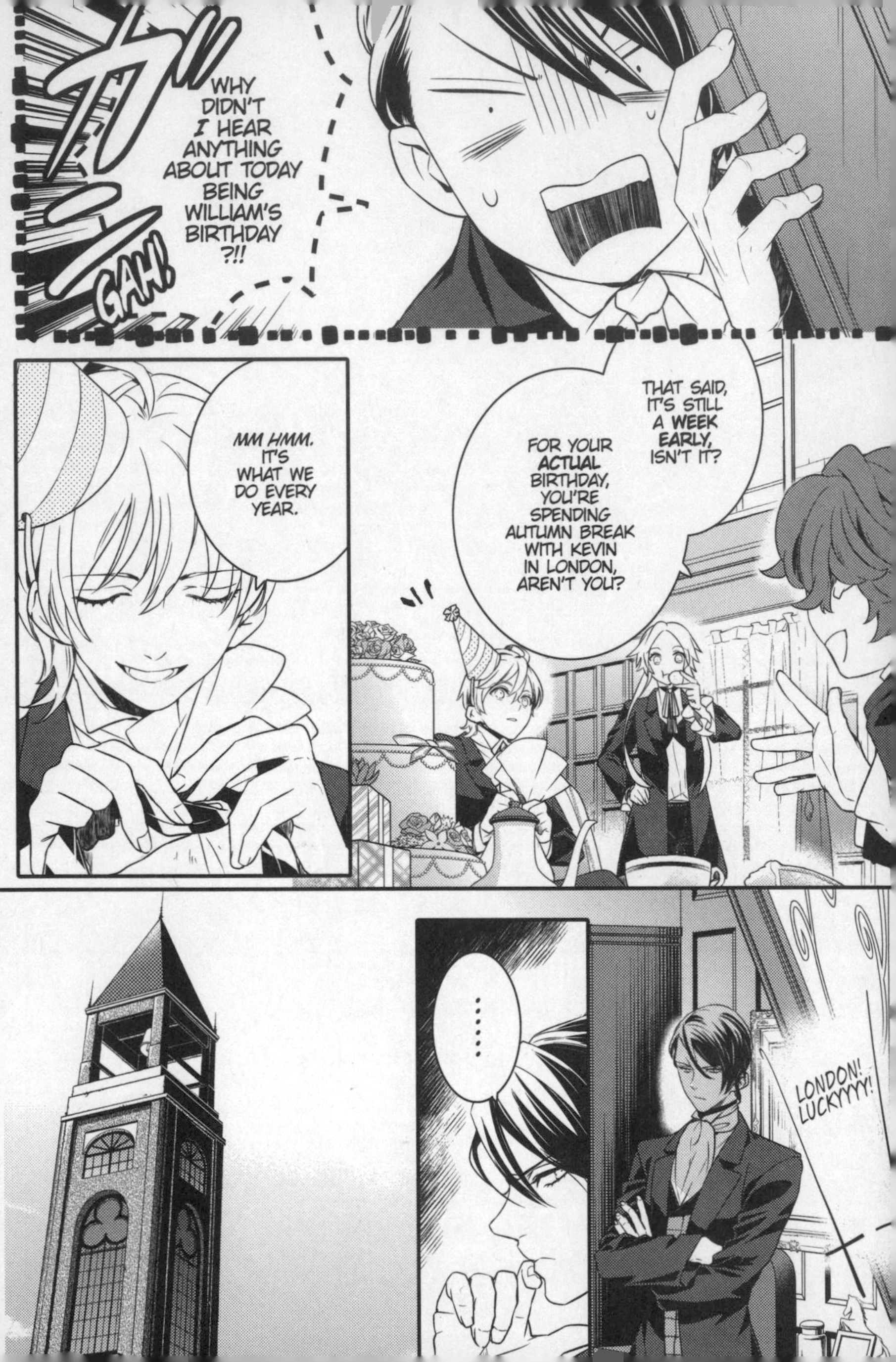
GAH!
WHY DIDN'T I HEAR ANYTHING ABOUT TODAY BEING WILLIAM'S BIRTHDAY ?!!
THAT SAID, IT'S STILL A WEEK EARLY, ISN'T IT?
FOR YOUR ACTUAL BIRTHDAY, YOU'RE SPENDING AUTUMN BREAK WITH KEVIN IN LONDON, AREN'T YOU?
MM HMM. IT'S WHAT WE DO EVERY YEAR.
LONDON! LUCKYYYY!
......

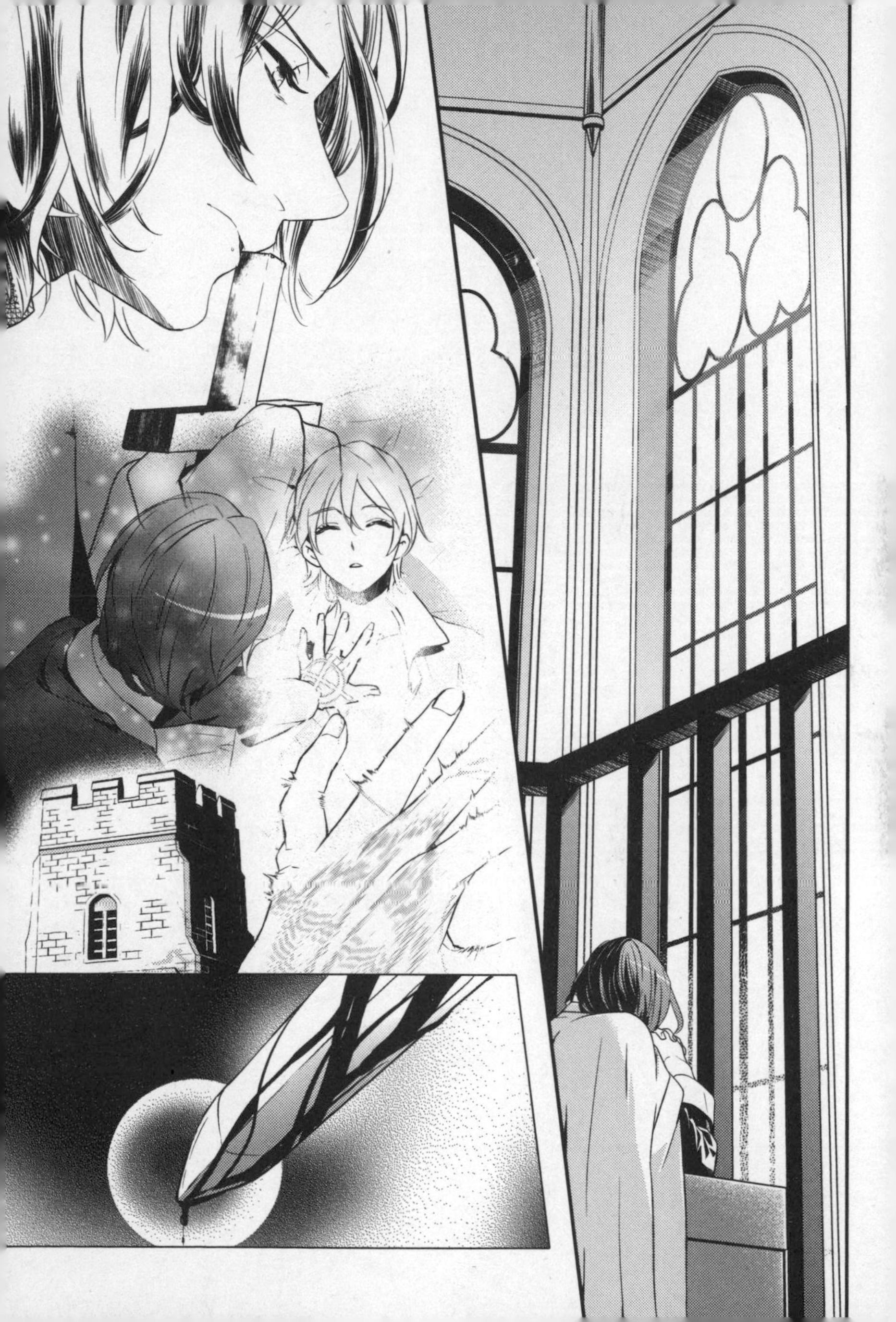

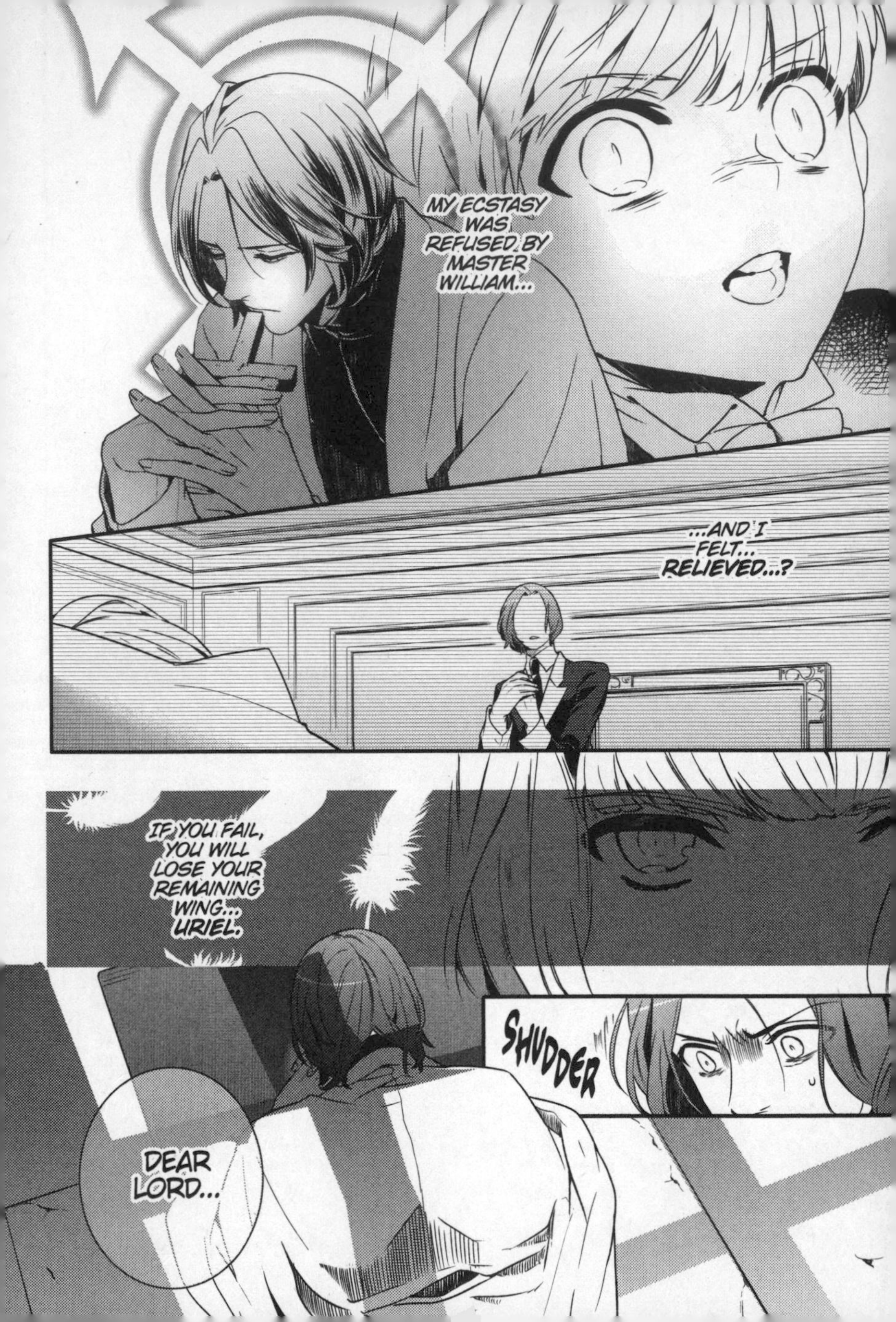
MY ECSTASY WAS REFUSED BY MASTER WILLIAM...
...AND I FELT... RELIEVED...?
IF YOU FAIL, YOU WILL LOSE YOUR REMAINING WING... URIEL.
SHUDDER
DEAR LORD...

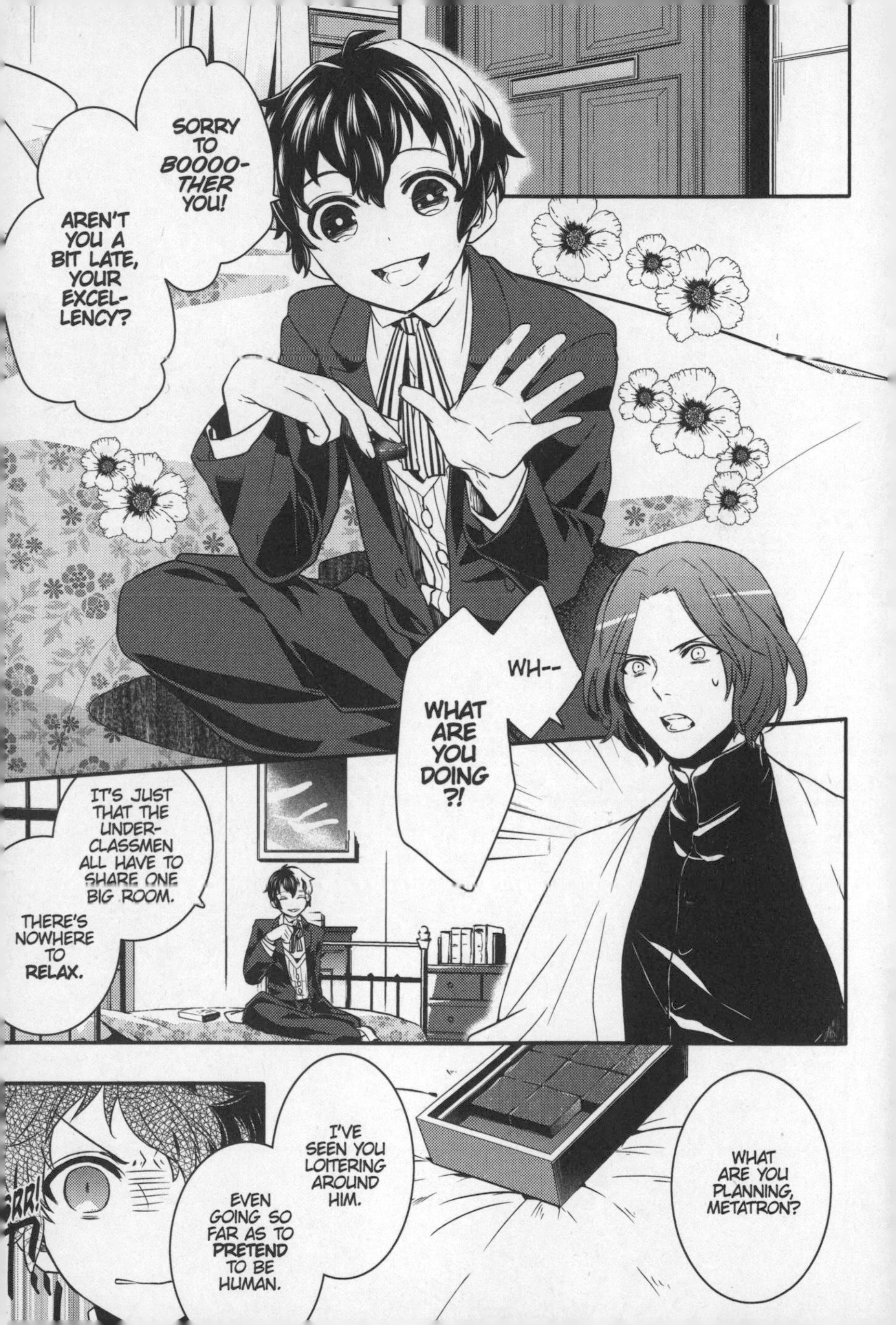
SORRY TO BOOOO-THER YOU!
AREN'T YOU A BIT LATE, YOUR EXCEL-LENCY?
WH--
WHAT ARE YOU DOING ?!
IT'S JUST THAT THE UNDER-CLASSMEN ALL HAVE TO SHARE ONE BIG ROOM.
THERE'S NOWHERE TO RELAX.
WHAT ARE YOU PLANNING, METATRON?
I'VE SEEN YOU LOITERING AROUND HIM.
EVEN GOING SO FAR AS TO PRETEND TO BE HUMAN.

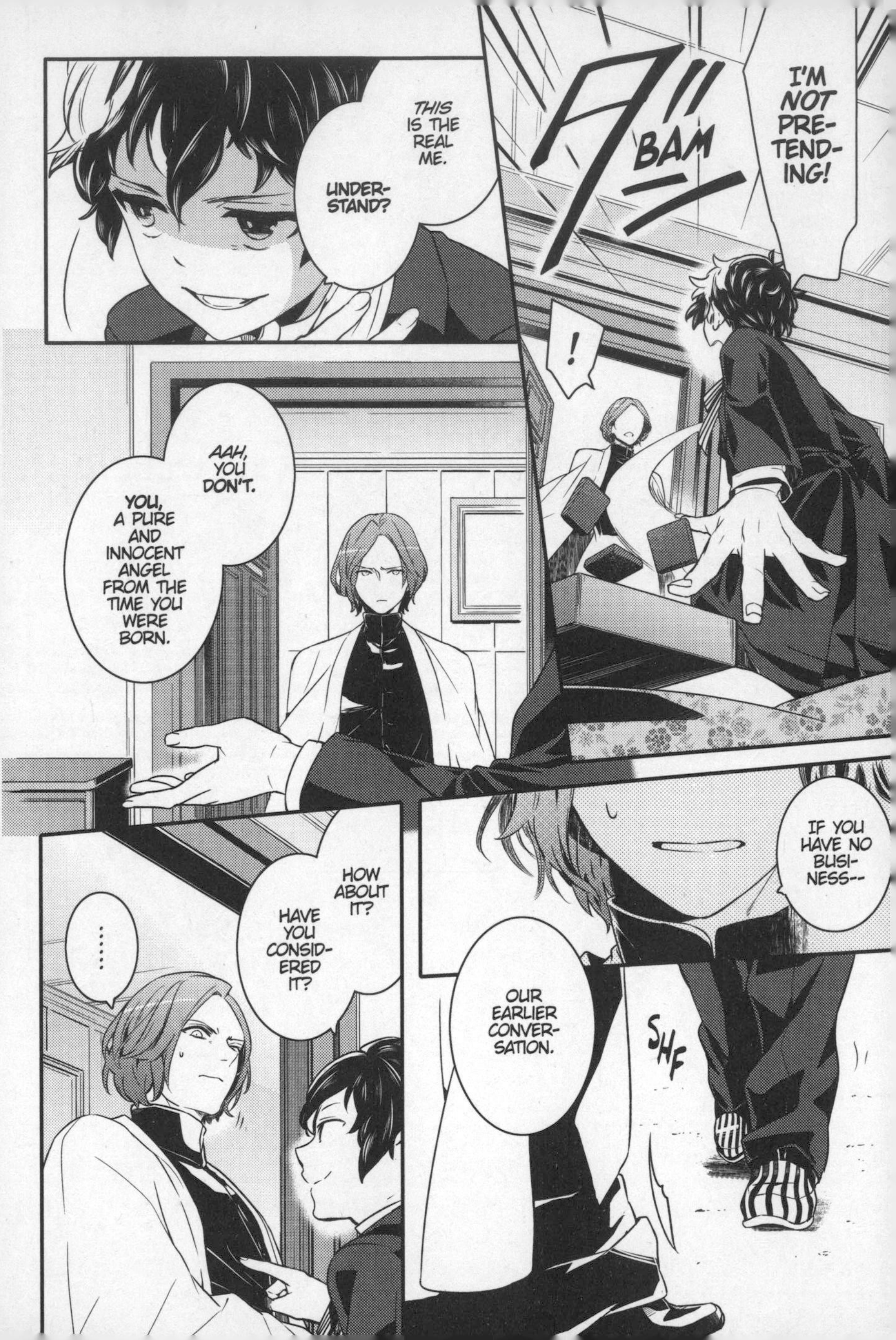
I'M NOT PRETENDING!
BAM
!
THIS IS THE REAL ME.
UNDERSTAND?
AAH, YOU DON'T.
YOU, A PURE AND INNOCENT ANGEL FROM THE TIME YOU WERE BORN.
IF YOU HAVE NO BUSINESS--
OUR EARLIER CONVERSATION.
SHF
HOW ABOUT IT?
HAVE YOU CONSIDERED IT?
......

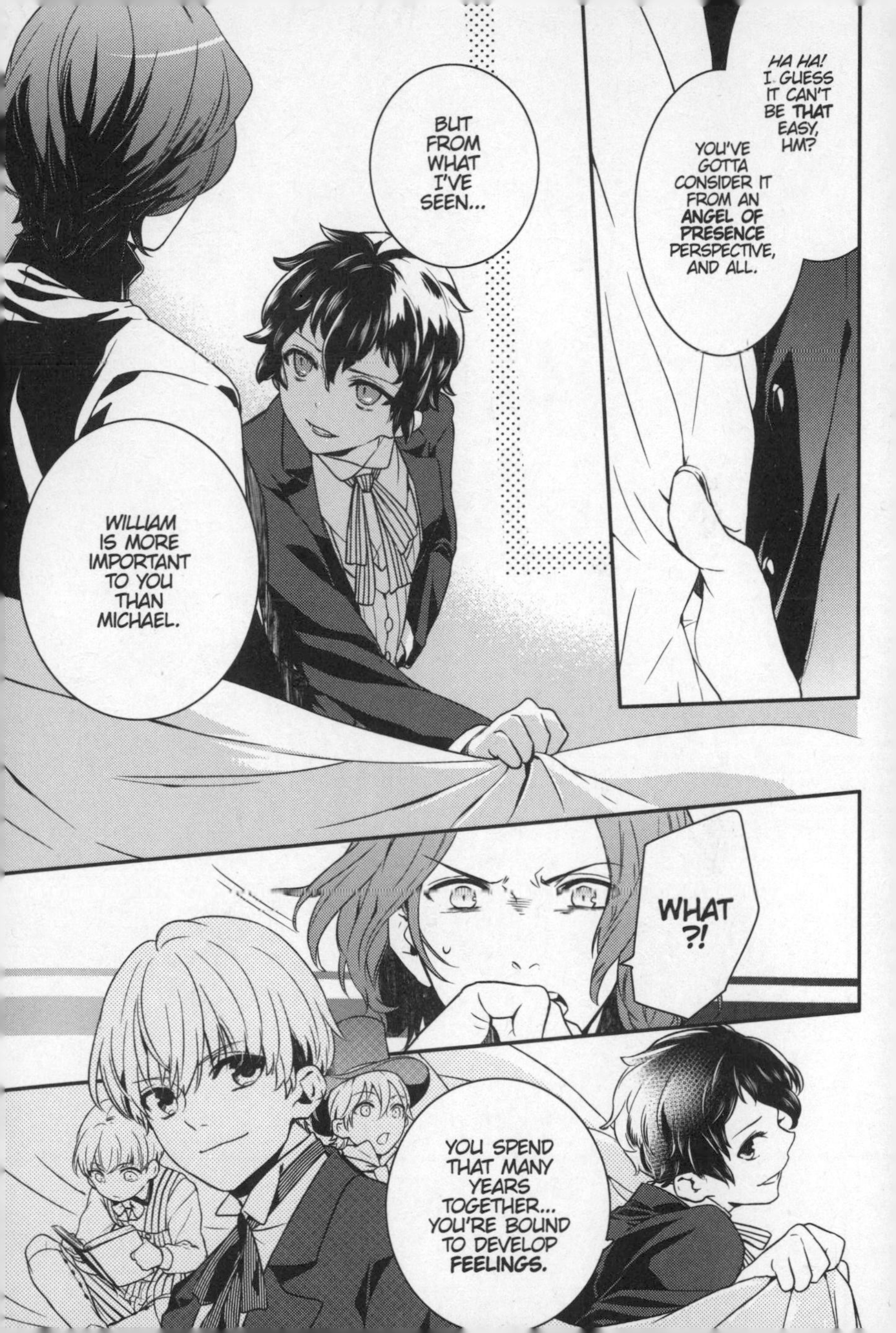
HA HA! I GUESS IT CAN'T BE THAT EASY, HM?
YOU'VE GOTTA CONSIDER IT FROM AN ANGEL OF PRESENCE PERSPECTIVE, AND ALL.
BUT FROM WHAT I'VE SEEN...
WILLIAM IS MORE IMPORTANT TO YOU THAN MICHAEL.
WHAT?!
YOU SPEND THAT MANY YEARS TOGETHER... YOU'RE BOUND TO DEVELOP FEELINGS.

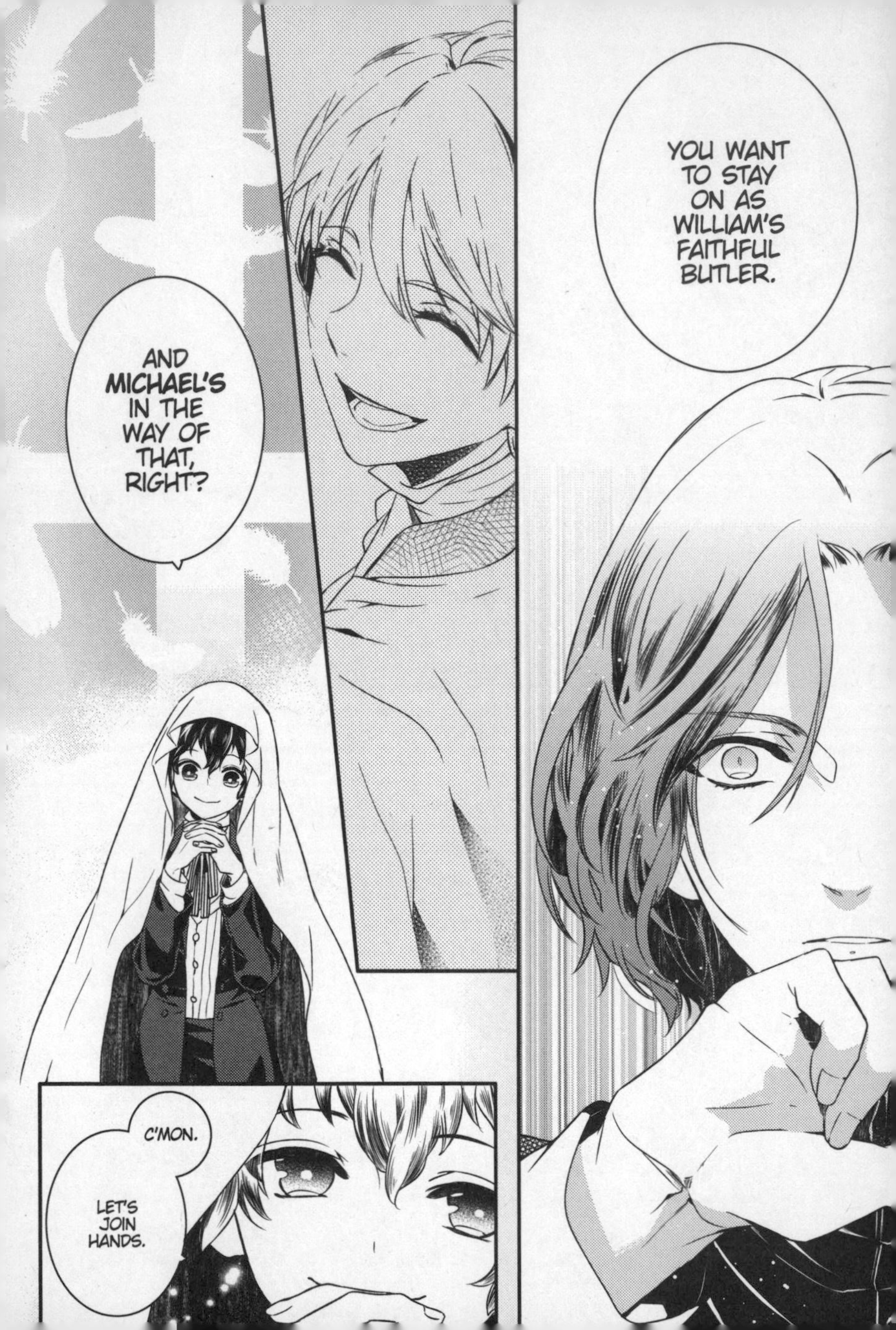
YOU WANT TO STAY ON AS WILLIAM'S FAITHFUL BUTLER.
AND MICHAEL'S IN THE WAY OF THAT, RIGHT?
C'MON.
LET'S JOIN HANDS.

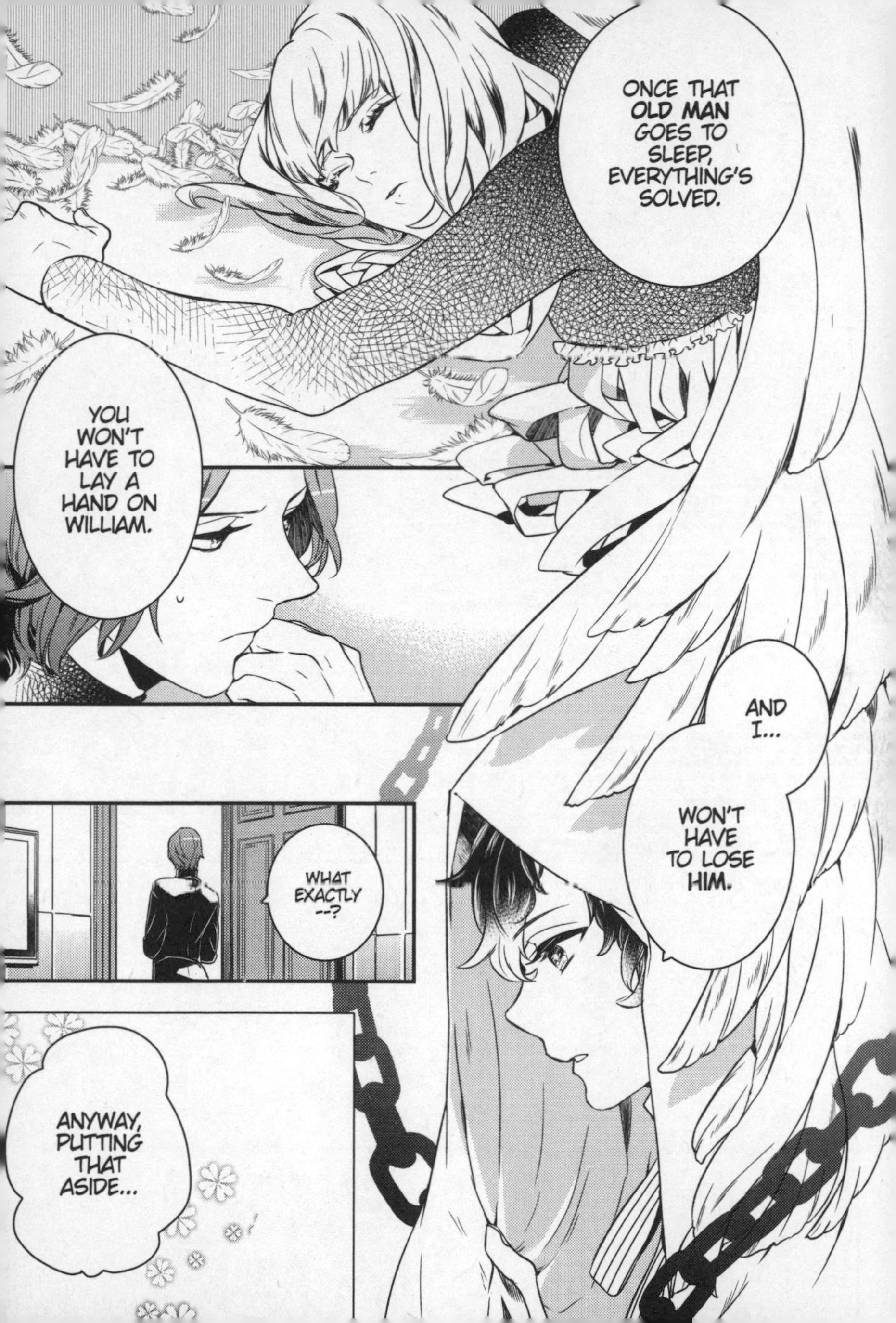
ONCE THAT OLD MAN GOES TO SLEEP, EVERYTHING'S SOLVED.
YOU WON'T HAVE TO LAY A HAND ON WILLIAM.
AND I...
WON'T HAVE TO LOSE HIM.
WHAT EXACTLY --?
ANYWAY, PUTTING THAT ASIDE...

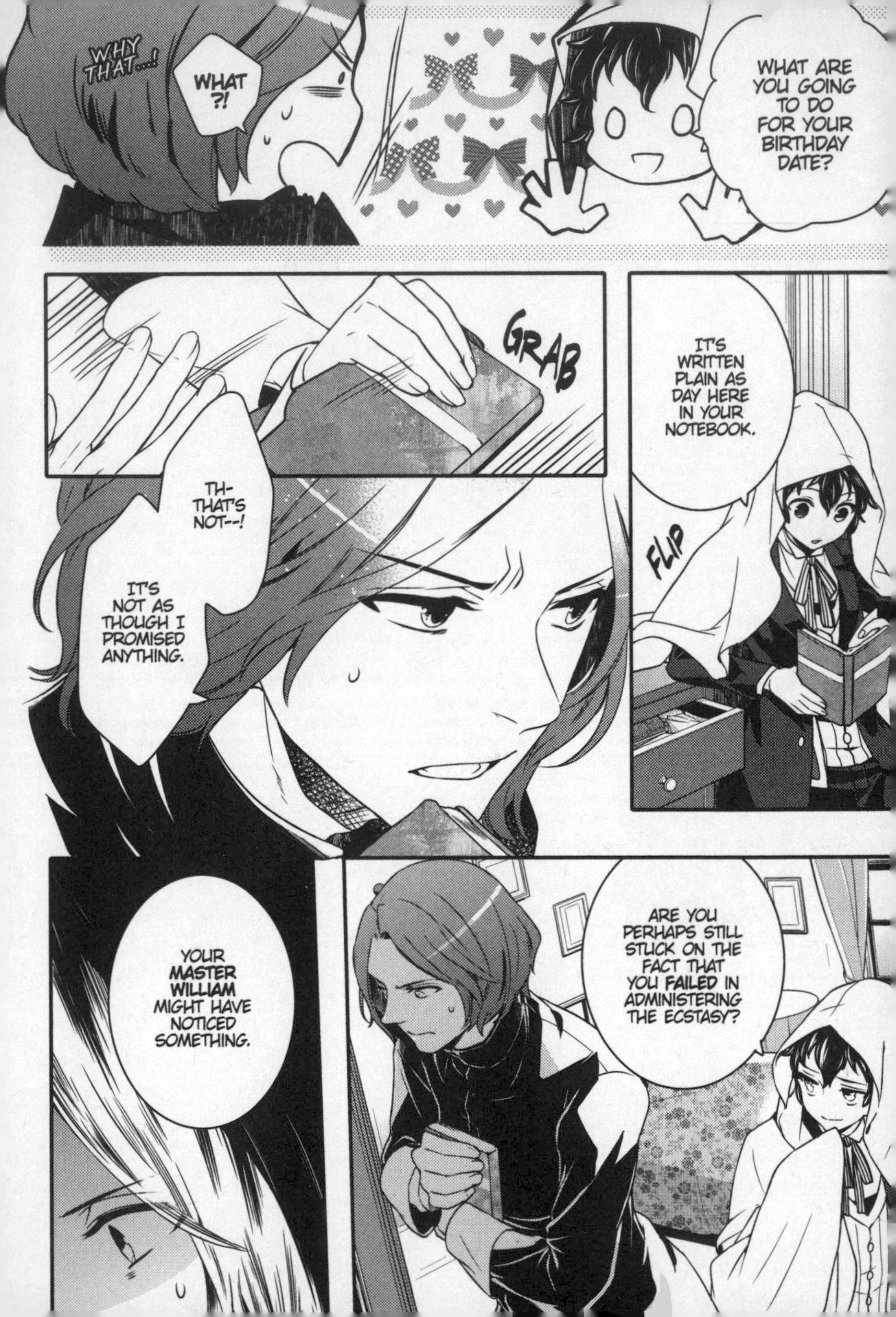
WHAT ARE YOU GOING TO DO FOR YOUR BIRTHDAY DATE?
WHAT ?!
WHY THAT...!
IT'S WRITTEN PLAIN AS DAY HERE IN YOUR NOTEBOOK.
FLIP
GRAB
TH-THAT'S NOT--!
IT'S NOT AS THOUGH I PROMISED ANYTHING.
ARE YOU PERHAPS STILL STUCK ON THE FACT THAT YOU FAILED IN ADMINISTERING THE ECSTASY?
YOUR MASTER WILLIAM MIGHT HAVE NOTICED SOMETHING.

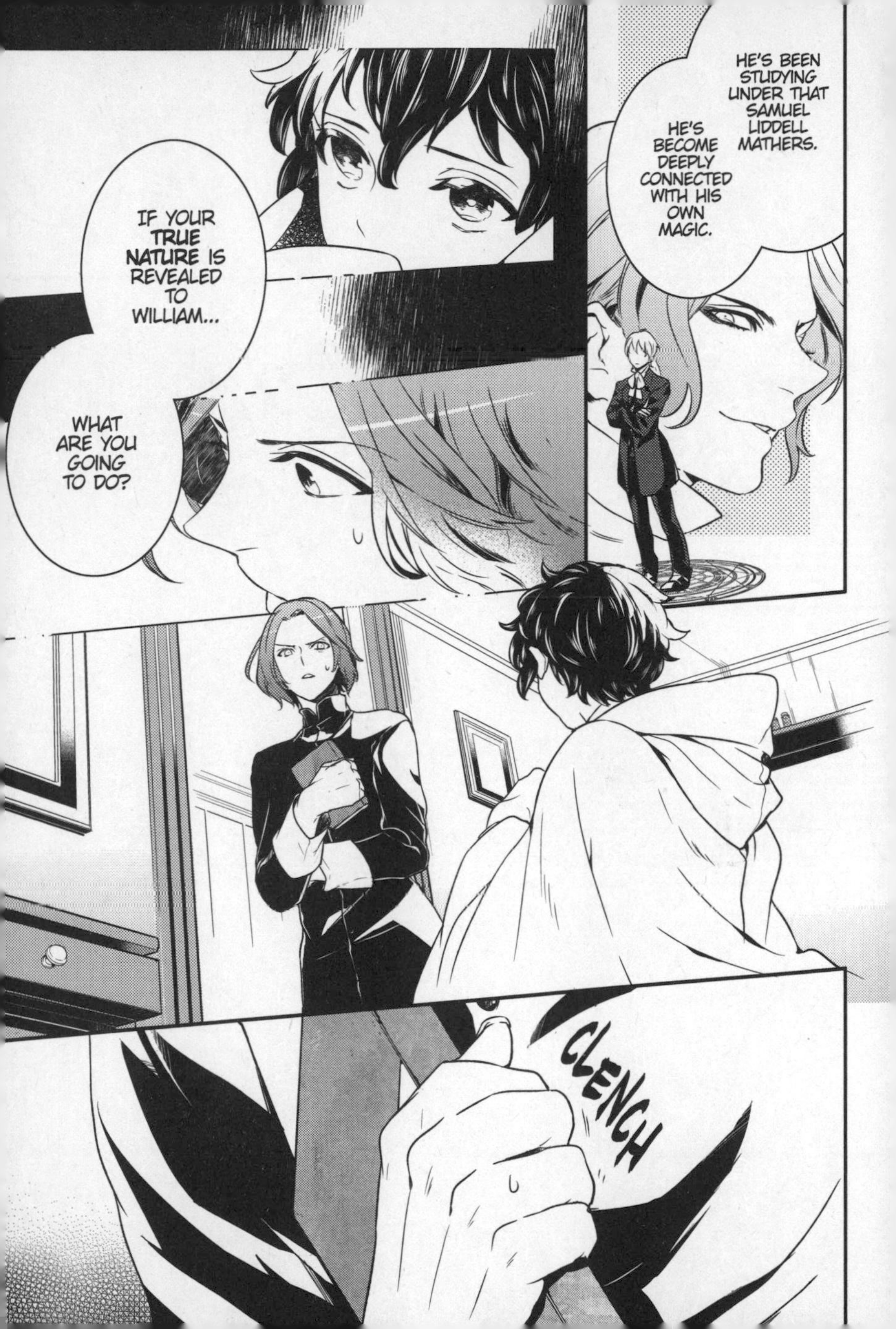
HE'S BEEN STUDYING UNDER THAT SAMUEL LIDDELL MATHERS.
HE'S BECOME DEEPLY CONNECTED WITH HIS OWN MAGIC.
IF YOUR TRUE NATURE IS REVEALED TO WILLIAM...
WHAT ARE YOU GOING TO DO?
CLENCH

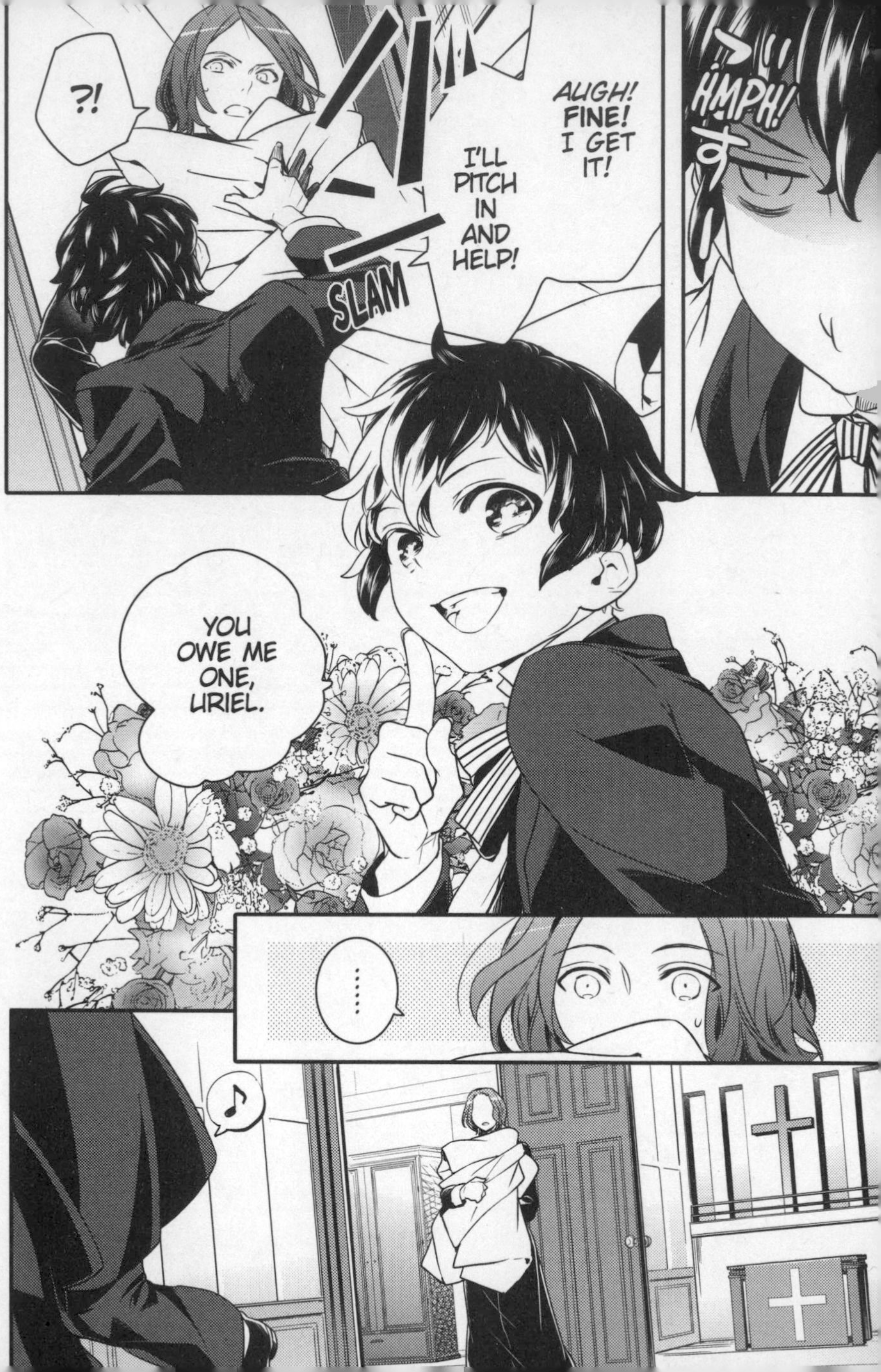
HMPH!
す
AUGH! FINE! I GET IT!
I'LL PITCH IN AND HELP!
SLAM
?!
YOU OWE ME ONE, URIEL.
......
♪

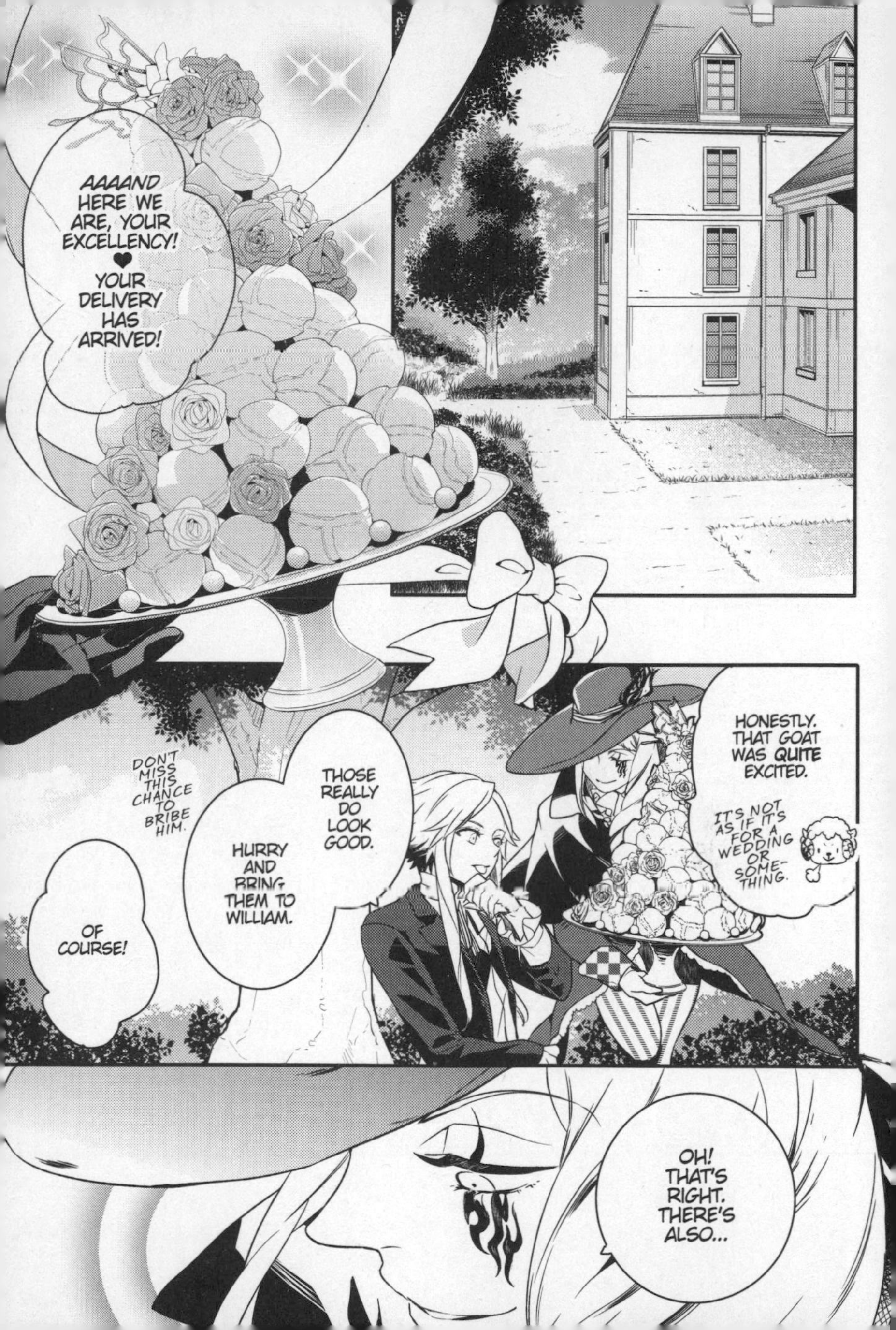
AAAAND HERE WE ARE, YOUR EXCELLENCY! ❤ YOUR DELIVERY HAS ARRIVED!
HONESTLY. THAT GOAT WAS QUITE EXCITED.
IT'S NOT AS IF IT'S FOR A WEDDING OR SOMETHING.
THOSE REALLY DO LOOK GOOD.
HURRY AND BRING THEM TO WILLIAM.
DON'T MISS THIS CHANCE TO BRIBE HIM.
OF COURSE!
OH! THAT'S RIGHT. THERE'S ALSO...

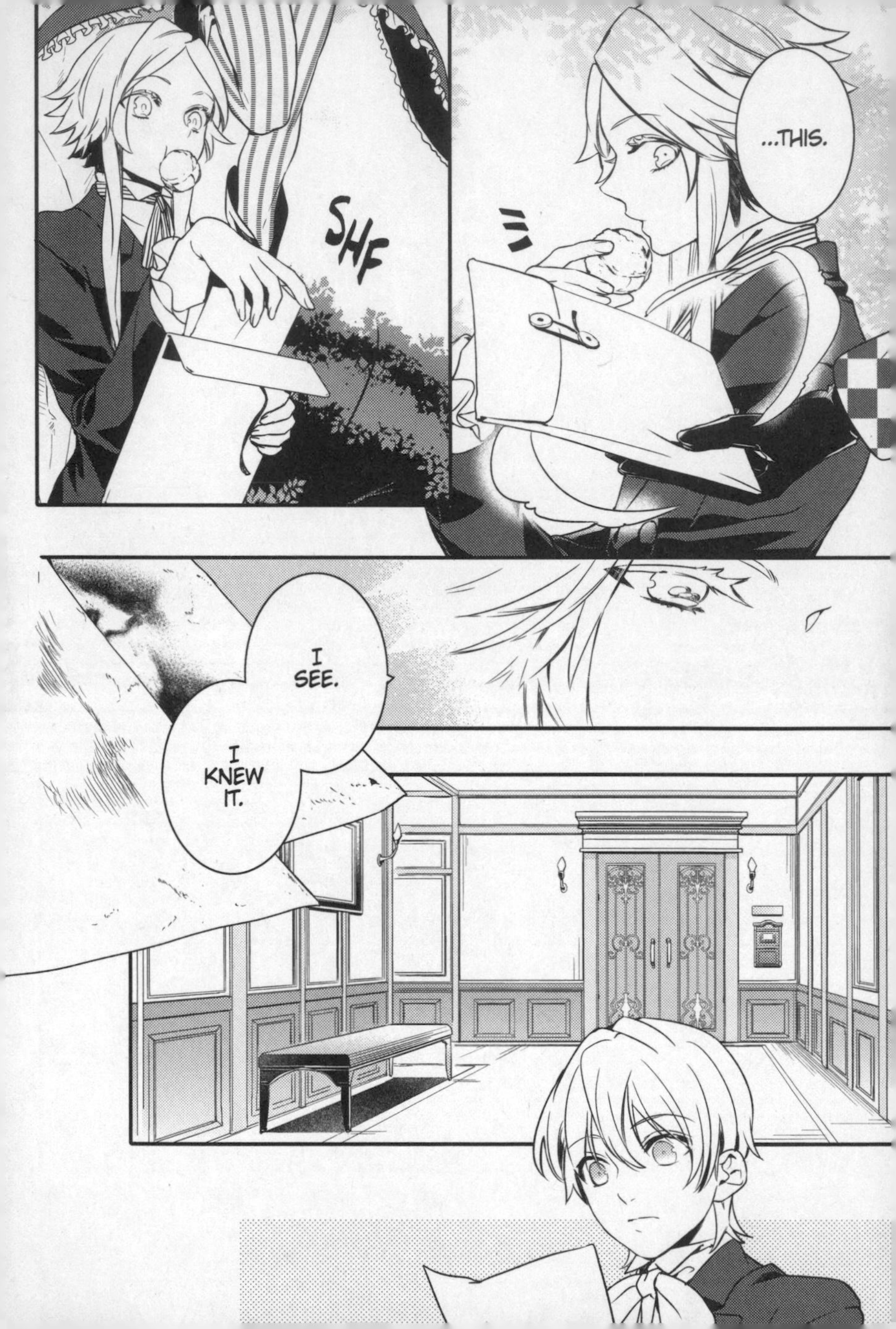
...THIS.
SHF
I SEE.
I KNEW IT.

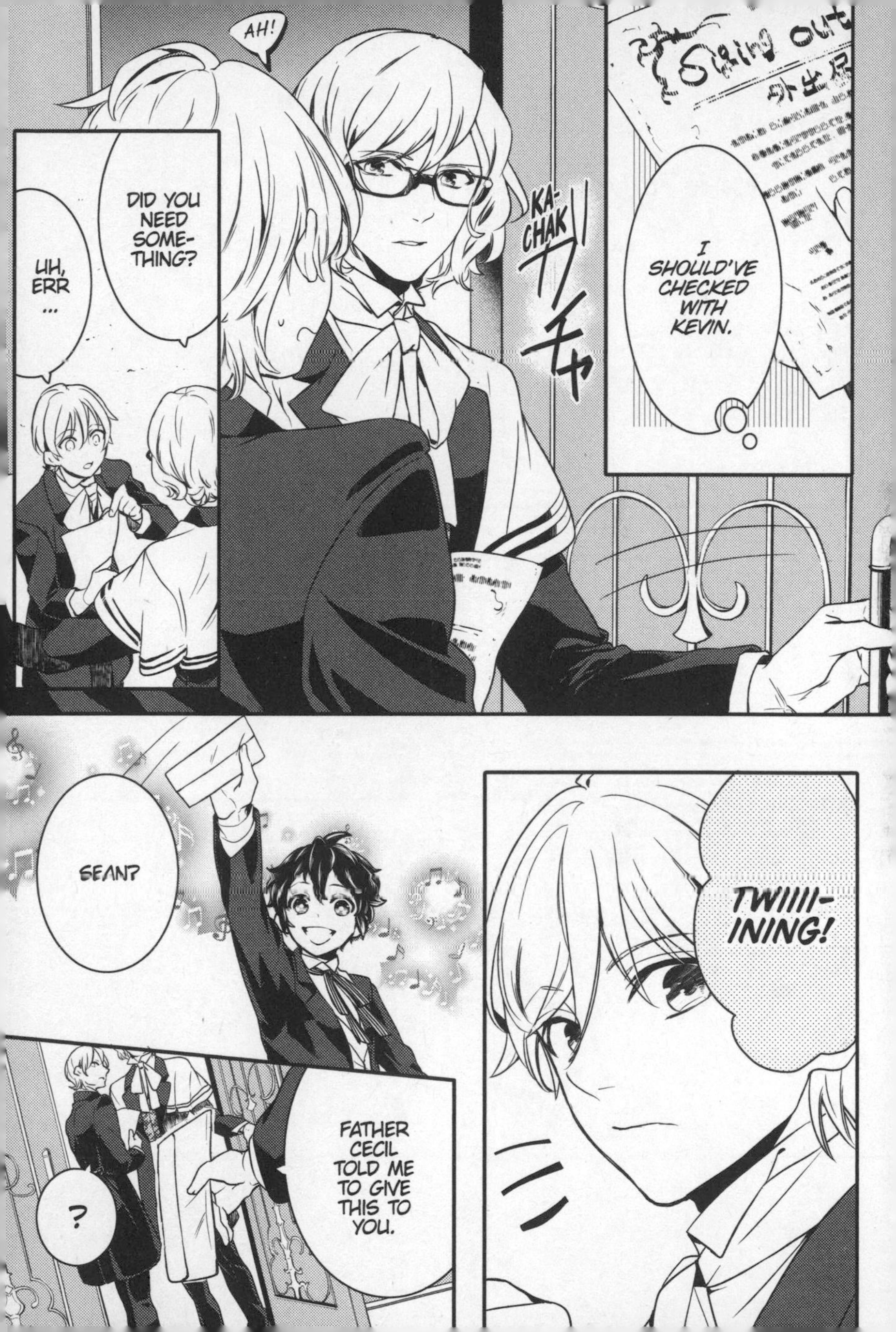
I SHOULD'VE CHECKED WITH KEVIN.
KA-CHAK
AH!
DID YOU NEED SOME-THING?
UH, ERR ...
TWIIII-INING!
SEAN?
FATHER CECIL TOLD ME TO GIVE THIS TO YOU.
?

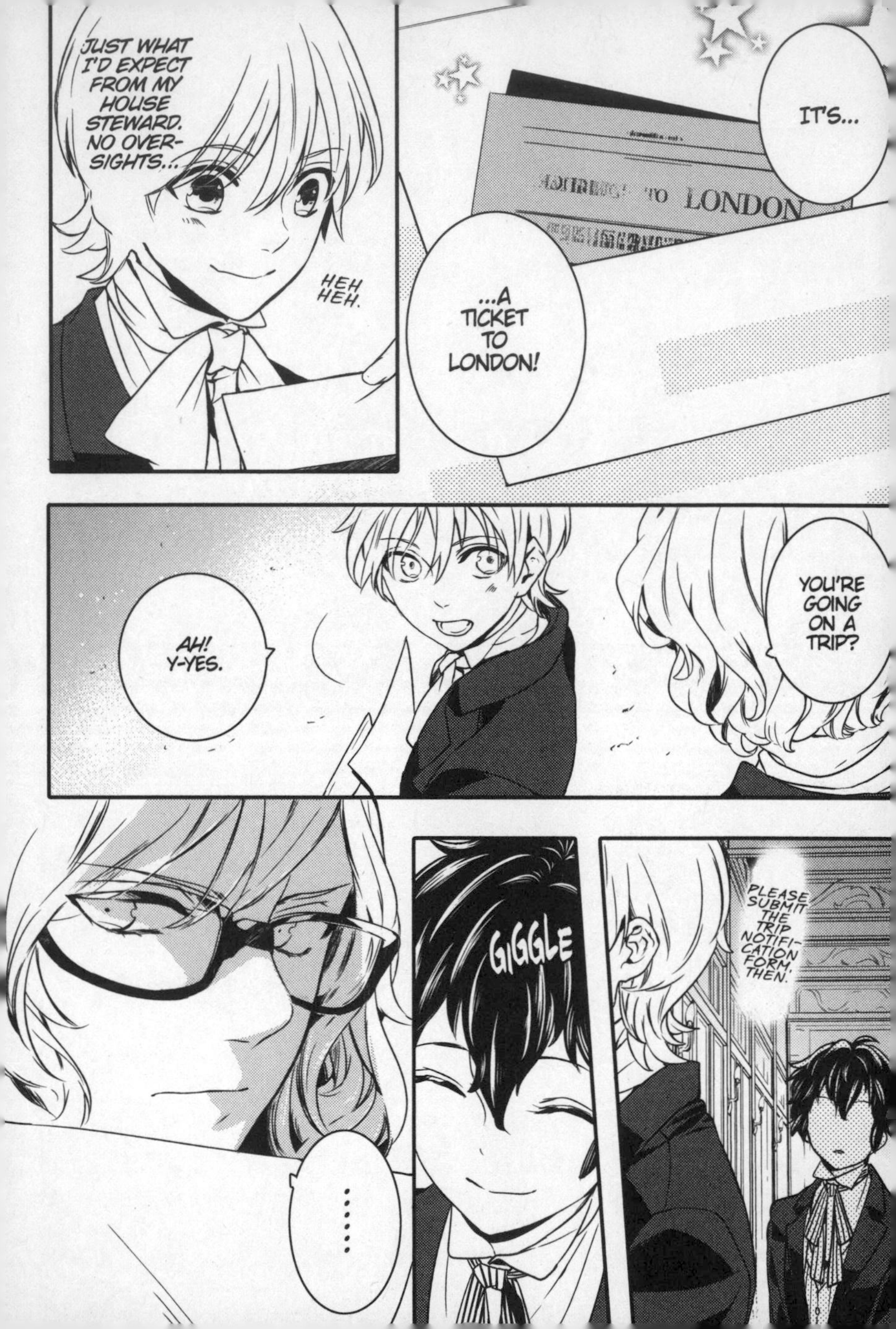
IT'S...
TO LONDON
...A TICKET TO LONDON!
JUST WHAT I'D EXPECT FROM MY HOUSE STEWARD. NO OVER-SIGHTS...
HEH HEH.
YOU'RE GOING ON A TRIP?
AH! Y-YES.
PLEASE SUBMIT THE TRIP NOTIFI-CATION FORM, THEN.
GIGGLE
......

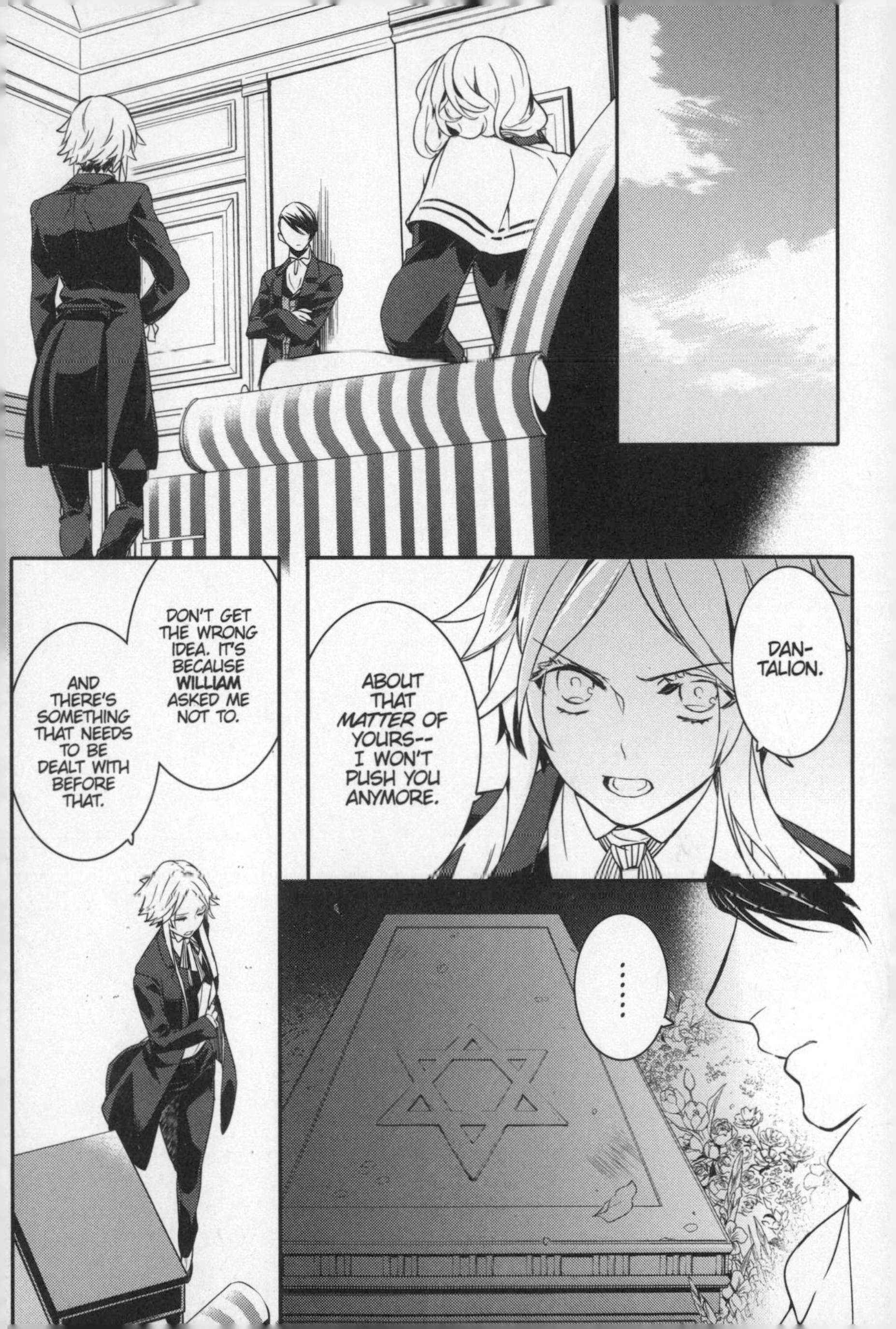
DAN-TALION.
ABOUT THAT MATTER OF YOURS-- I WON'T PUSH YOU ANYMORE.
......
DON'T GET THE WRONG IDEA. IT'S BECAUSE WILLIAM ASKED ME NOT TO.
AND THERE'S SOMETHING THAT NEEDS TO BE DEALT WITH BEFORE THAT.

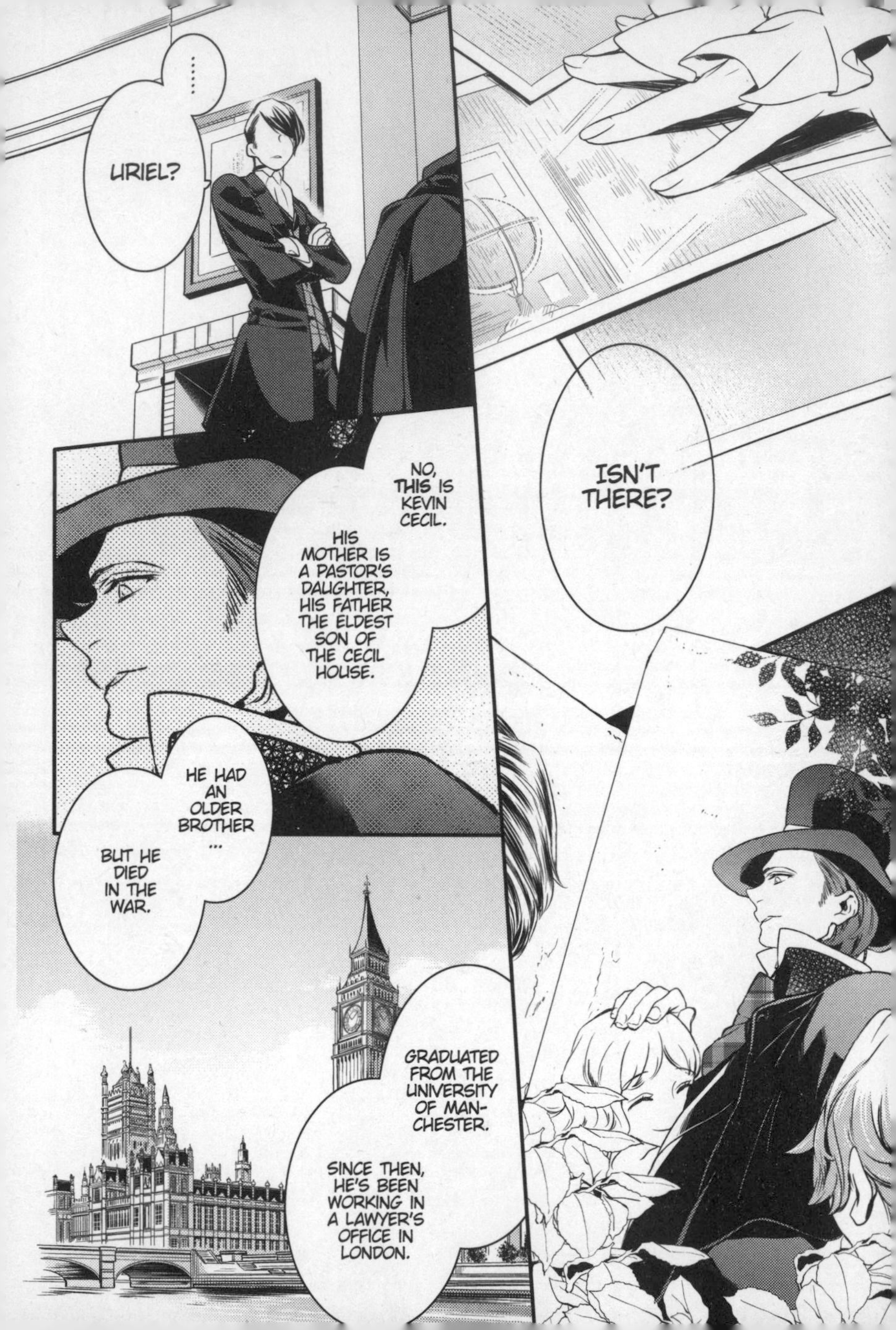
ISN'T THERE?
......
URIEL?
NO, THIS IS KEVIN CECIL.
HIS MOTHER IS A PASTOR'S DAUGHTER, HIS FATHER THE ELDEST SON OF THE CECIL HOUSE.
HE HAD AN OLDER BROTHER ...
BUT HE DIED IN THE WAR.
GRADUATED FROM THE UNIVERSITY OF MAN-CHESTER.
SINCE THEN, HE'S BEEN WORKING IN A LAWYER'S OFFICE IN LONDON.

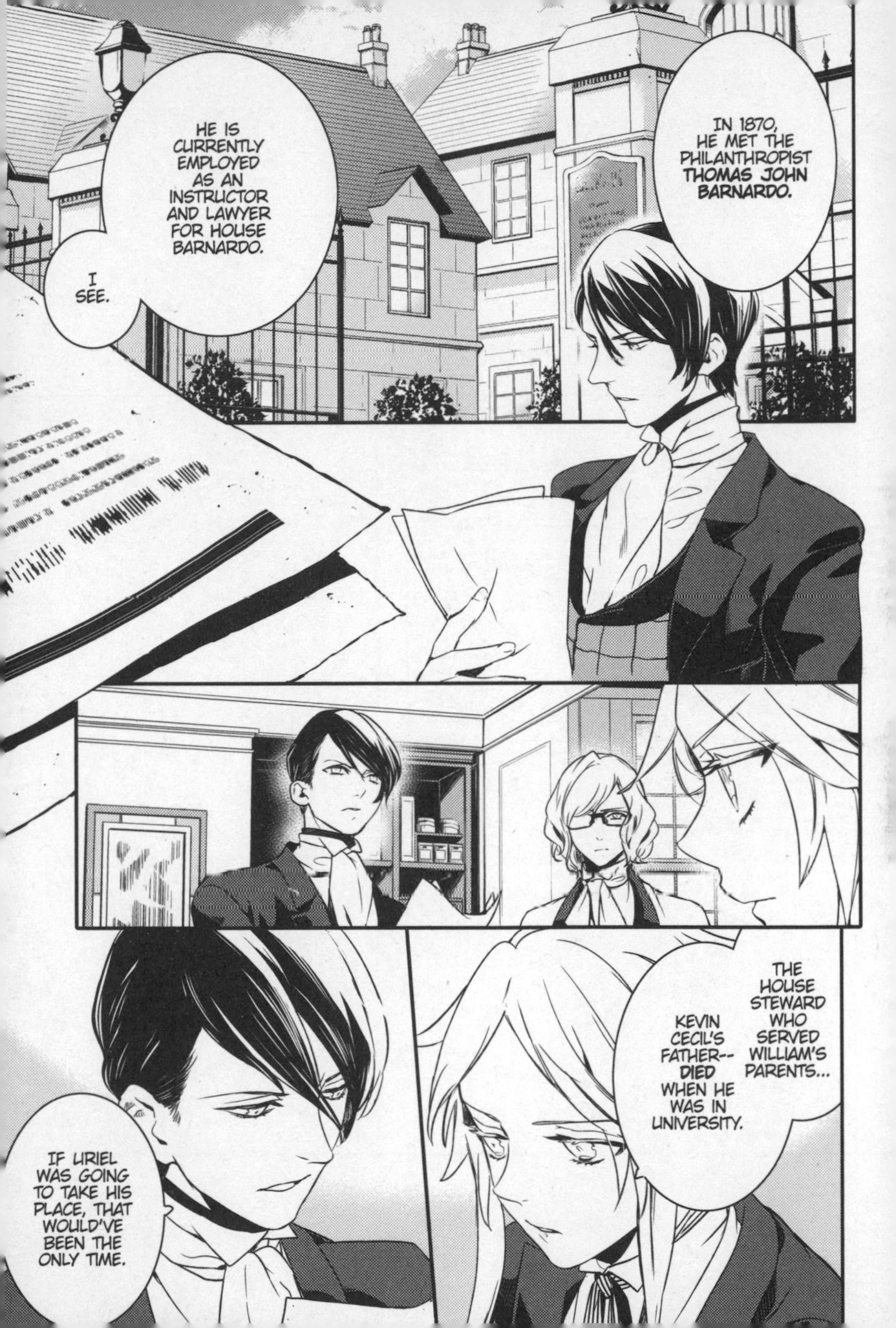
IN 1870, HE MET THE PHILANTHROPIST THOMAS JOHN BARNARDO.
HE IS CURRENTLY EMPLOYED AS AN INSTRUCTOR AND LAWYER FOR HOUSE BARNARDO.
I SEE.
THE HOUSE STEWARD WHO SERVED WILLIAM'S PARENTS...
KEVIN CECIL'S FATHER-- DIED WHEN HE WAS IN UNIVERSITY.
IF URIEL WAS GOING TO TAKE HIS PLACE, THAT WOULD'VE BEEN THE ONLY TIME.

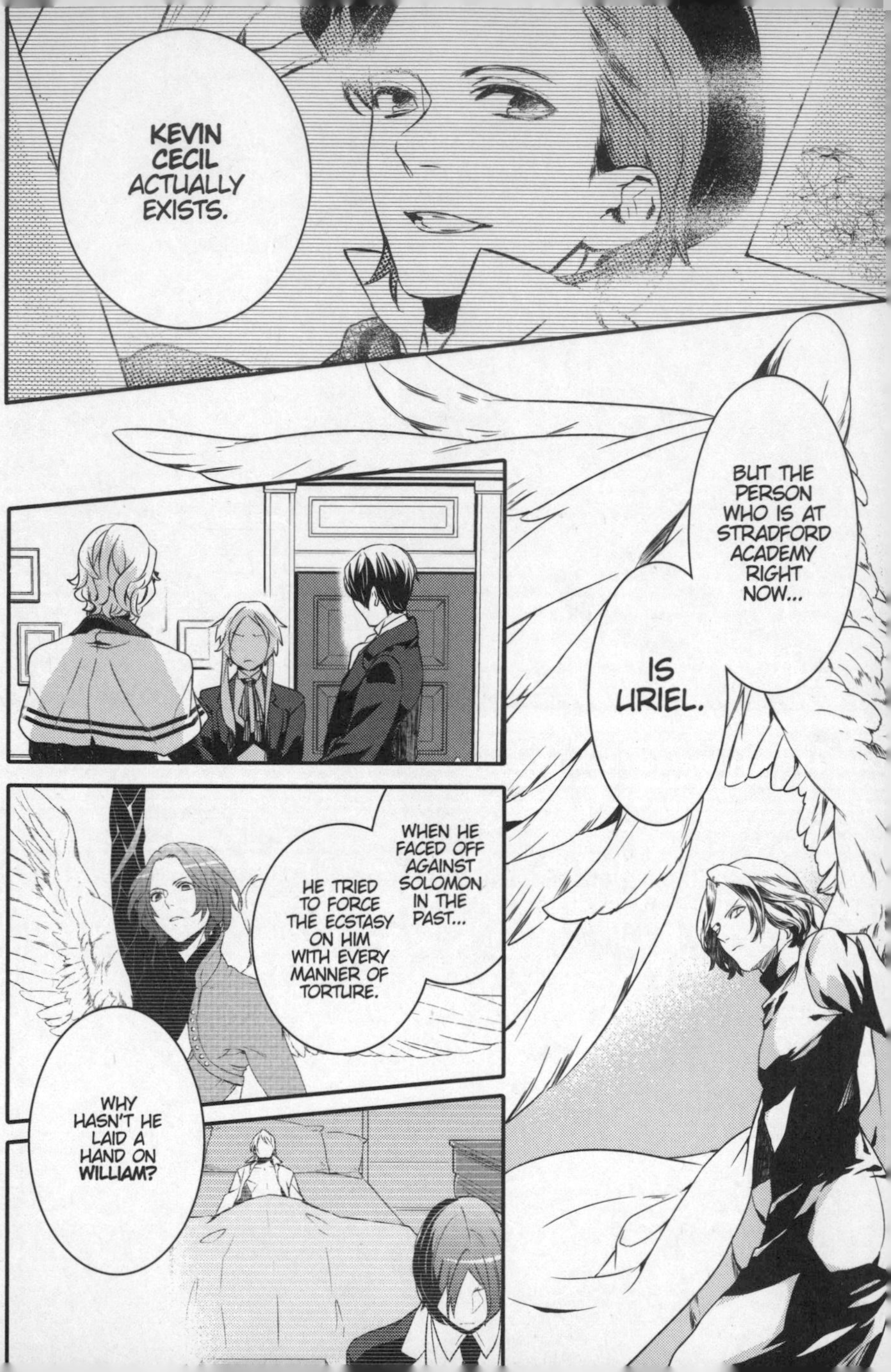
KEVIN CECIL ACTUALLY EXISTS.
BUT THE PERSON WHO IS AT STRADFORD ACADEMY RIGHT NOW...
IS URIEL.
WHEN HE FACED OFF AGAINST SOLOMON IN THE PAST...
HE TRIED TO FORCE THE ECSTASY ON HIM WITH EVERY MANNER OF TORTURE.
WHY HASN'T HE LAID A HAND ON WILLIAM?

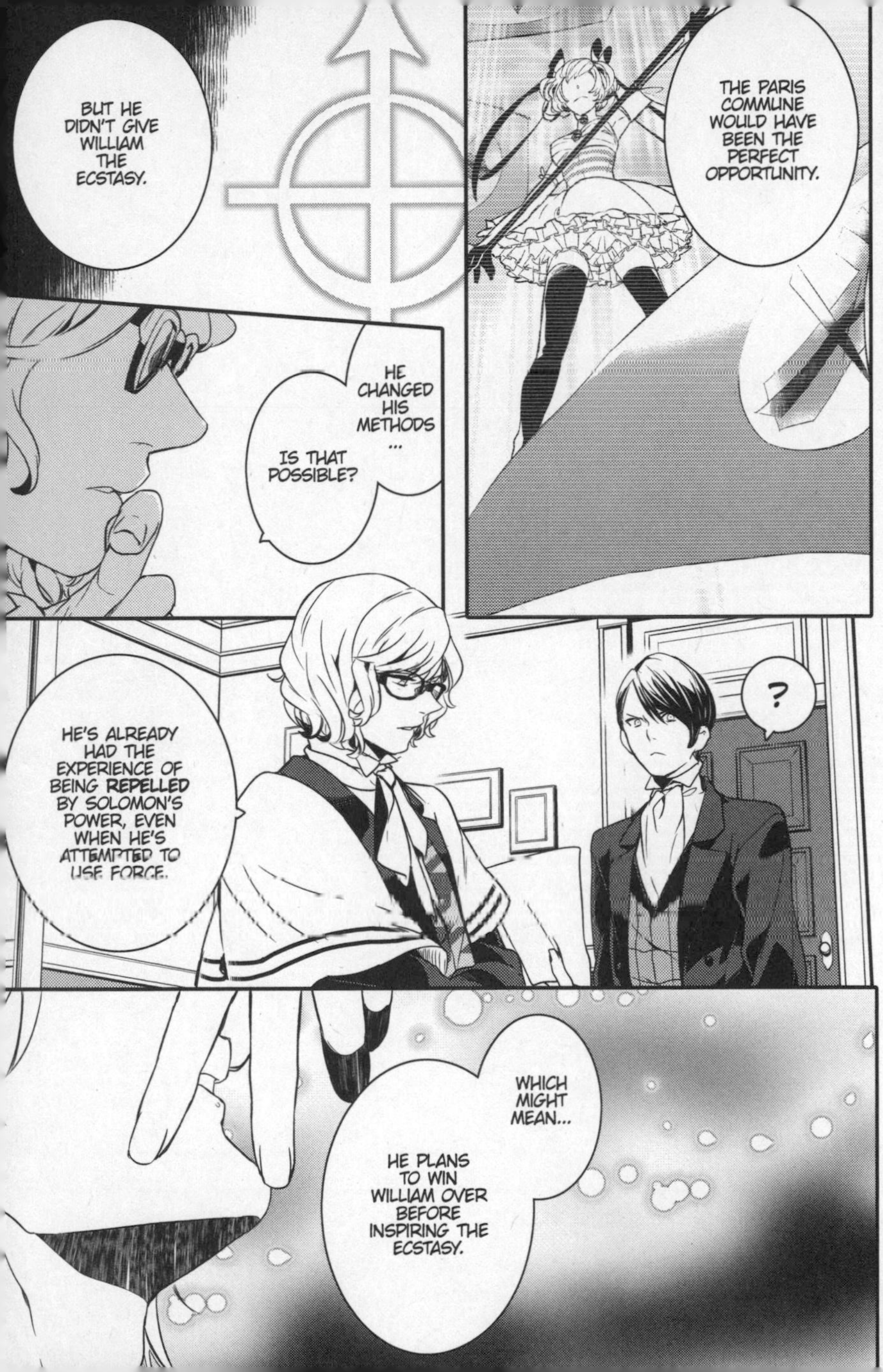
THE PARIS COMMUNE WOULD HAVE BEEN THE PERFECT OPPORTUNITY.
BUT HE DIDN'T GIVE WILLIAM THE ECSTASY.
HE CHANGED HIS METHODS ...
IS THAT POSSIBLE?
?
HE'S ALREADY HAD THE EXPERIENCE OF BEING **REPELLED** BY SOLOMON'S POWER, EVEN WHEN HE'S ATTEMPTED TO USE FORCE.
WHICH MIGHT MEAN...
HE PLANS TO WIN WILLIAM OVER BEFORE INSPIRING THE ECSTASY.

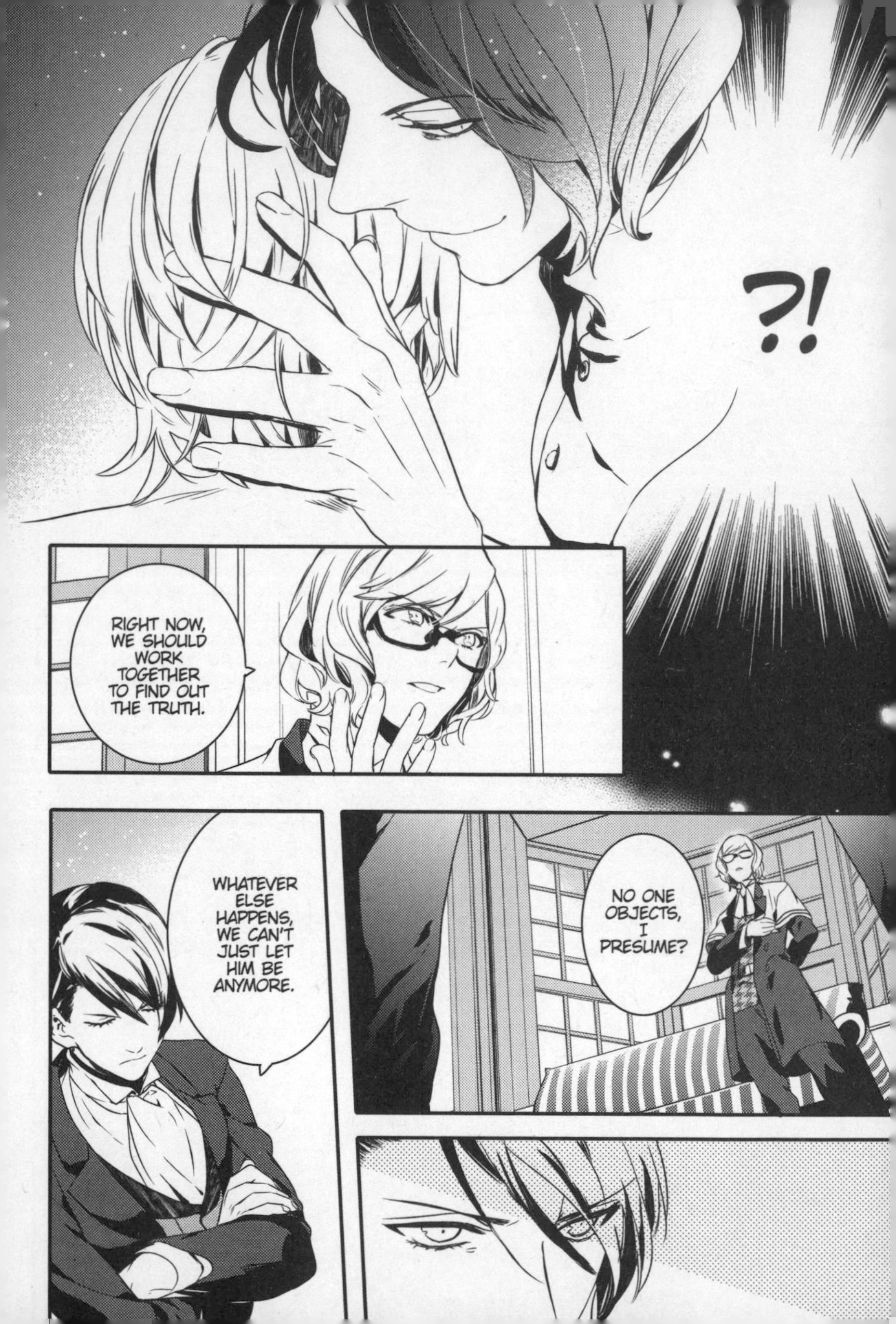
?!
RIGHT NOW, WE SHOULD WORK TOGETHER TO FIND OUT THE TRUTH.
NO ONE OBJECTS, I PRESUME?
WHATEVER ELSE HAPPENS, WE CAN'T JUST LET HIM BE ANYMORE.

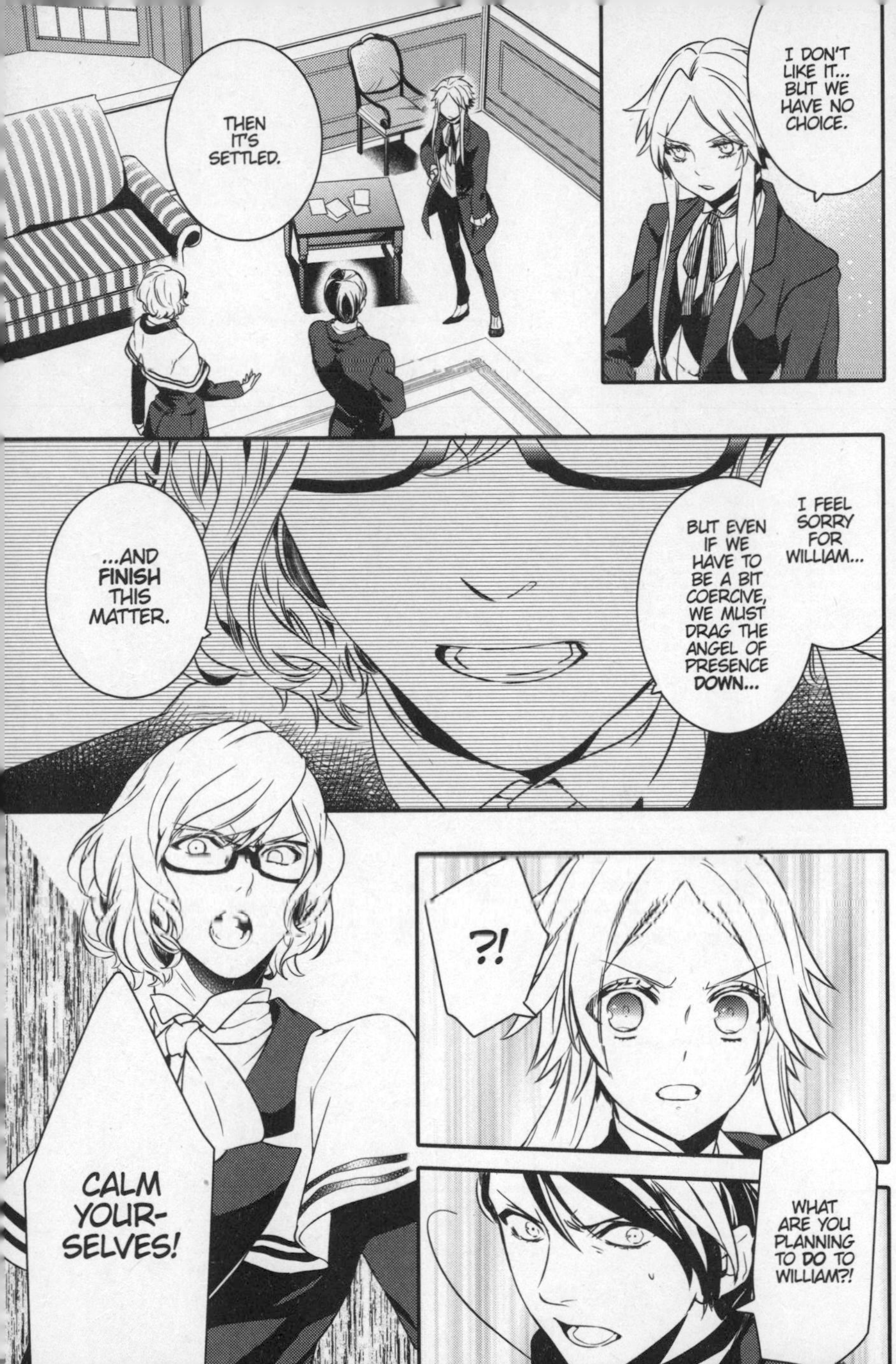
I DON'T LIKE IT... BUT WE HAVE NO CHOICE.
THEN IT'S SETTLED.
I FEEL SORRY FOR WILLIAM...
BUT EVEN IF WE HAVE TO BE A BIT COERCIVE, WE MUST DRAG THE ANGEL OF PRESENCE DOWN...
...AND FINISH THIS MATTER.
?!
WHAT ARE YOU PLANNING TO DO TO WILLIAM?!
CALM YOUR-SELVES!

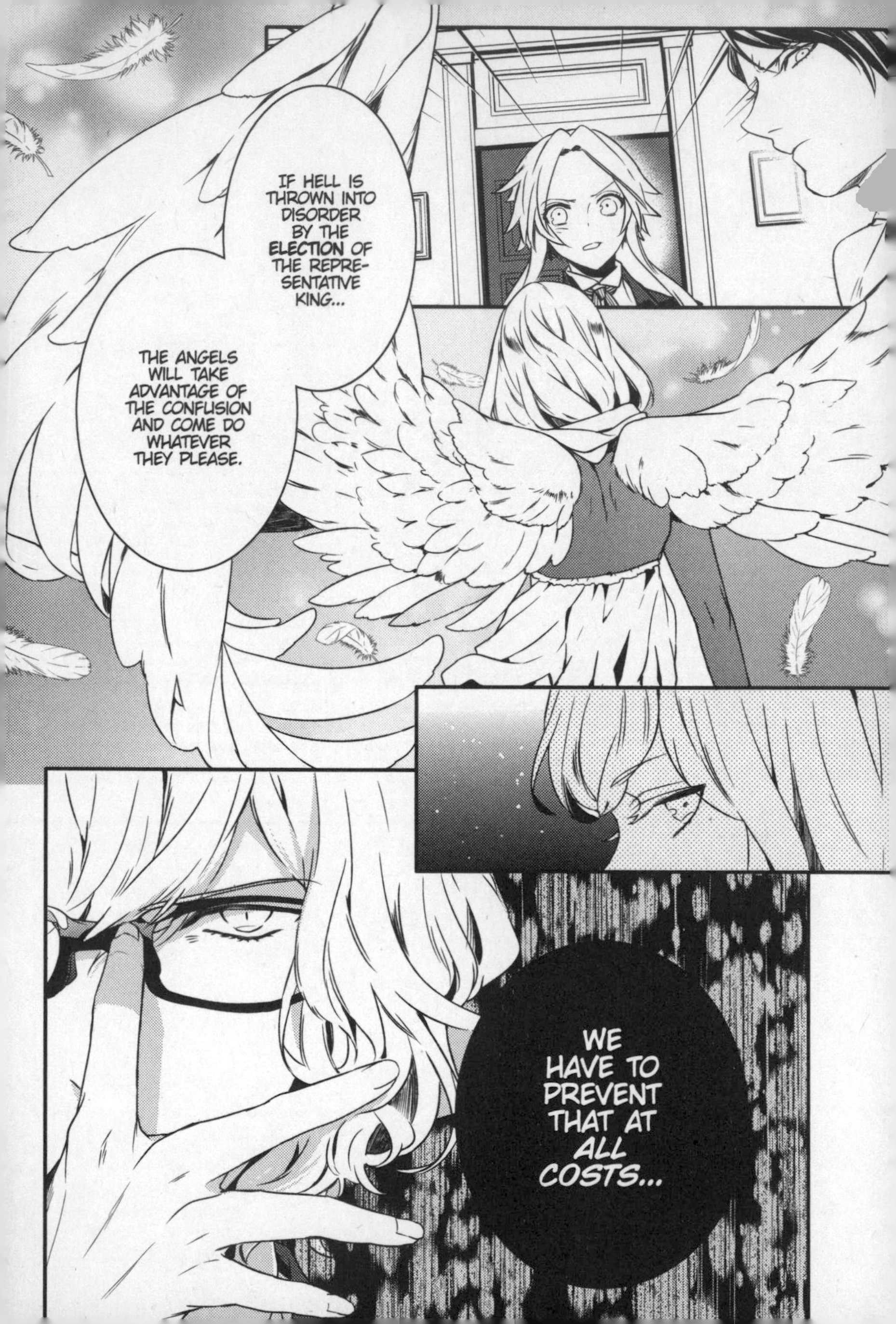
IF HELL IS THROWN INTO DISORDER BY THE ELECTION OF THE REPRE-SENTATIVE KING...
THE ANGELS WILL TAKE ADVANTAGE OF THE CONFUSION AND COME DO WHATEVER THEY PLEASE.
WE HAVE TO PREVENT THAT AT ALL COSTS...

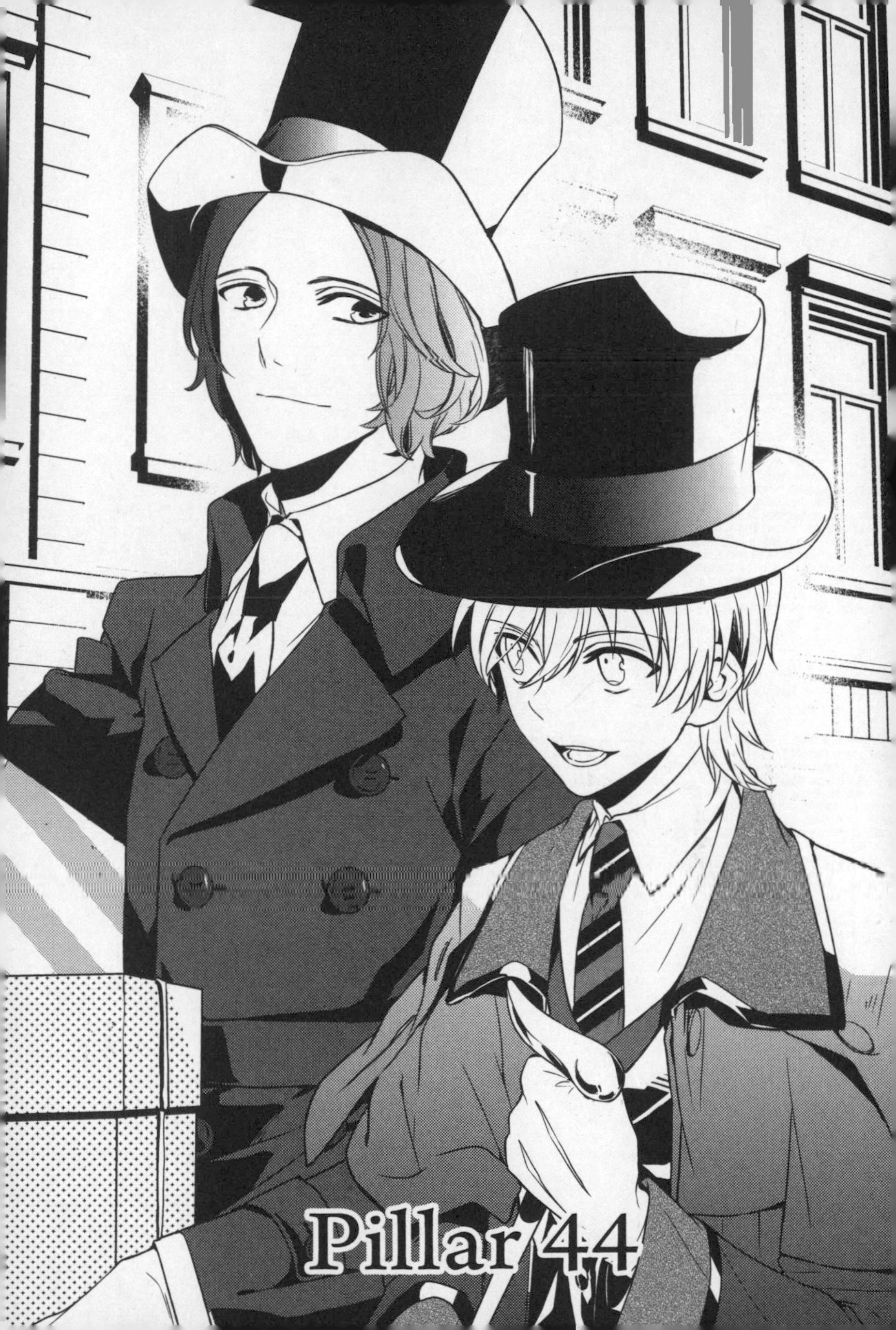
Pillar 44

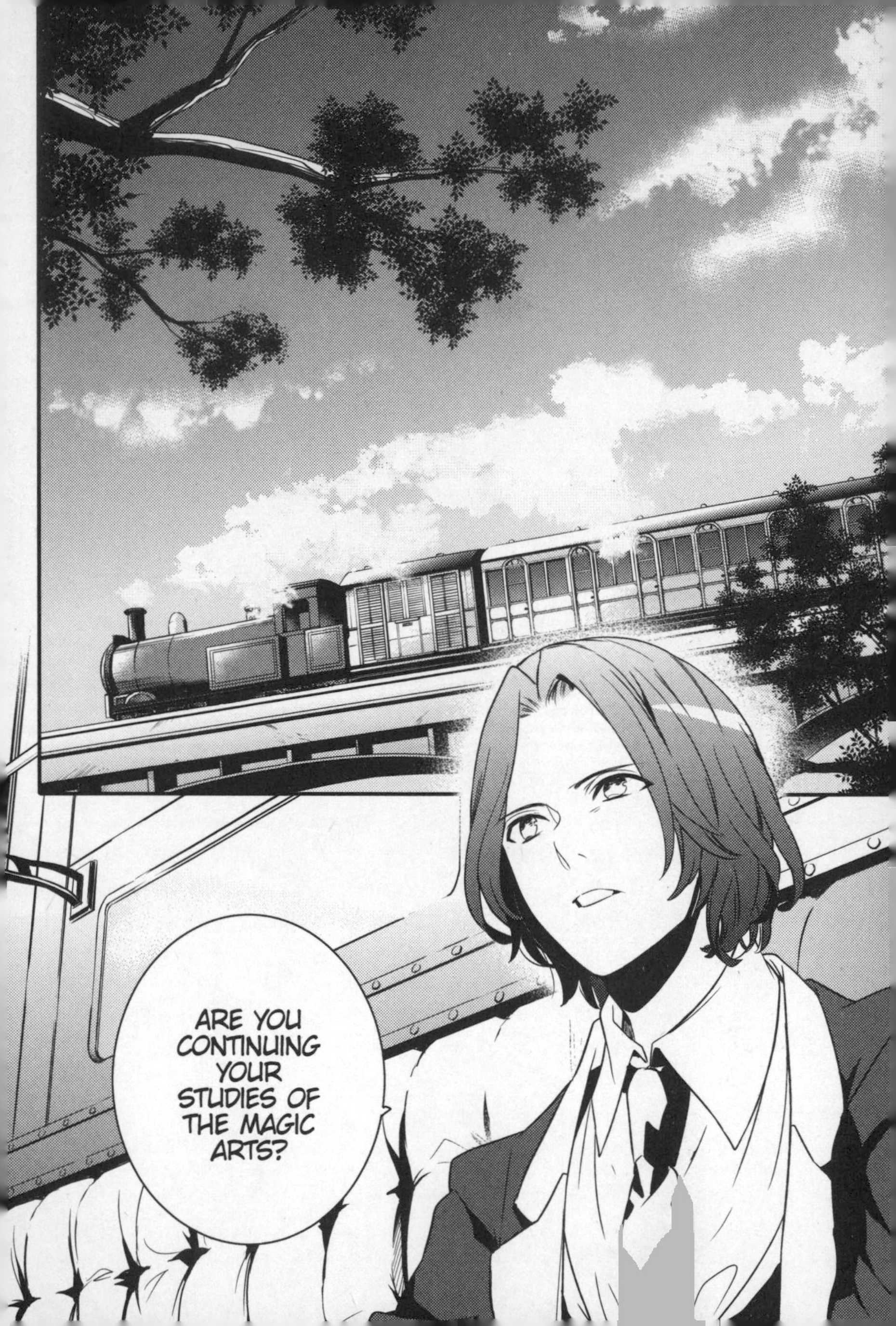
ARE YOU CONTINUING YOUR STUDIES OF THE MAGIC ARTS?

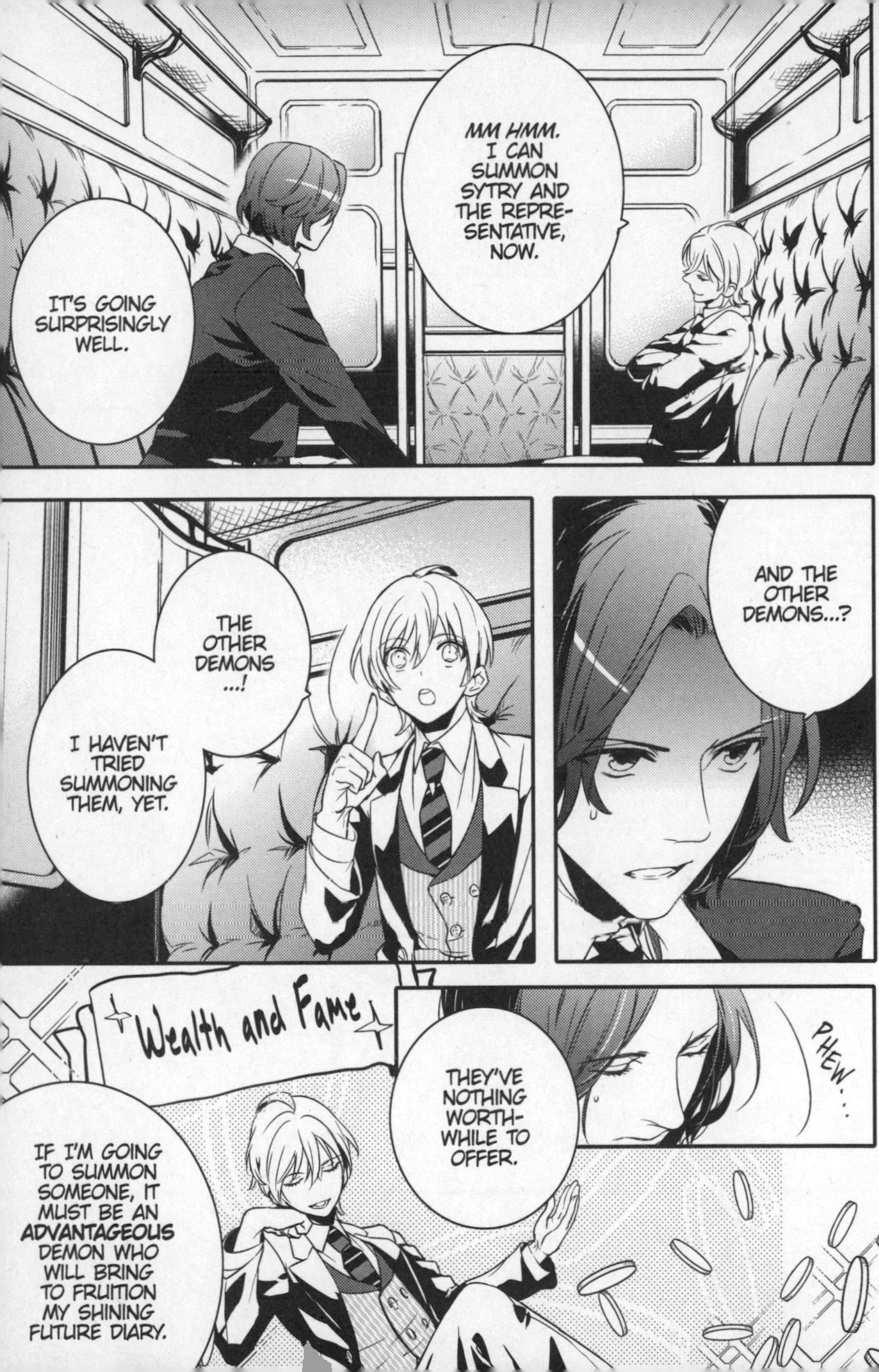
MM HMM. I CAN SUMMON SYTRY AND THE REPRE-SENTATIVE, NOW.
IT'S GOING SURPRISINGLY WELL.
AND THE OTHER DEMONS...?
THE OTHER DEMONS ...!
I HAVEN'T TRIED SUMMONING THEM, YET.
PHEW...
THEY'VE NOTHING WORTH-WHILE TO OFFER.
Wealth and Fame
IF I'M GOING TO SUMMON SOMEONE, IT MUST BE AN **ADVANTAGEOUS** DEMON WHO WILL BRING TO FRUITION MY SHINING FUTURE DIARY.

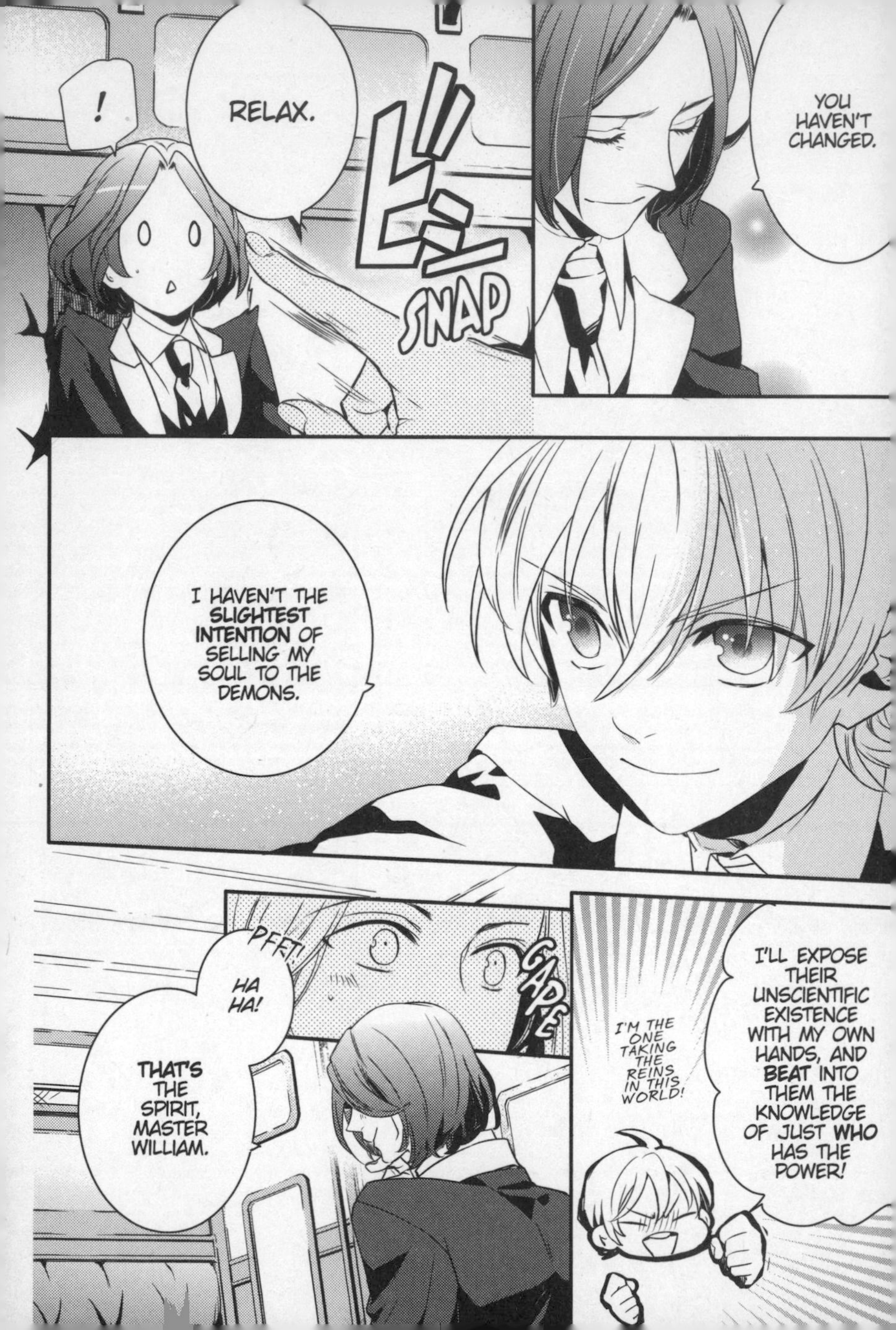
YOU HAVEN'T CHANGED.
RELAX.
!
SNAP
I HAVEN'T THE SLIGHTEST INTENTION OF SELLING MY SOUL TO THE DEMONS.
I'LL EXPOSE THEIR UNSCIENTIFIC EXISTENCE WITH MY OWN HANDS, AND BEAT INTO THEM THE KNOWLEDGE OF JUST WHO HAS THE POWER!
I'M THE ONE TAKING THE REINS IN THIS WORLD!
GAPE
PFFT!
HA HA!
THAT'S THE SPIRIT, MASTER WILLIAM.

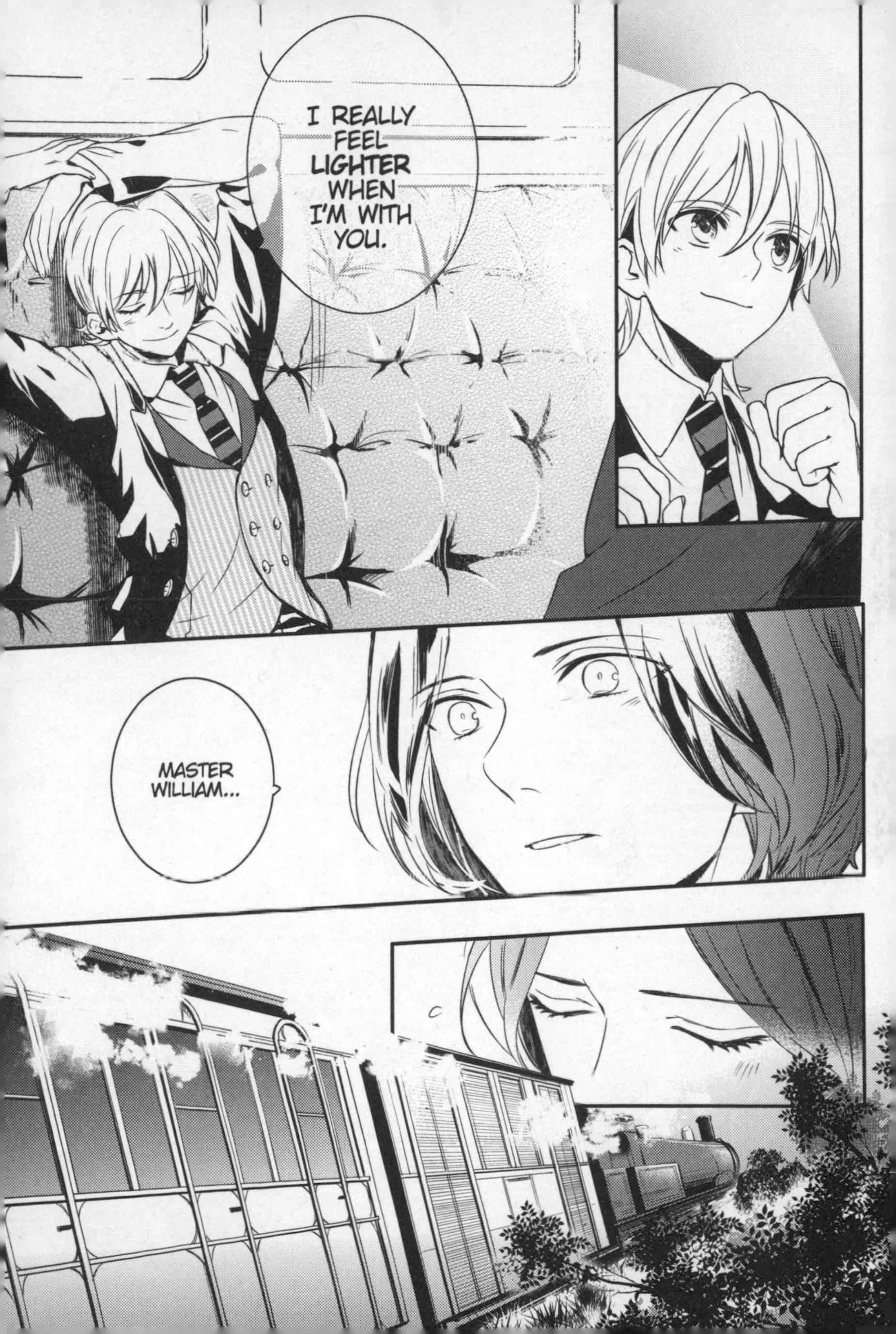
I REALLY FEEL LIGHTER WHEN I'M WITH YOU.
MASTER WILLIAM...

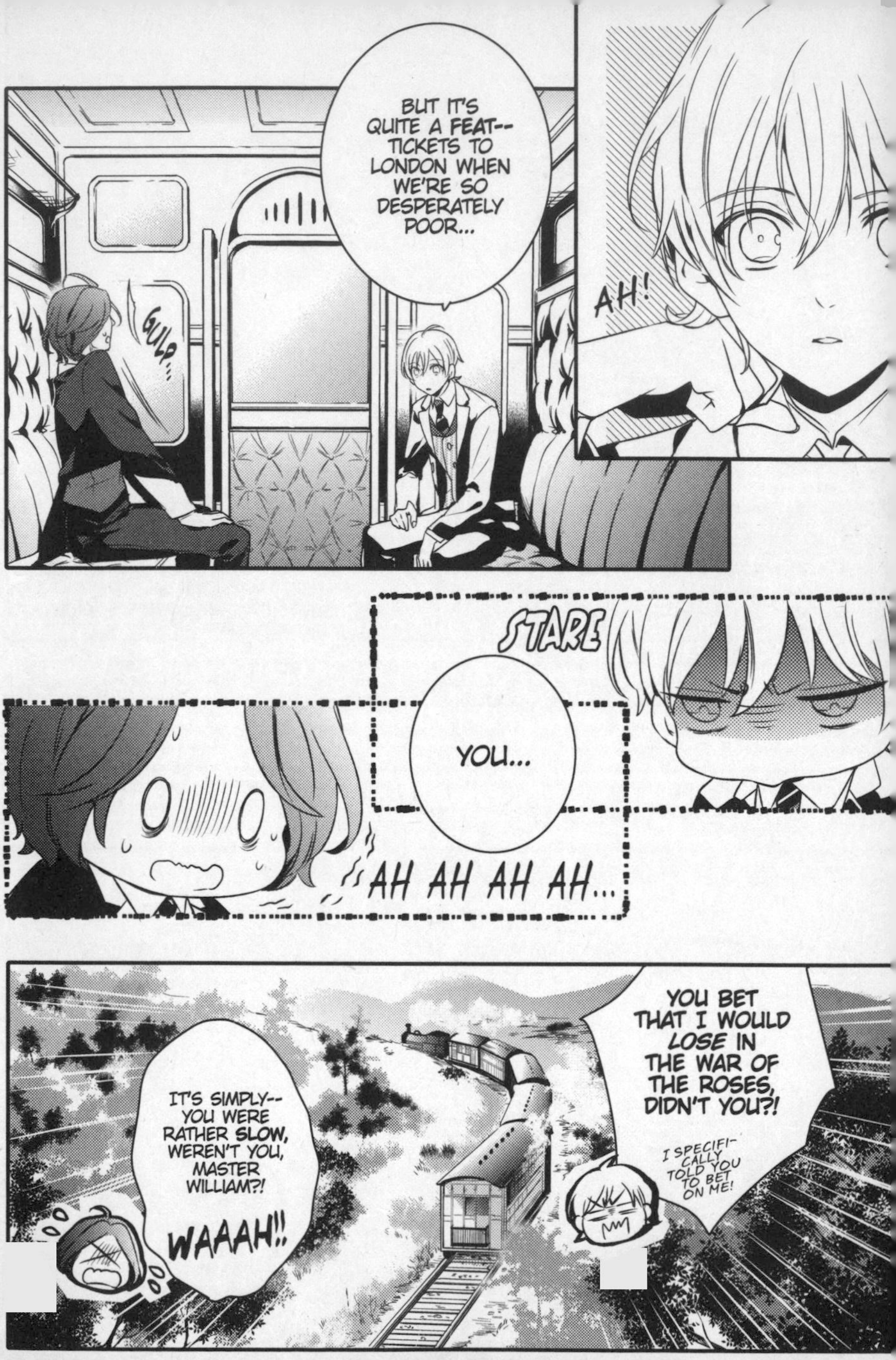
AH!
BUT IT'S QUITE A FEAT--TICKETS TO LONDON WHEN WE'RE SO DESPERATELY POOR...
GULP...
STARE
YOU...
AH AH AH AH...
YOU BET THAT I WOULD LOSE IN THE WAR OF THE ROSES, DIDN'T YOU?!
I SPECIFICALLY TOLD YOU TO BET ON ME!
IT'S SIMPLY--YOU WERE RATHER SLOW, WEREN'T YOU, MASTER WILLIAM?!
WAAAH!!

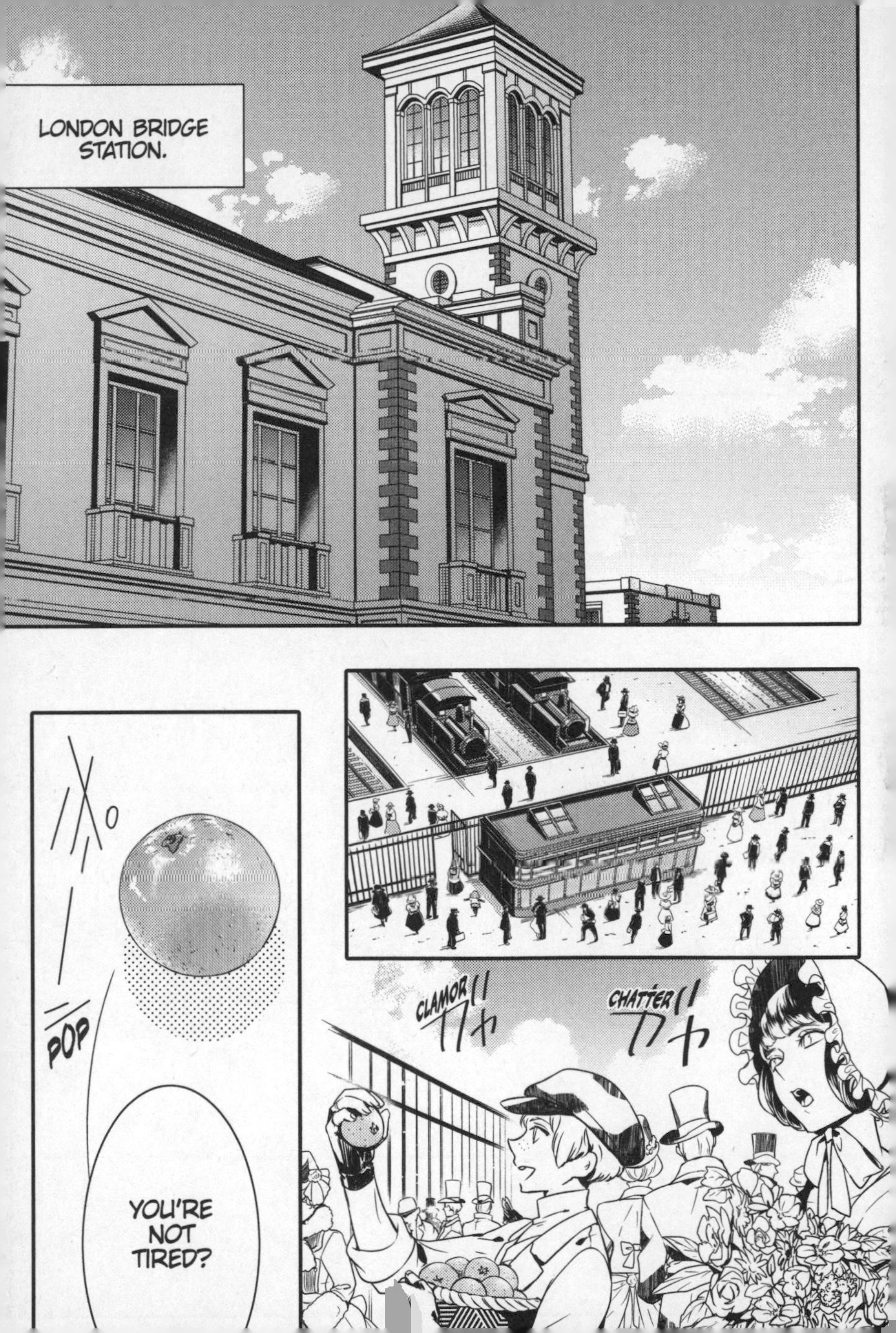
LONDON BRIDGE STATION.
CHATTER
CLAMOR
POP
YOU'RE NOT TIRED?

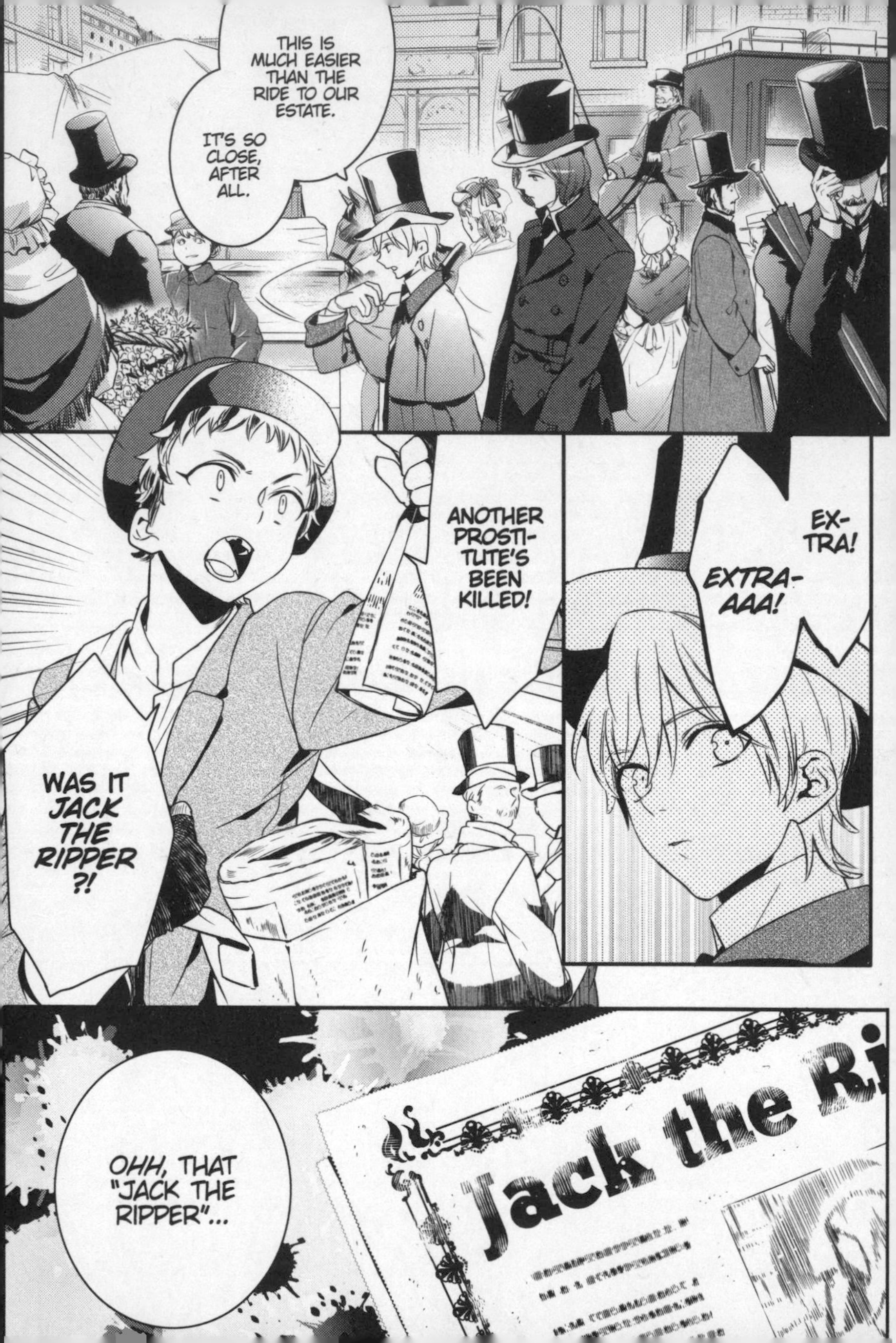
THIS IS MUCH EASIER THAN THE RIDE TO OUR ESTATE.
IT'S SO CLOSE, AFTER ALL.
EX-TRA!
EXTRA-AAA!
ANOTHER PROSTI-TUTE'S BEEN KILLED!
WAS IT JACK THE RIPPER?!
Jack the Ri
OHH, THAT "JACK THE RIPPER"...

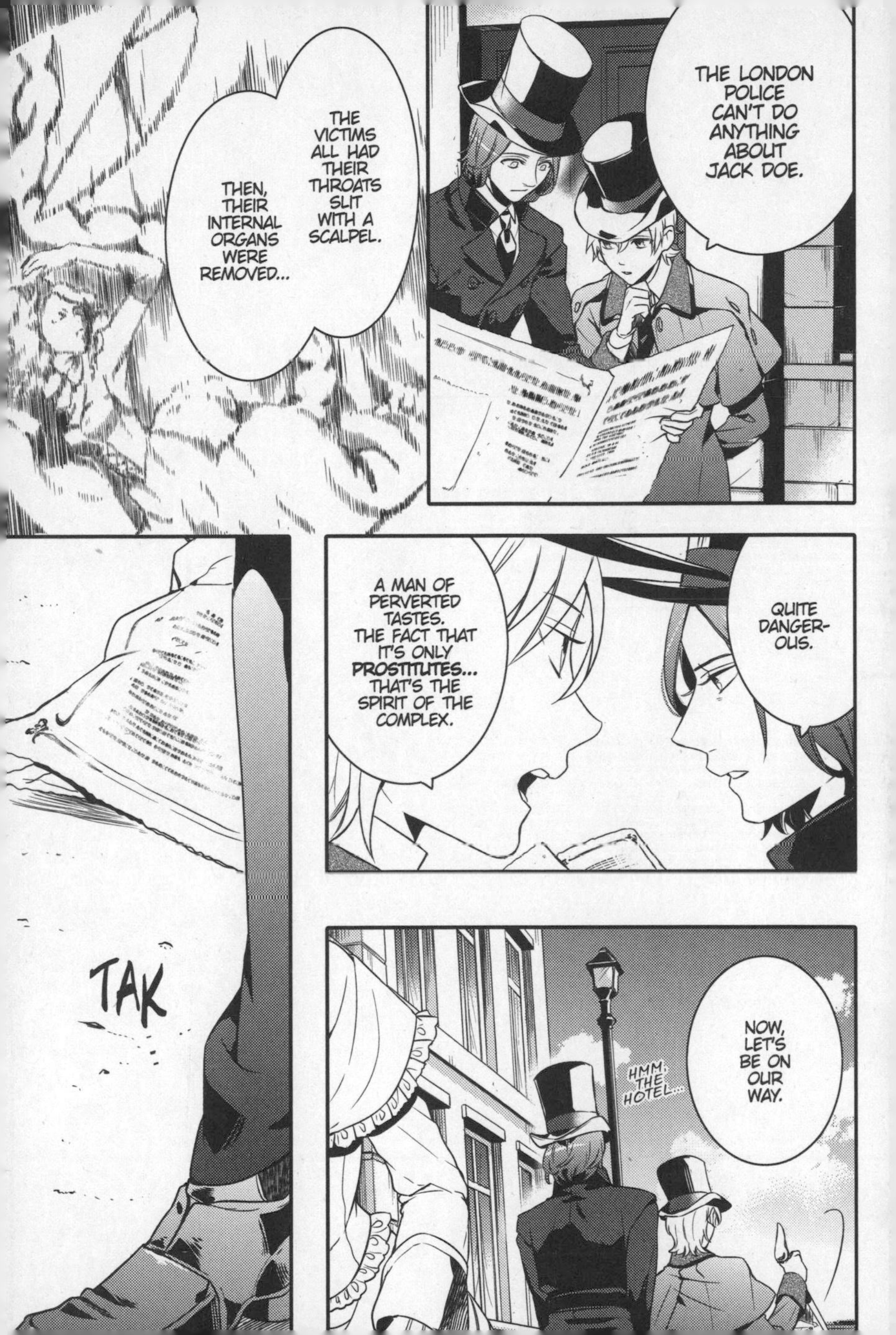
THE LONDON POLICE CAN'T DO ANYTHING ABOUT JACK DOE.
THE VICTIMS ALL HAD THEIR THROATS SLIT WITH A SCALPEL.
THEN, THEIR INTERNAL ORGANS WERE REMOVED...
QUITE DANGER-OUS.
A MAN OF PERVERTED TASTES. THE FACT THAT IT'S ONLY **PROSTITUTES...** THAT'S THE SPIRIT OF THE COMPLEX.
NOW, LET'S BE ON OUR WAY.
HMM, THE HOTEL...
TAK

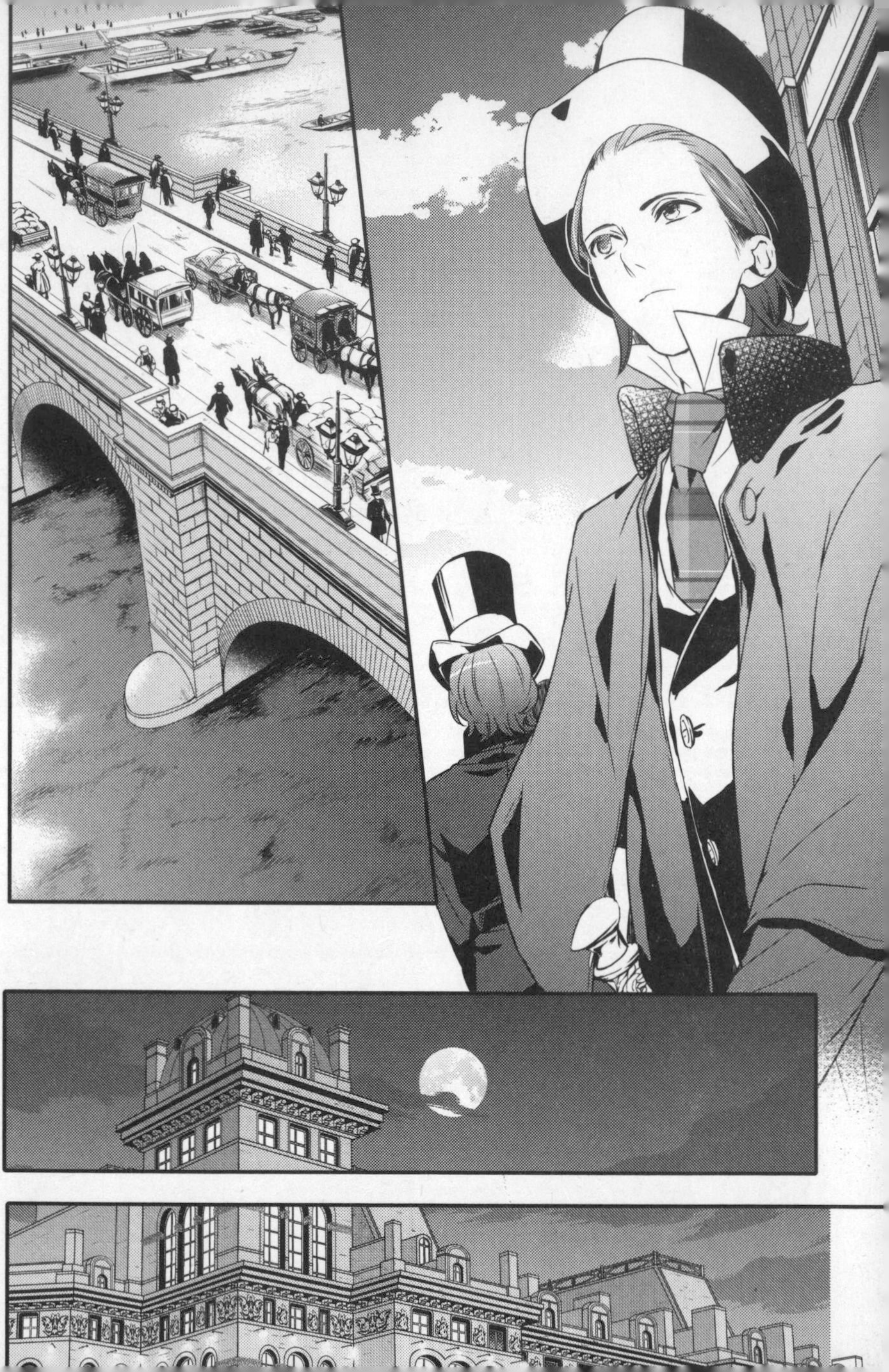

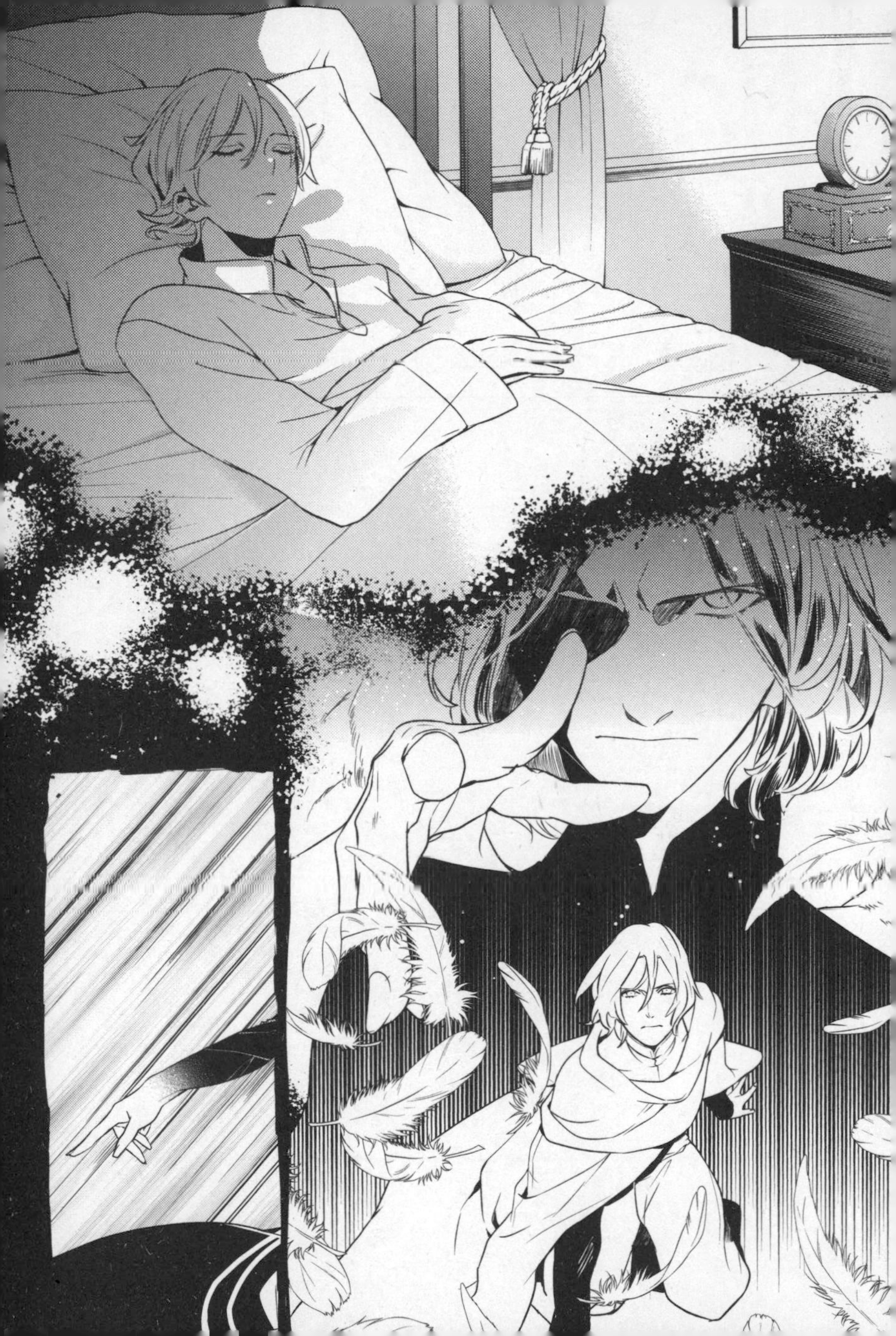

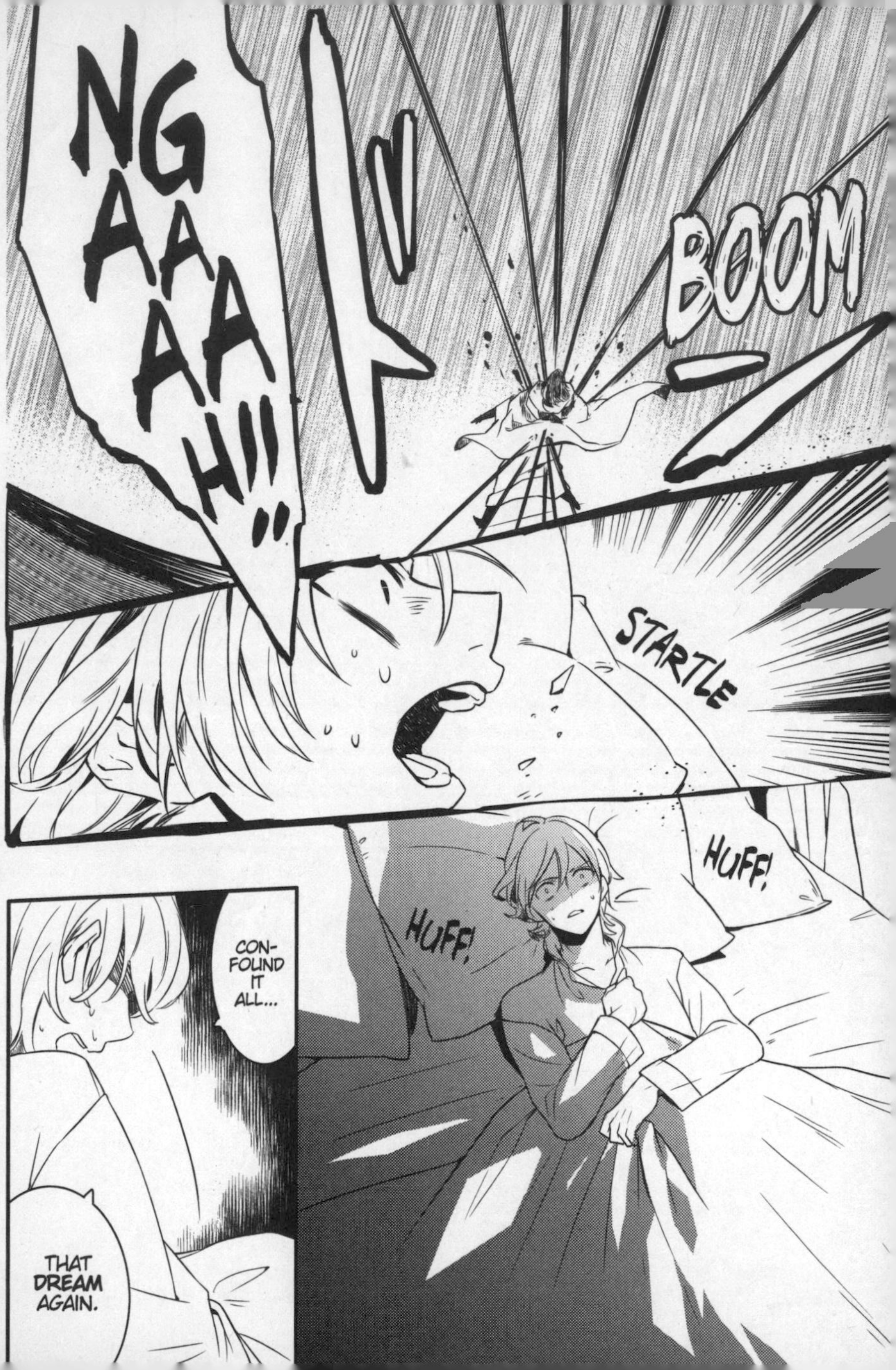
BOOM
NGAAAAH!!
STARTLE
HUFF!
HUFF!
CON-FOUND IT ALL...
THAT DREAM AGAIN.

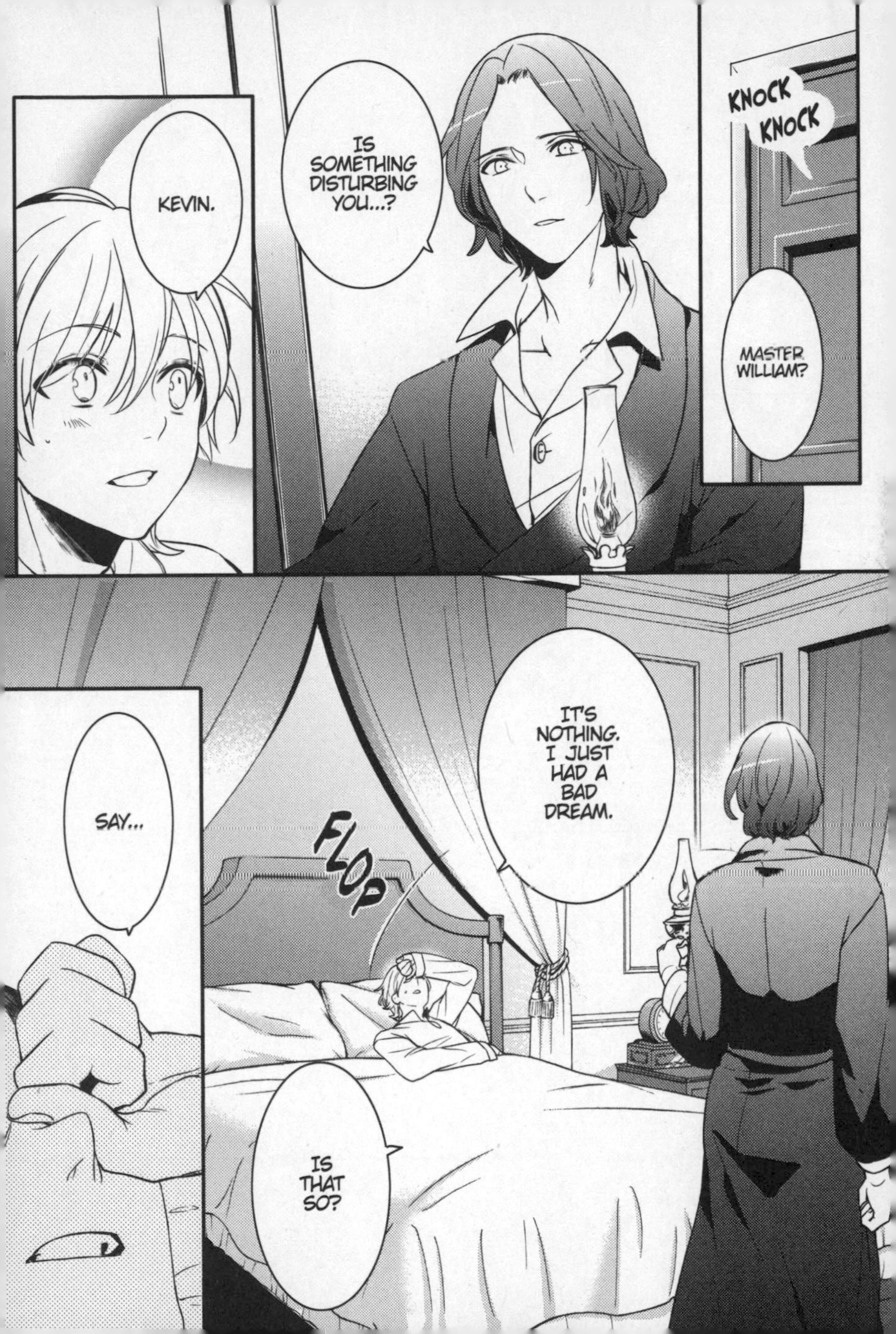
KNOCK KNOCK
MASTER WILLIAM?
IS SOMETHING DISTURBING YOU...?
KEVIN.
IT'S NOTHING. I JUST HAD A BAD DREAM.
FLOP
IS THAT SO?
SAY...

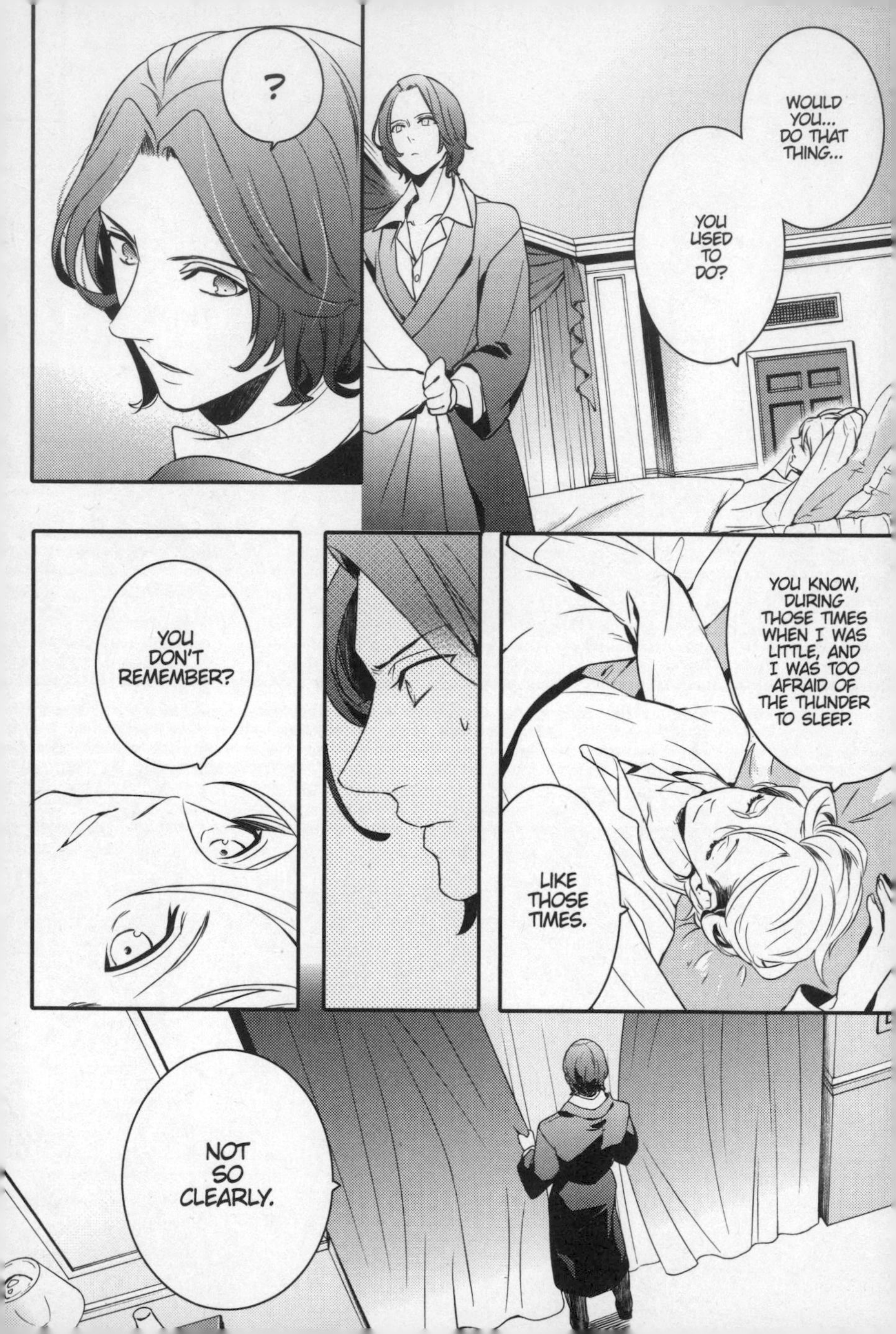
WOULD YOU... DO THAT THING...
YOU USED TO DO?
?
YOU KNOW, DURING THOSE TIMES WHEN I WAS LITTLE, AND I WAS TOO AFRAID OF THE THUNDER TO SLEEP.
LIKE THOSE TIMES.
YOU DON'T REMEMBER?
NOT SO CLEARLY.

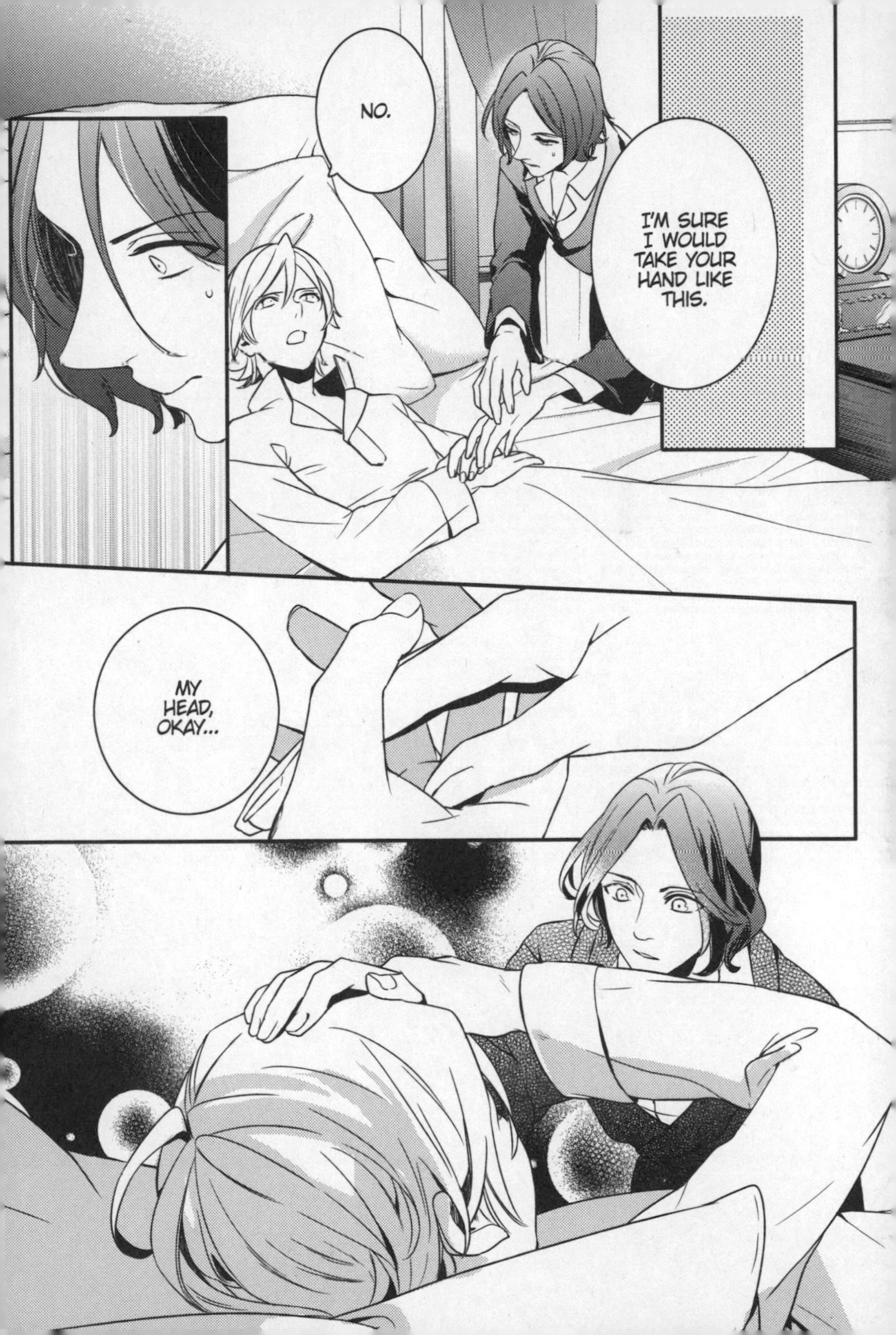
I'M SURE I WOULD TAKE YOUR HAND LIKE THIS.
NO.
MY HEAD, OKAY...

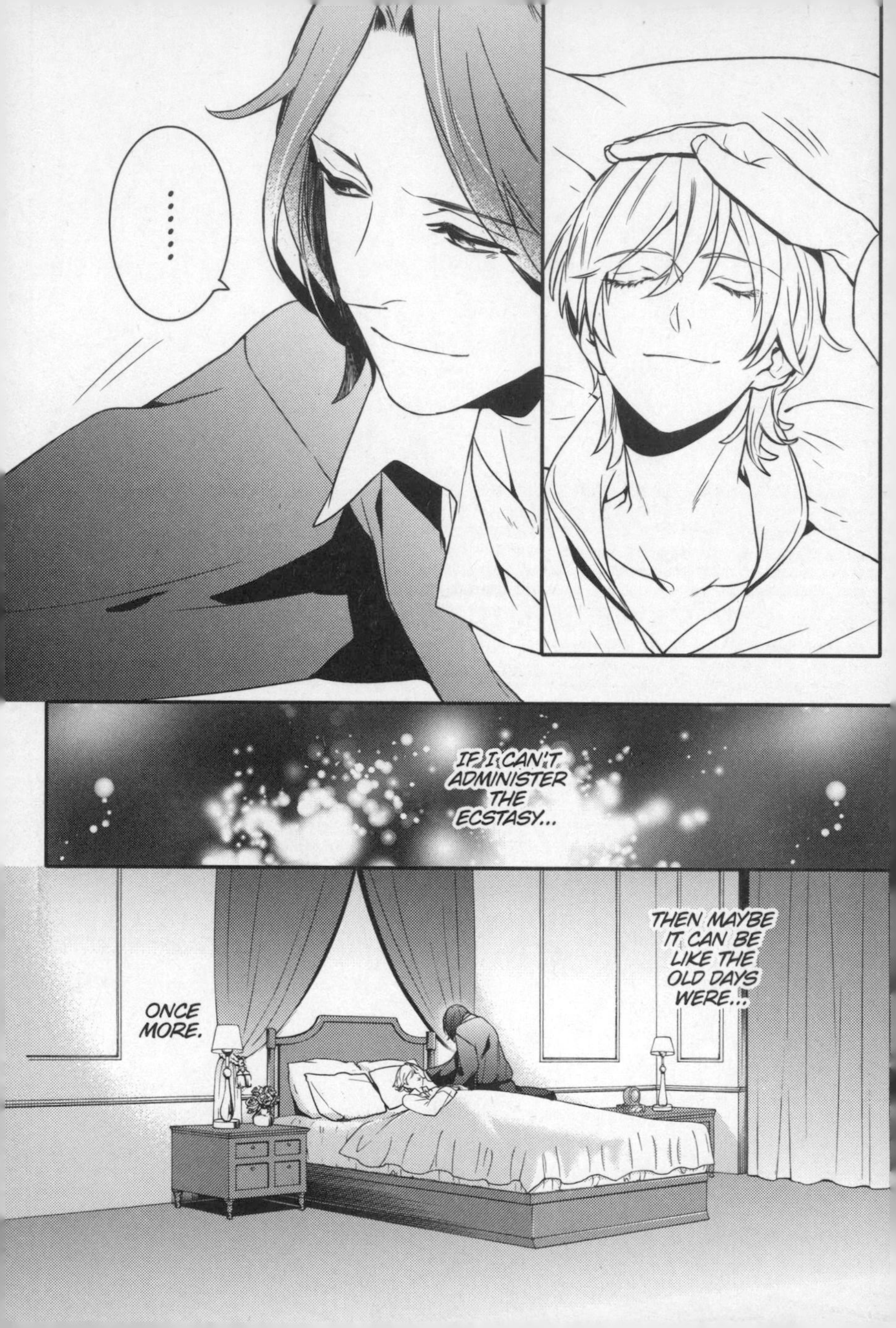
......
IF I CAN'T ADMINISTER THE ECSTASY...
THEN MAYBE IT CAN BE LIKE THE OLD DAYS WERE...
ONCE MORE.

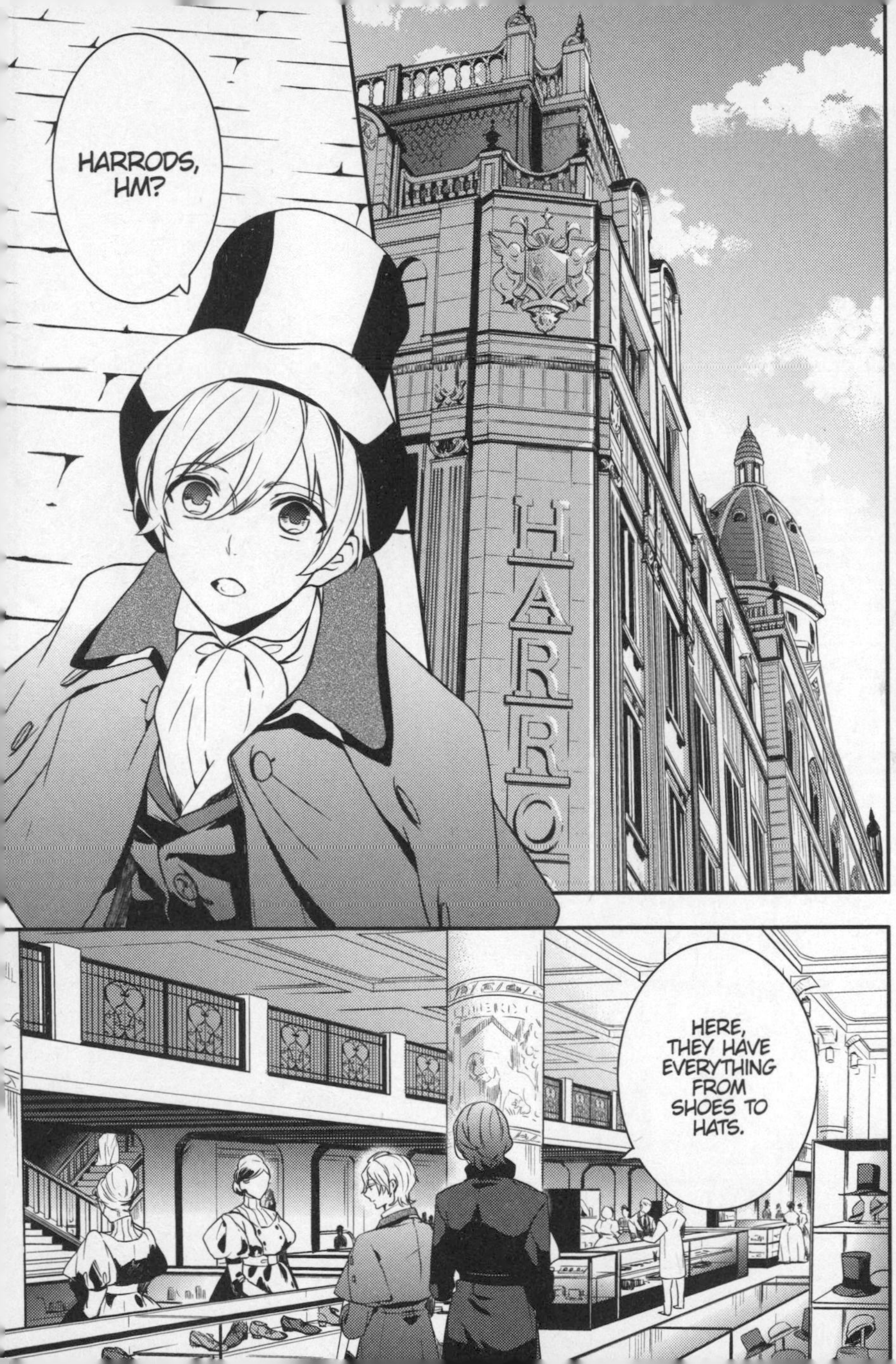
HARRODS, HM?
HERE, THEY HAVE EVERYTHING FROM SHOES TO HATS.

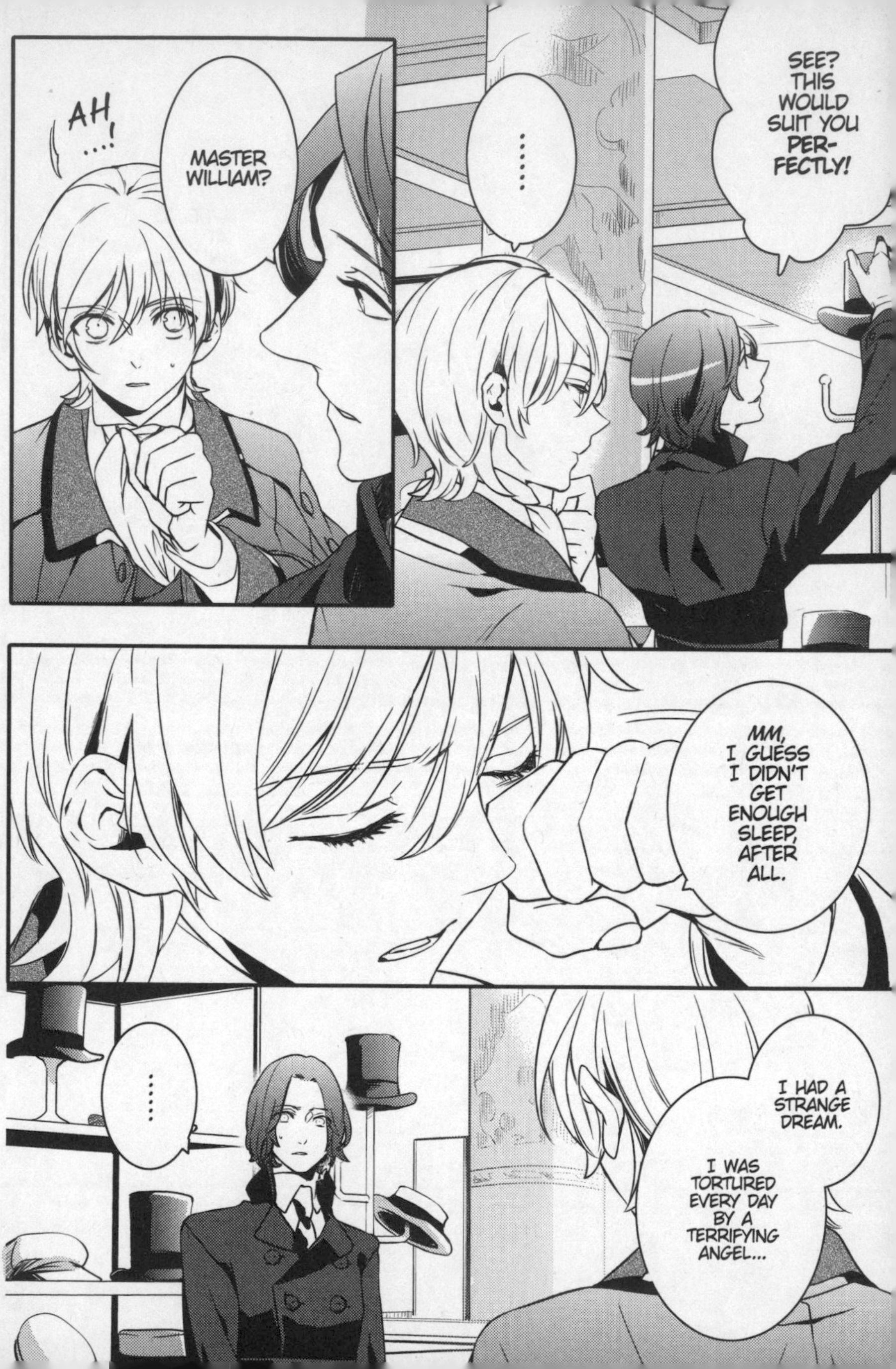

SEE? THIS WOULD SUIT YOU PER-FECTLY!
......
MASTER WILLIAM?
AH ...!
MM, I GUESS I DIDN'T GET ENOUGH SLEEP, AFTER ALL.
I HAD A STRANGE DREAM.
I WAS TORTURED EVERY DAY BY A TERRIFYING ANGEL...
......

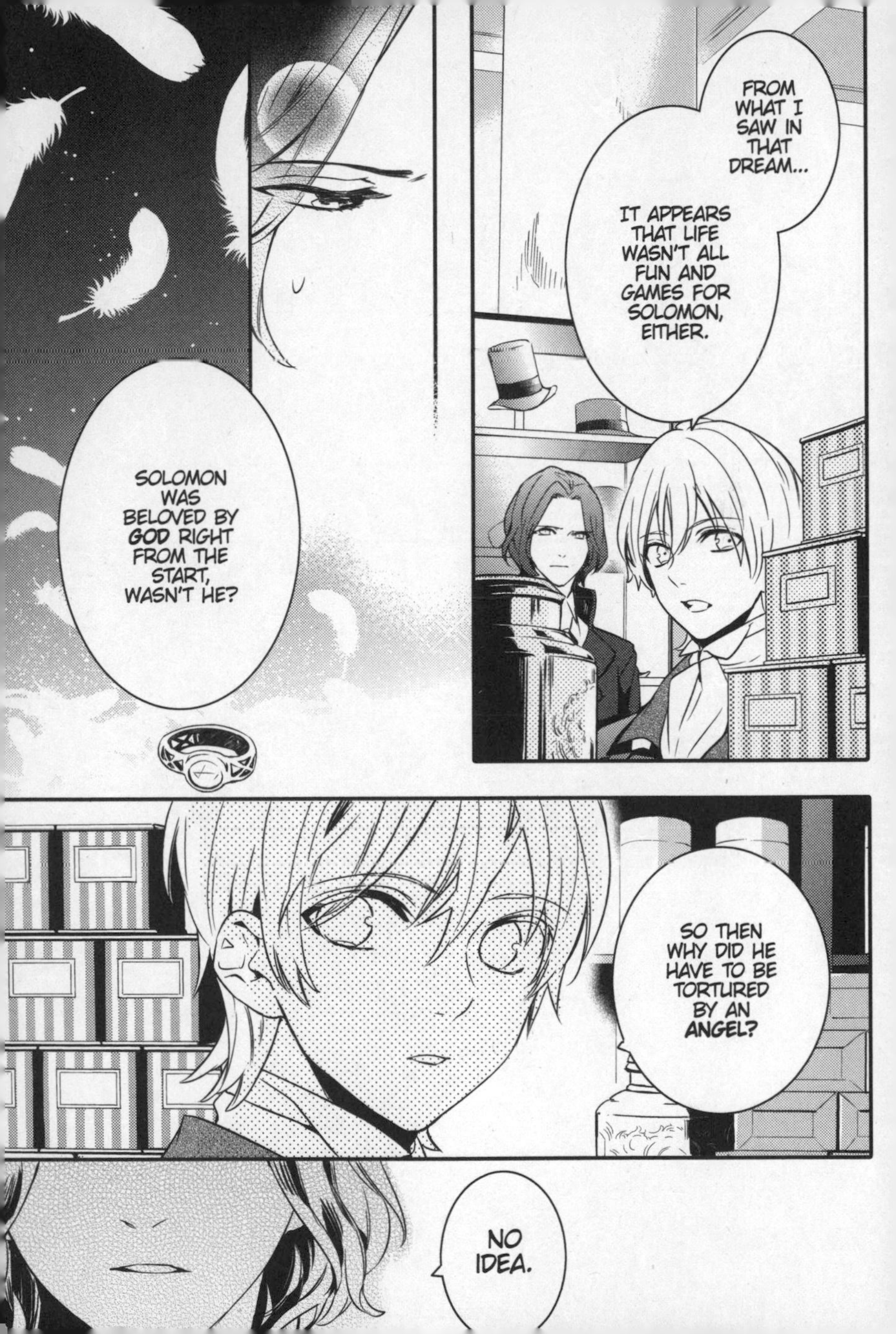
FROM WHAT I SAW IN THAT DREAM...
IT APPEARS THAT LIFE WASN'T ALL FUN AND GAMES FOR SOLOMON, EITHER.
SOLOMON WAS BELOVED BY GOD RIGHT FROM THE START, WASN'T HE?
SO THEN WHY DID HE HAVE TO BE TORTURED BY AN ANGEL?
NO IDEA.

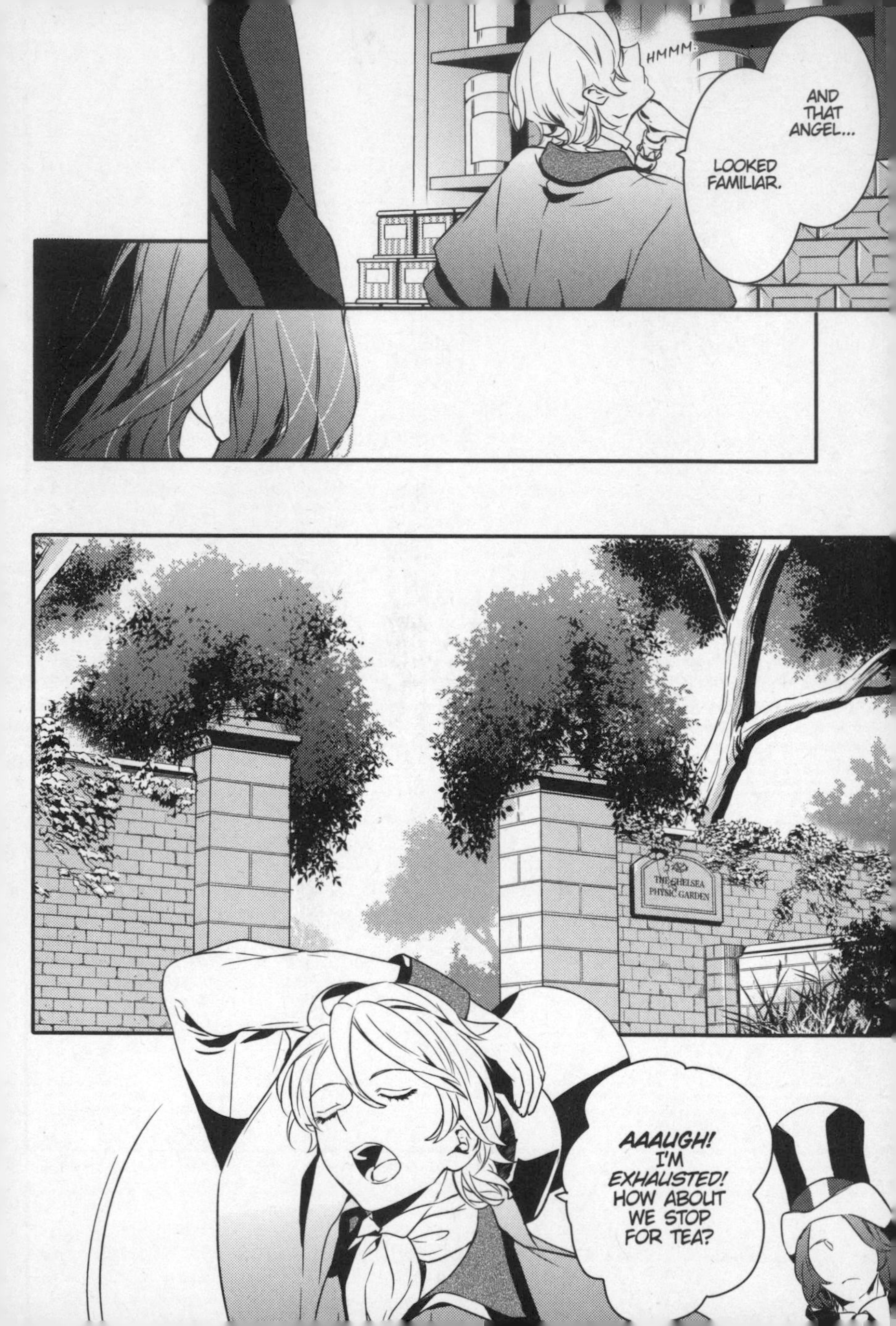
HMMM.
AND THAT ANGEL...
LOOKED FAMILIAR.
THE CHELSEA PHYSIC GARDEN
AAAUGH! I'M EXHAUSTED! HOW ABOUT WE STOP FOR TEA?

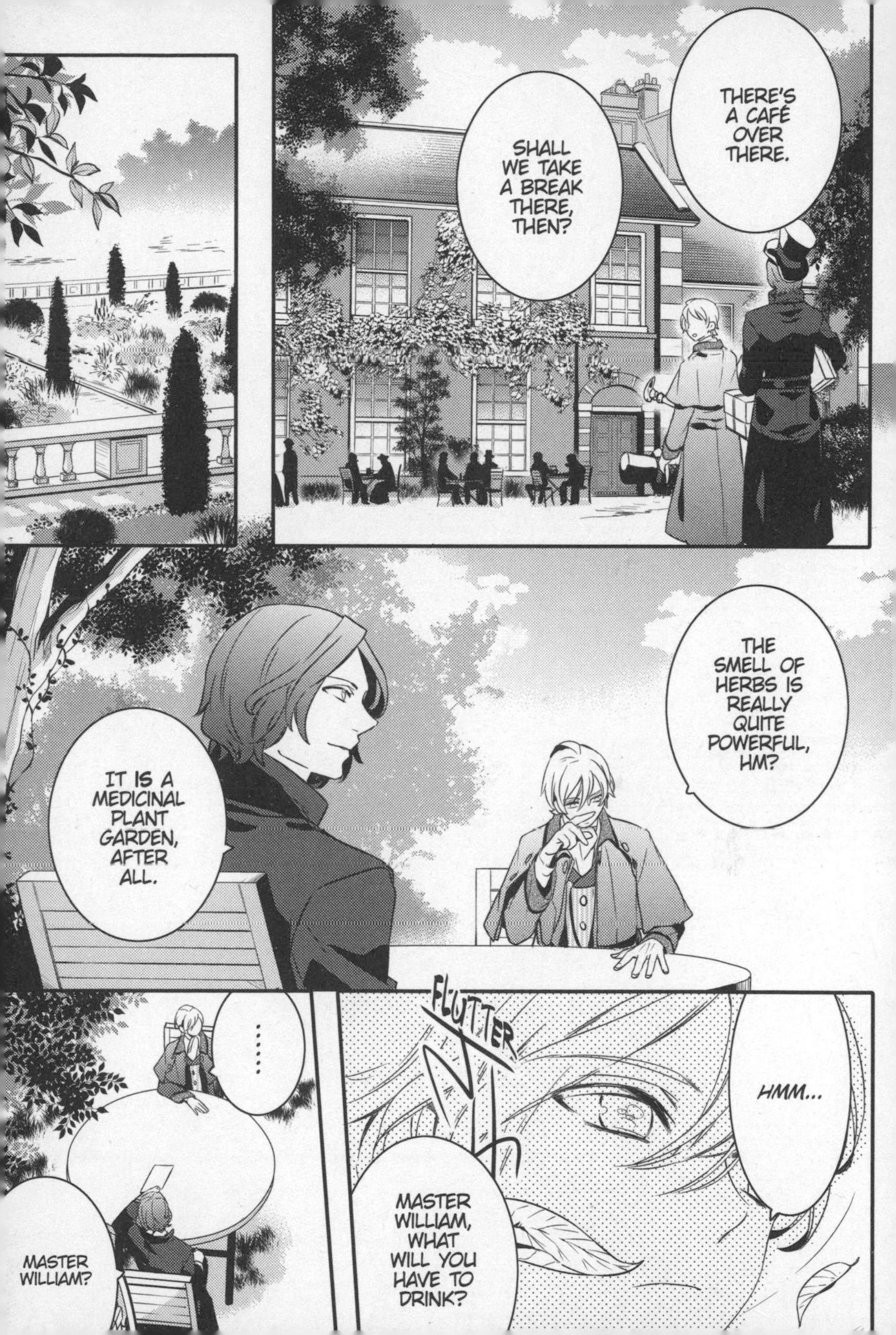
THERE'S A CAFÉ OVER THERE.
SHALL WE TAKE A BREAK THERE, THEN?
THE SMELL OF HERBS IS REALLY QUITE POWERFUL, HM?
IT IS A MEDICINAL PLANT GARDEN, AFTER ALL.
HMM...
FLUTTER
MASTER WILLIAM, WHAT WILL YOU HAVE TO DRINK?
......
MASTER WILLIAM?

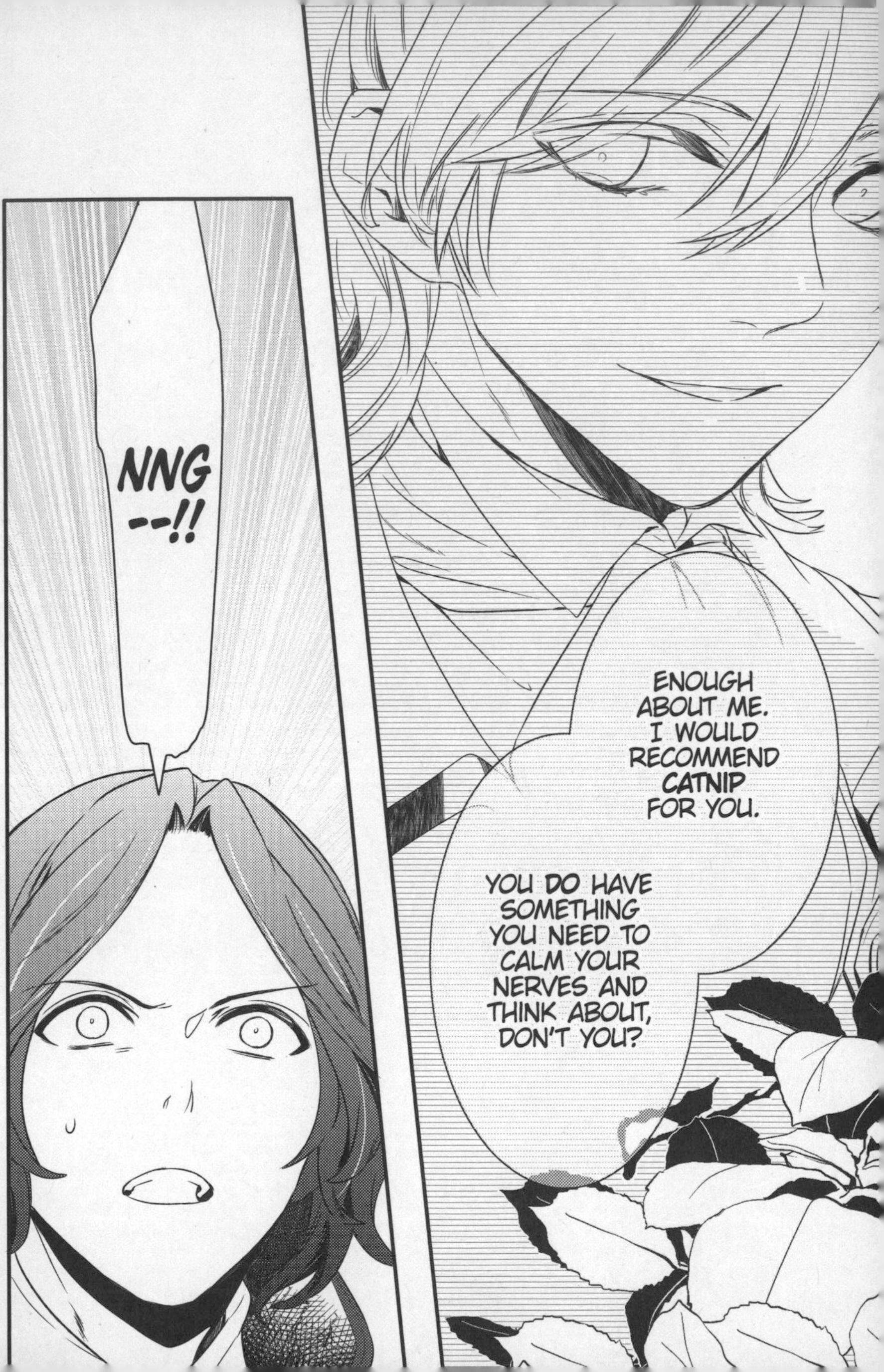
ENOUGH ABOUT ME. I WOULD RECOMMEND CATNIP FOR YOU.
YOU DO HAVE SOMETHING YOU NEED TO CALM YOUR NERVES AND THINK ABOUT, DON'T YOU?
NNG --!!

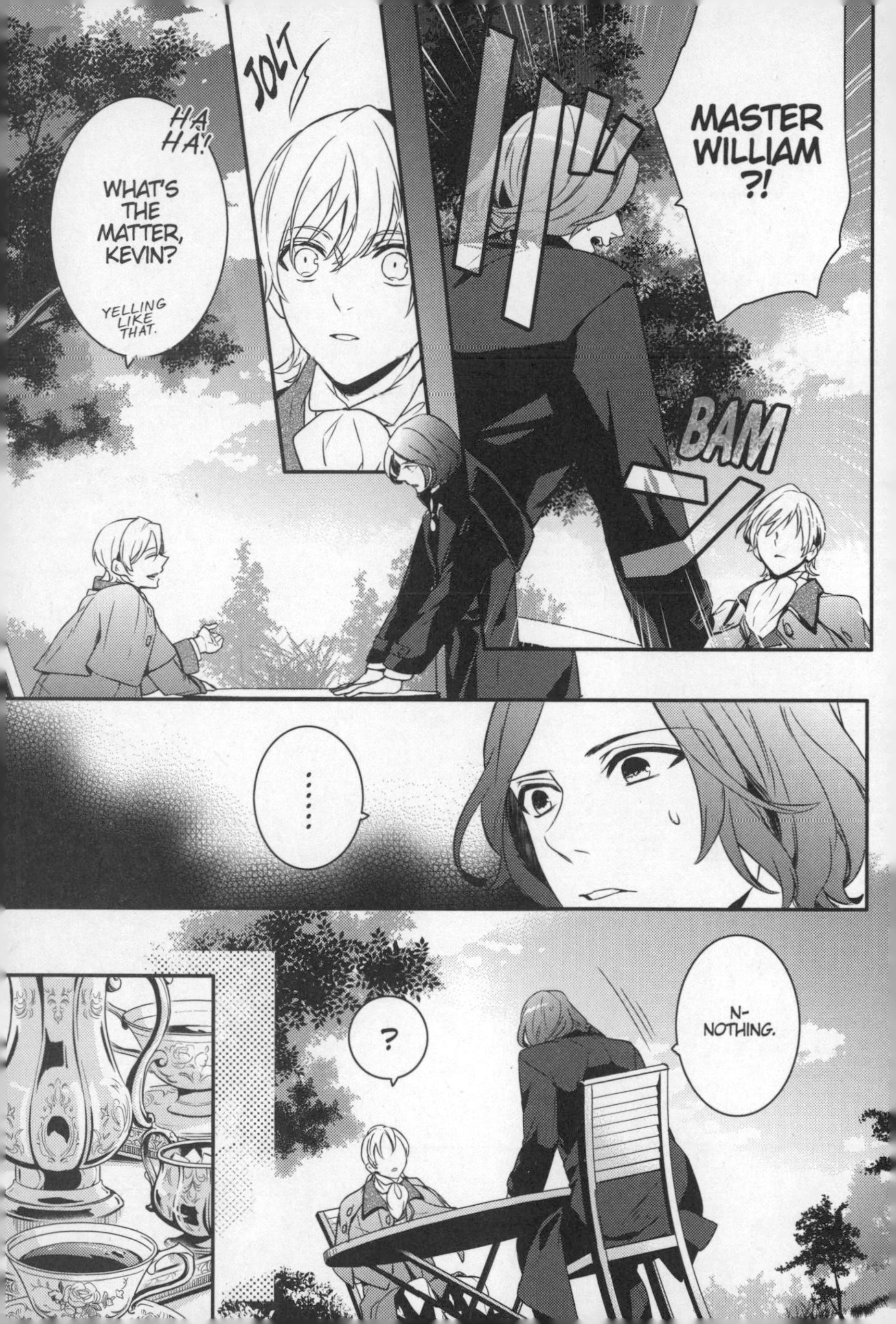
MASTER WILLIAM ?!
BAM
JOLT
HA HA!
WHAT'S THE MATTER, KEVIN?
YELLING LIKE THAT.
......
N- NOTHING.
?

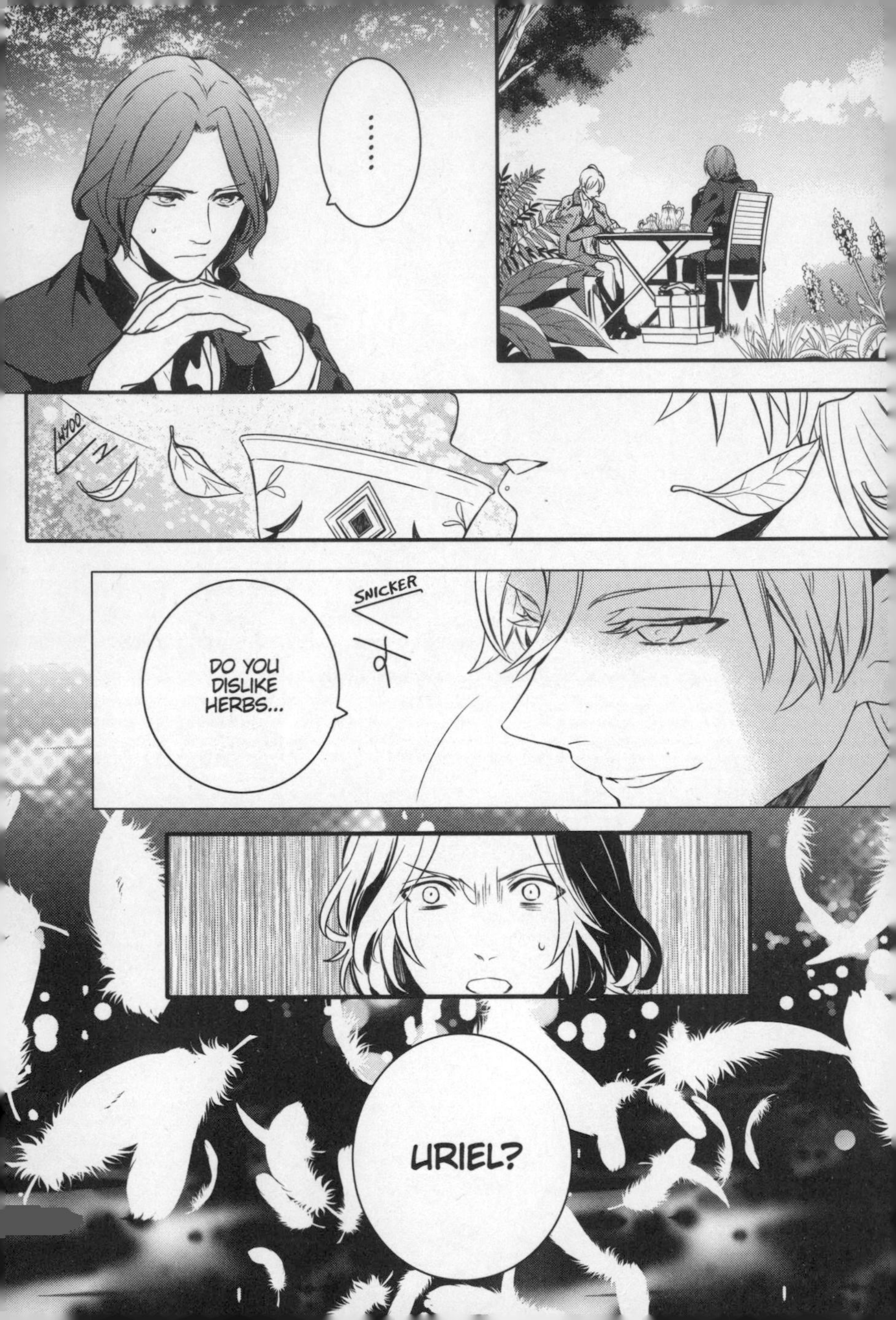
……
HYOO
SNICKER
DO YOU DISLIKE HERBS...
URIEL?

Pillar 45

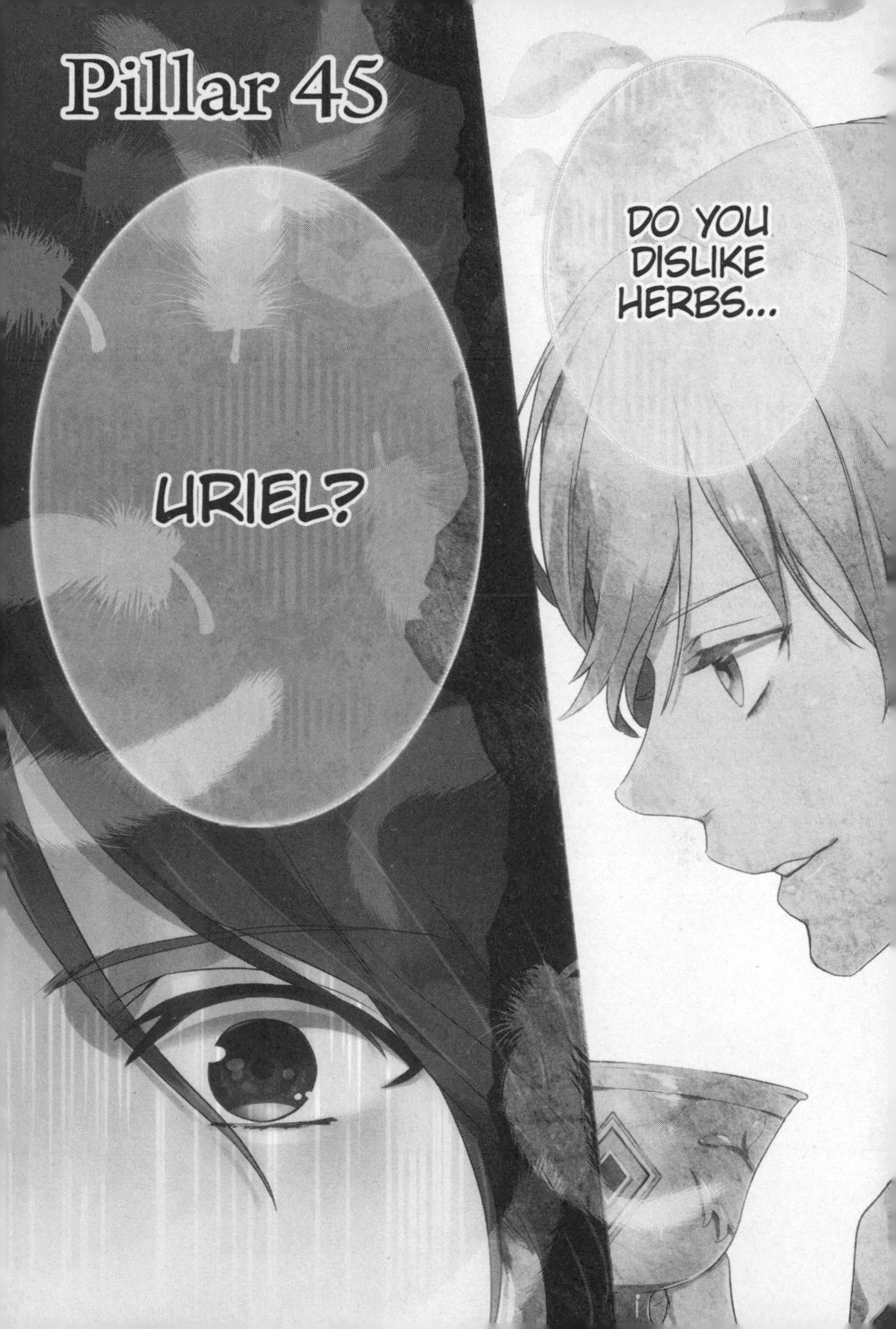
DO YOU DISLIKE HERBS...
URIEL?

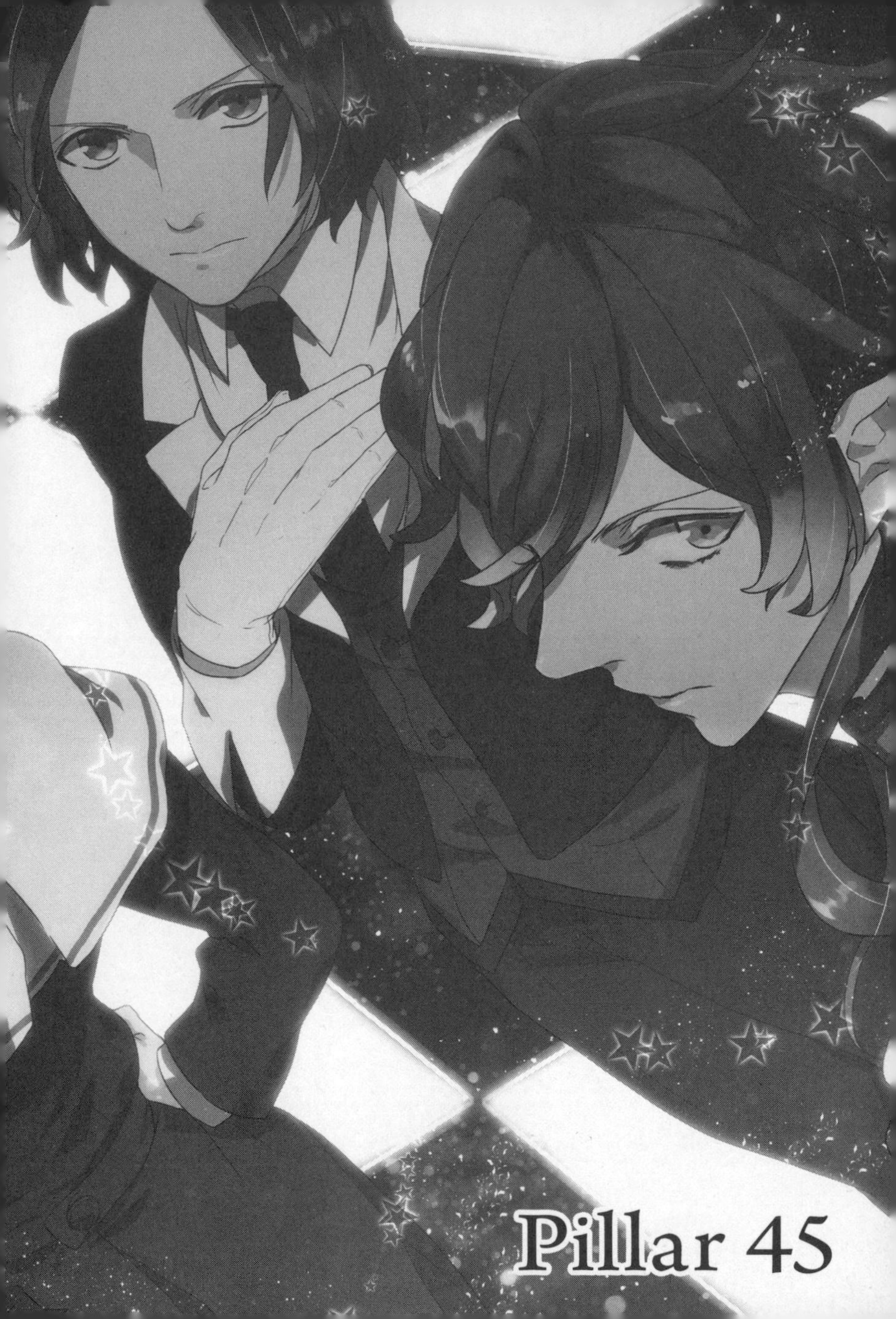

Pillar 45

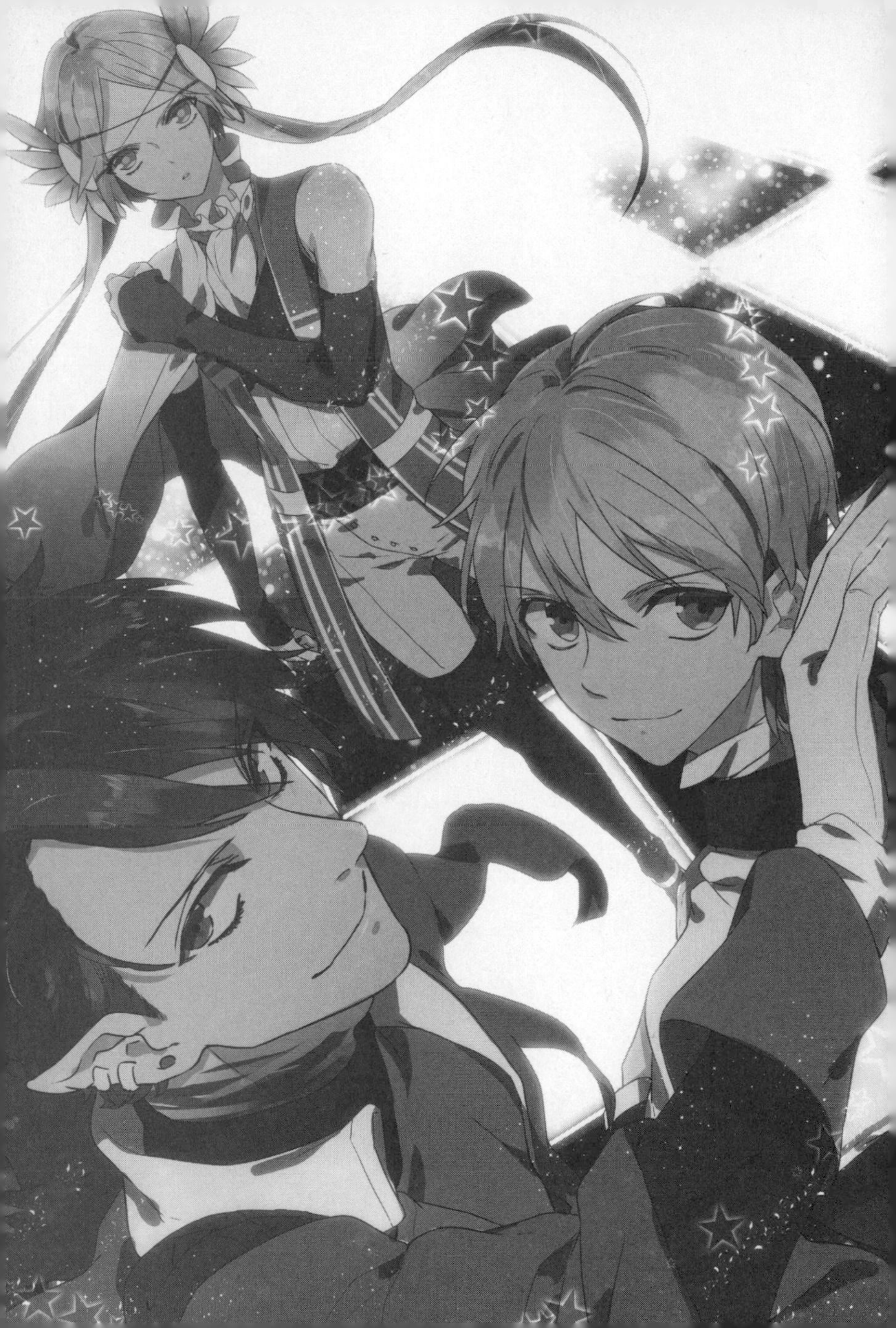

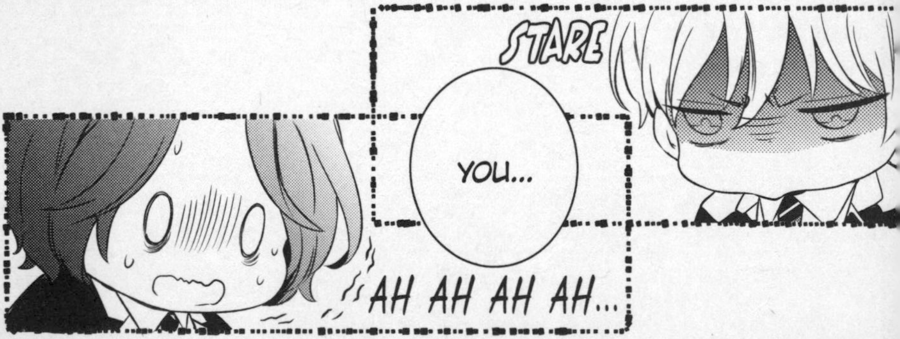
STARE
YOU...
AH AH AH AH...

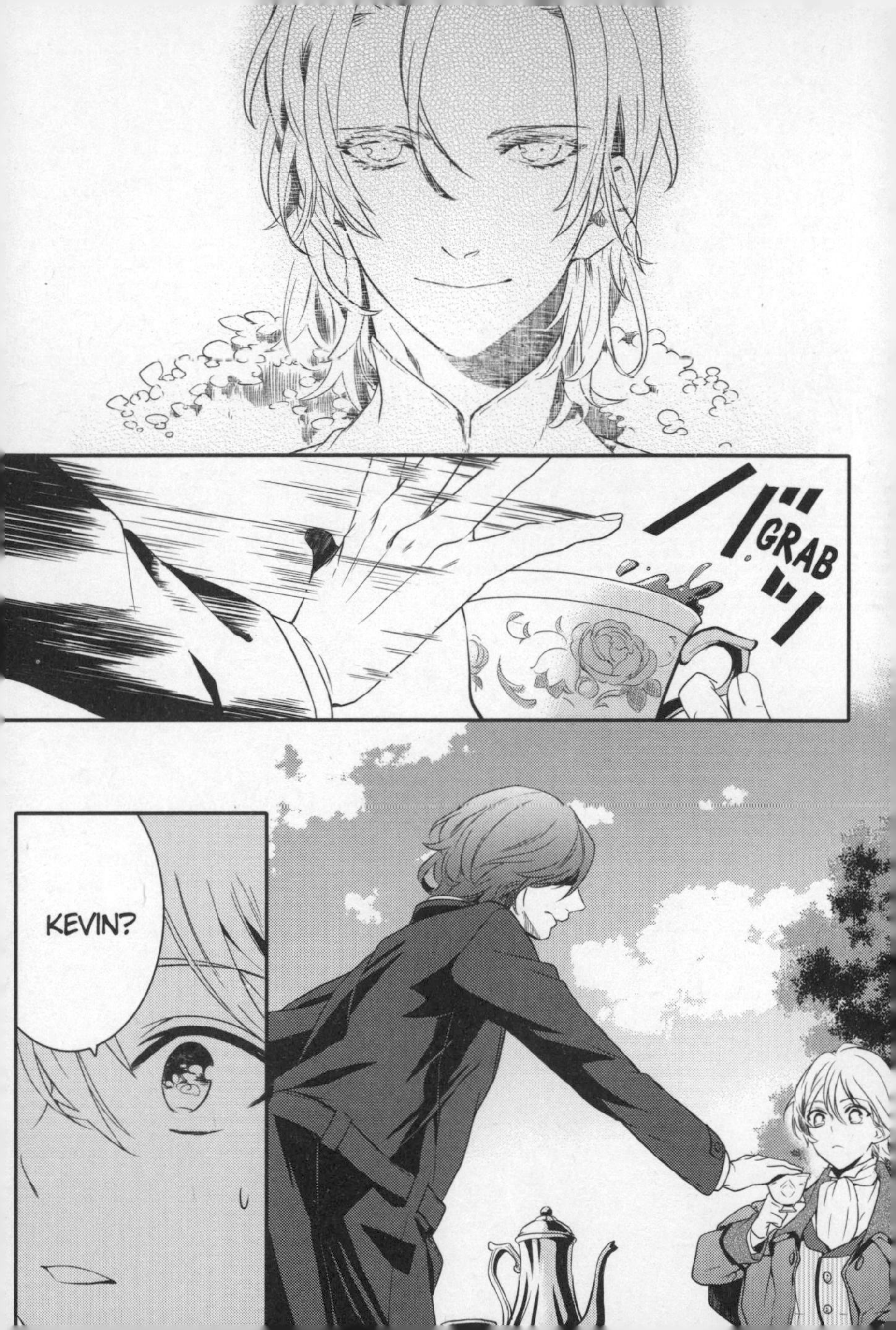
GRAB
KEVIN?

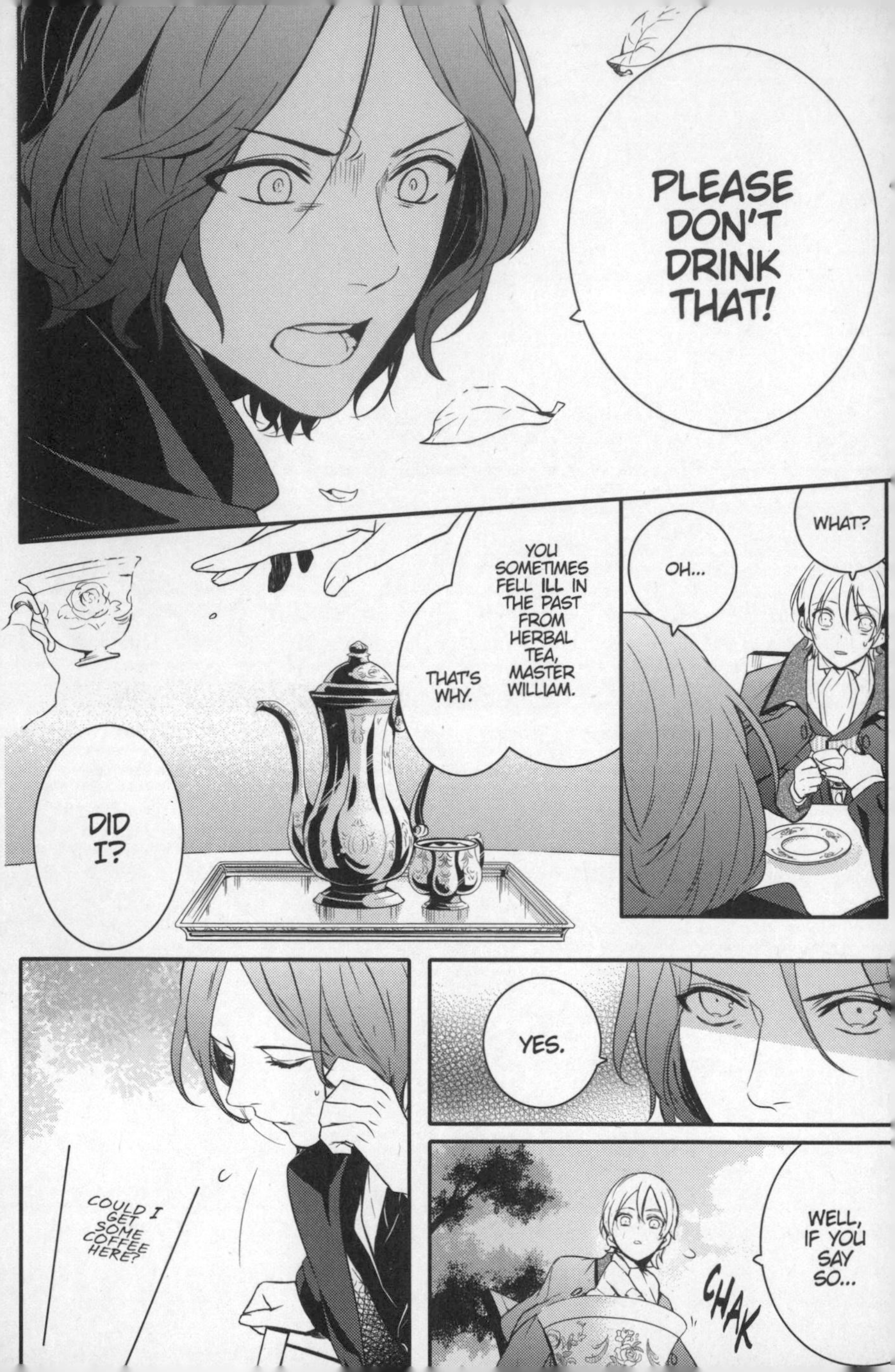
PLEASE DON'T DRINK THAT!
WHAT?
OH...
YOU SOMETIMES FELL ILL IN THE PAST FROM HERBAL TEA, MASTER WILLIAM.
THAT'S WHY.
DID I?
YES.
WELL, IF YOU SAY SO...
CHAK
COULD I GET SOME COFFEE HERE?

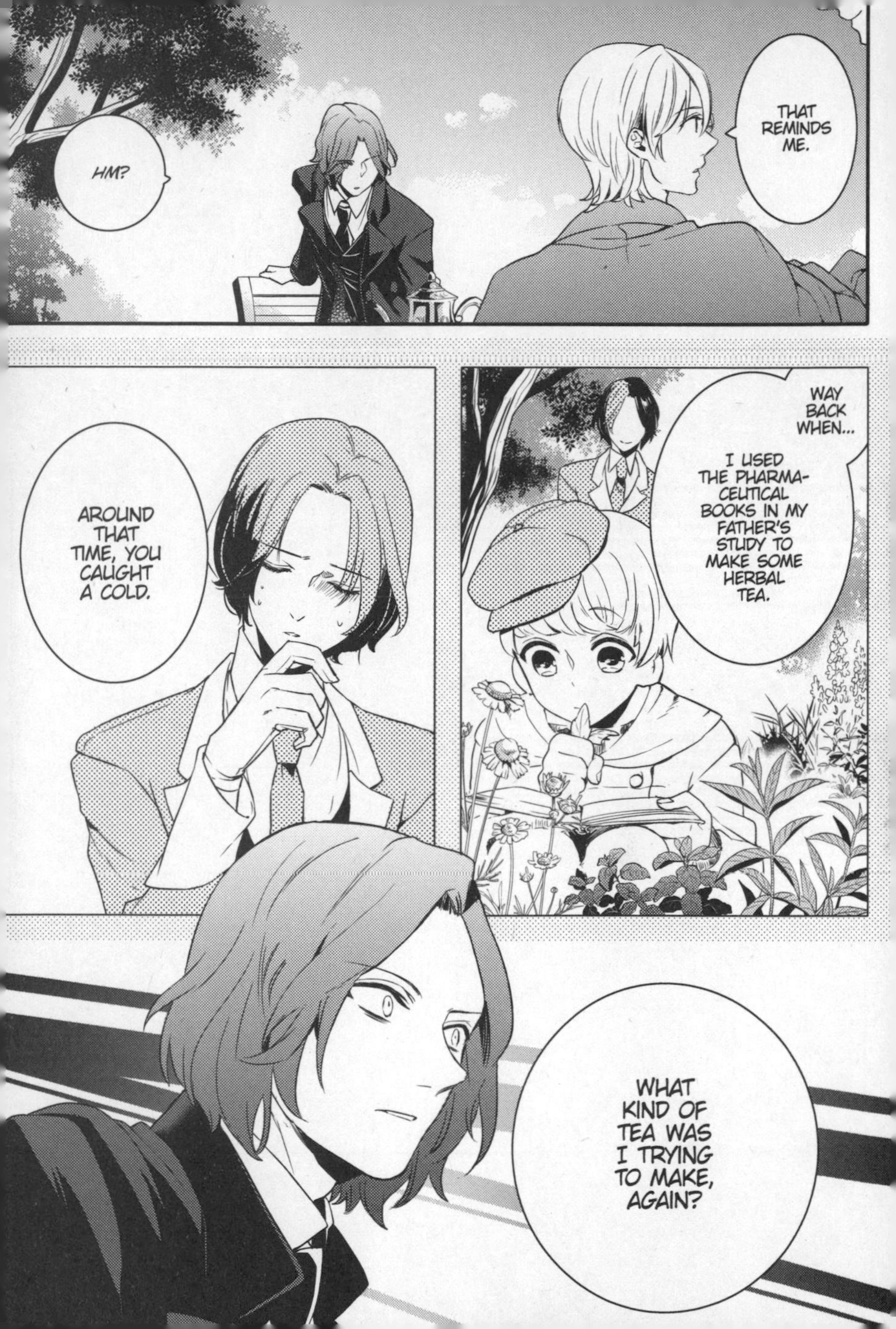
THAT REMINDS ME.
HM?
WAY BACK WHEN...
I USED THE PHARMACEUTICAL BOOKS IN MY FATHER'S STUDY TO MAKE SOME HERBAL TEA.
AROUND THAT TIME, YOU CAUGHT A COLD.
WHAT KIND OF TEA WAS I TRYING TO MAKE, AGAIN?

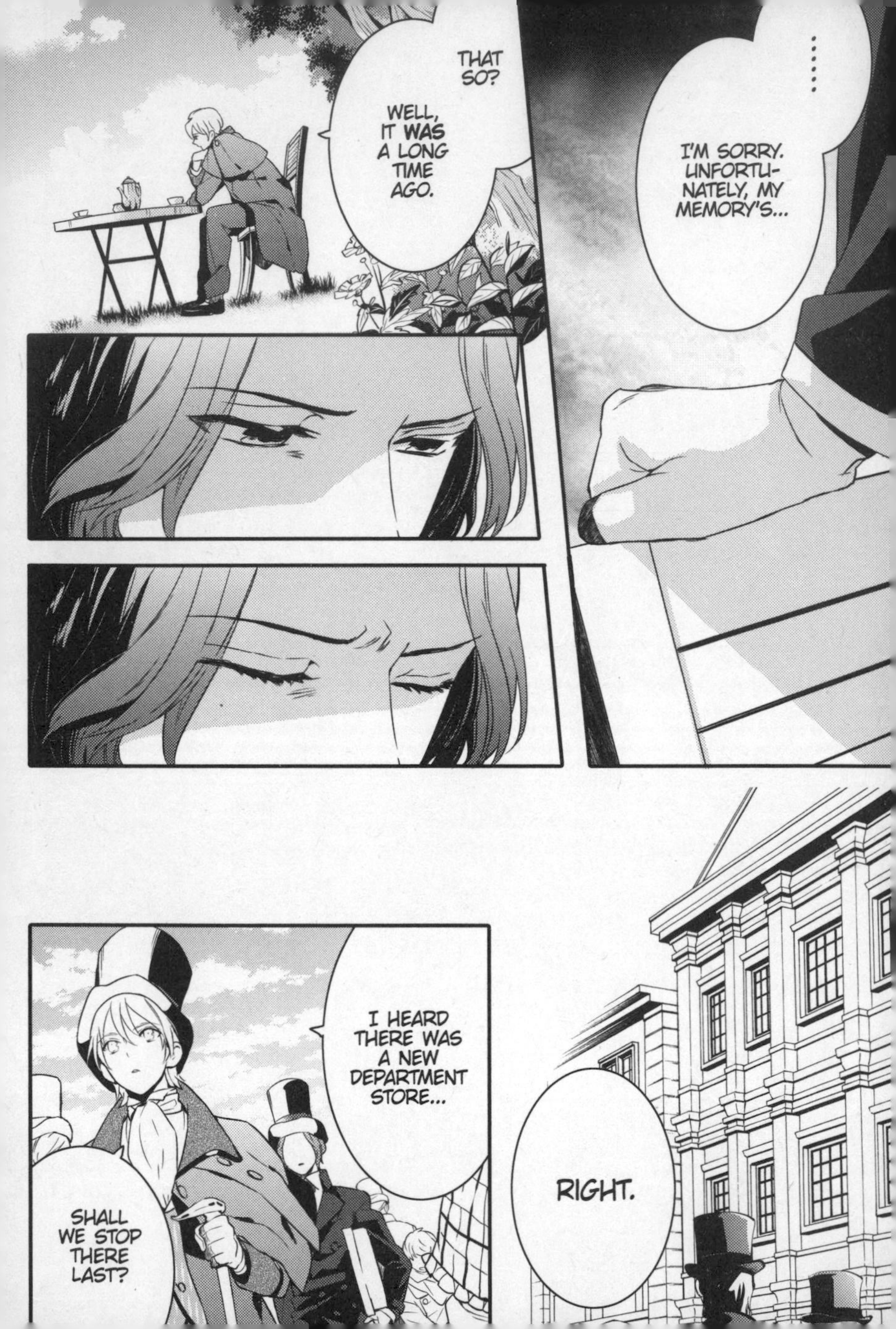
......
I'M SORRY. UNFORTU-NATELY, MY MEMORY'S...
THAT SO?
WELL, IT WAS A LONG TIME AGO.
RIGHT.
I HEARD THERE WAS A NEW DEPARTMENT STORE...
SHALL WE STOP THERE LAST?

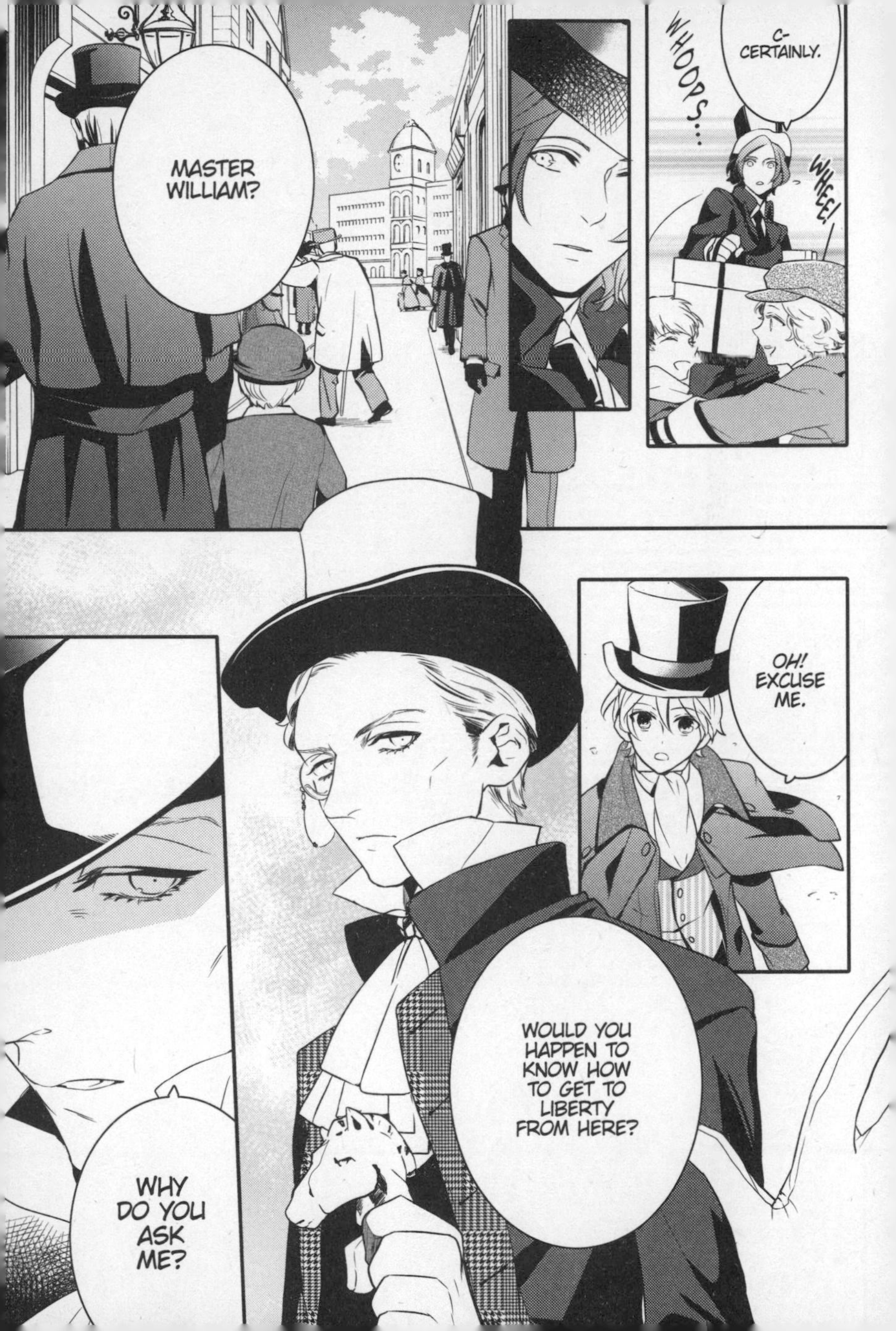
C-CERTAINLY.
WHOOPS...
WHEE!
MASTER WILLIAM?
OH! EXCUSE ME.
WOULD YOU HAPPEN TO KNOW HOW TO GET TO LIBERTY FROM HERE?
WHY DO YOU ASK ME?

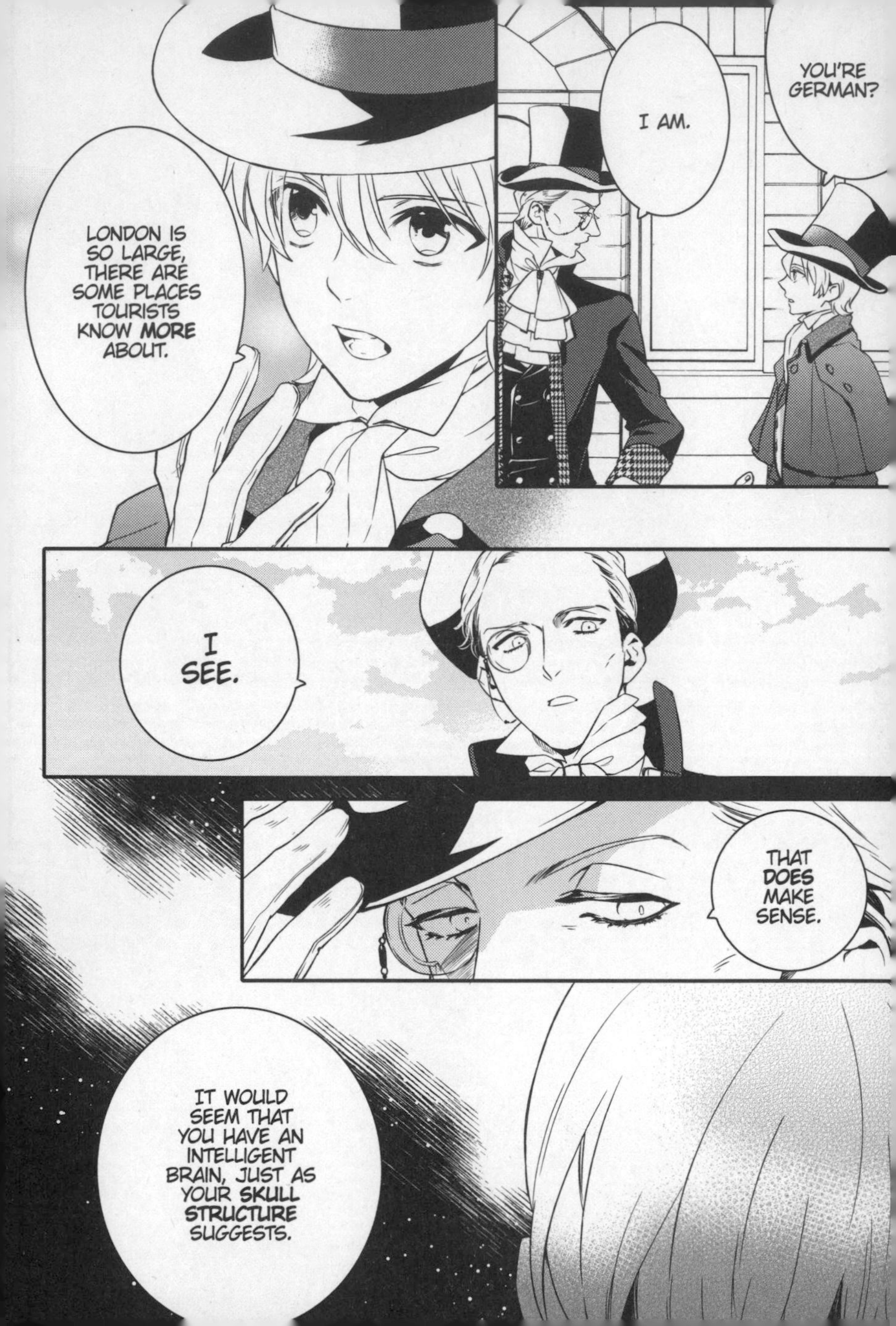
YOU'RE GERMAN?
I AM.
LONDON IS SO LARGE, THERE ARE SOME PLACES TOURISTS KNOW MORE ABOUT.
I SEE.
THAT DOES MAKE SENSE.
IT WOULD SEEM THAT YOU HAVE AN INTELLIGENT BRAIN, JUST AS YOUR SKULL STRUCTURE SUGGESTS.

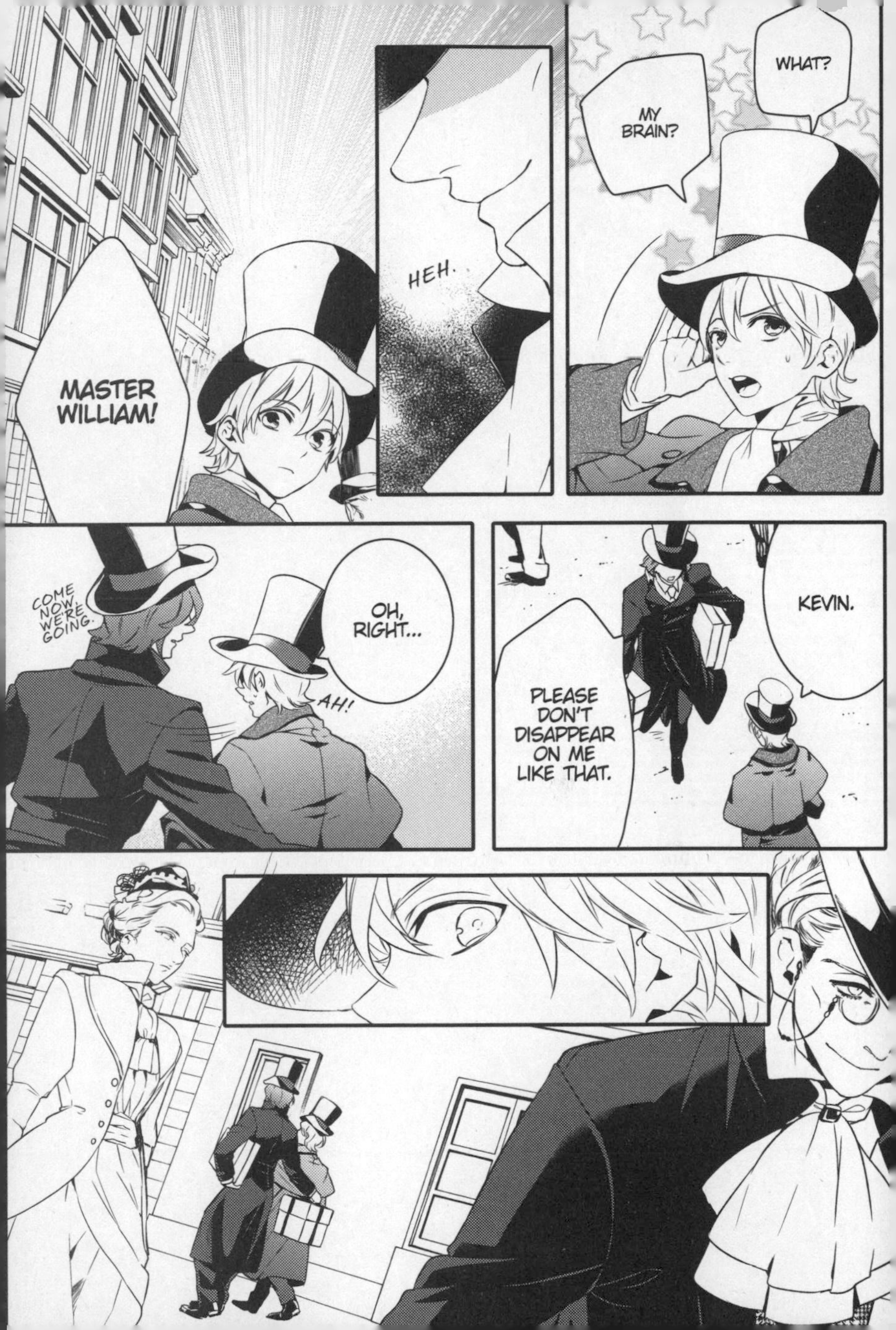
WHAT?
MY BRAIN?
HEH.
MASTER WILLIAM!
KEVIN.
PLEASE DON'T DISAPPEAR ON ME LIKE THAT.
OH, RIGHT...
AH!
COME NOW, WE'RE GOING.

AARGH! THIS IS SO ANNOYING!

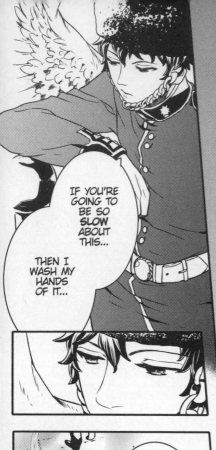

IF YOU'RE GOING TO BE SO SLOW ABOUT THIS...

THEN I WASH MY HANDS OF IT...

URIEL.

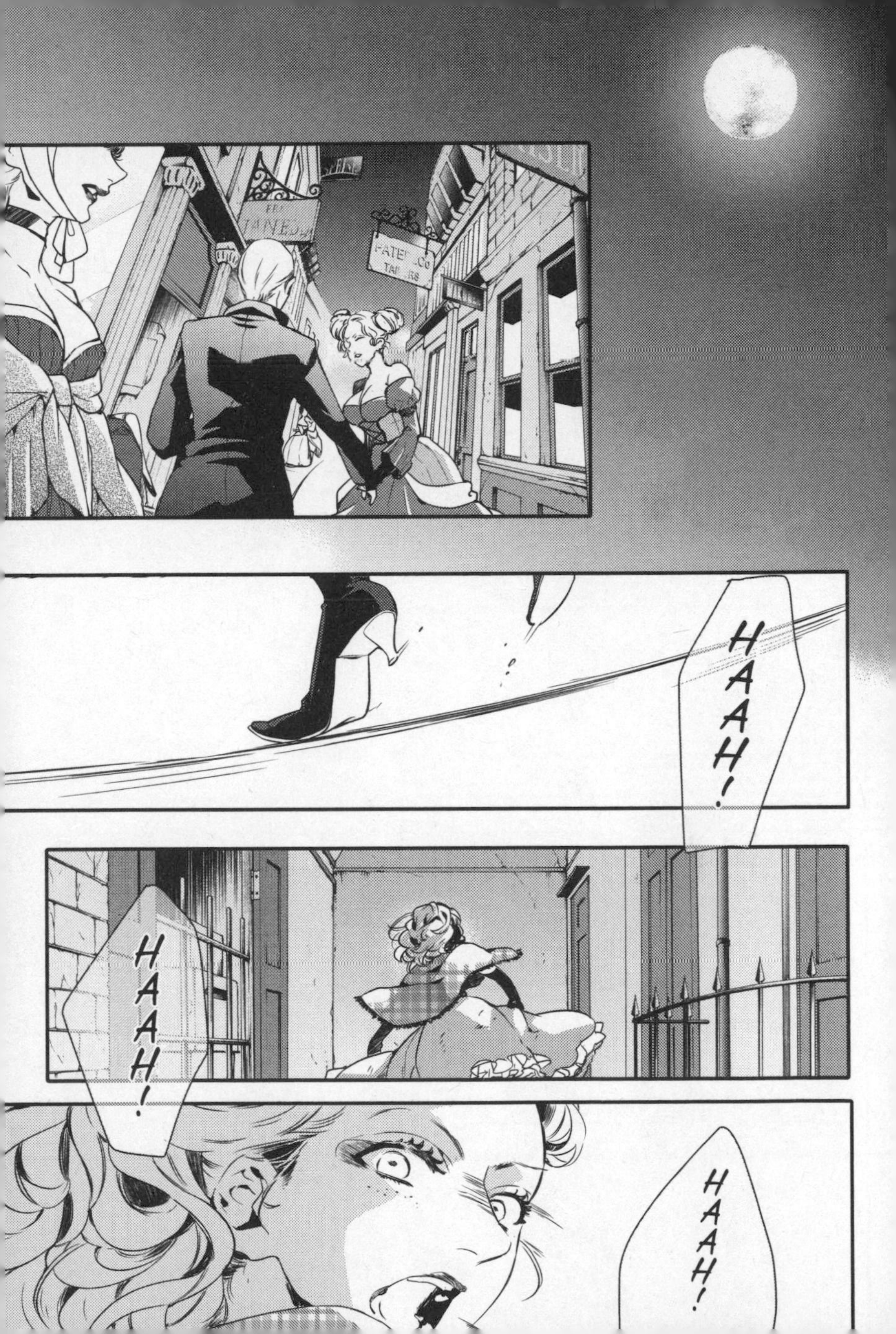
HAAAH!
HAAAH!
HAAAH!

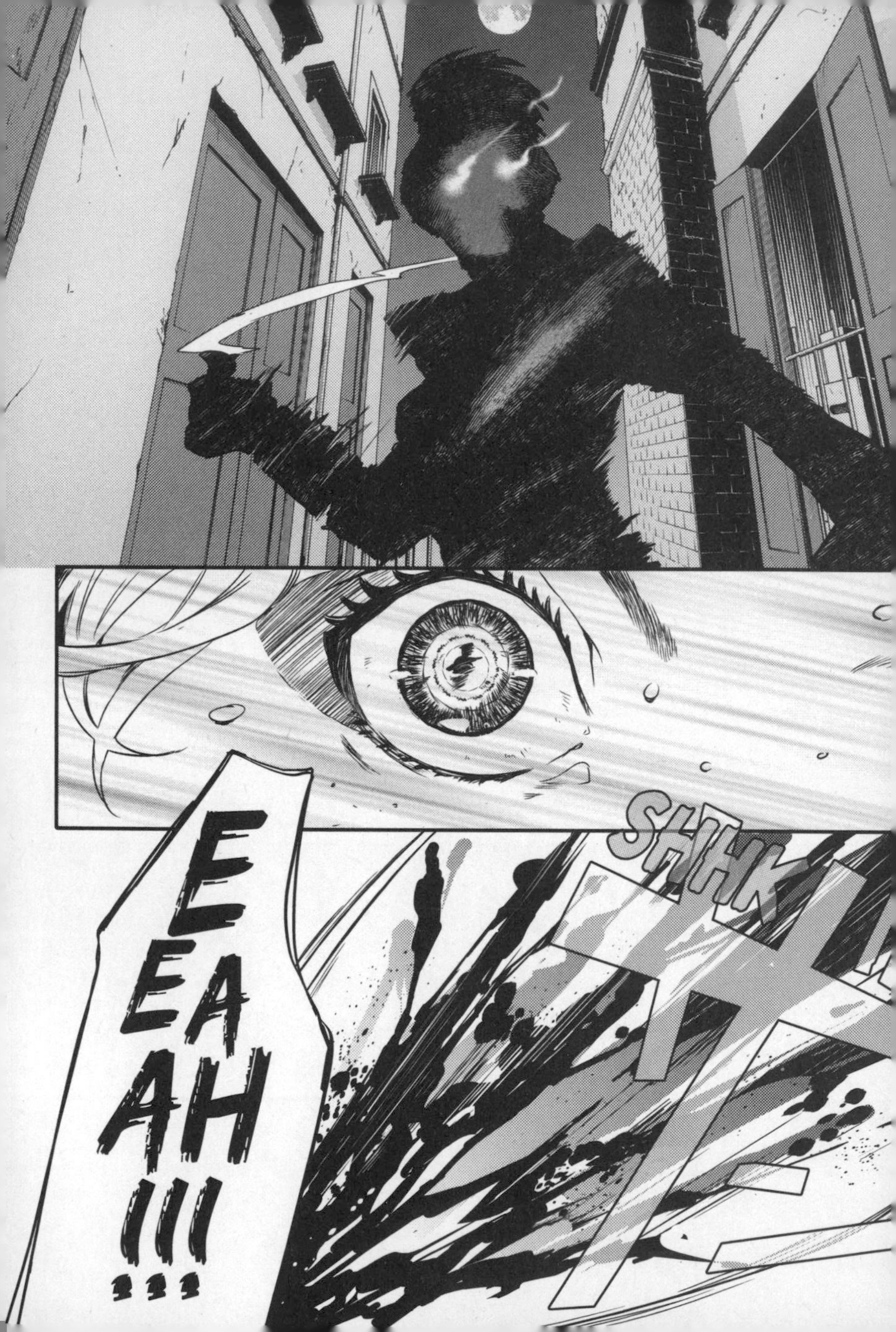
SHHK
EEEAAAHH!!!!!!

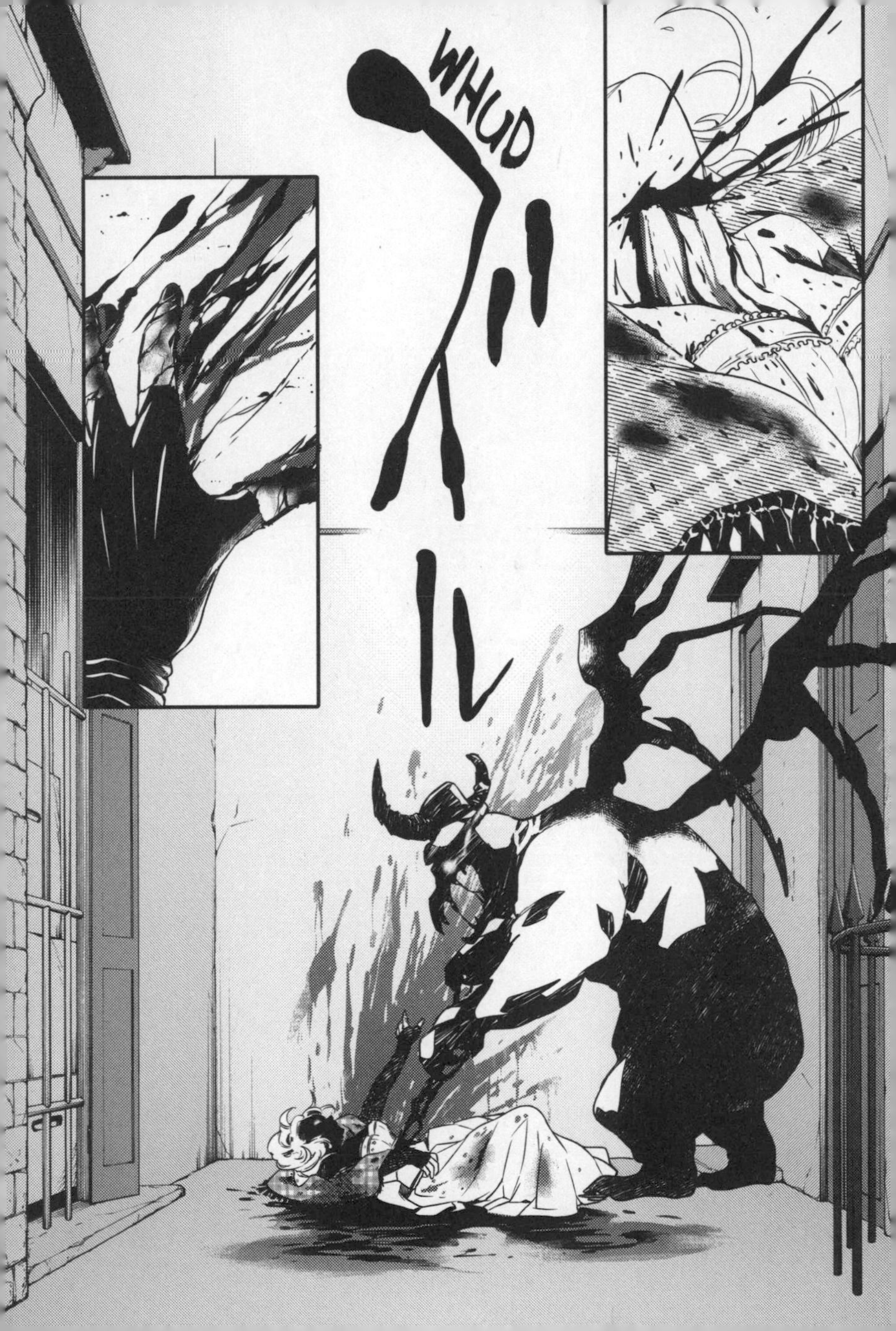
WHUD

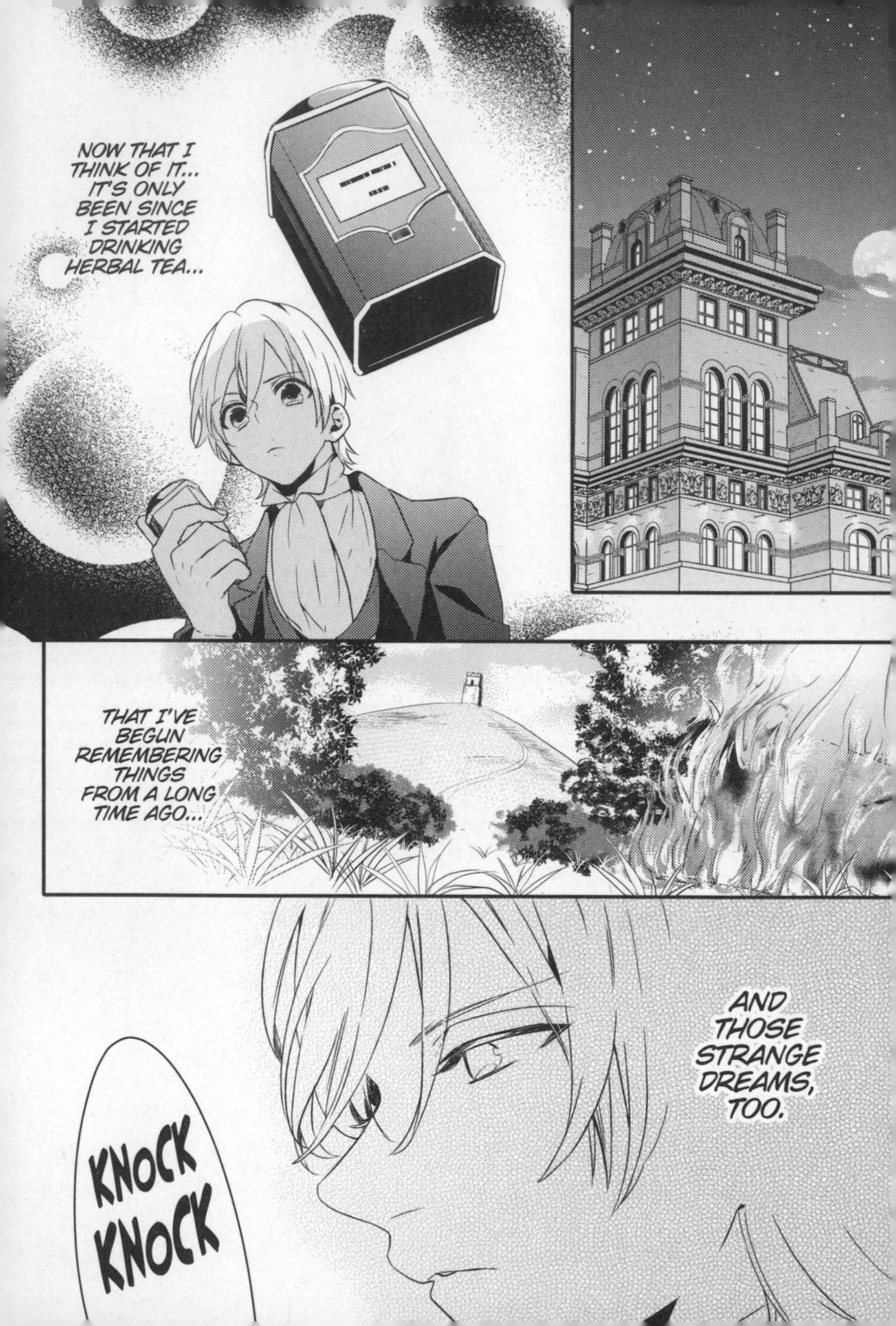
NOW THAT I THINK OF IT... IT'S ONLY BEEN SINCE I STARTED DRINKING HERBAL TEA...
THAT I'VE BEGUN REMEMBERING THINGS FROM A LONG TIME AGO...
AND THOSE STRANGE DREAMS, TOO.
KNOCK KNOCK

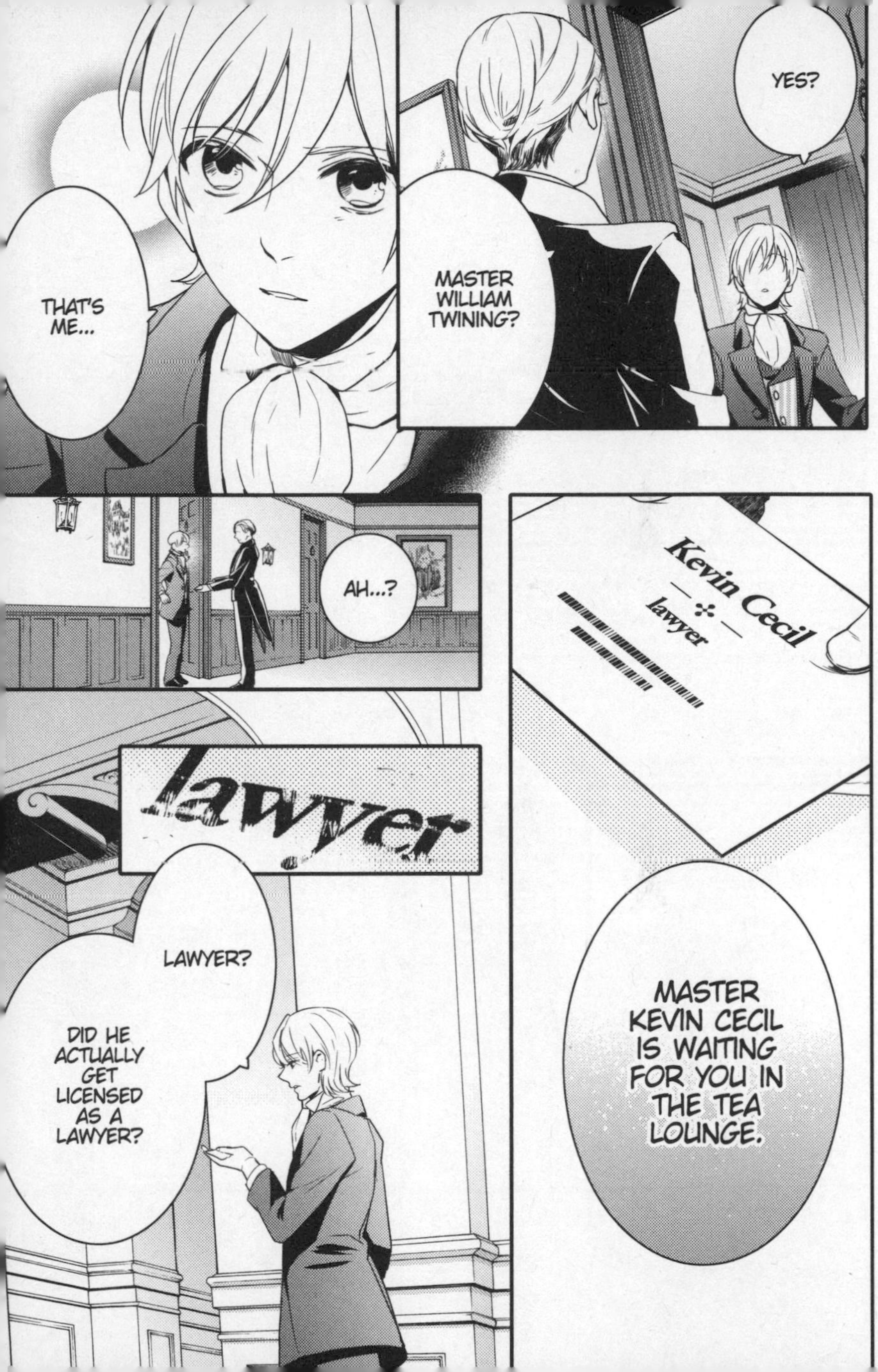
YES?
MASTER WILLIAM TWINING?
THAT'S ME...
Kevin Cecil
lawyer
MASTER KEVIN CECIL IS WAITING FOR YOU IN THE TEA LOUNGE.
AH...?
lawyer
LAWYER?
DID HE ACTUALLY GET LICENSED AS A LAWYER?

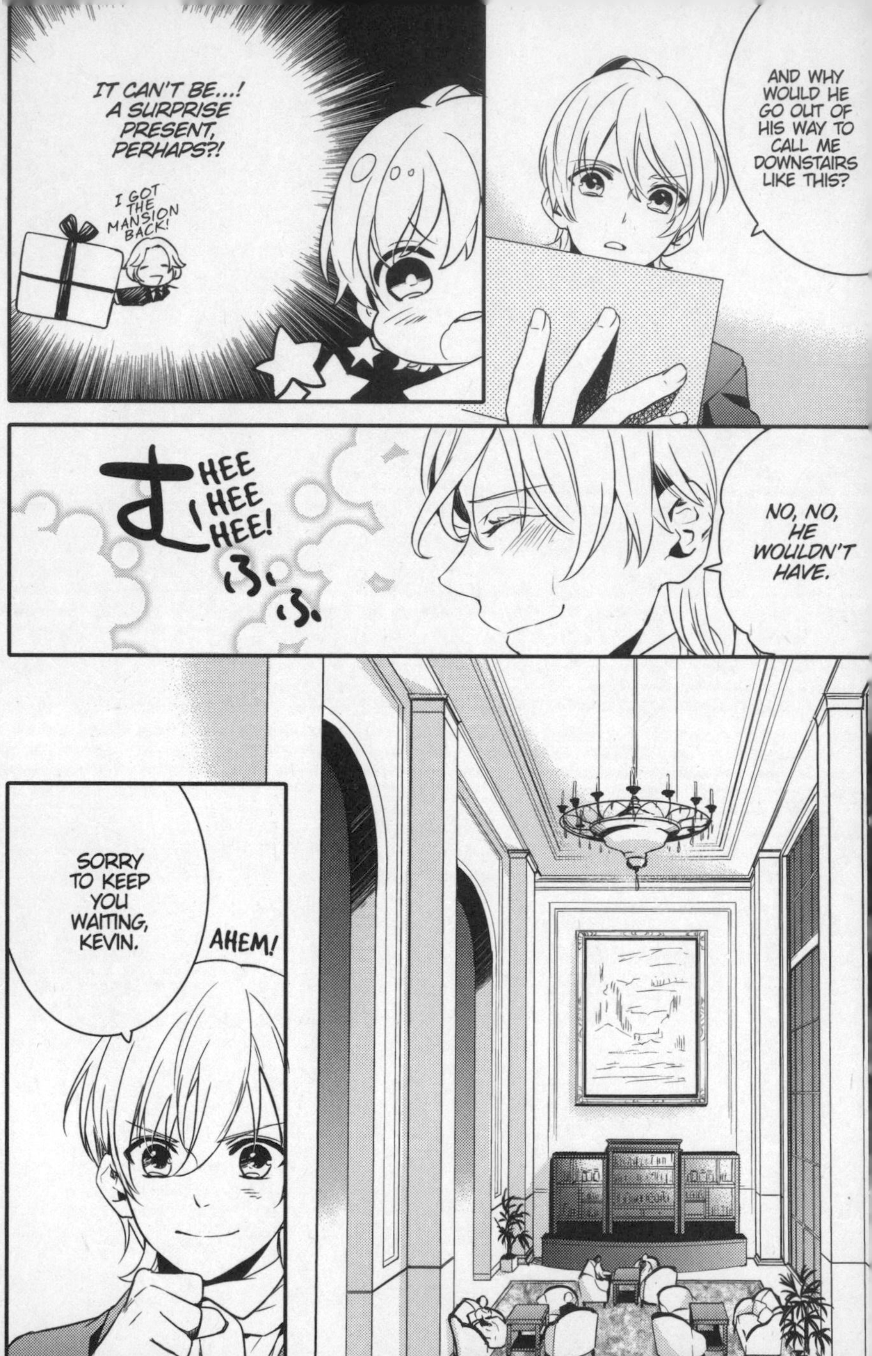
AND WHY WOULD HE GO OUT OF HIS WAY TO CALL ME DOWNSTAIRS LIKE THIS?
IT CAN'T BE...! A SURPRISE PRESENT, PERHAPS?!
I GOT THE MANSION BACK!
NO, NO, HE WOULDN'T HAVE.
HEE HEE HEE!
ふふ
AHEM!
SORRY TO KEEP YOU WAITING, KEVIN.

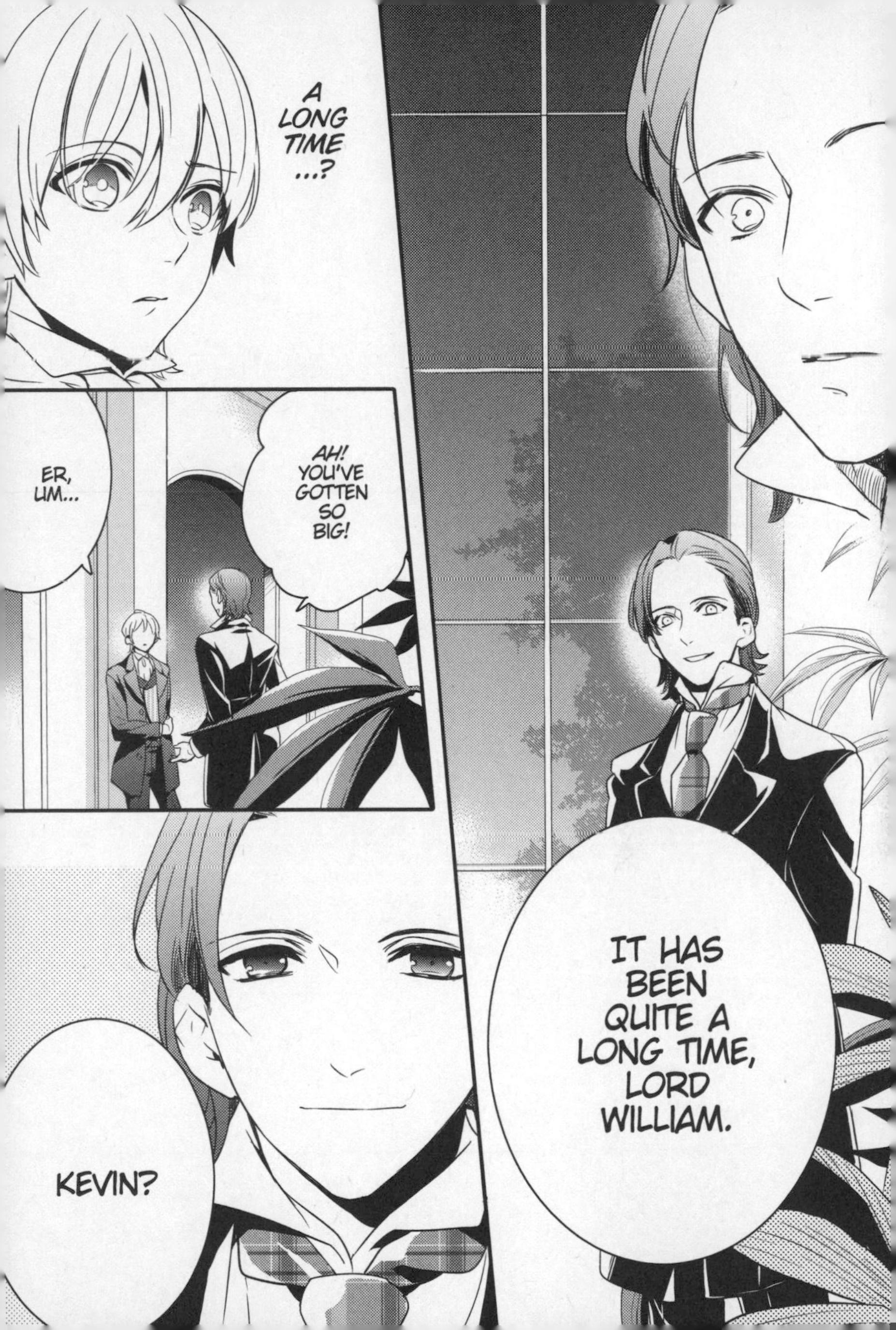
IT HAS BEEN QUITE A LONG TIME, LORD WILLIAM.
A LONG TIME ...?
AH! YOU'VE GOTTEN SO BIG!
ER, UM...
KEVIN?

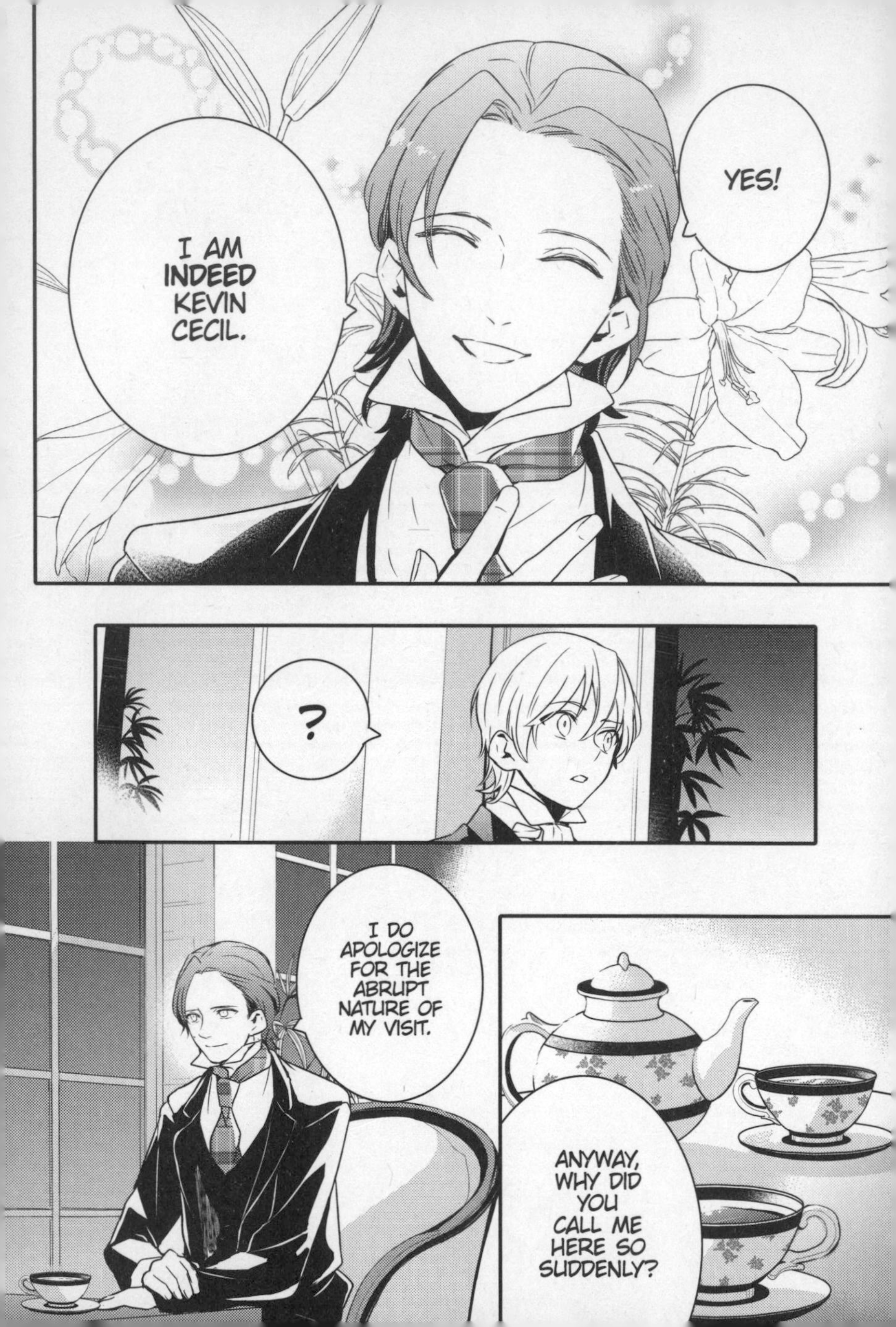
YES!
I AM INDEED KEVIN CECIL.
?
ANYWAY, WHY DID YOU CALL ME HERE SO SUDDENLY?
I DO APOLOGIZE FOR THE ABRUPT NATURE OF MY VISIT.

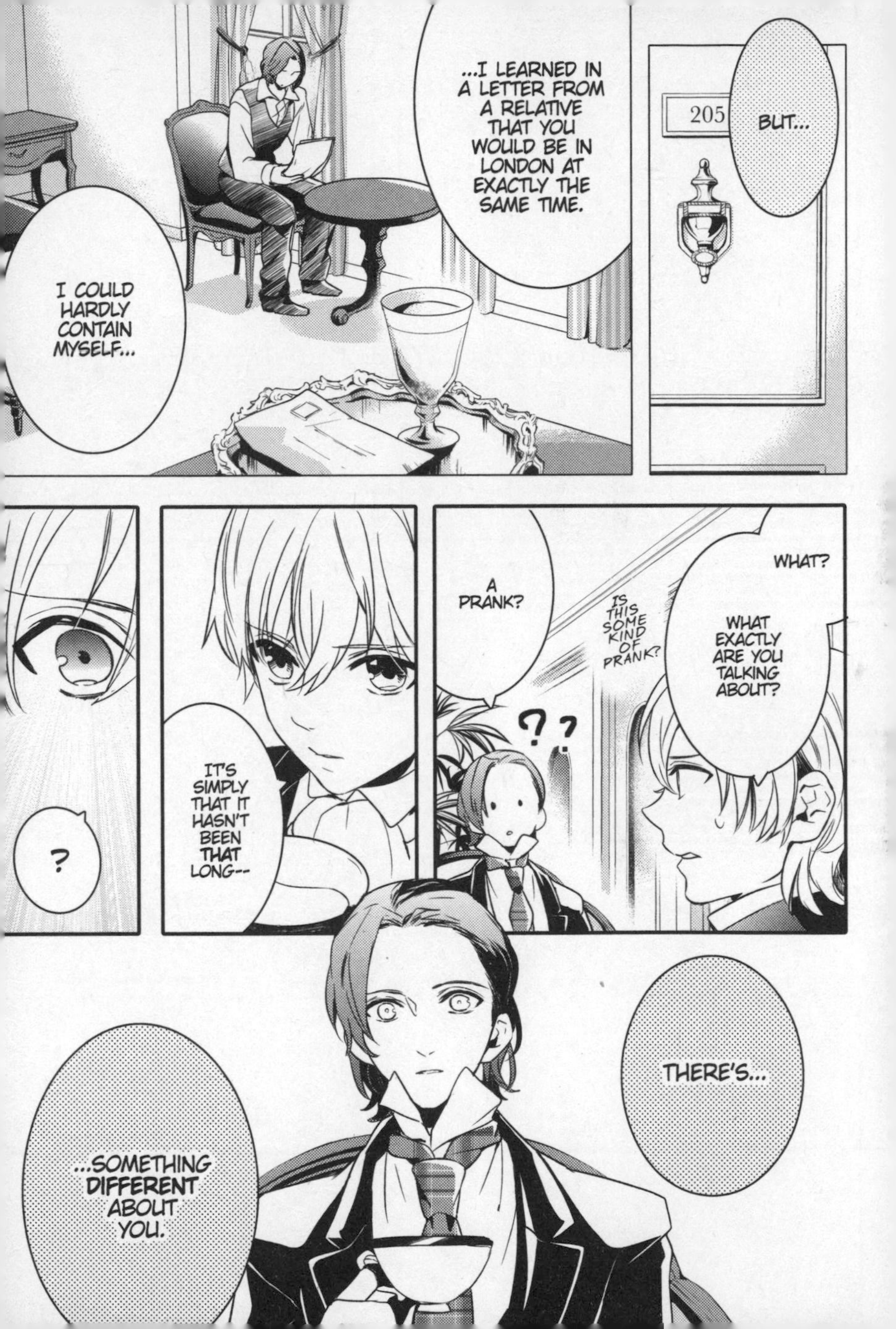
205
BUT...
...I LEARNED IN A LETTER FROM A RELATIVE THAT YOU WOULD BE IN LONDON AT EXACTLY THE SAME TIME.
I COULD HARDLY CONTAIN MYSELF...
WHAT?
WHAT EXACTLY ARE YOU TALKING ABOUT?
IS THIS SOME KIND OF PRANK?
A PRANK?
??
IT'S SIMPLY THAT IT HASN'T BEEN THAT LONG--
?
THERE'S...
...SOMETHING DIFFERENT ABOUT YOU.

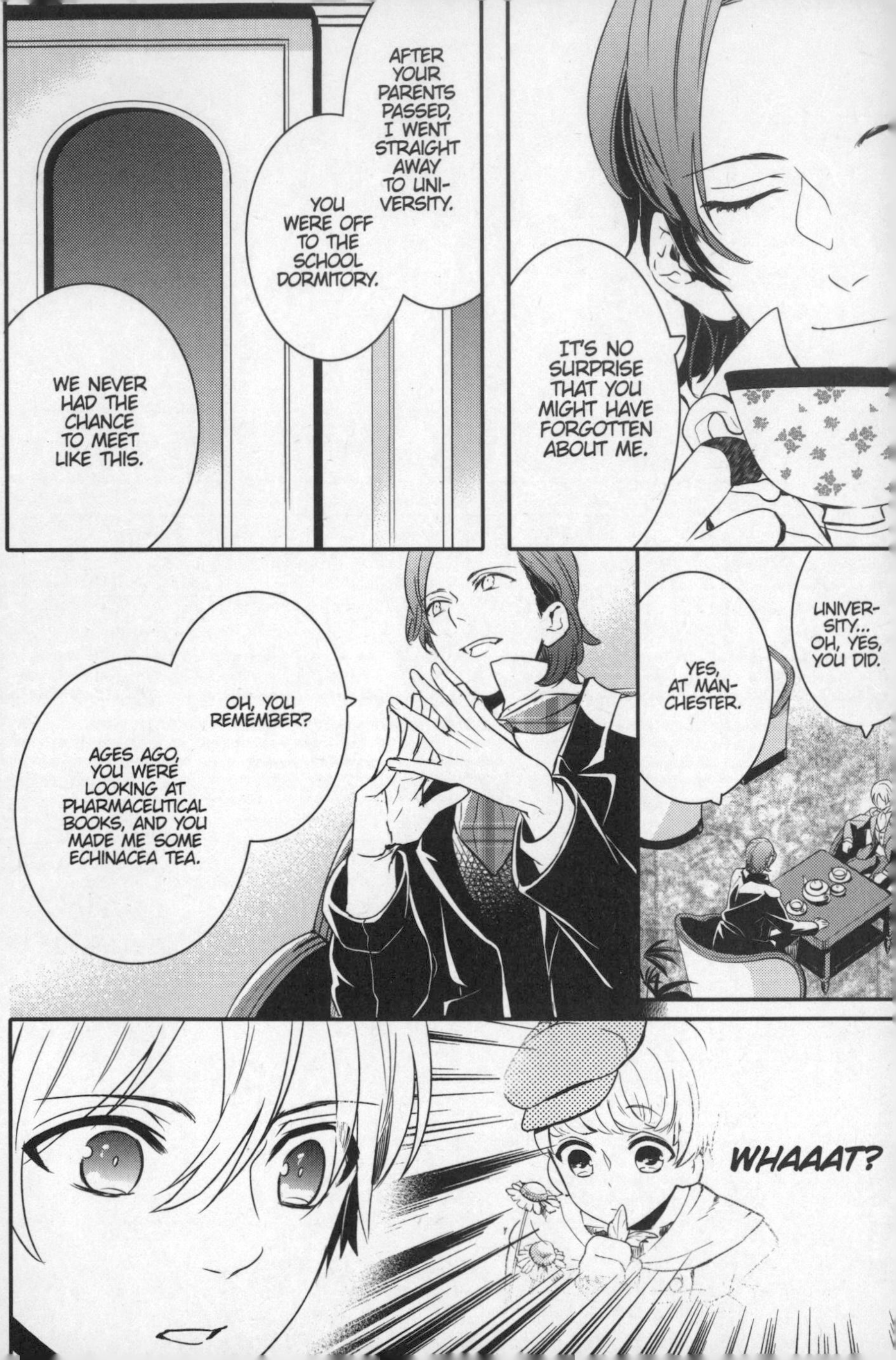
IT'S NO SURPRISE THAT YOU MIGHT HAVE FORGOTTEN ABOUT ME.
AFTER YOUR PARENTS PASSED, I WENT STRAIGHT AWAY TO UNI-VERSITY.
YOU WERE OFF TO THE SCHOOL DORMITORY.
WE NEVER HAD THE CHANCE TO MEET LIKE THIS.
UNIVER-SITY... OH, YES, YOU DID.
YES, AT MAN-CHESTER.
OH, YOU REMEMBER?
AGES AGO, YOU WERE LOOKING AT PHARMACEUTICAL BOOKS, AND YOU MADE ME SOME ECHINACEA TEA.
WHAAAT?

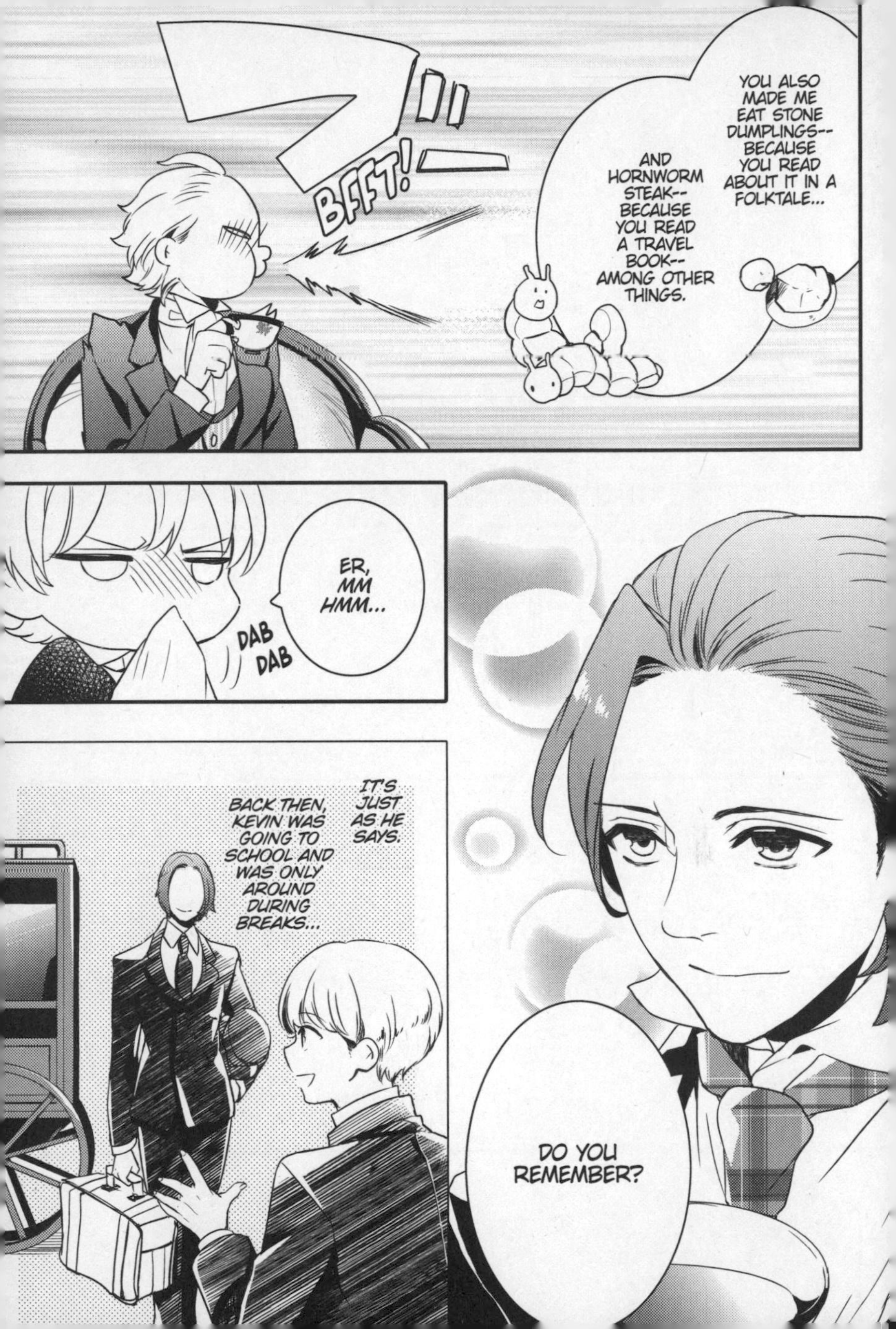
YOU ALSO MADE ME EAT STONE DUMPLINGS-- BECAUSE YOU READ ABOUT IT IN A FOLKTALE...
AND HORNWORM STEAK-- BECAUSE YOU READ A TRAVEL BOOK-- AMONG OTHER THINGS.
BFFT!
DO YOU REMEMBER?
ER, MM HMM...
DAB DAB
IT'S JUST AS HE SAYS.
BACK THEN, KEVIN WAS GOING TO SCHOOL AND WAS ONLY AROUND DURING BREAKS...

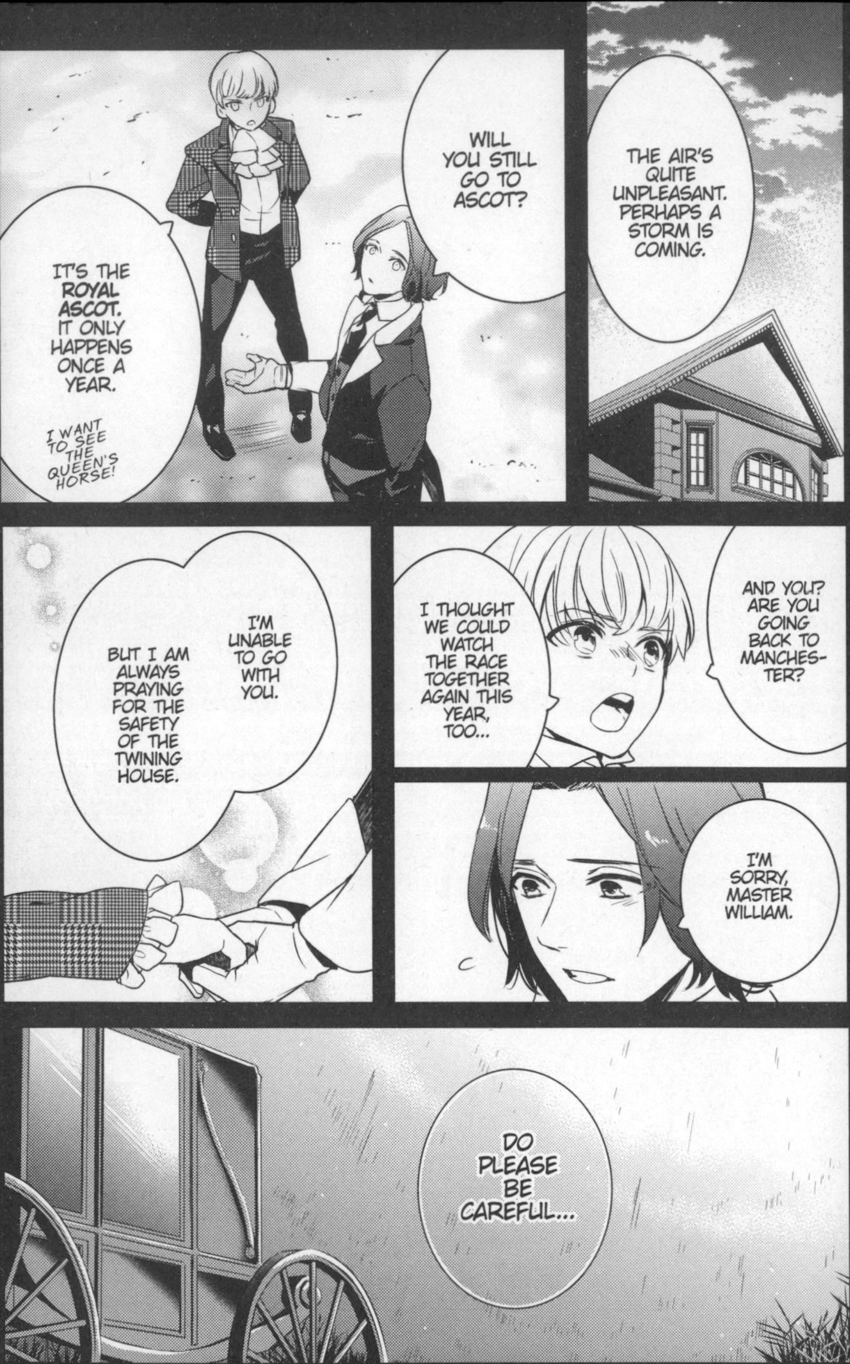
THE AIR'S QUITE UNPLEASANT. PERHAPS A STORM IS COMING.
WILL YOU STILL GO TO ASCOT?
...
IT'S THE ROYAL ASCOT. IT ONLY HAPPENS ONCE A YEAR.
I WANT TO SEE THE QUEEN'S HORSE!
AND YOU? ARE YOU GOING BACK TO MANCHESTER?
I THOUGHT WE COULD WATCH THE RACE TOGETHER AGAIN THIS YEAR, TOO...
I'M SORRY, MASTER WILLIAM.
I'M UNABLE TO GO WITH YOU.
BUT I AM ALWAYS PRAYING FOR THE SAFETY OF THE TWINING HOUSE.
DO PLEASE BE CAREFUL...

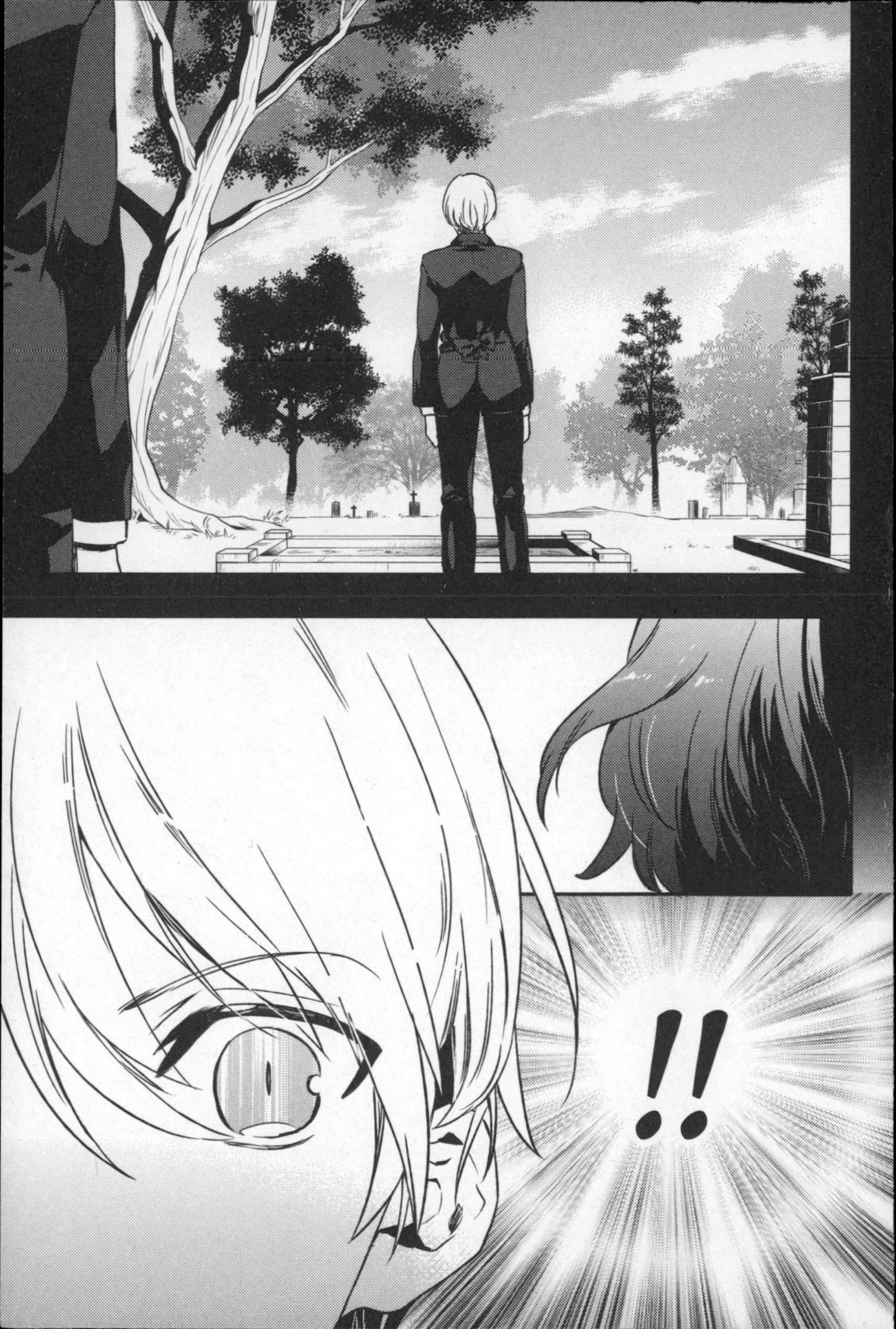
!!

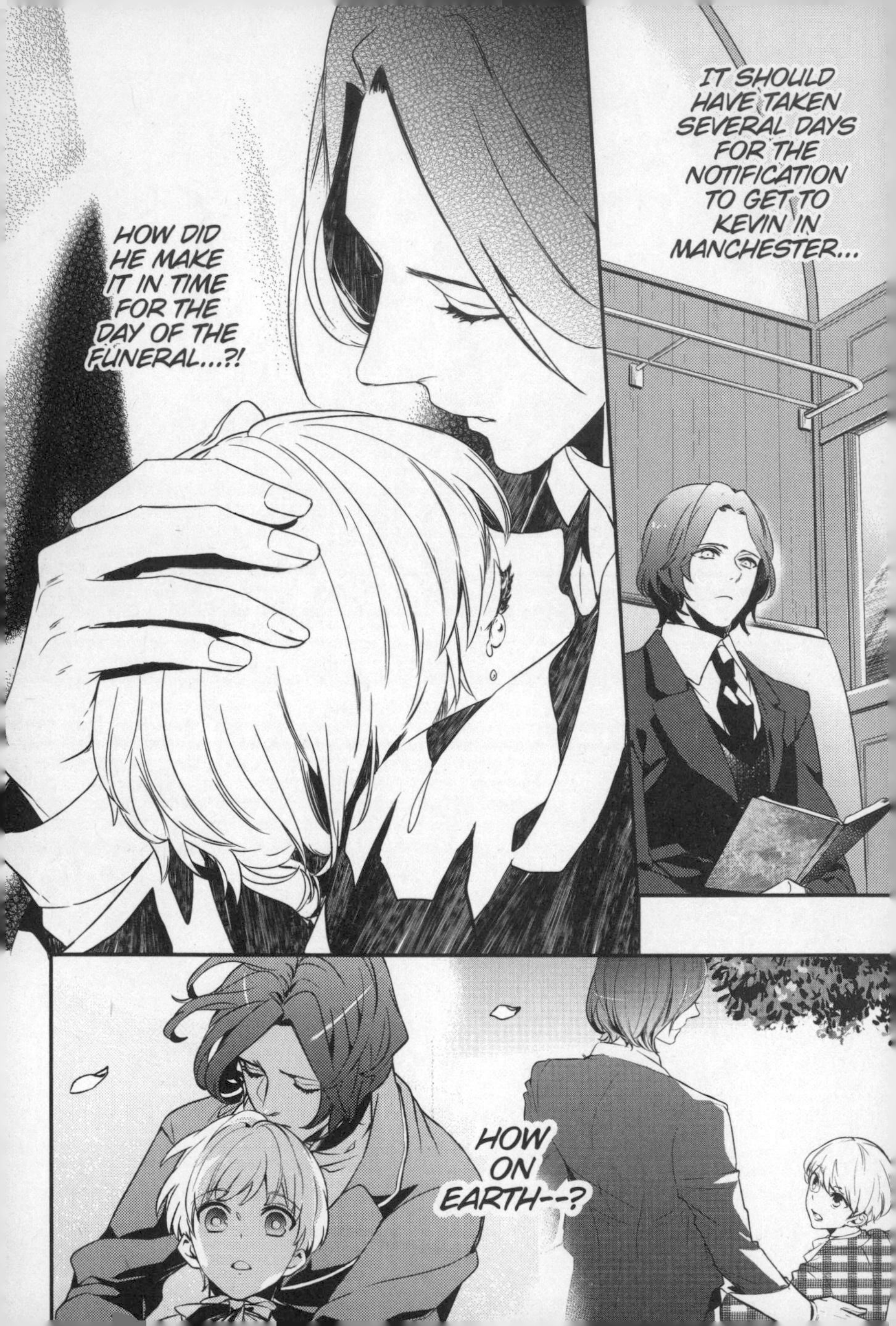
IT SHOULD HAVE TAKEN SEVERAL DAYS FOR THE NOTIFICATION TO GET TO KEVIN IN MANCHESTER...
HOW DID HE MAKE IT IN TIME FOR THE DAY OF THE FUNERAL...?!
HOW ON EARTH--?

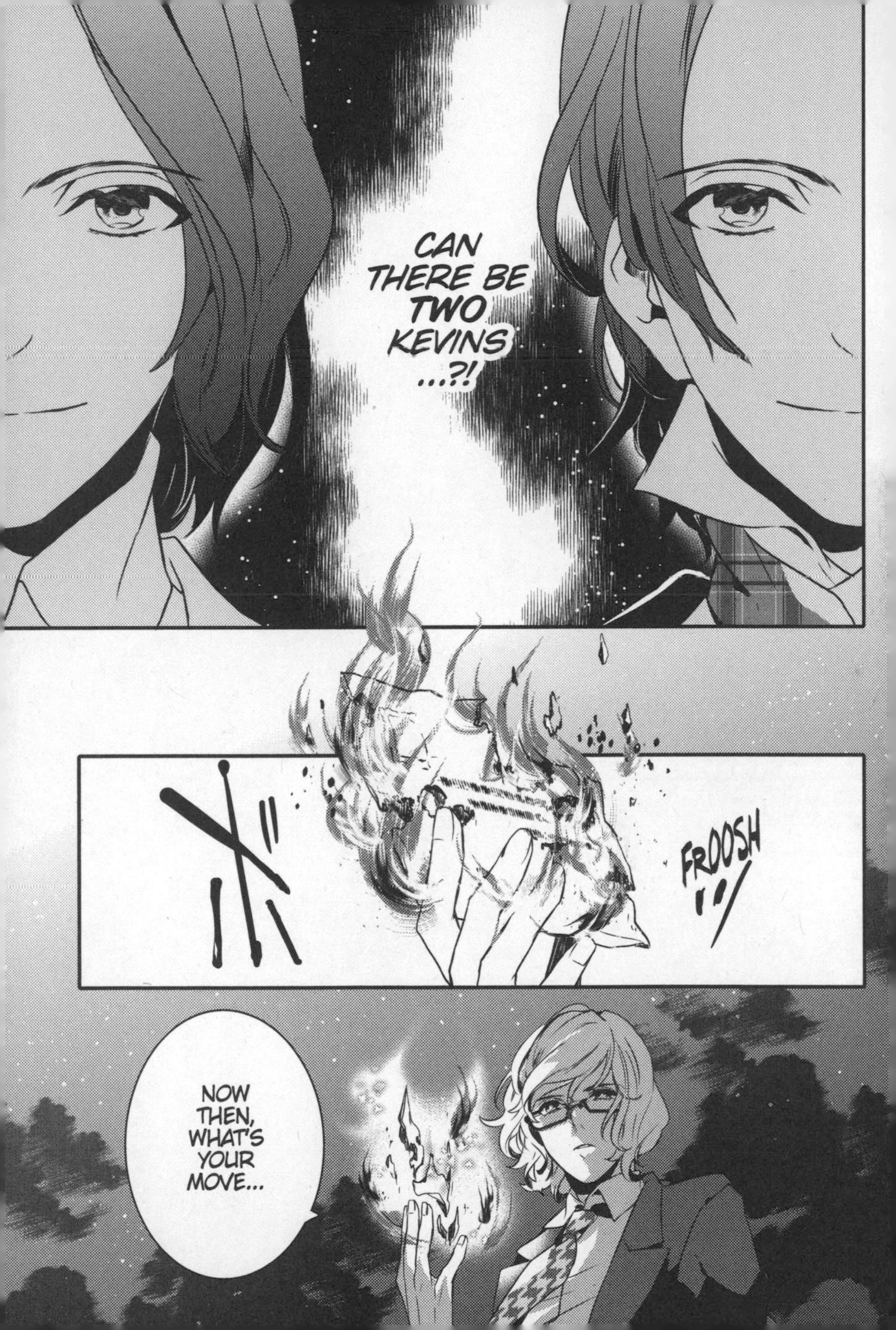
CAN THERE BE TWO KEVINS ...?!
FROOSH
NOW THEN, WHAT'S YOUR MOVE...

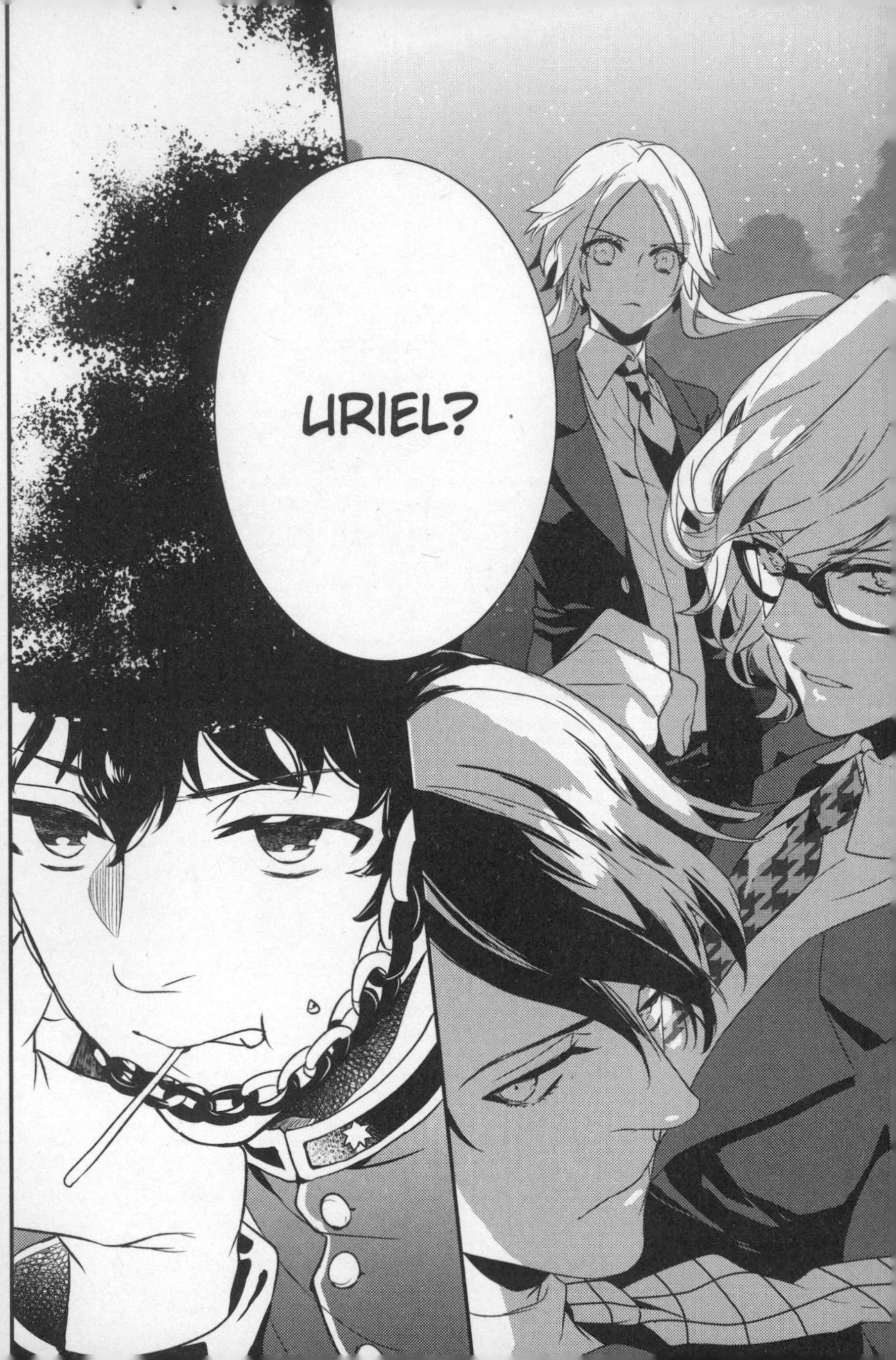
URIEL?

魔界王子
devils and realist

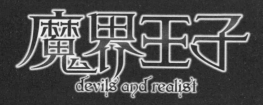

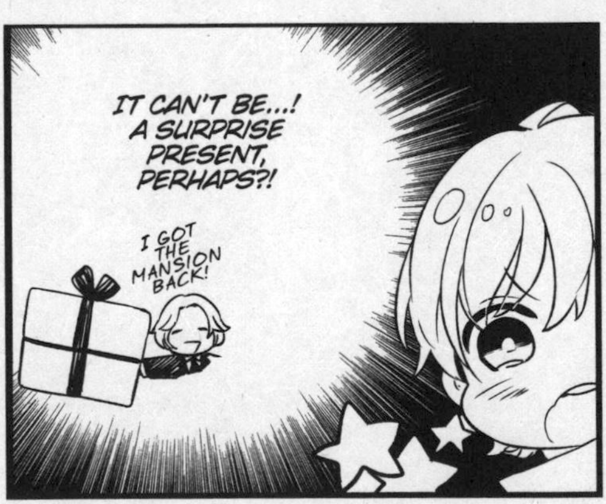
IT CAN'T BE...! A SURPRISE PRESENT, PERHAPS?!
I GOT THE MANSION BACK!

Pillar 46

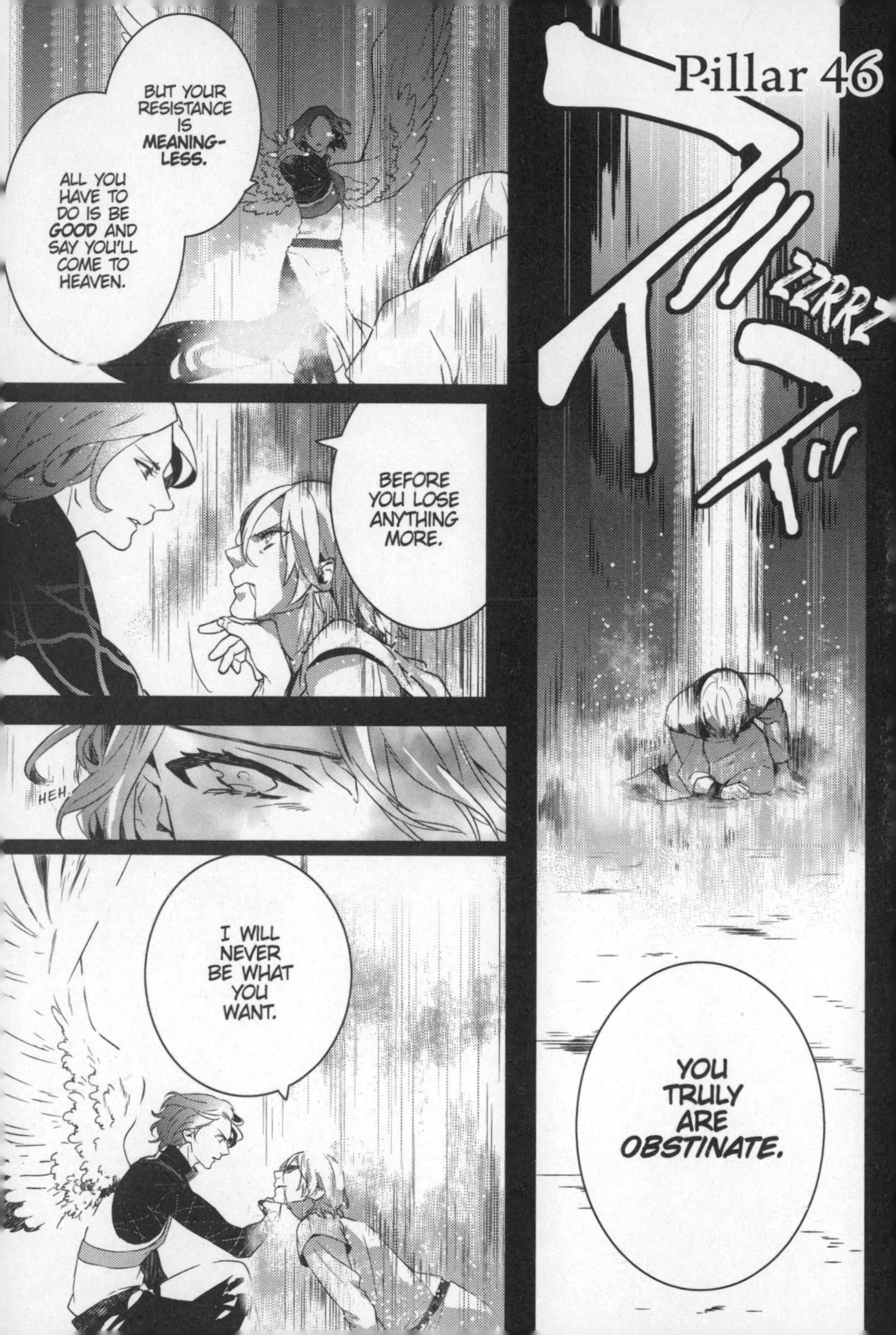
ZZRRZ
YOU TRULY ARE OBSTINATE.
BUT YOUR RESISTANCE IS MEANING-LESS.
ALL YOU HAVE TO DO IS BE GOOD AND SAY YOU'LL COME TO HEAVEN.
BEFORE YOU LOSE ANYTHING MORE.
HEH.
I WILL NEVER BE WHAT YOU WANT.

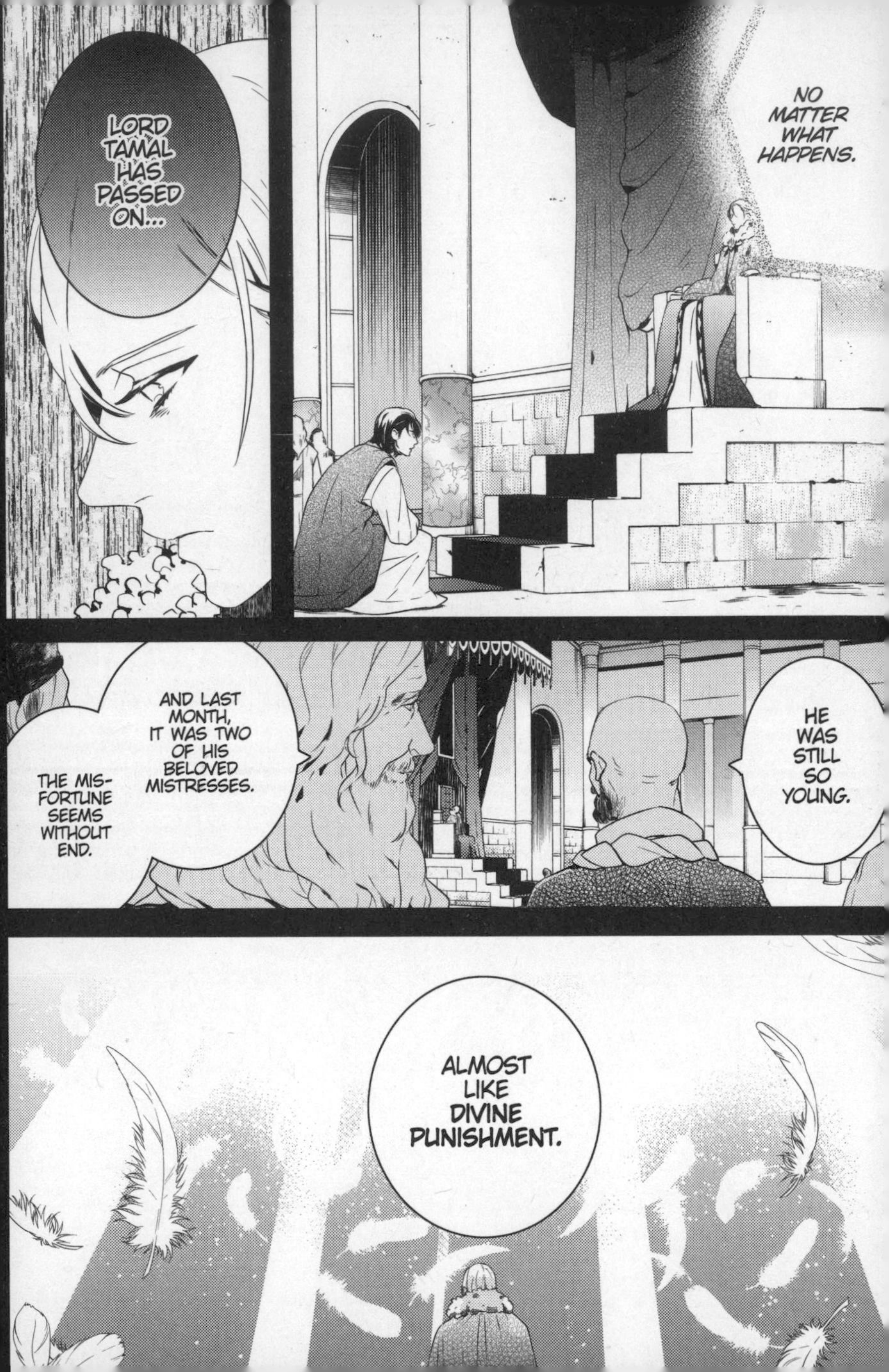
NO MATTER WHAT HAPPENS.
LORD TAMAL HAS PASSED ON...
HE WAS STILL SO YOUNG.
AND LAST MONTH, IT WAS TWO OF HIS BELOVED MISTRESSES.
THE MIS-FORTUNE SEEMS WITHOUT END.
ALMOST LIKE DIVINE PUNISHMENT.

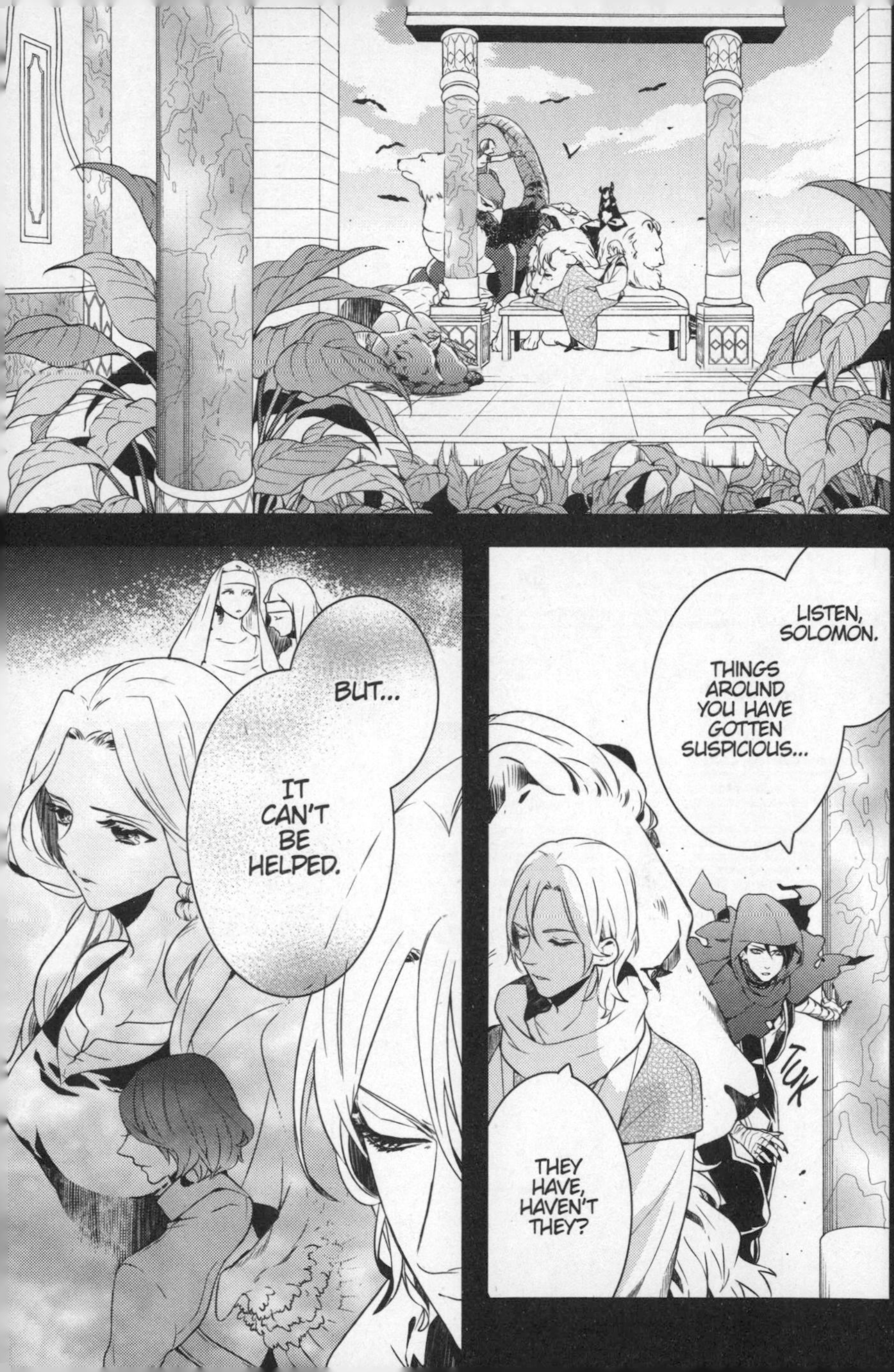
LISTEN, SOLOMON.
THINGS AROUND YOU HAVE GOTTEN SUSPICIOUS...
TUK
THEY HAVE, HAVEN'T THEY?
BUT...
IT CAN'T BE HELPED.

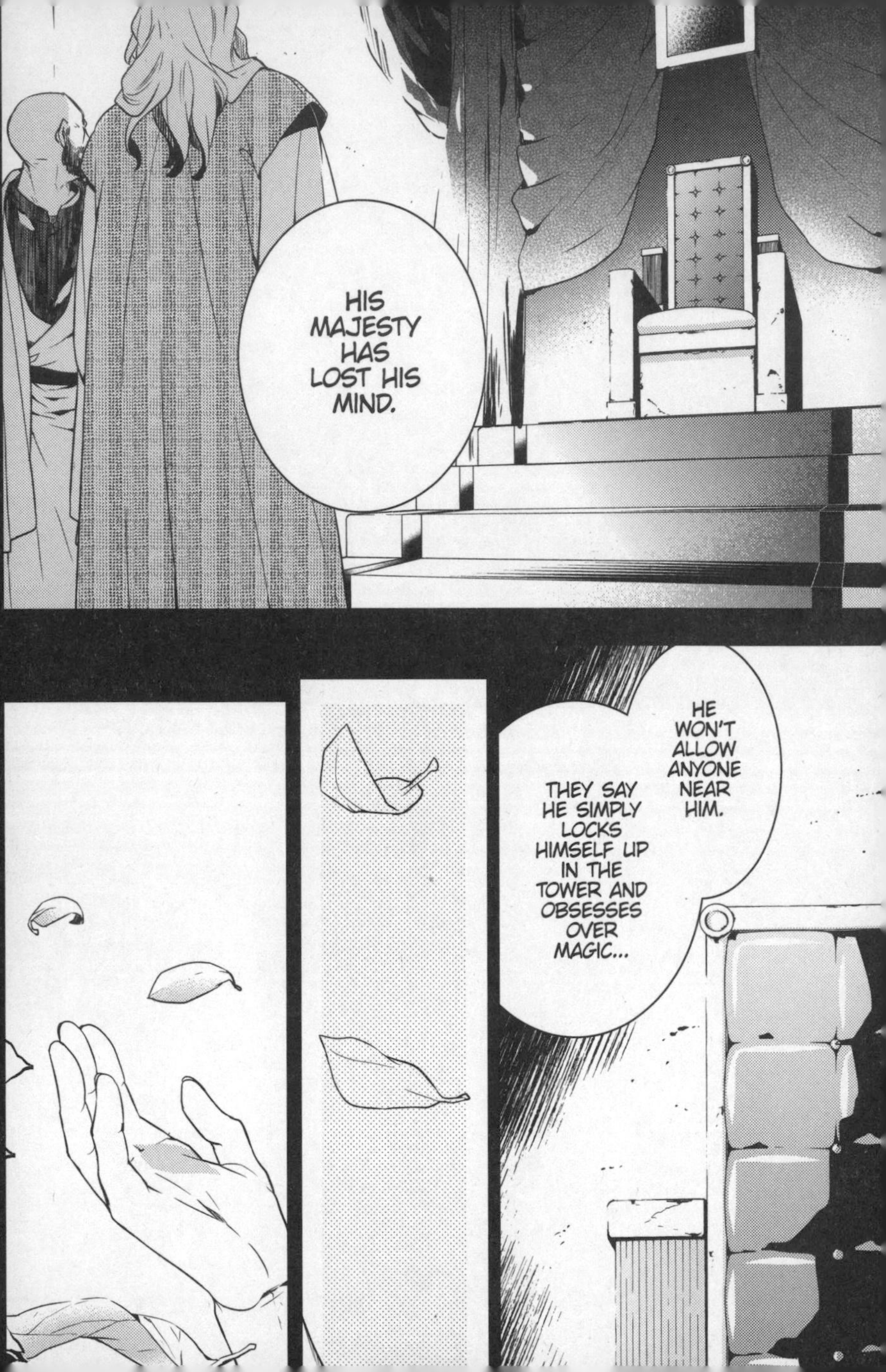
HIS MAJESTY HAS LOST HIS MIND.
HE WON'T ALLOW ANYONE NEAR HIM.
THEY SAY HE SIMPLY LOCKS HIMSELF UP IN THE TOWER AND OBSESSES OVER MAGIC...

Pillar 46

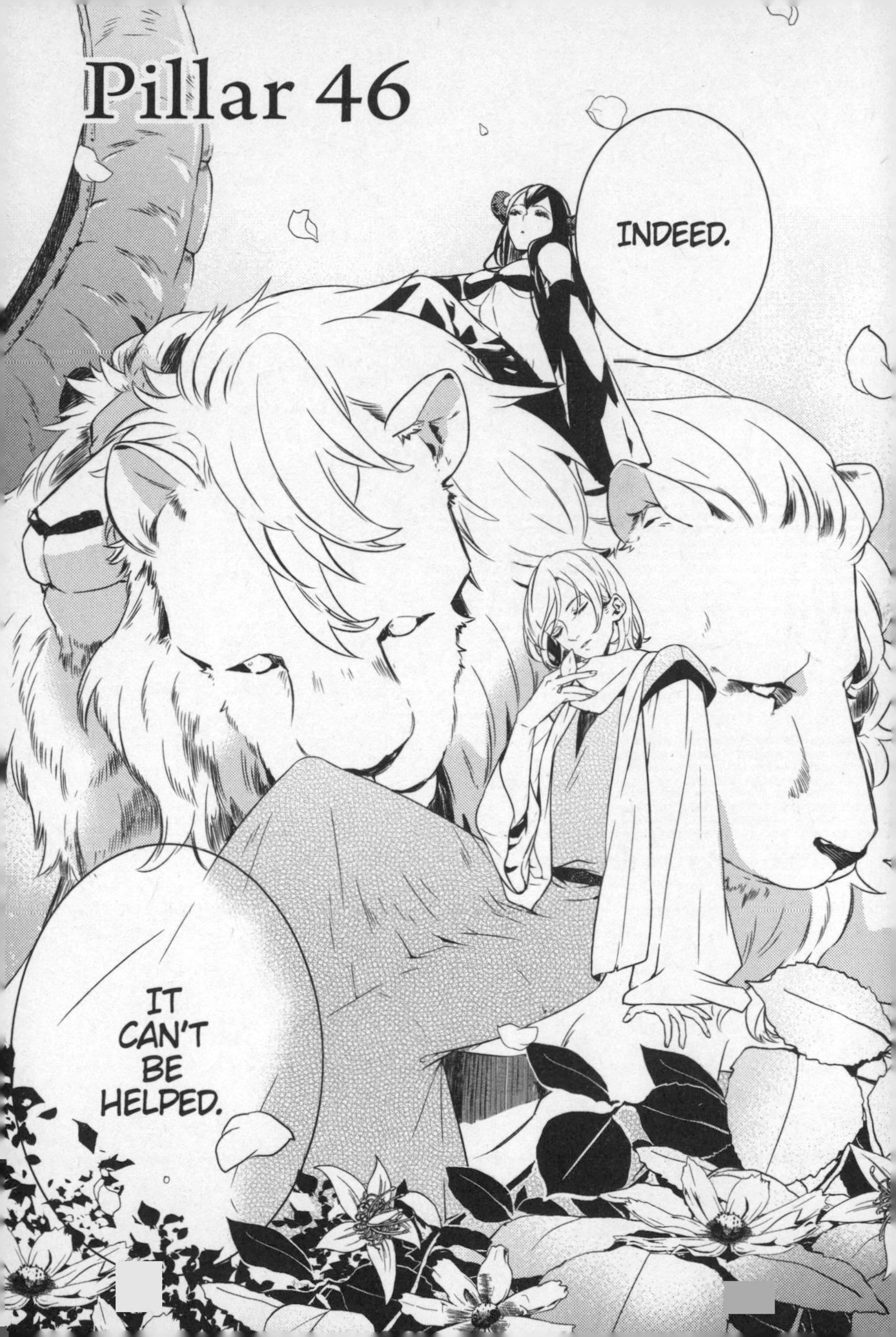
INDEED.
IT CAN'T BE HELPED.

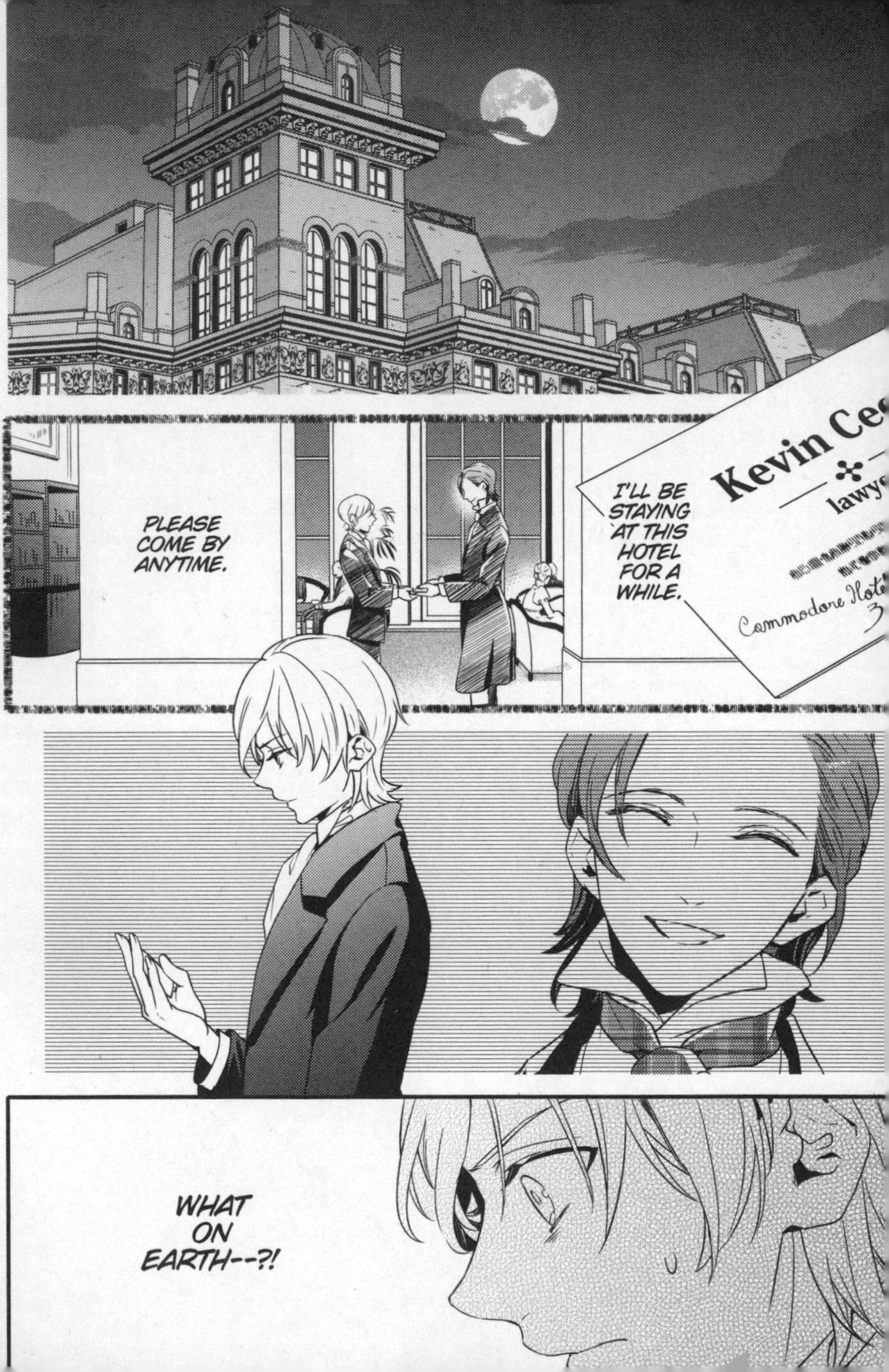
I'LL BE STAYING AT THIS HOTEL FOR A WHILE.
PLEASE COME BY ANYTIME.
WHAT ON EARTH--?!

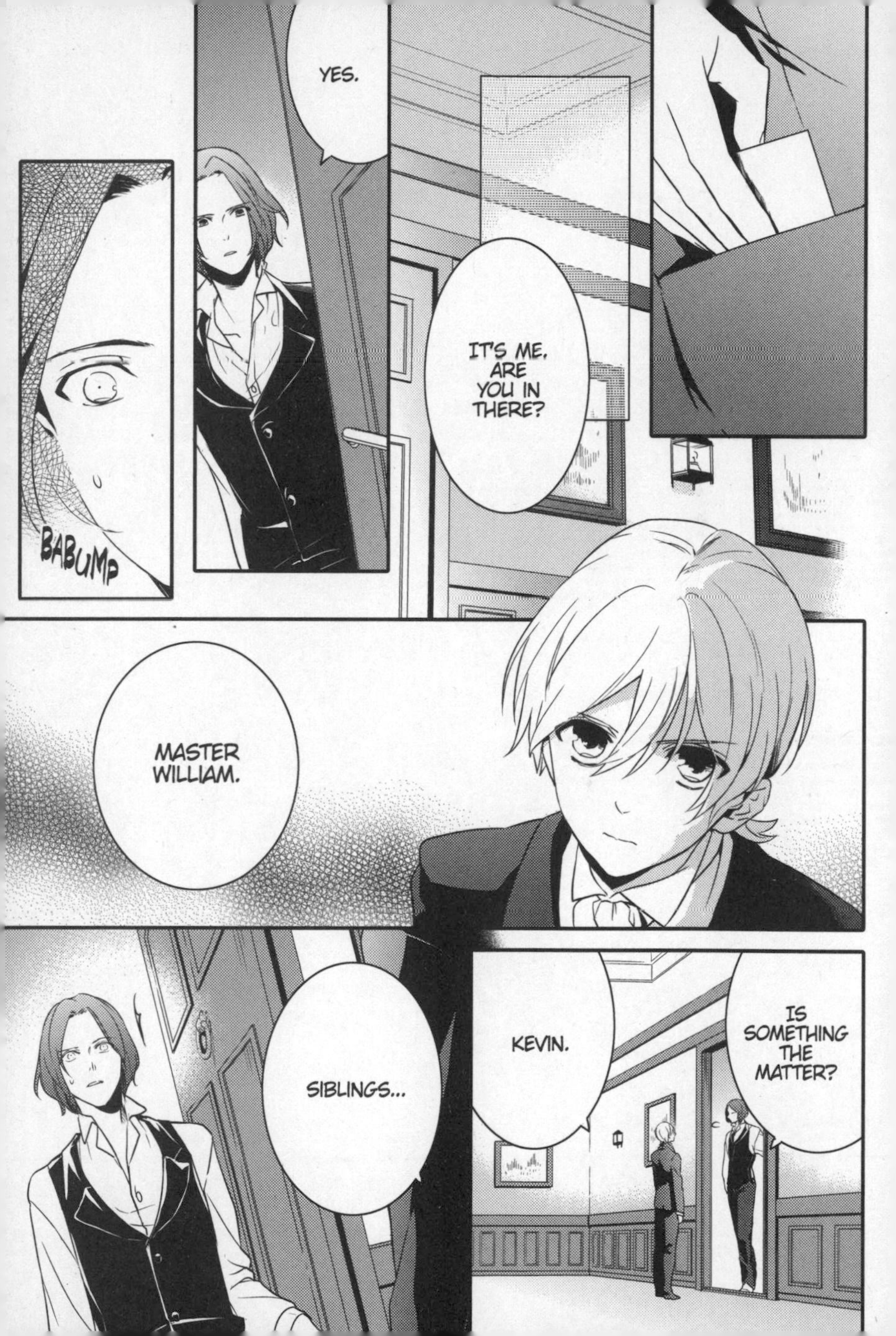
IT'S ME. ARE YOU IN THERE?
YES.
BABUMP
MASTER WILLIAM.
IS SOMETHING THE MATTER?
KEVIN.
SIBLINGS...

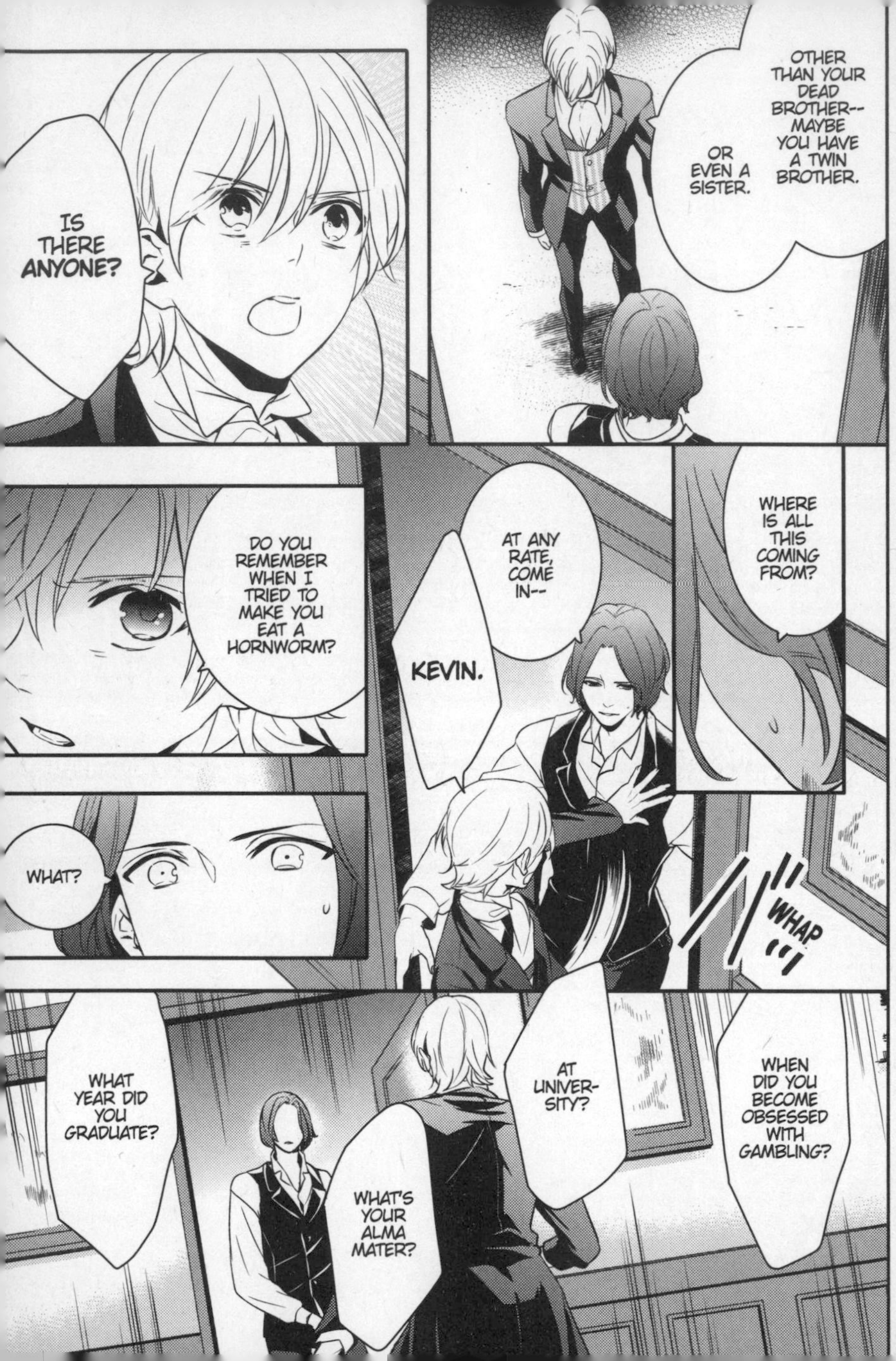
OTHER THAN YOUR DEAD BROTHER-- MAYBE YOU HAVE A TWIN BROTHER.
OR EVEN A SISTER.
IS THERE ANYONE?
WHERE IS ALL THIS COMING FROM?
AT ANY RATE, COME IN--
KEVIN.
WHAP
DO YOU REMEMBER WHEN I TRIED TO MAKE YOU EAT A HORNWORM?
WHAT?
WHEN DID YOU BECOME OBSESSED WITH GAMBLING?
AT UNIVER-SITY?
WHAT'S YOUR ALMA MATER?
WHAT YEAR DID YOU GRADUATE?

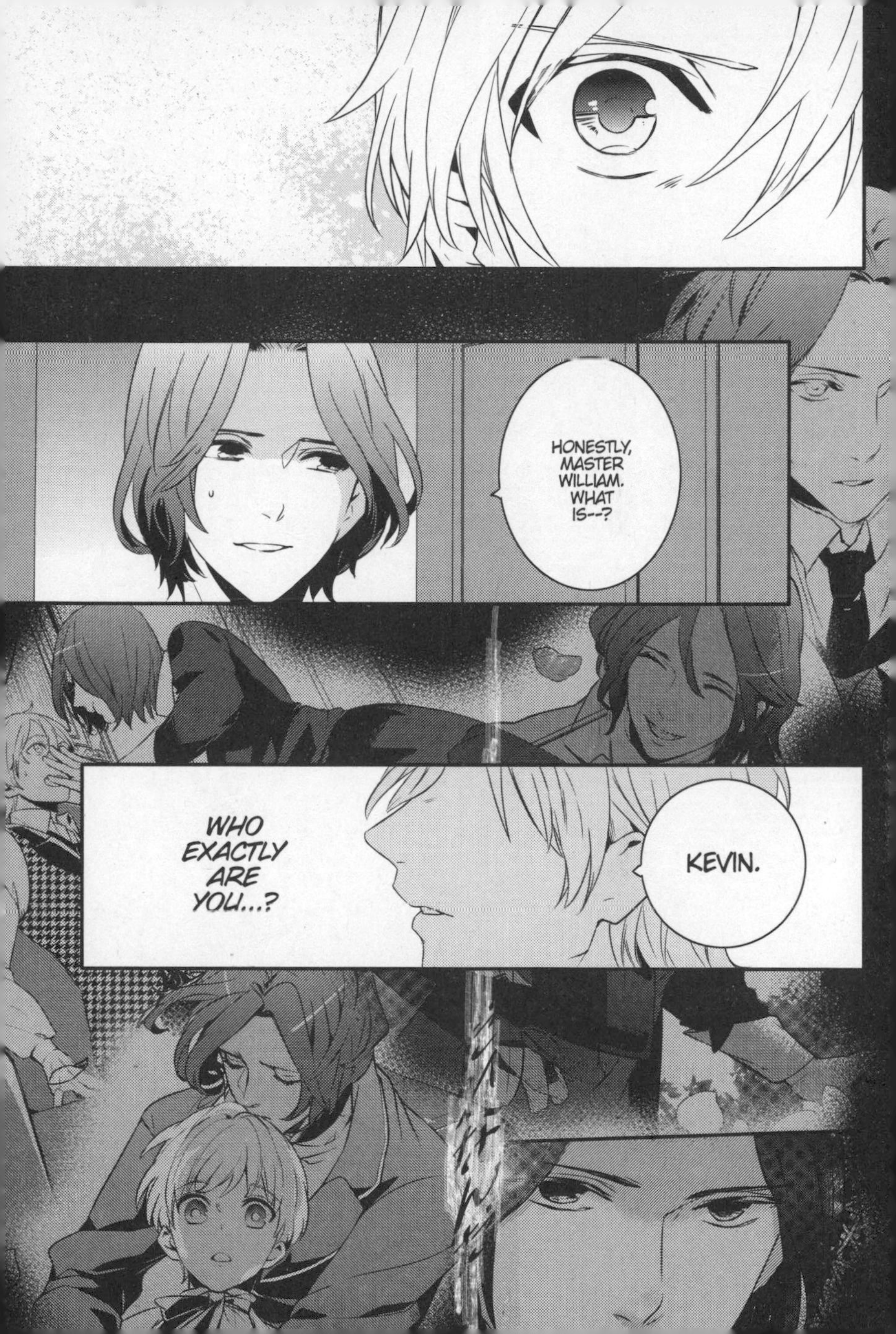
HONESTLY, MASTER WILLIAM. WHAT IS--?
KEVIN.
WHO EXACTLY ARE YOU...?

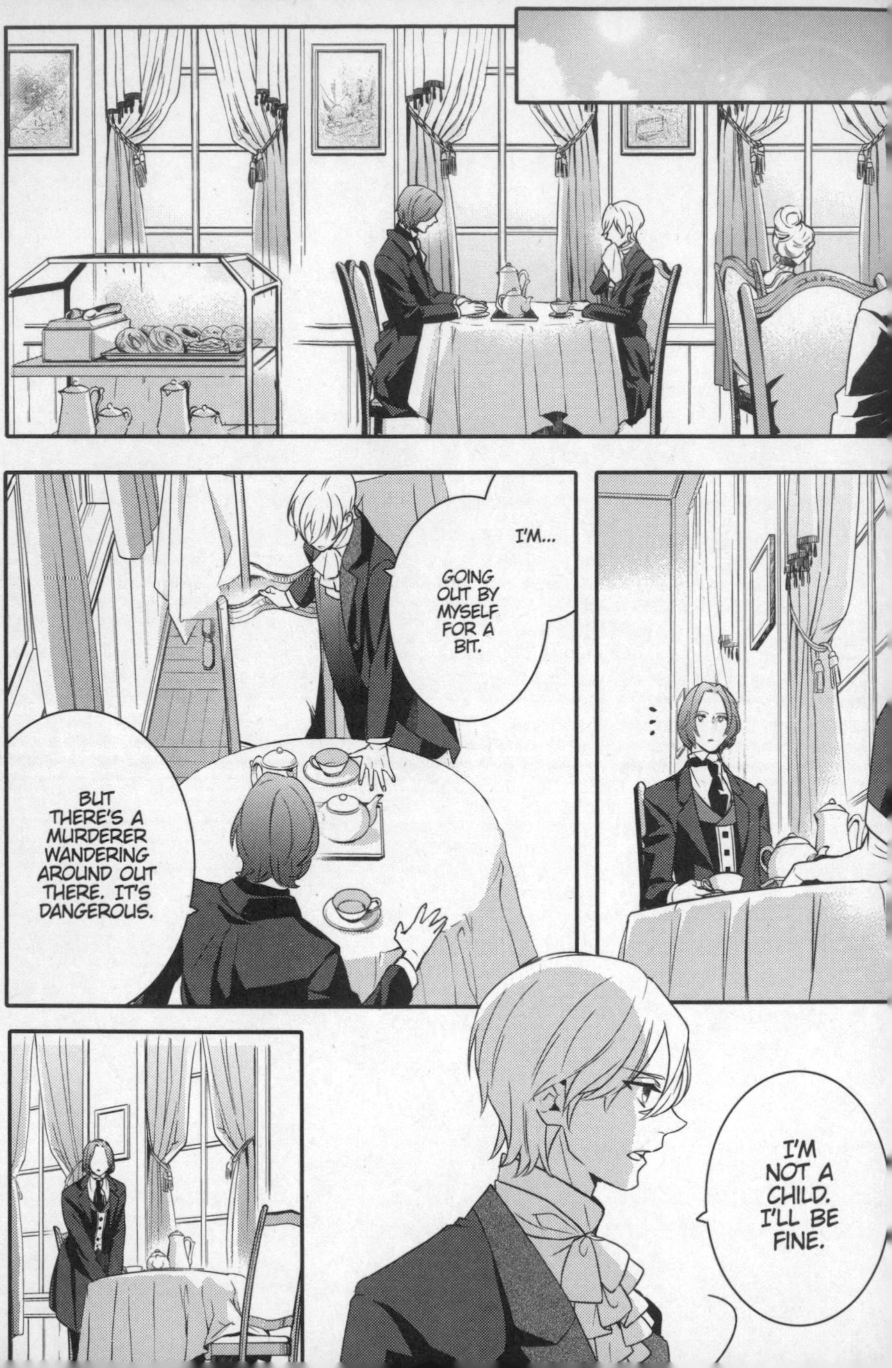
I'M...
GOING OUT BY MYSELF FOR A BIT.
BUT THERE'S A MURDERER WANDERING AROUND OUT THERE. IT'S DANGEROUS.
I'M NOT A CHILD. I'LL BE FINE.

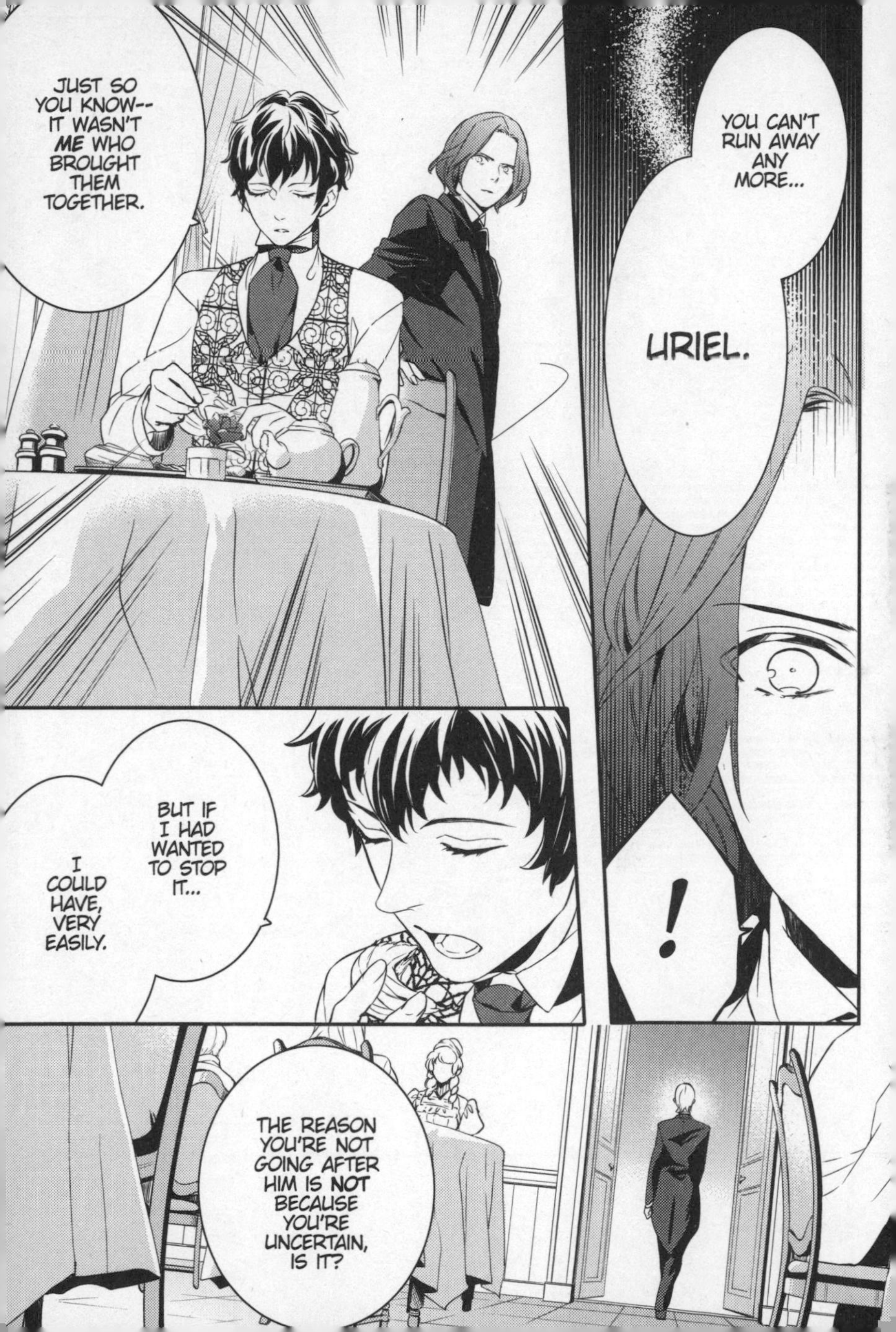
YOU CAN'T RUN AWAY ANY MORE...
URIEL.
!
JUST SO YOU KNOW-- IT WASN'T *ME* WHO BROUGHT THEM TOGETHER.
BUT IF I HAD WANTED TO STOP IT...
I COULD HAVE, VERY EASILY.
THE REASON YOU'RE NOT GOING AFTER HIM IS **NOT** BECAUSE YOU'RE UNCERTAIN, IS IT?

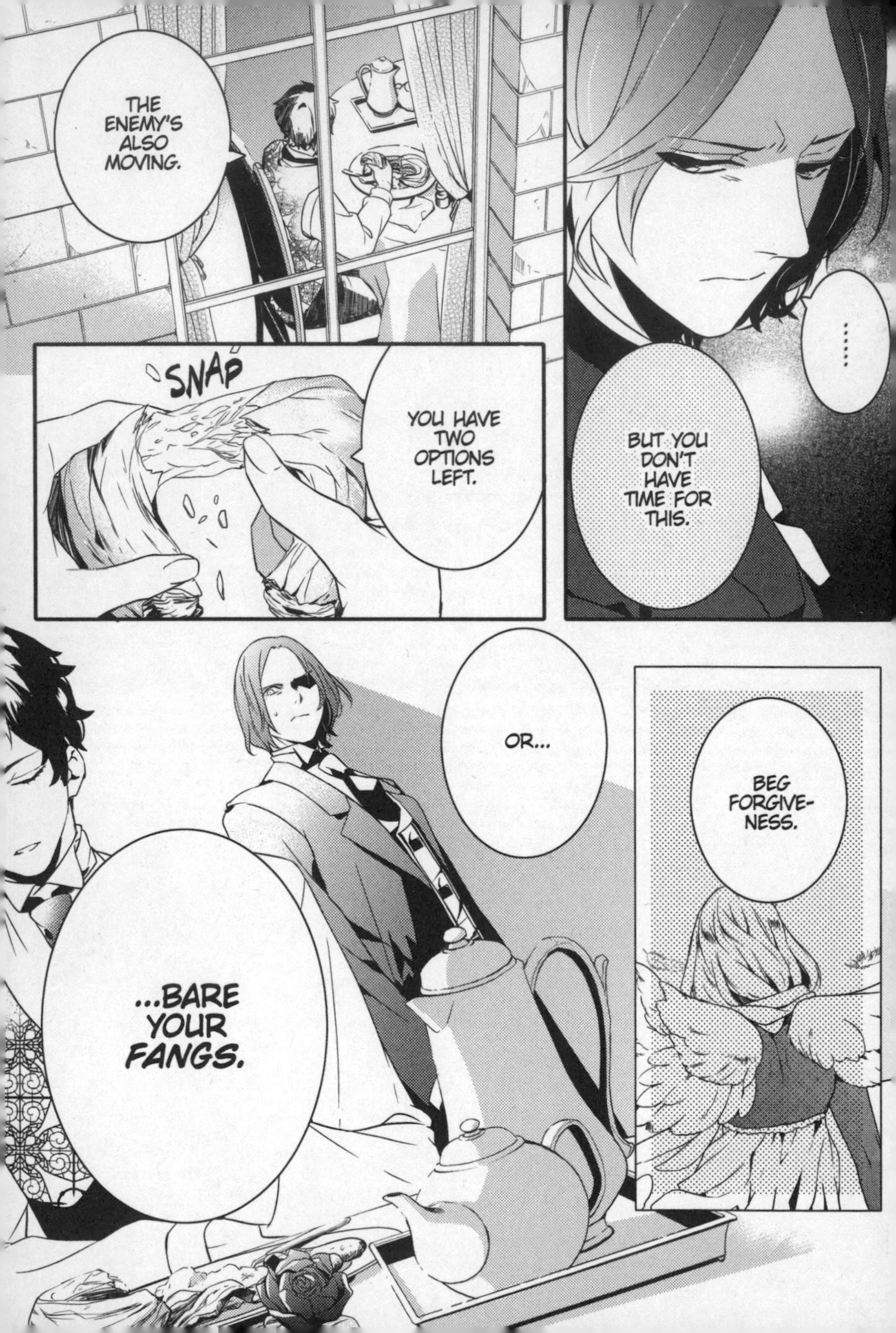
……
BUT YOU DON'T HAVE TIME FOR THIS.
THE ENEMY'S ALSO MOVING.
SNAP
YOU HAVE TWO OPTIONS LEFT.
BEG FORGIVENESS.
OR...
...BARE YOUR FANGS.

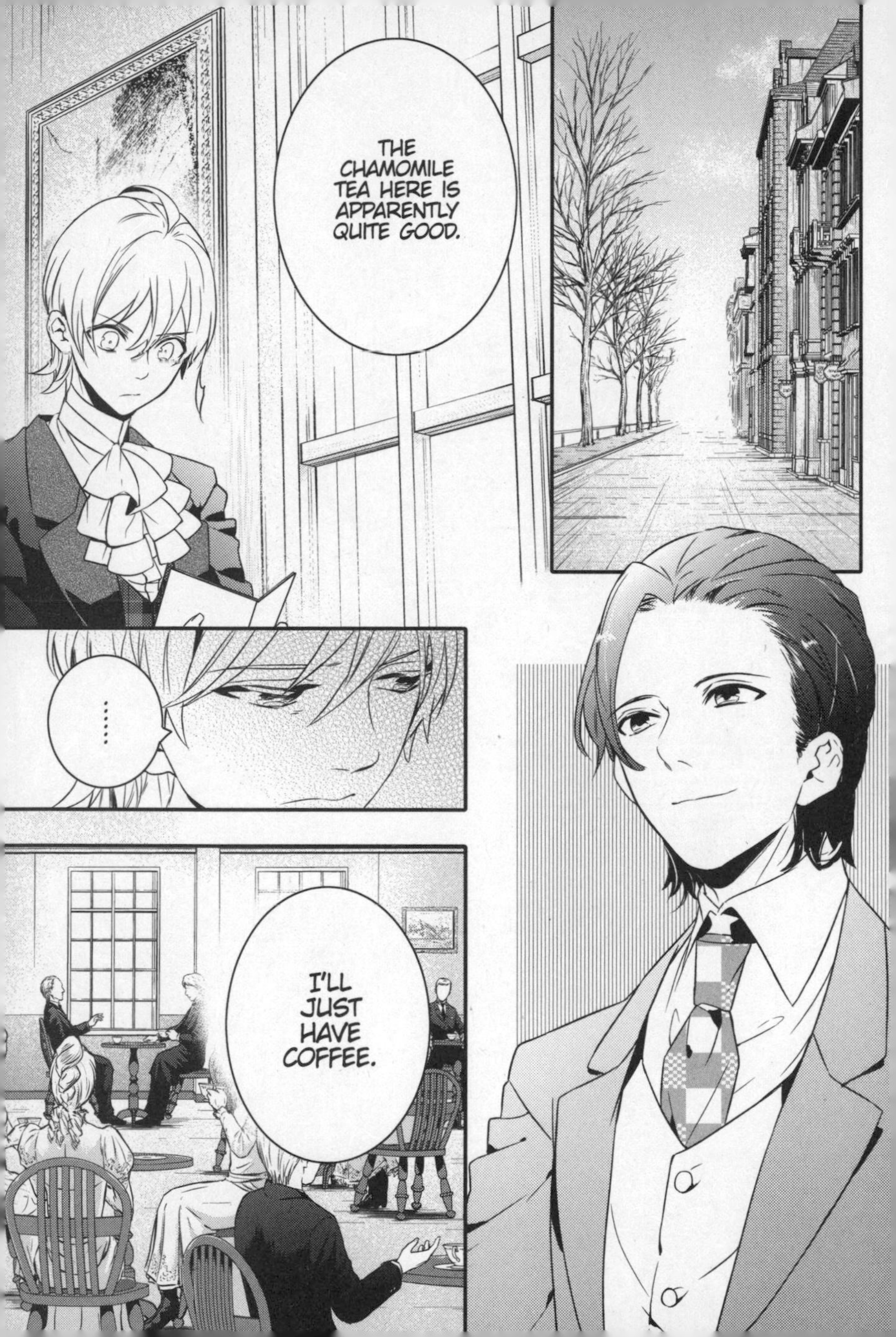
THE CHAMOMILE TEA HERE IS APPARENTLY QUITE GOOD.
......
I'LL JUST HAVE COFFEE.

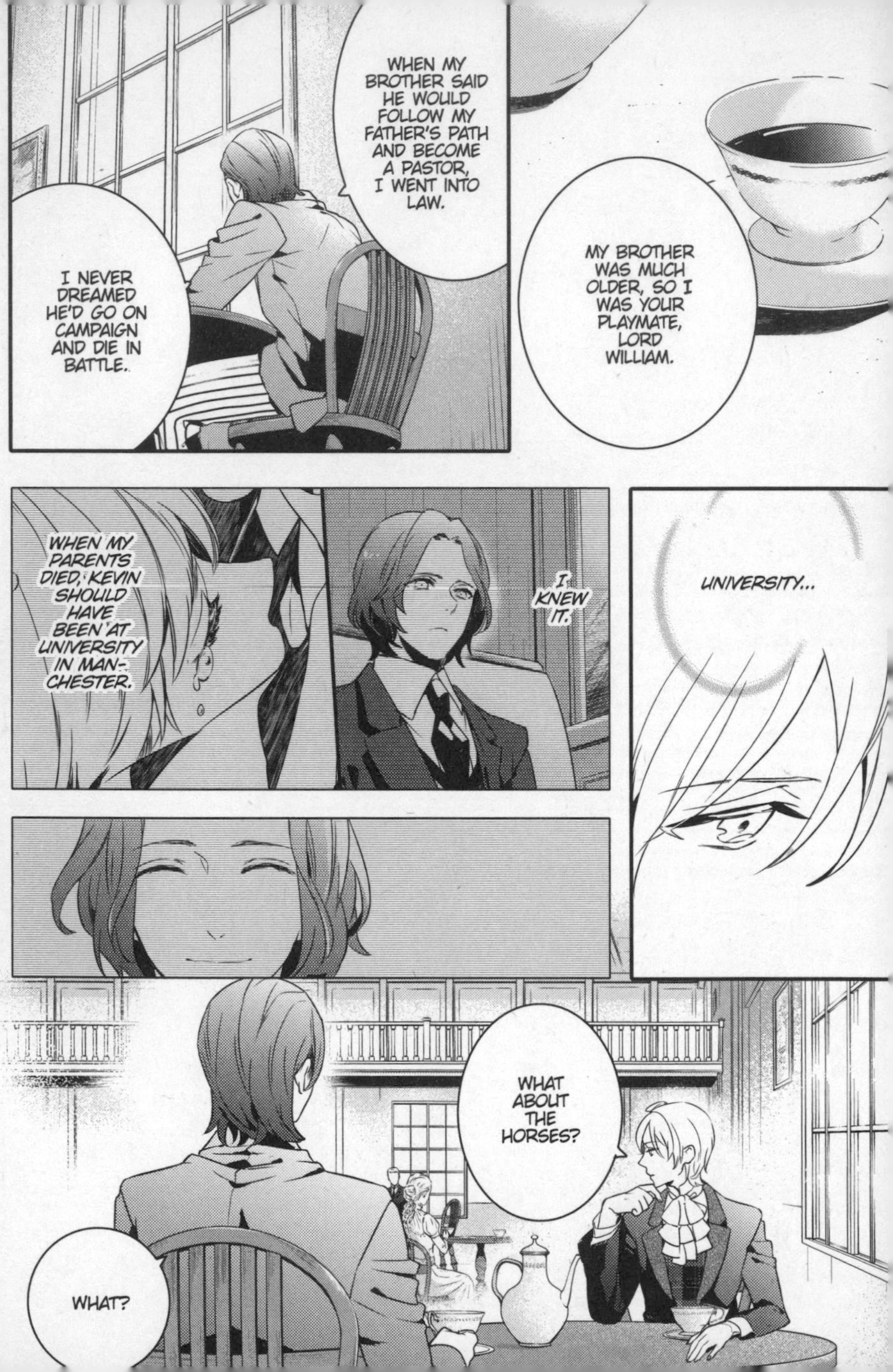
MY BROTHER WAS MUCH OLDER, SO I WAS YOUR PLAYMATE, LORD WILLIAM.
WHEN MY BROTHER SAID HE WOULD FOLLOW MY FATHER'S PATH AND BECOME A PASTOR, I WENT INTO LAW.
I NEVER DREAMED HE'D GO ON CAMPAIGN AND DIE IN BATTLE.
UNIVERSITY...
I KNEW IT.
WHEN MY PARENTS DIED, KEVIN SHOULD HAVE BEEN AT UNIVERSITY IN MAN-CHESTER.
WHAT ABOUT THE HORSES?
WHAT?

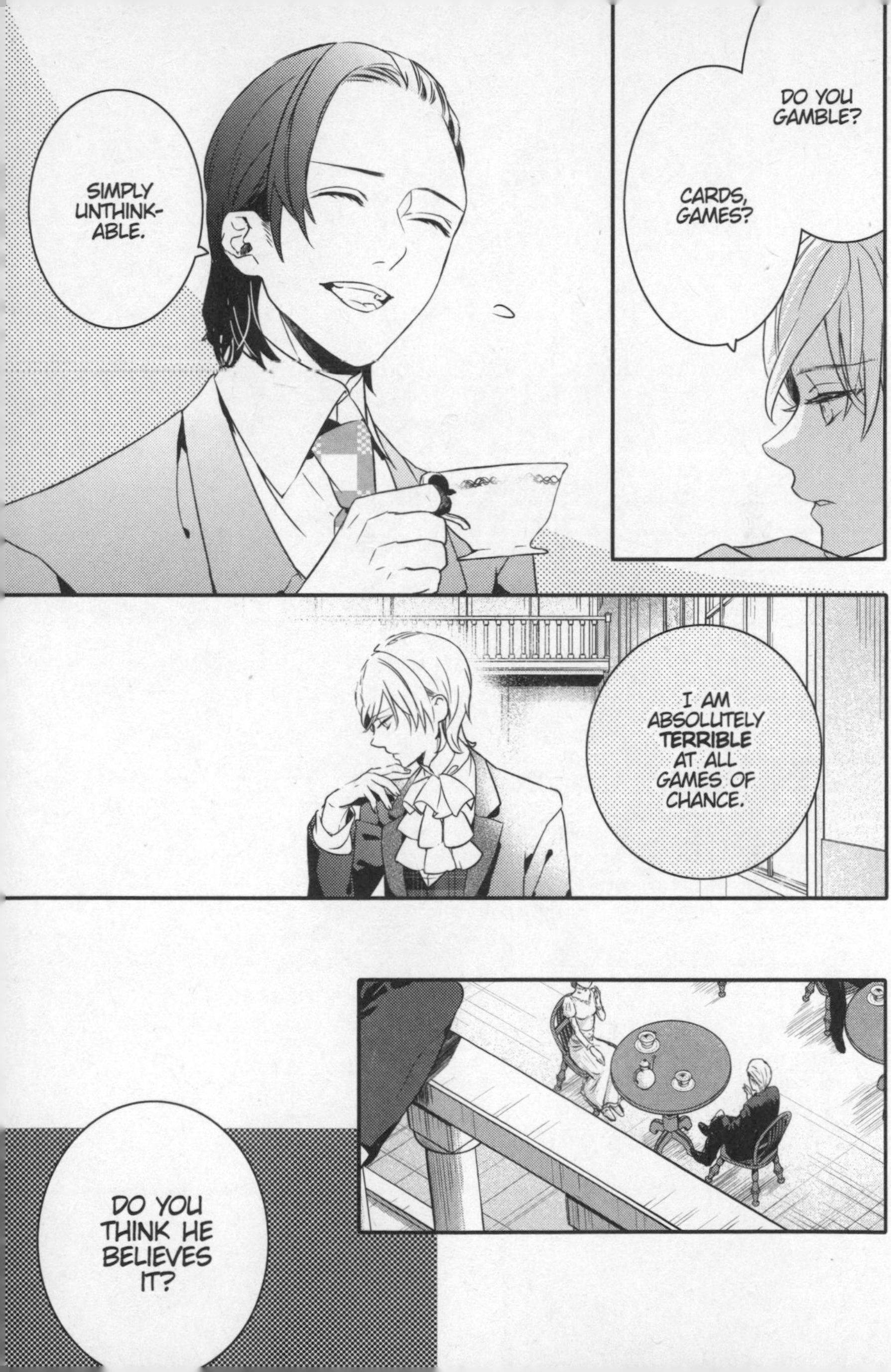
DO YOU GAMBLE?
CARDS, GAMES?
SIMPLY UNTHINK-ABLE.
I AM ABSOLUTELY TERRIBLE AT ALL GAMES OF CHANCE.
DO YOU THINK HE BELIEVES IT?

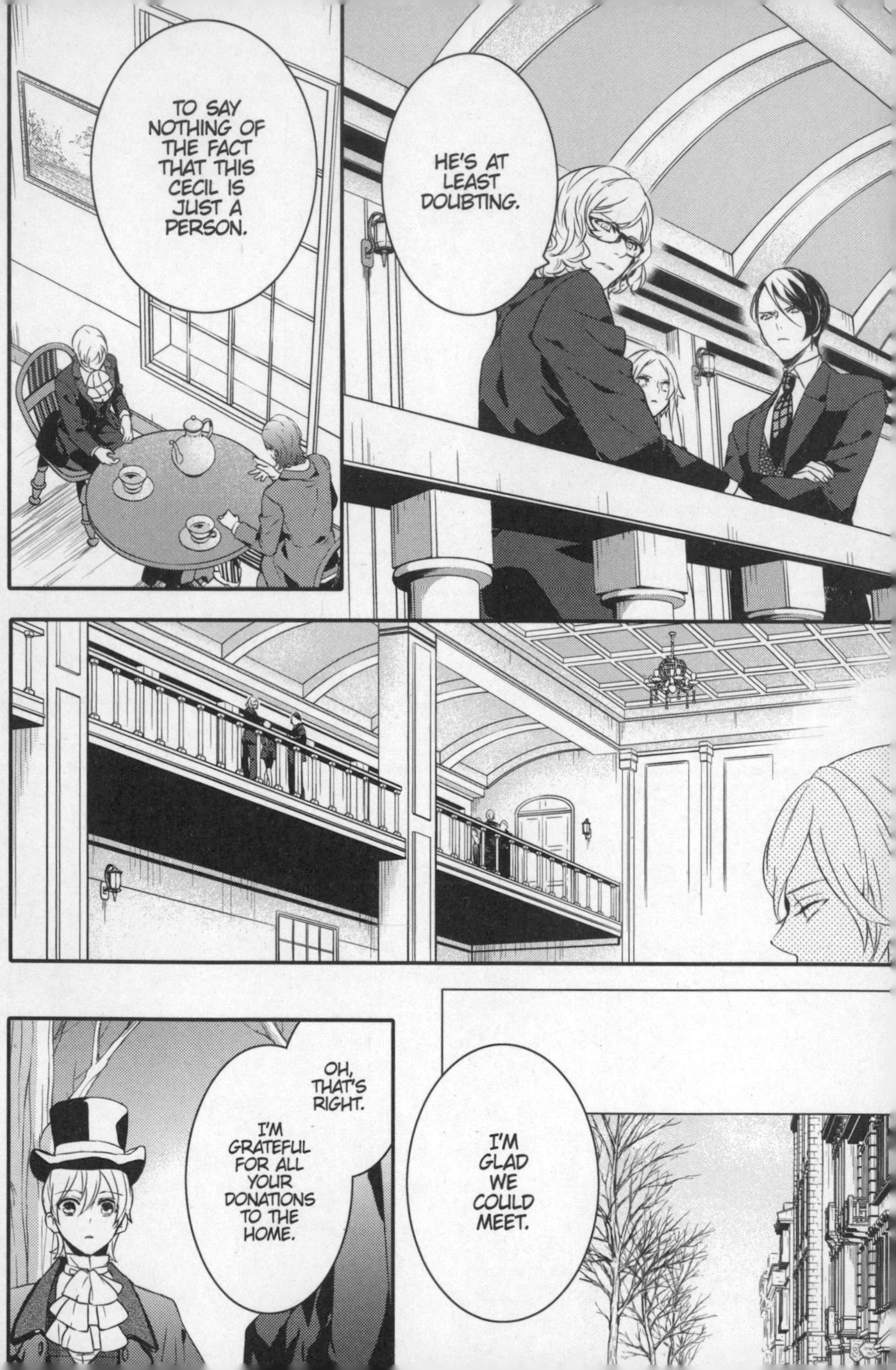
HE'S AT LEAST DOUBTING.
TO SAY NOTHING OF THE FACT THAT THIS CECIL IS JUST A PERSON.
I'M GLAD WE COULD MEET.
OH, THAT'S RIGHT.
I'M GRATEFUL FOR ALL YOUR DONATIONS TO THE HOME.

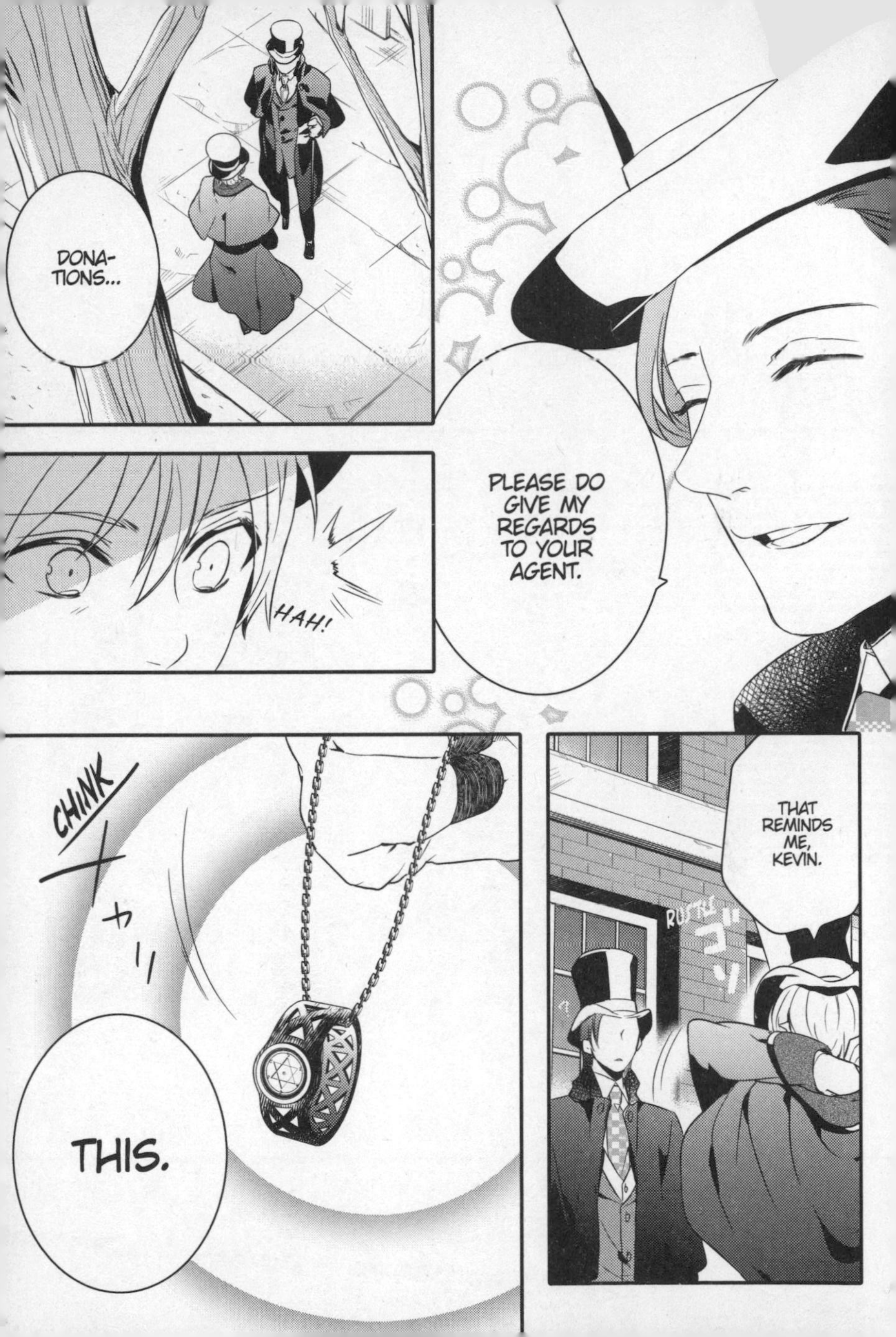
PLEASE DO GIVE MY REGARDS TO YOUR AGENT.
DONA-TIONS...
HAH!
THAT REMINDS ME, KEVIN.
RUSTL
ゴソ
CHINK
カリ
THIS.

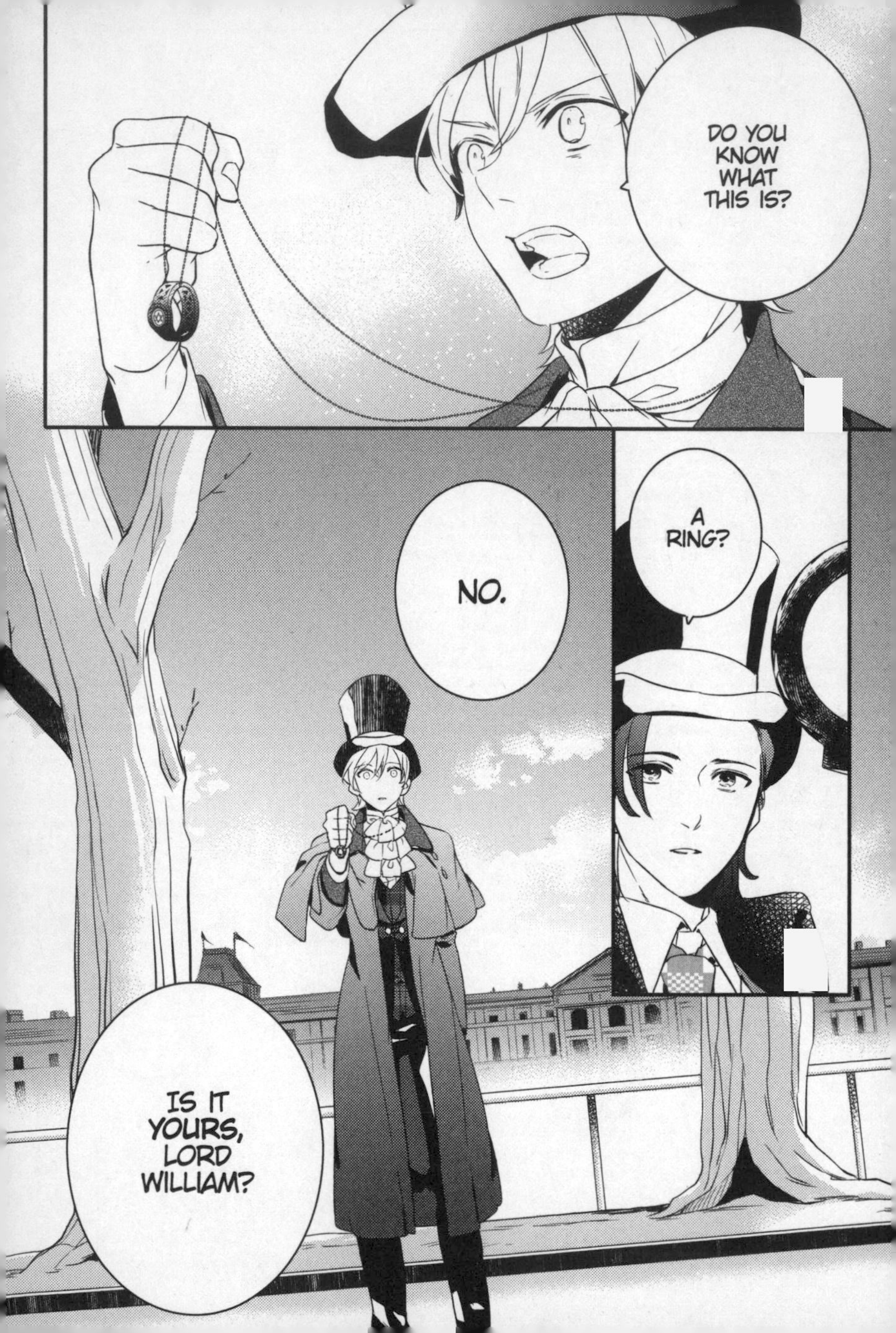
DO YOU KNOW WHAT THIS IS?
A RING?
NO.
IS IT YOURS, LORD WILLIAM?

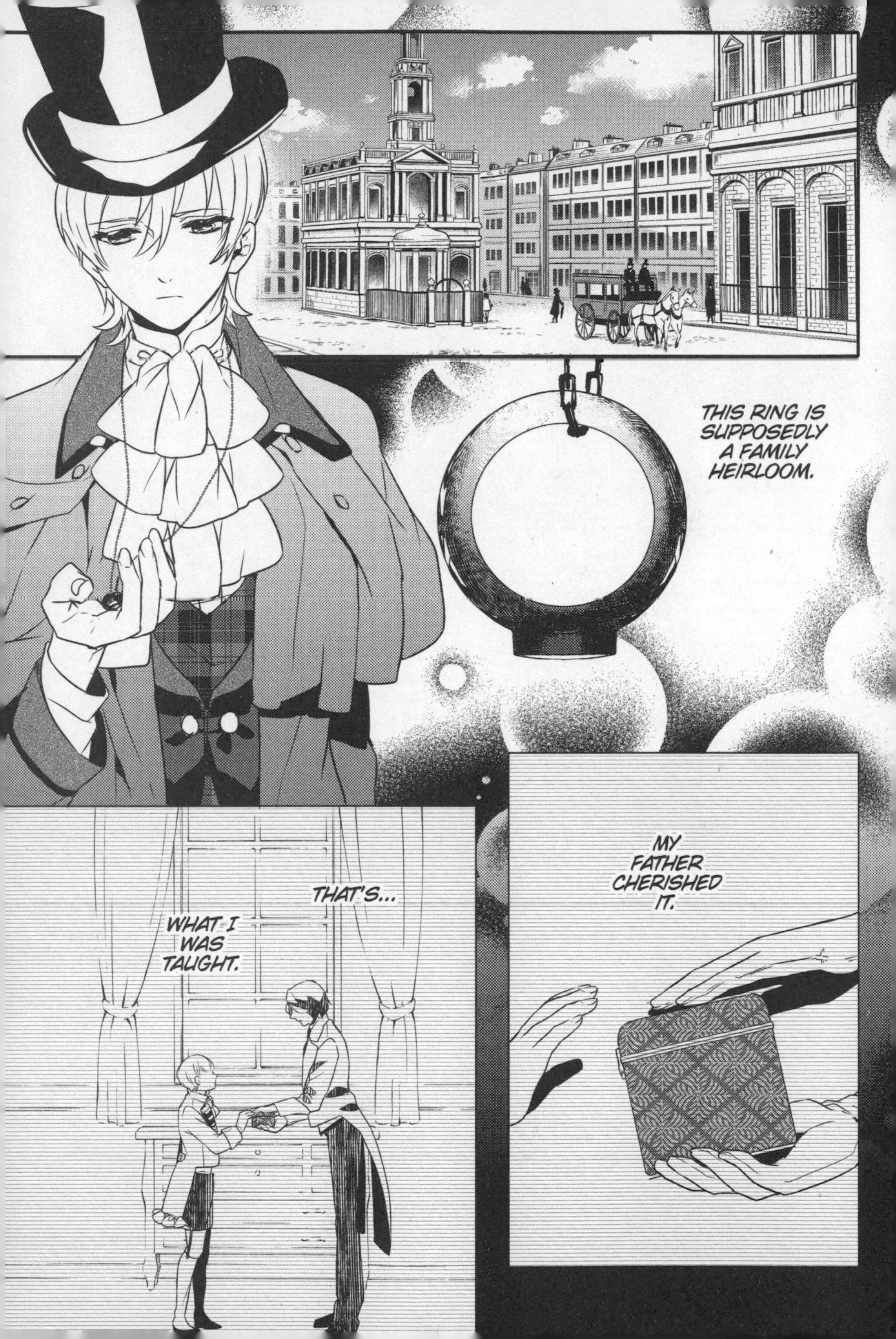
THIS RING IS SUPPOSEDLY A FAMILY HEIRLOOM.
MY FATHER CHERISHED IT.
THAT'S...
WHAT I WAS TAUGHT.

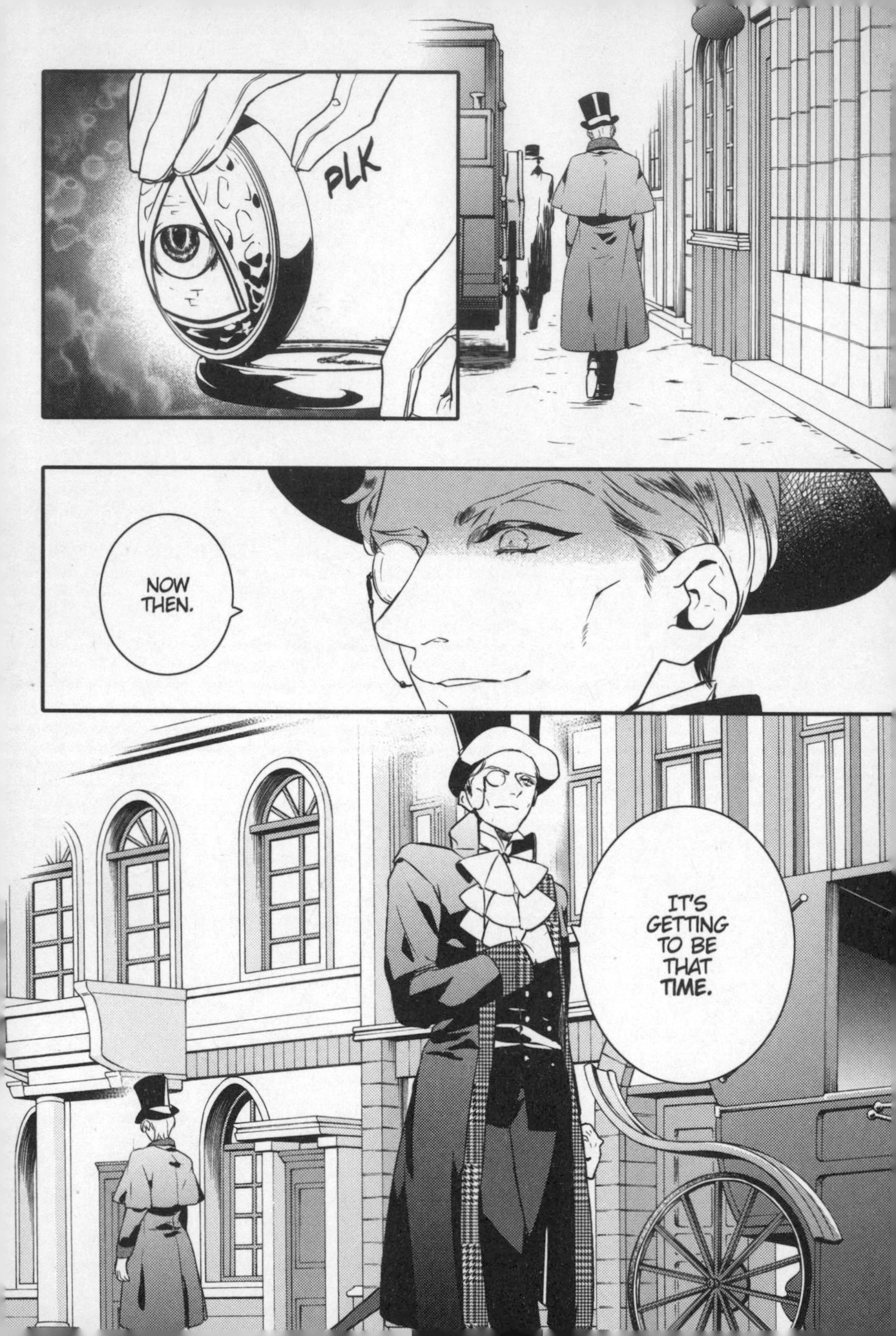
PLK
NOW THEN.
IT'S GETTING TO BE THAT TIME.

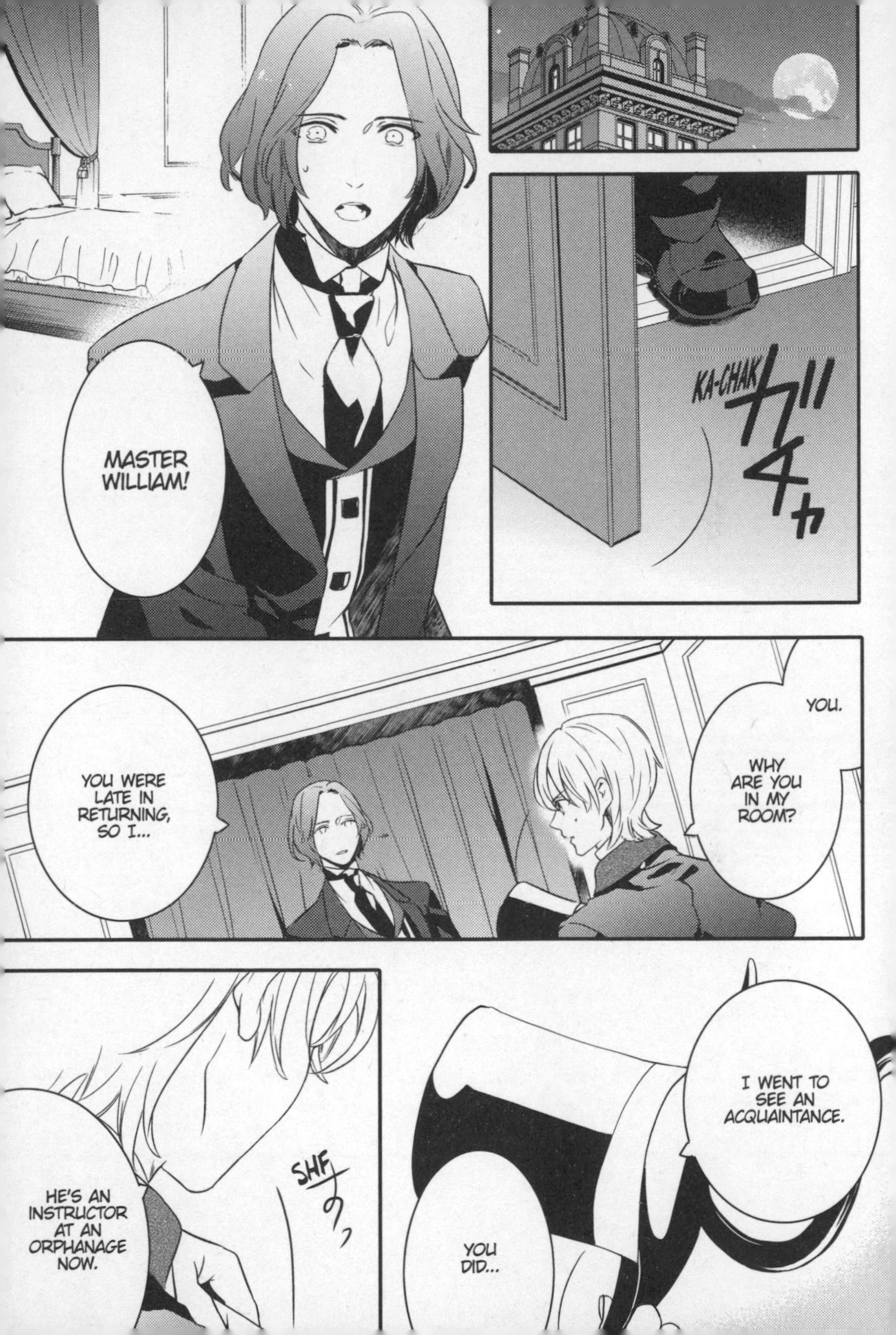
KA-CHAK
MASTER WILLIAM!
YOU.
WHY ARE YOU IN MY ROOM?
YOU WERE LATE IN RETURNING, SO I...
I WENT TO SEE AN ACQUAINTANCE.
YOU DID...
SHF
HE'S AN INSTRUCTOR AT AN ORPHANAGE NOW.

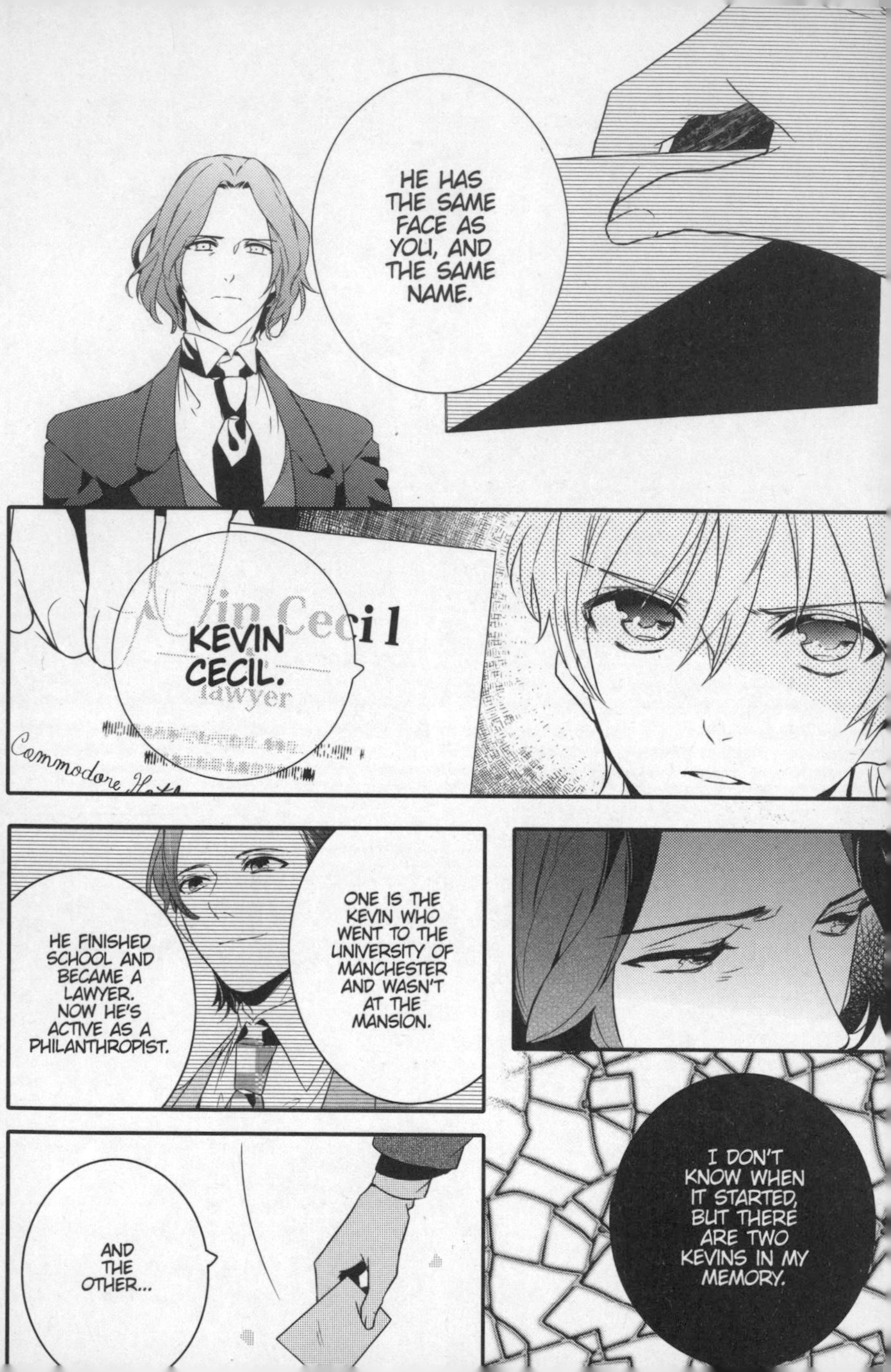
HE HAS THE SAME FACE AS YOU, AND THE SAME NAME.
KEVIN CECIL.
lawyer
ONE IS THE KEVIN WHO WENT TO THE UNIVERSITY OF MANCHESTER AND WASN'T AT THE MANSION.
HE FINISHED SCHOOL AND BECAME A LAWYER. NOW HE'S ACTIVE AS A PHILANTHROPIST.
I DON'T KNOW WHEN IT STARTED, BUT THERE ARE TWO KEVINS IN MY MEMORY.
AND THE OTHER...

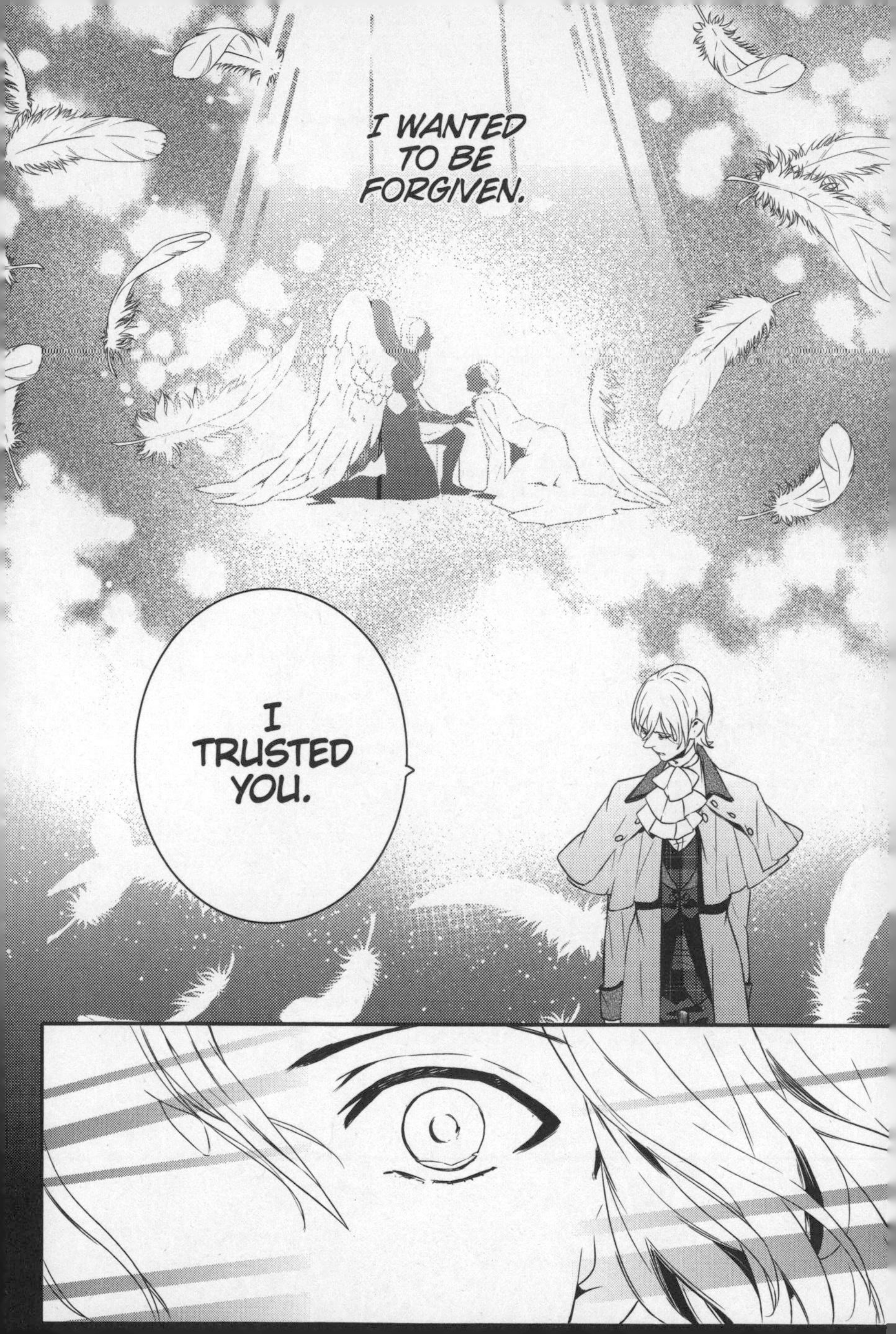
I WANTED TO BE FORGIVEN.
I TRUSTED YOU.

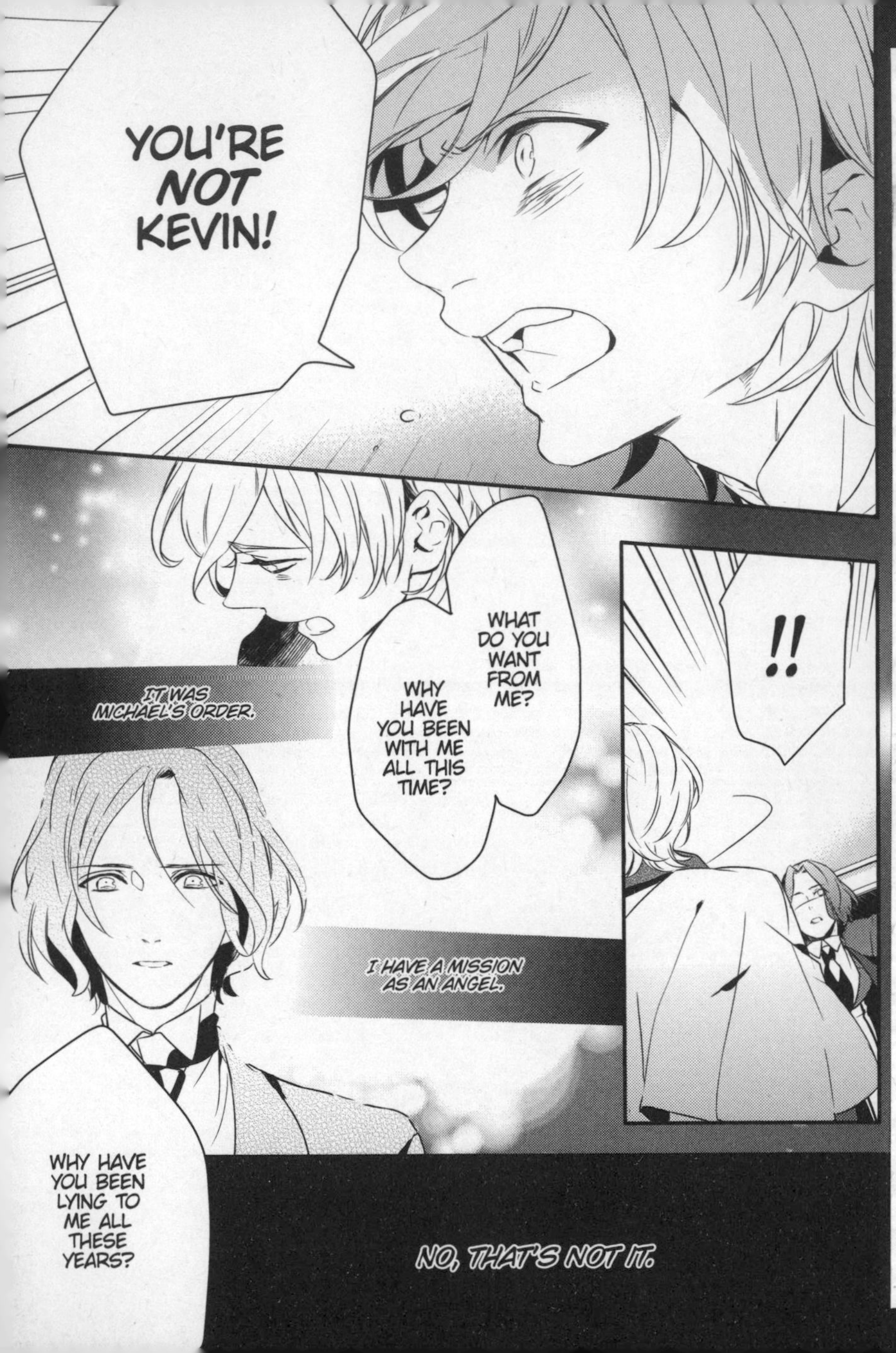
YOU'RE NOT KEVIN!
!!
WHAT DO YOU WANT FROM ME?
WHY HAVE YOU BEEN WITH ME ALL THIS TIME?
IT WAS MICHAEL'S ORDER.
I HAVE A MISSION AS AN ANGEL.
WHY HAVE YOU BEEN LYING TO ME ALL THESE YEARS?
NO, THAT'S NOT IT.

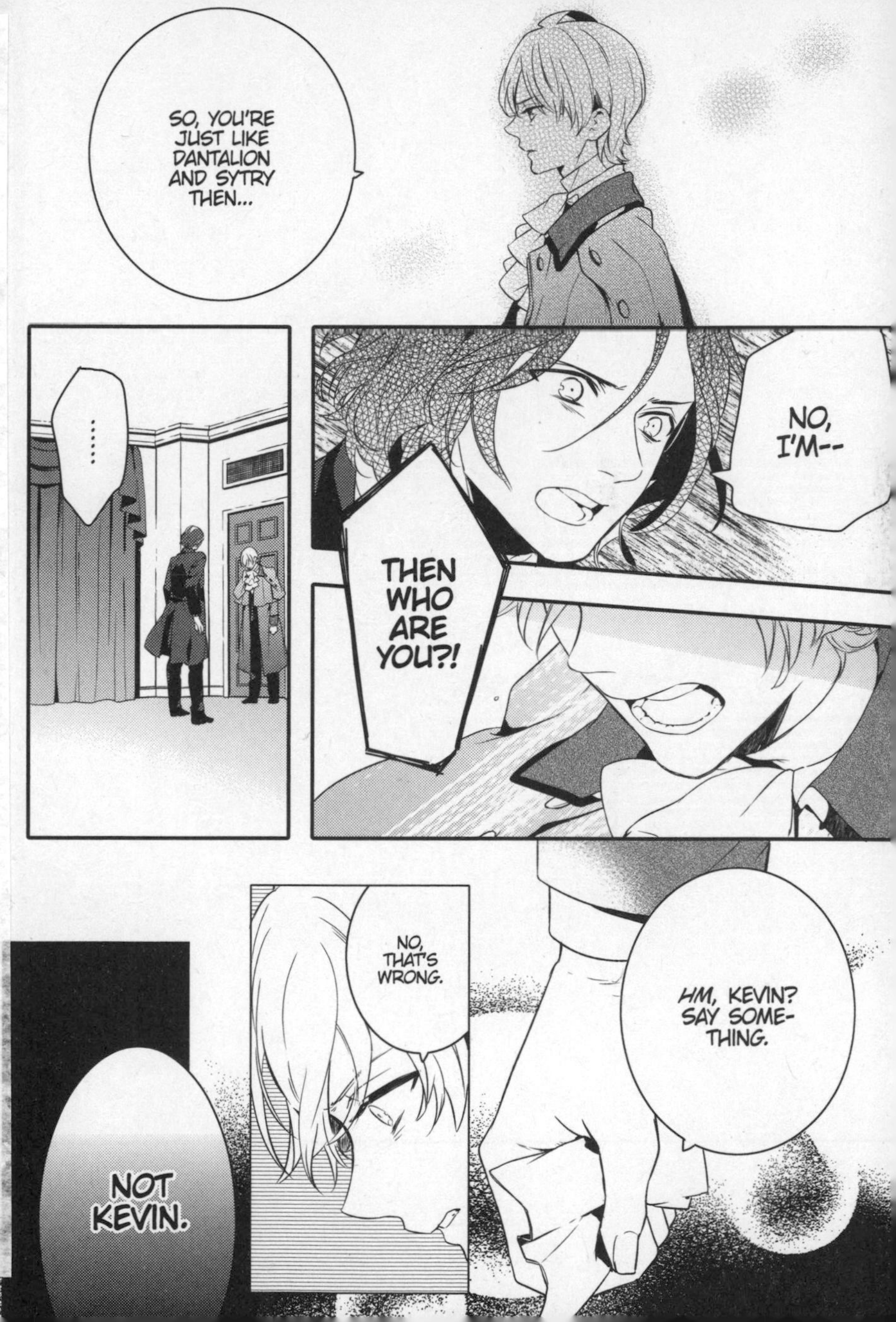
SO, YOU'RE JUST LIKE DANTALION AND SYTRY THEN...
NO, I'M--
THEN WHO ARE YOU?!
......
HM, KEVIN? SAY SOME-THING.
NO, THAT'S WRONG.
NOT KEVIN.

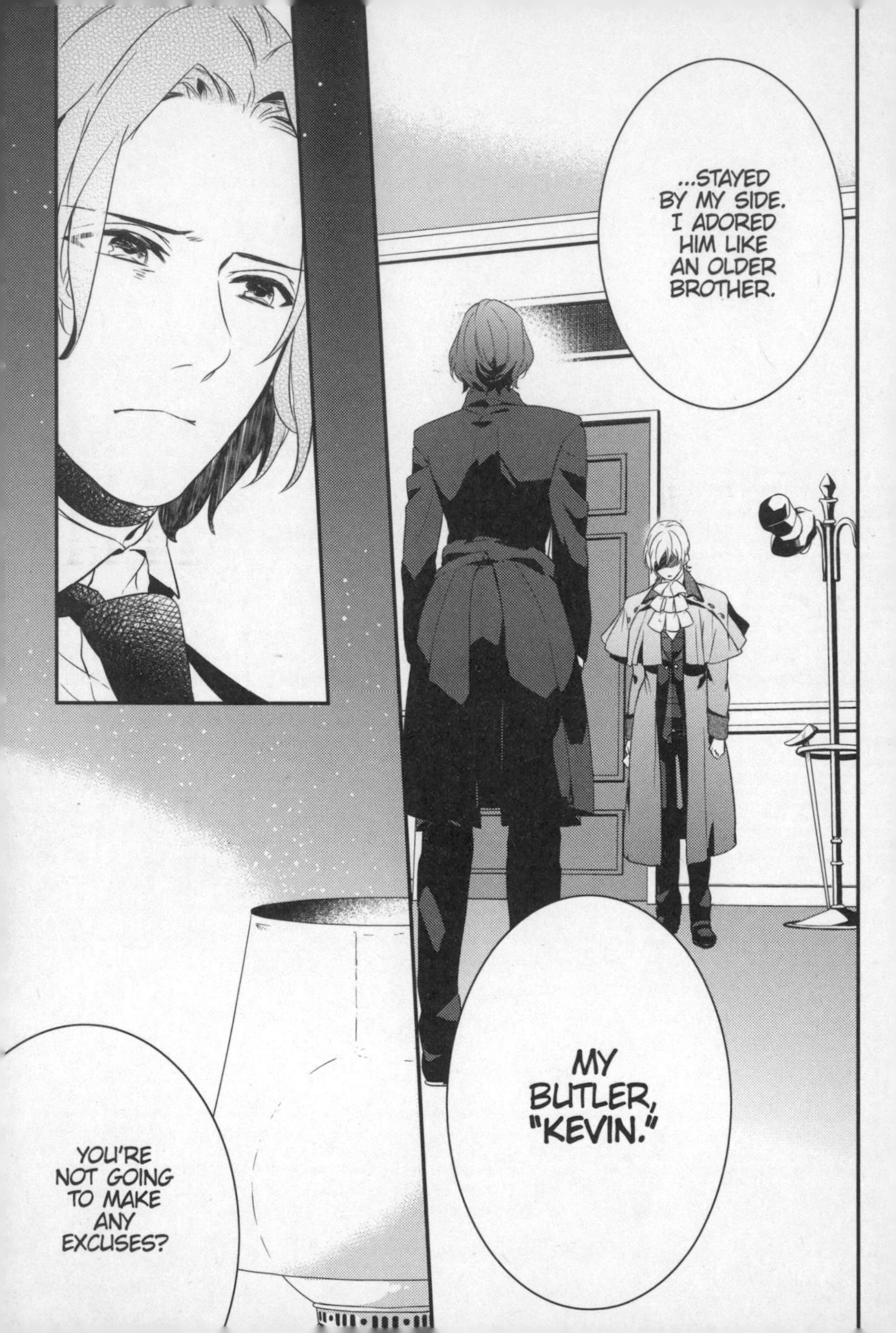
...STAYED BY MY SIDE. I ADORED HIM LIKE AN OLDER BROTHER.
MY BUTLER, "KEVIN."
YOU'RE NOT GOING TO MAKE ANY EXCUSES?

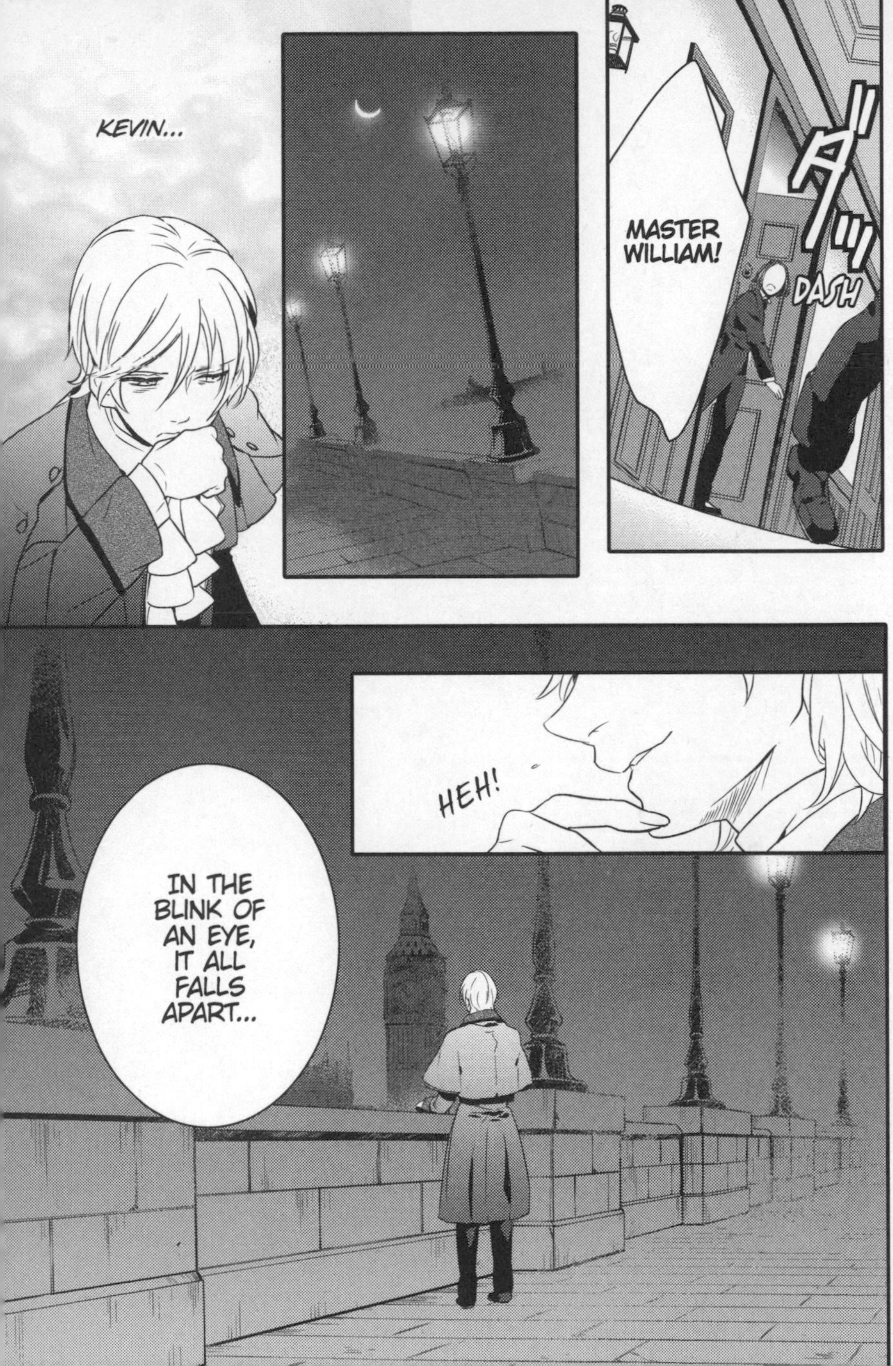
ダッ
DASH
MASTER WILLIAM!
KEVIN...
HEH!
IN THE BLINK OF AN EYE, IT ALL FALLS APART...

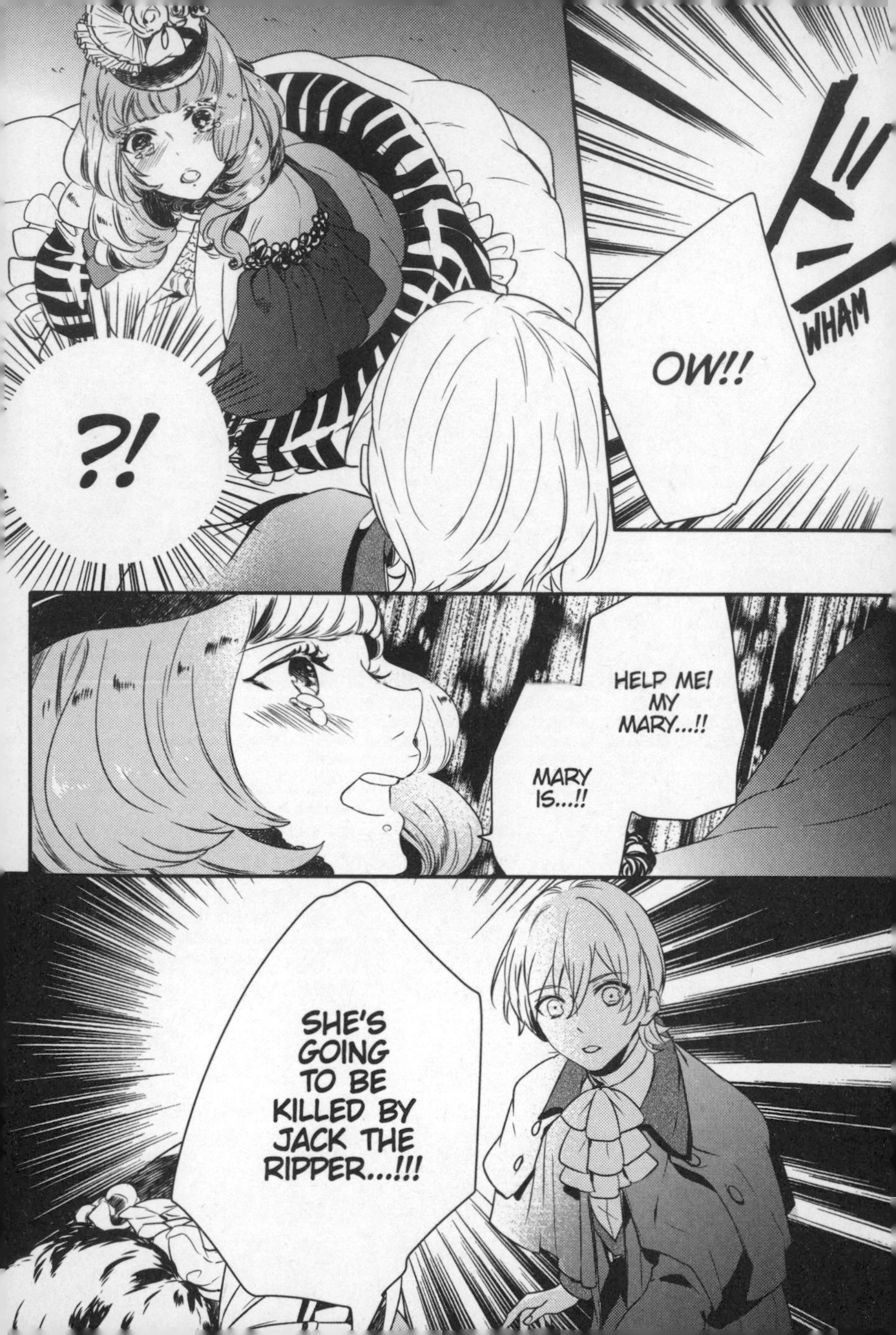
ドン
WHAM
OW!!
?!
HELP ME! MY MARY...!!
MARY IS...!!
SHE'S GOING TO BE KILLED BY JACK THE RIPPER...!!!

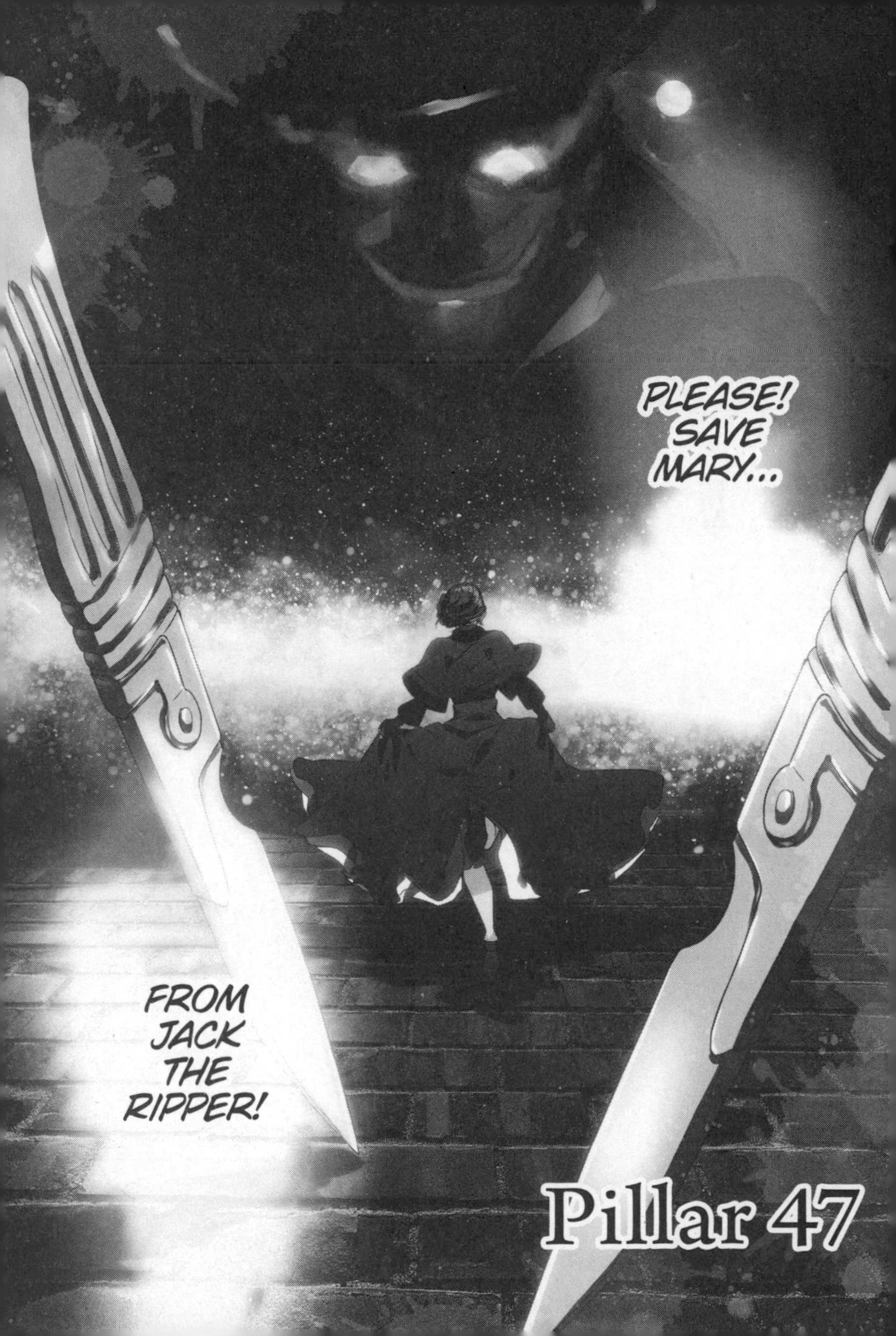
PLEASE! SAVE MARY...
FROM JACK THE RIPPER!
Pillar 47

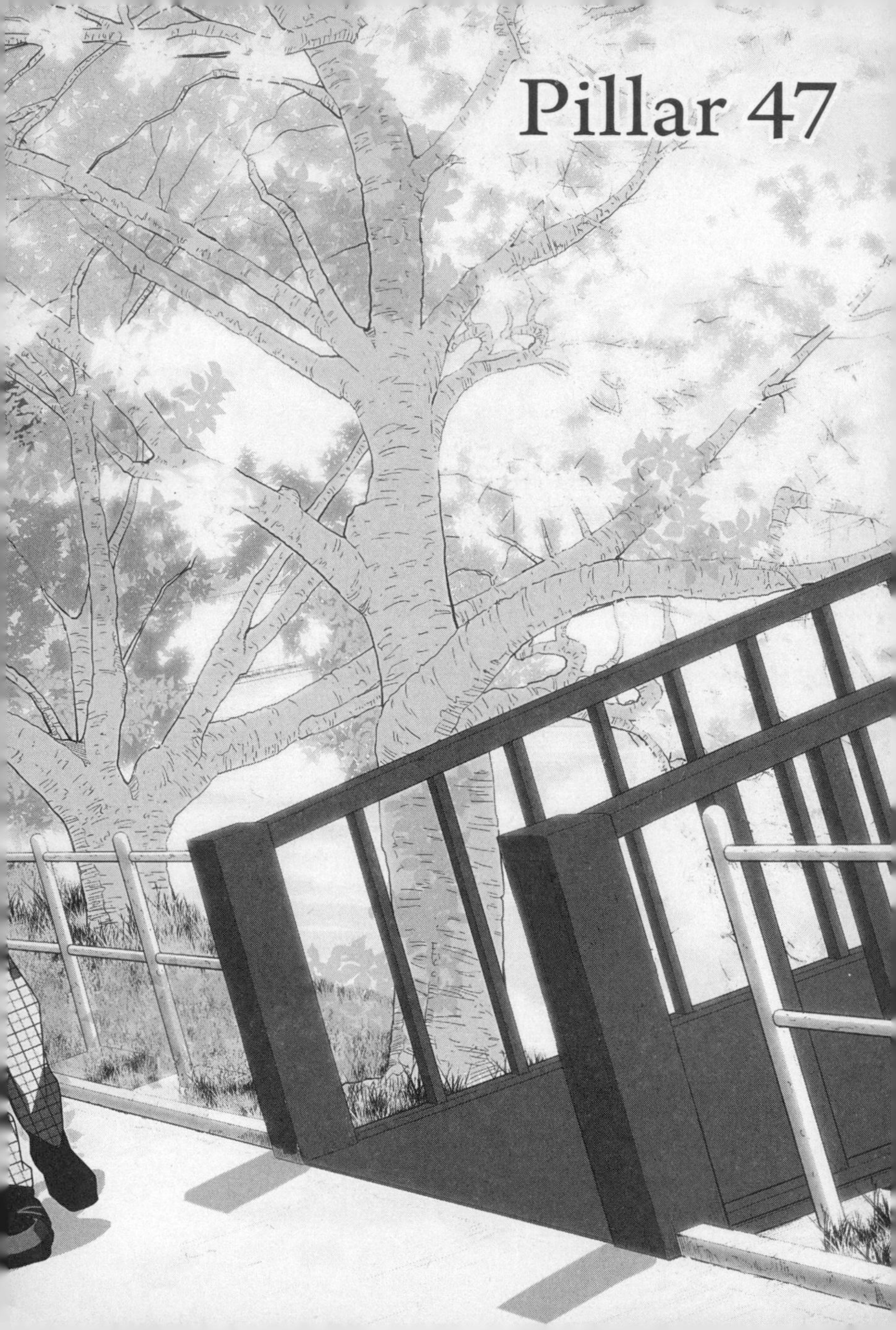
Pillar 47

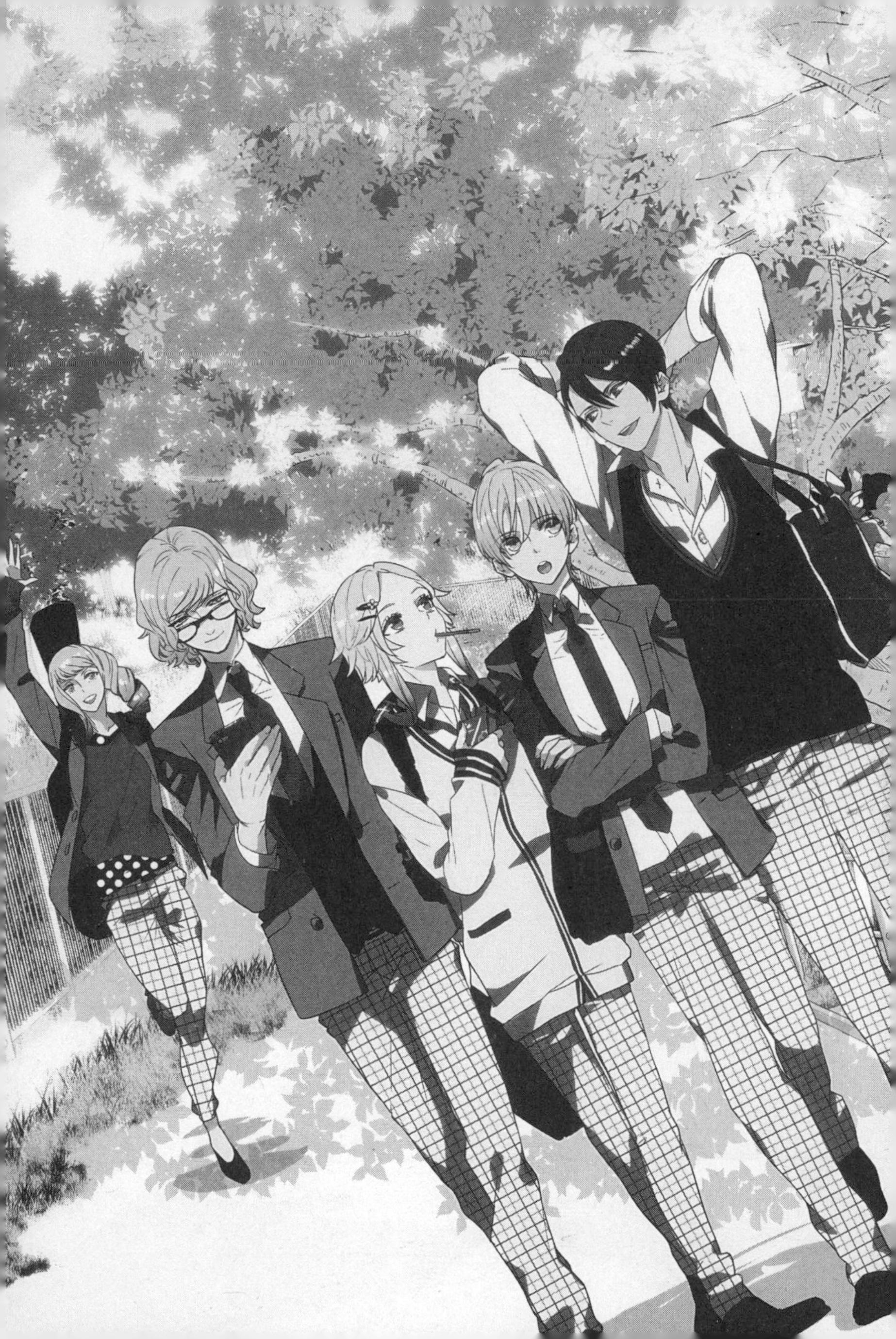

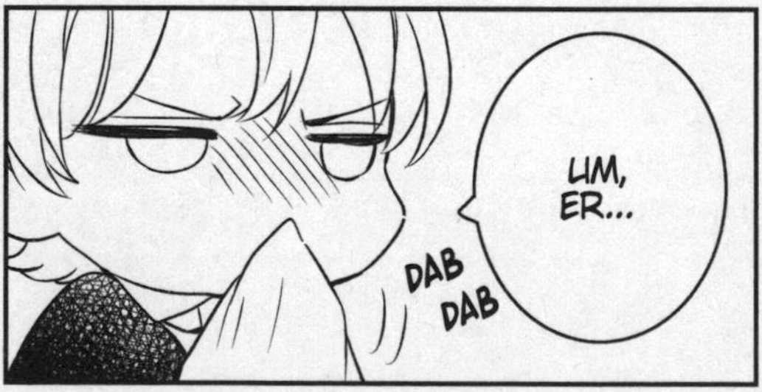
UM, ER...
DAB DAB

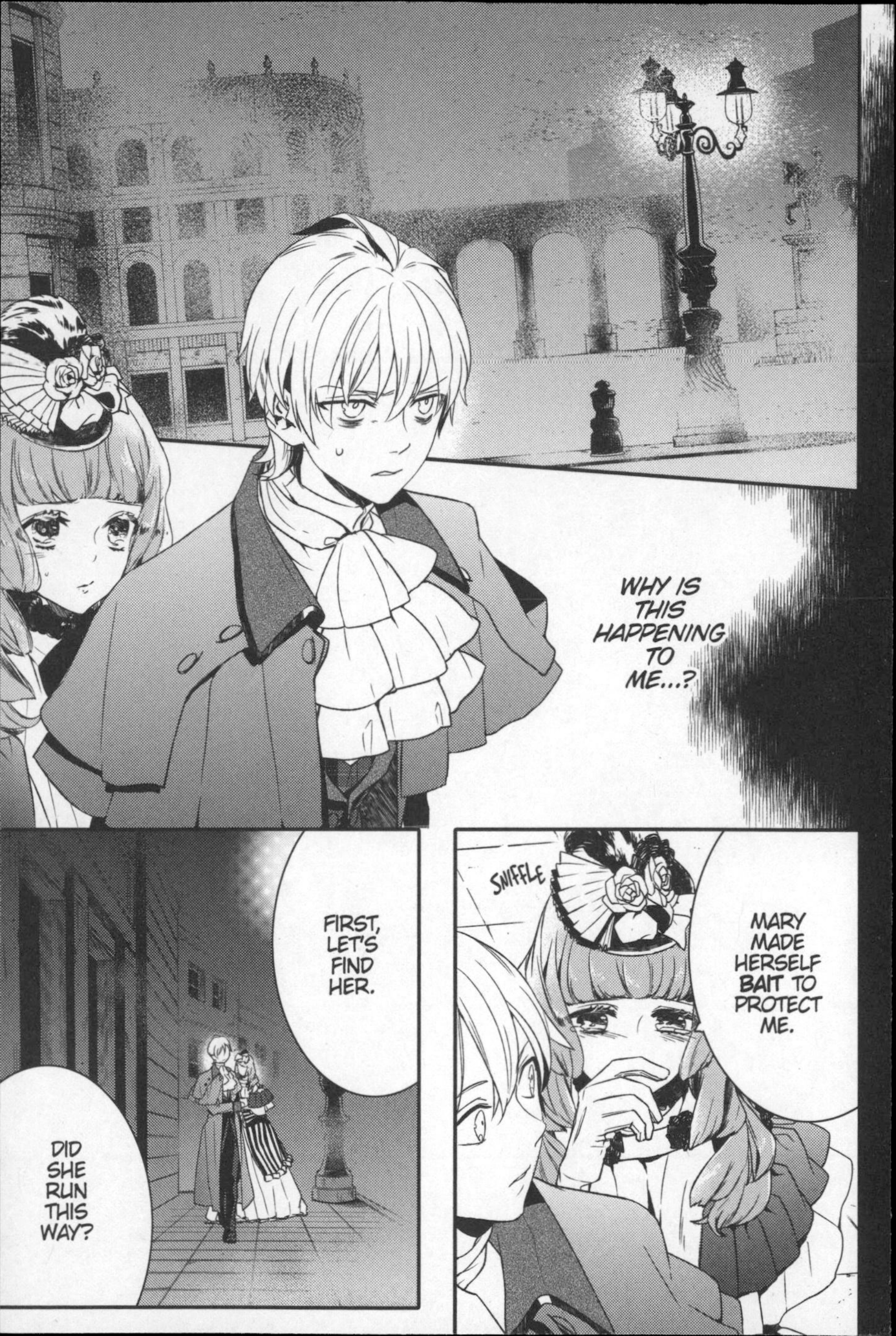
WHY IS THIS HAPPENING TO ME...?
SNIFFLE
MARY MADE HERSELF BAIT TO PROTECT ME.
FIRST, LET'S FIND HER.
DID SHE RUN THIS WAY?

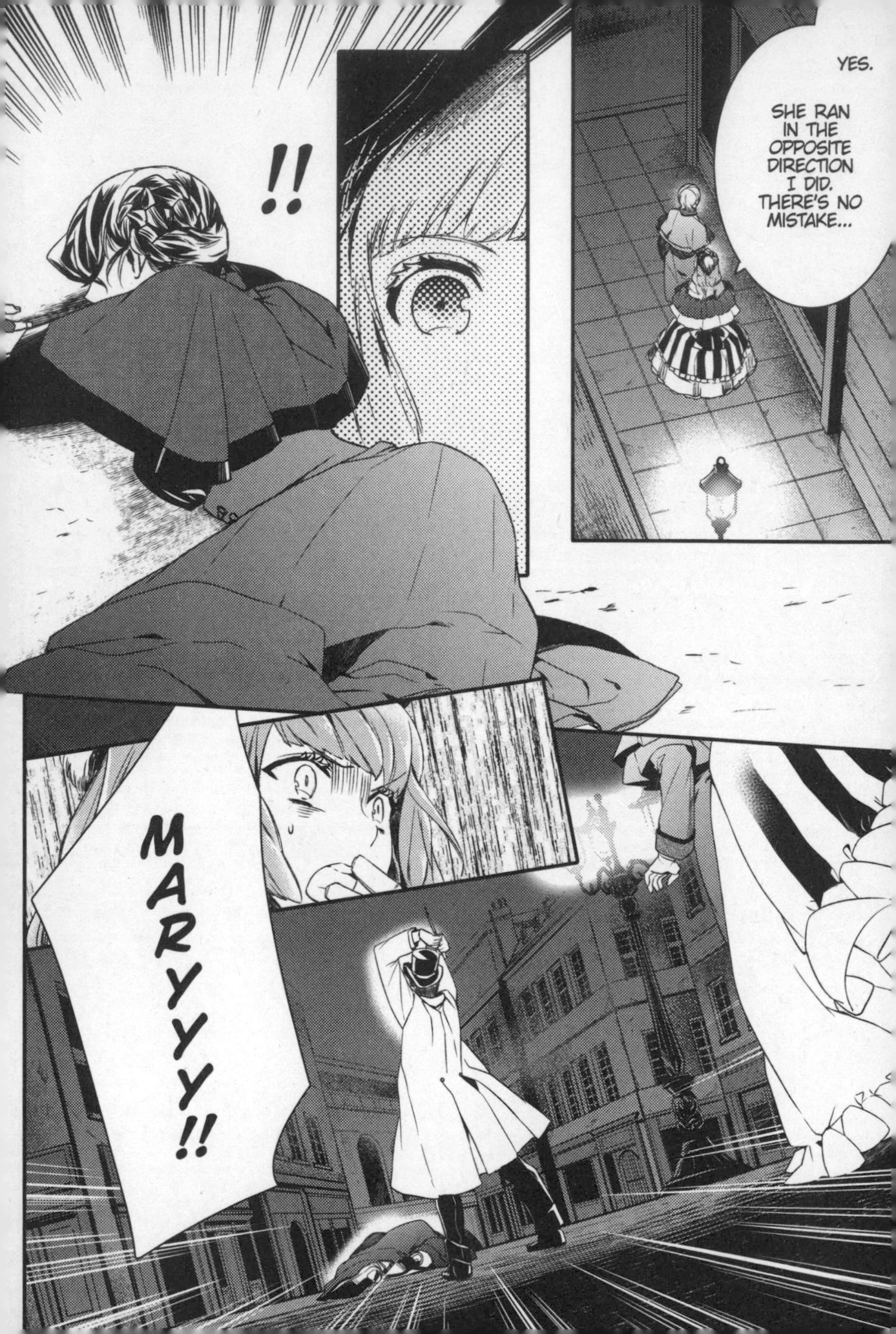
YES.
SHE RAN IN THE OPPOSITE DIRECTION I DID. THERE'S NO MISTAKE...
!!
MARYYY!!

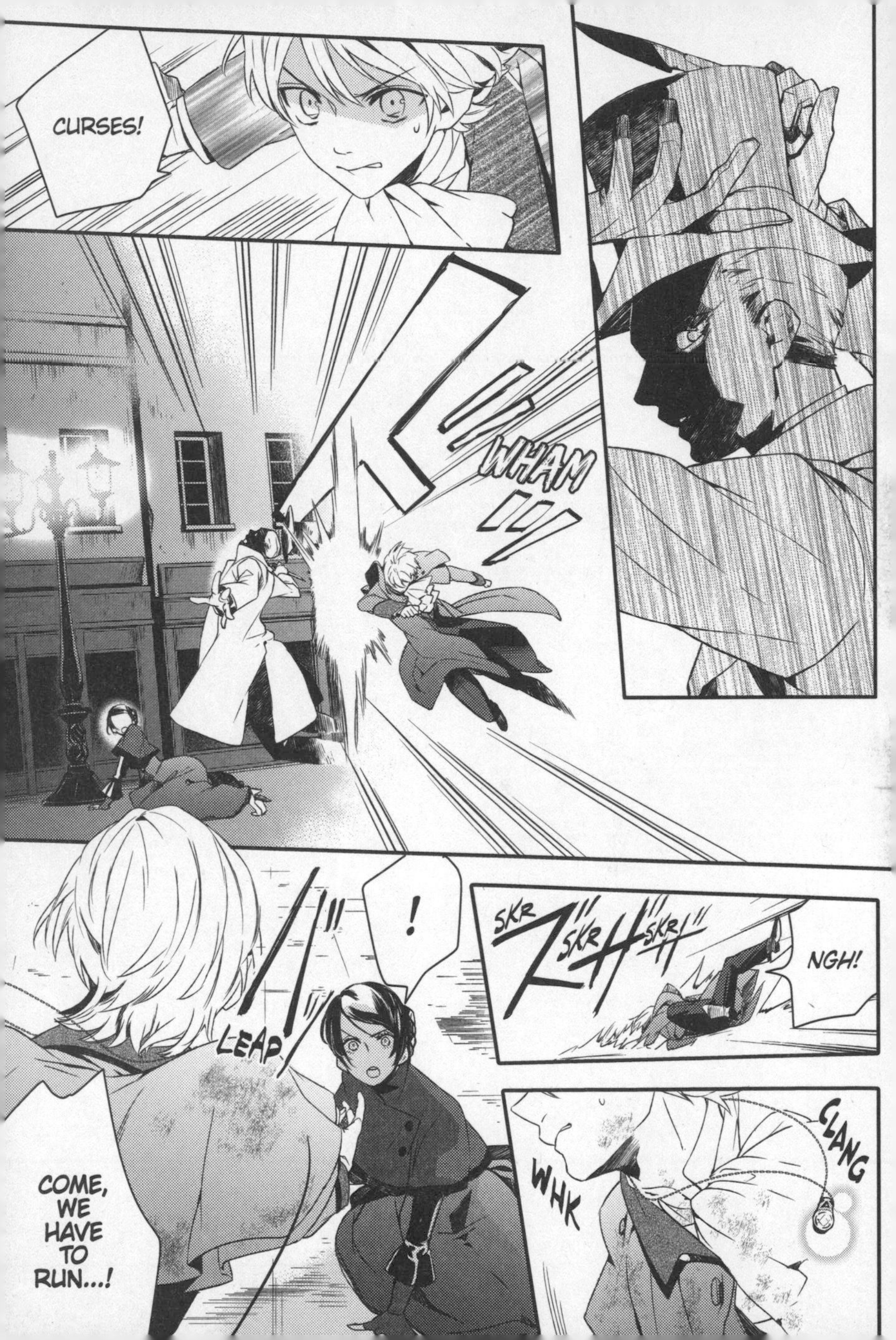
CURSES!
WHAM
SKR
SKR
SKR
NGH!
CLANG
WHK
!
LEAP
COME, WE HAVE TO RUN...!

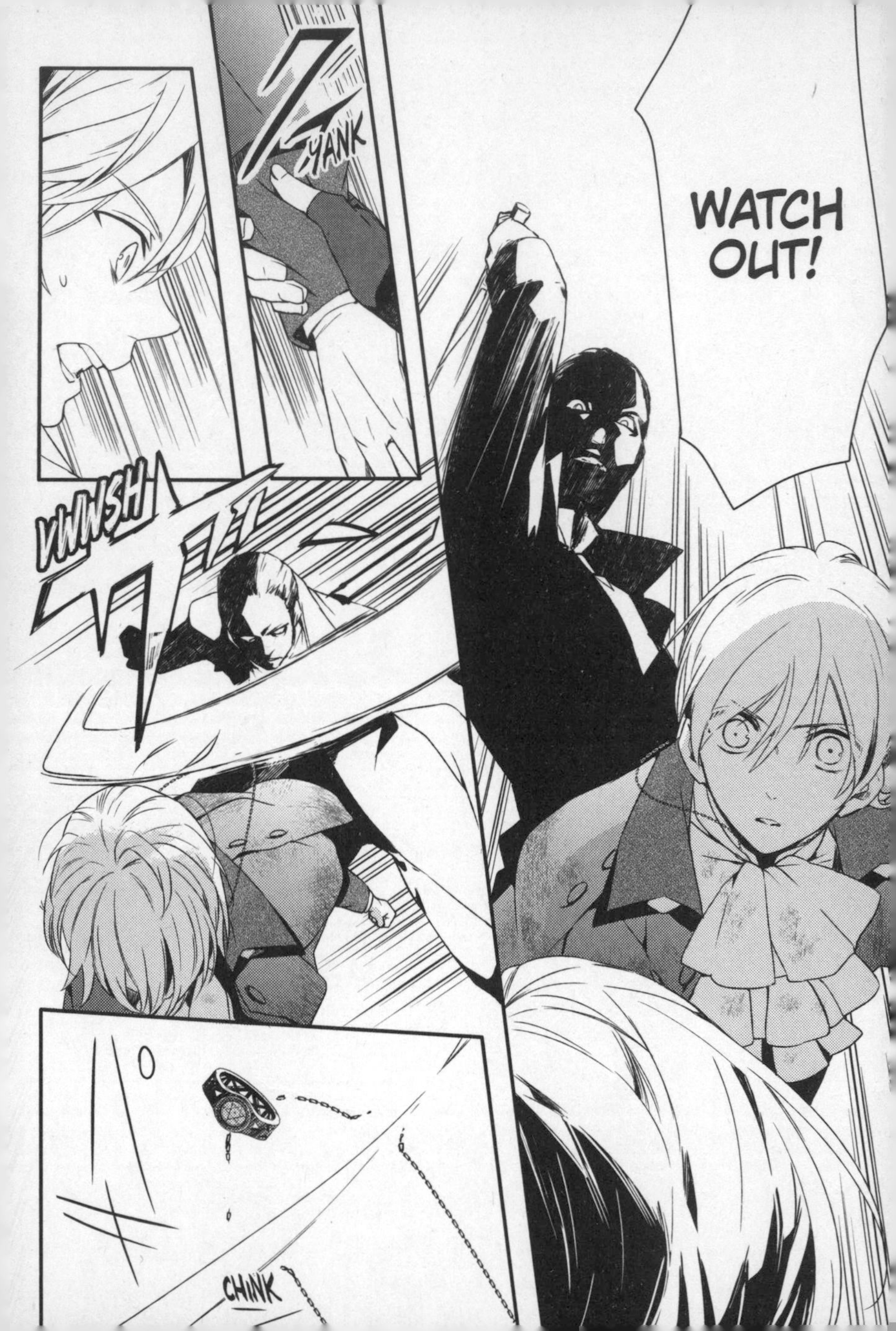
WATCH OUT!
YANK
VWWSH
CHINK

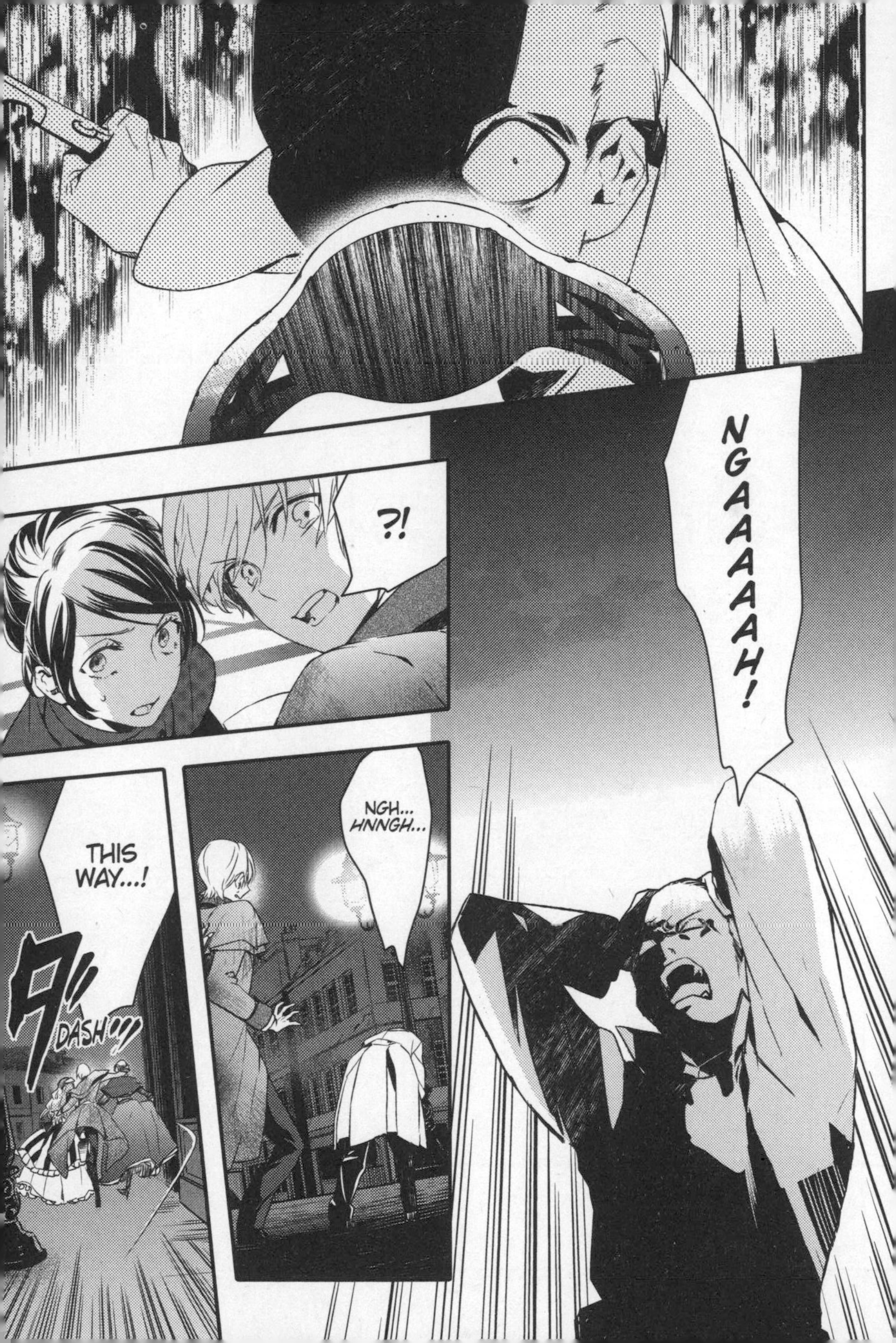
NGAAAAAAH!
?!
NGH... HNNGH...
THIS WAY...!
DASH!!

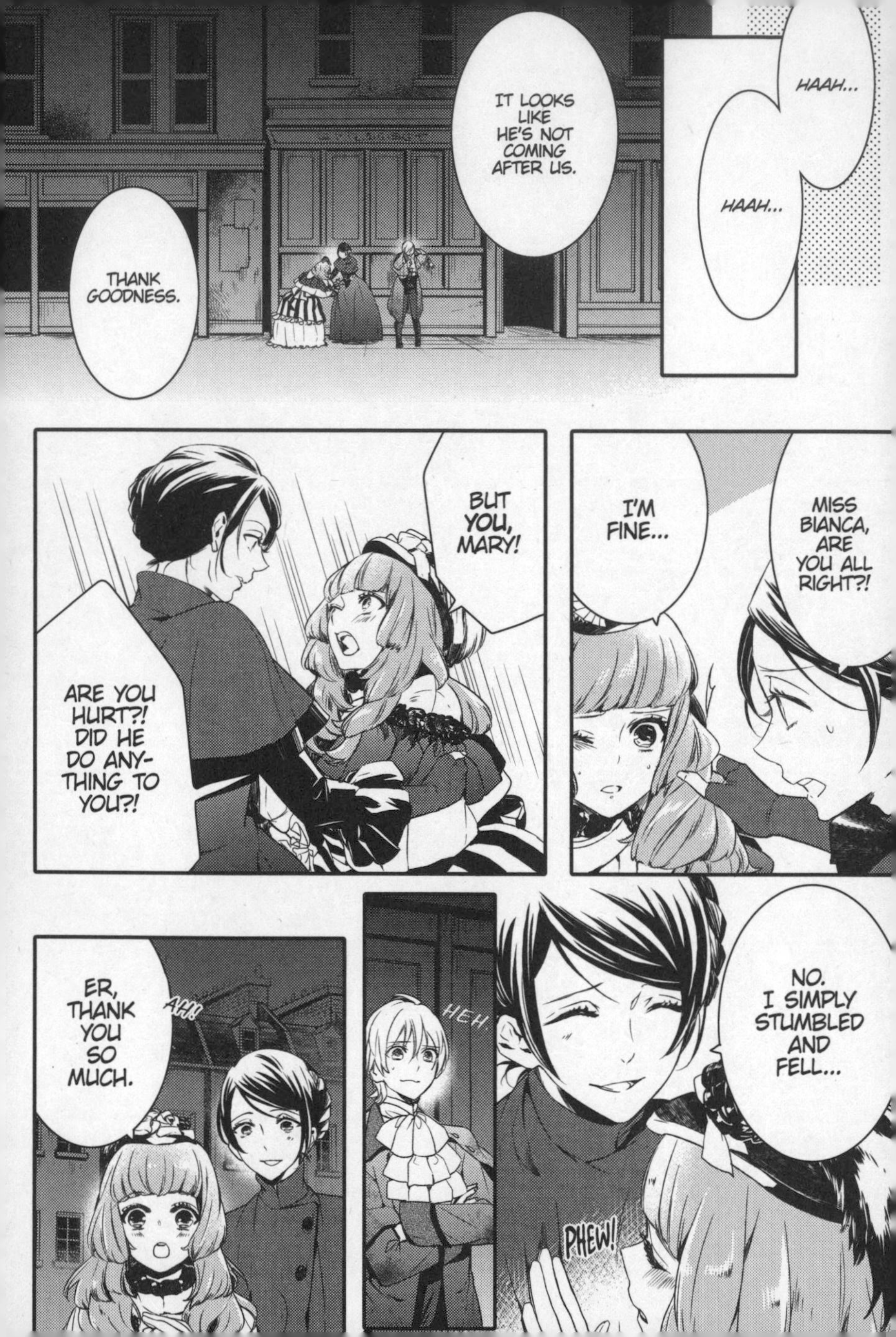
HAAH...
HAAH...
IT LOOKS LIKE HE'S NOT COMING AFTER US.
THANK GOODNESS.
MISS BIANCA, ARE YOU ALL RIGHT?!
I'M FINE...
BUT YOU, MARY!
ARE YOU HURT?! DID HE DO ANY-THING TO YOU?!
NO. I SIMPLY STUMBLED AND FELL...
PHEW!
HEH.
AH!
ER, THANK YOU SO MUCH.

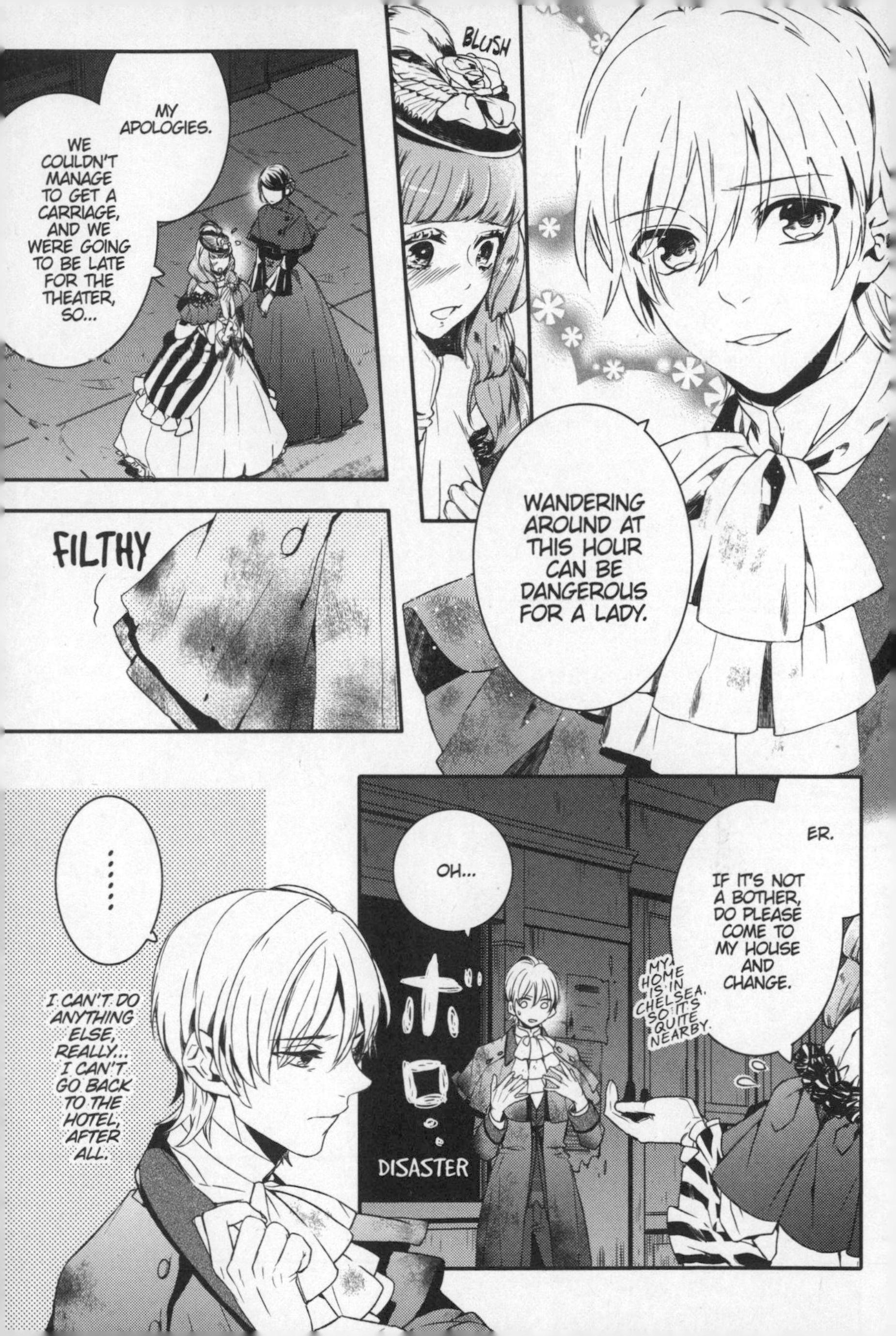
WANDERING AROUND AT THIS HOUR CAN BE DANGEROUS FOR A LADY.
BLUSH
MY APOLOGIES.
WE COULDN'T MANAGE TO GET A CARRIAGE, AND WE WERE GOING TO BE LATE FOR THE THEATER, SO...
FILTHY
ER.
IF IT'S NOT A BOTHER, DO PLEASE COME TO MY HOUSE AND CHANGE.
MY HOME IS IN CHELSEA, SO IT'S QUITE NEARBY.
OH...
DISASTER
......
I CAN'T DO ANYTHING ELSE, REALLY... I CAN'T GO BACK TO THE HOTEL, AFTER ALL.

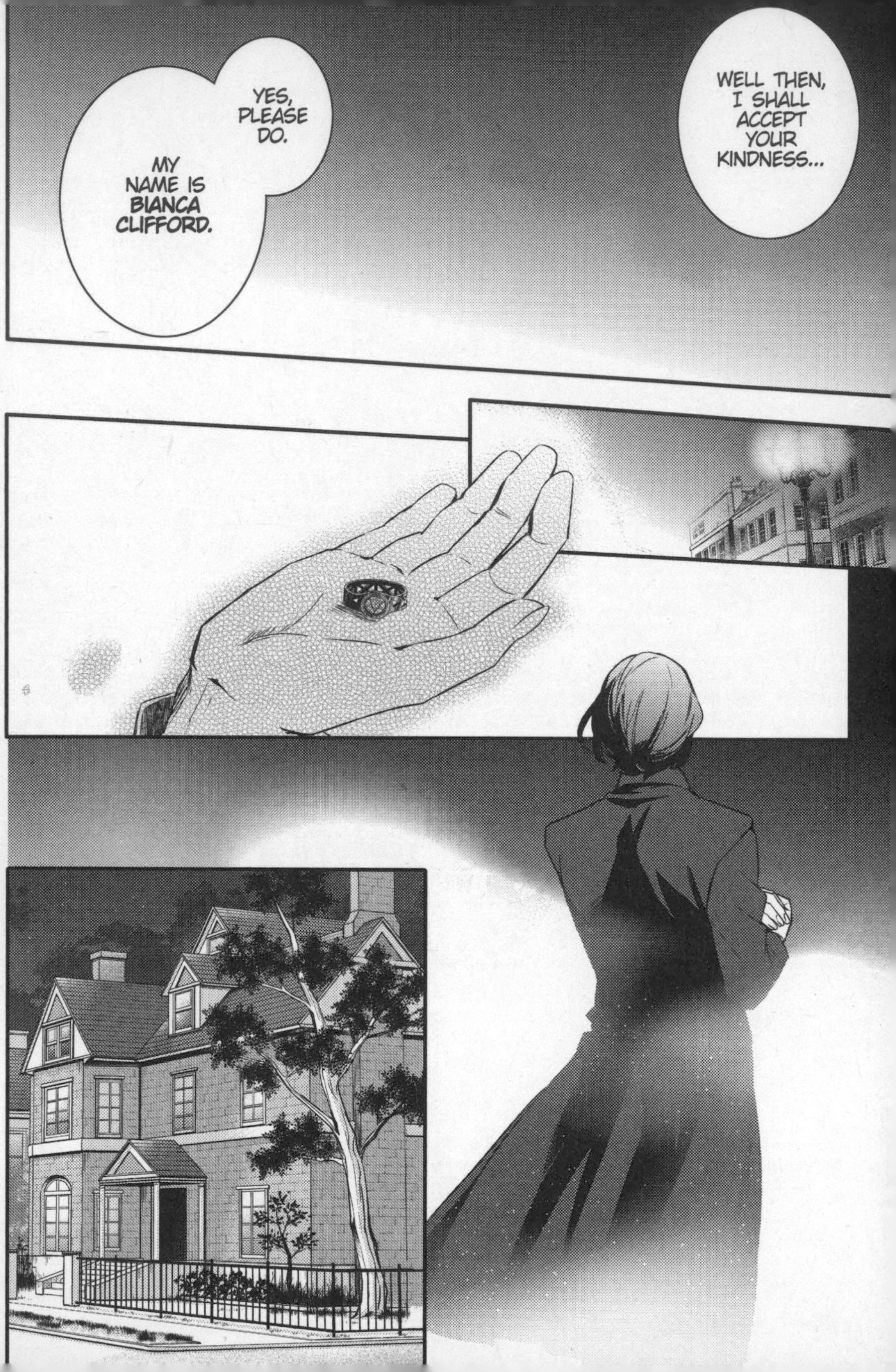
WELL THEN, I SHALL ACCEPT YOUR KINDNESS...
YES, PLEASE DO.
MY NAME IS BIANCA CLIFFORD.

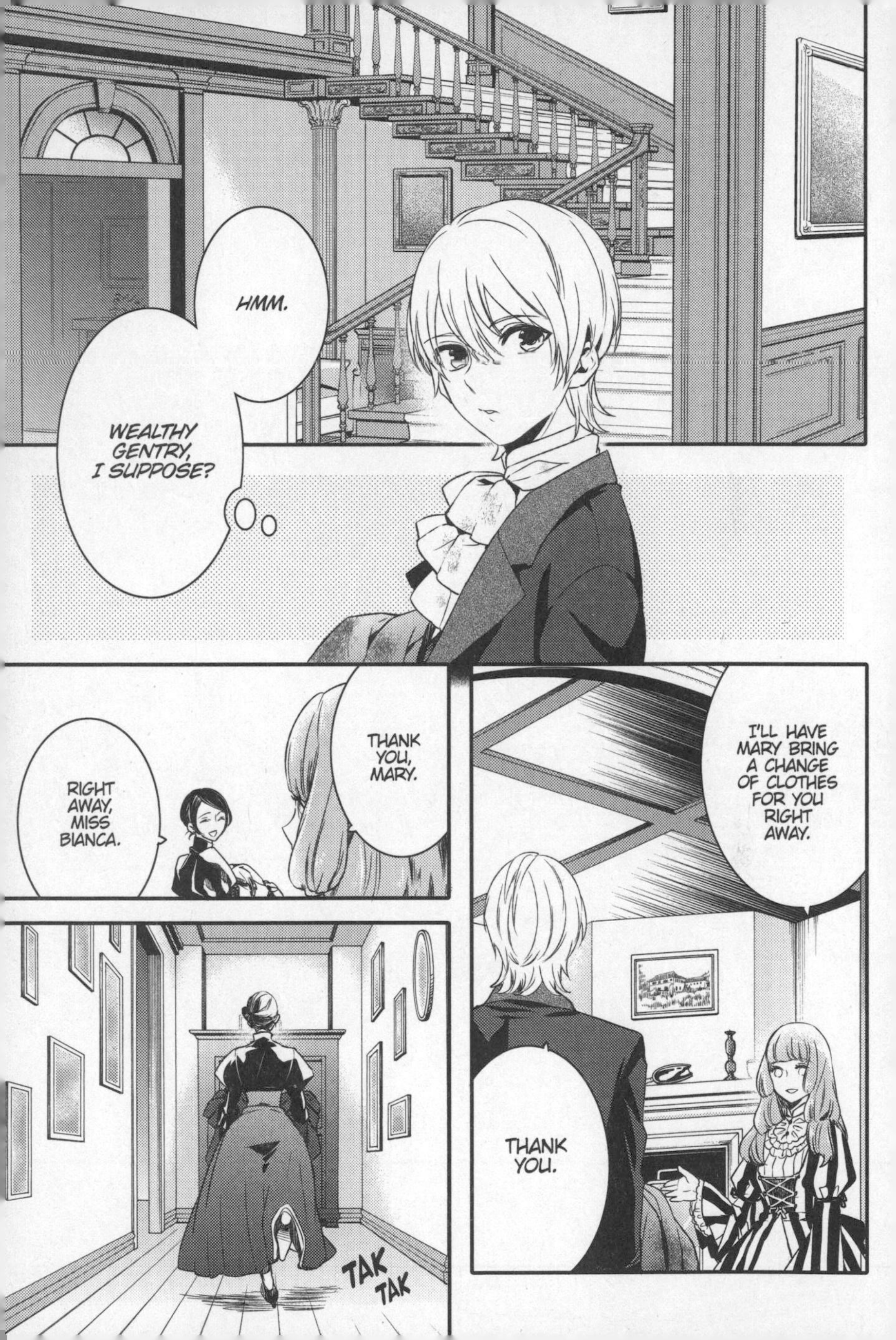
HMM.
WEALTHY GENTRY, I SUPPOSE?
I'LL HAVE MARY BRING A CHANGE OF CLOTHES FOR YOU RIGHT AWAY.
THANK YOU.
THANK YOU, MARY.
RIGHT AWAY, MISS BIANCA.
TAK TAK

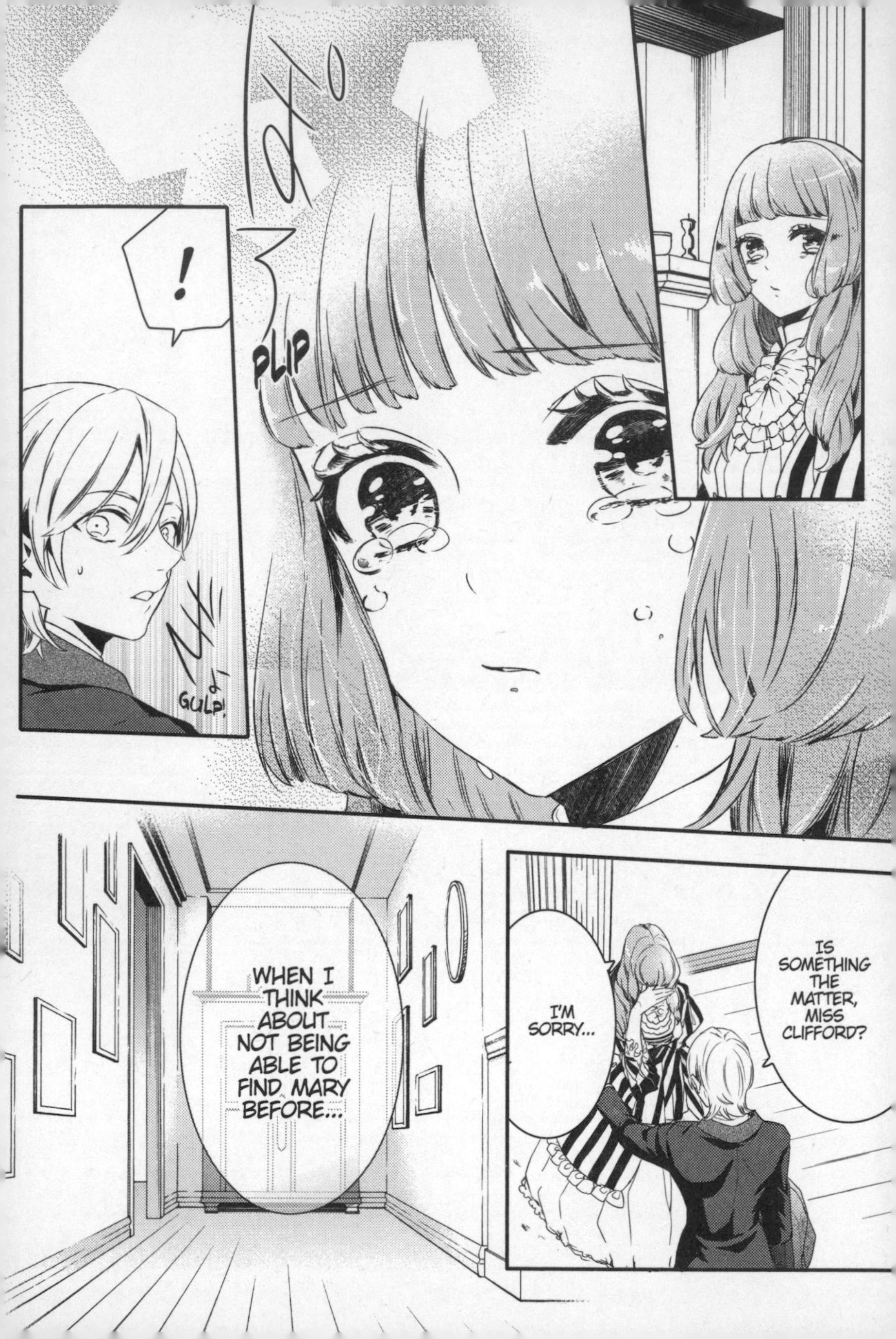
PLIP
!
GULP!
IS SOMETHING THE MATTER, MISS CLIFFORD?
I'M SORRY...
WHEN I THINK ABOUT NOT BEING ABLE TO FIND MARY BEFORE...

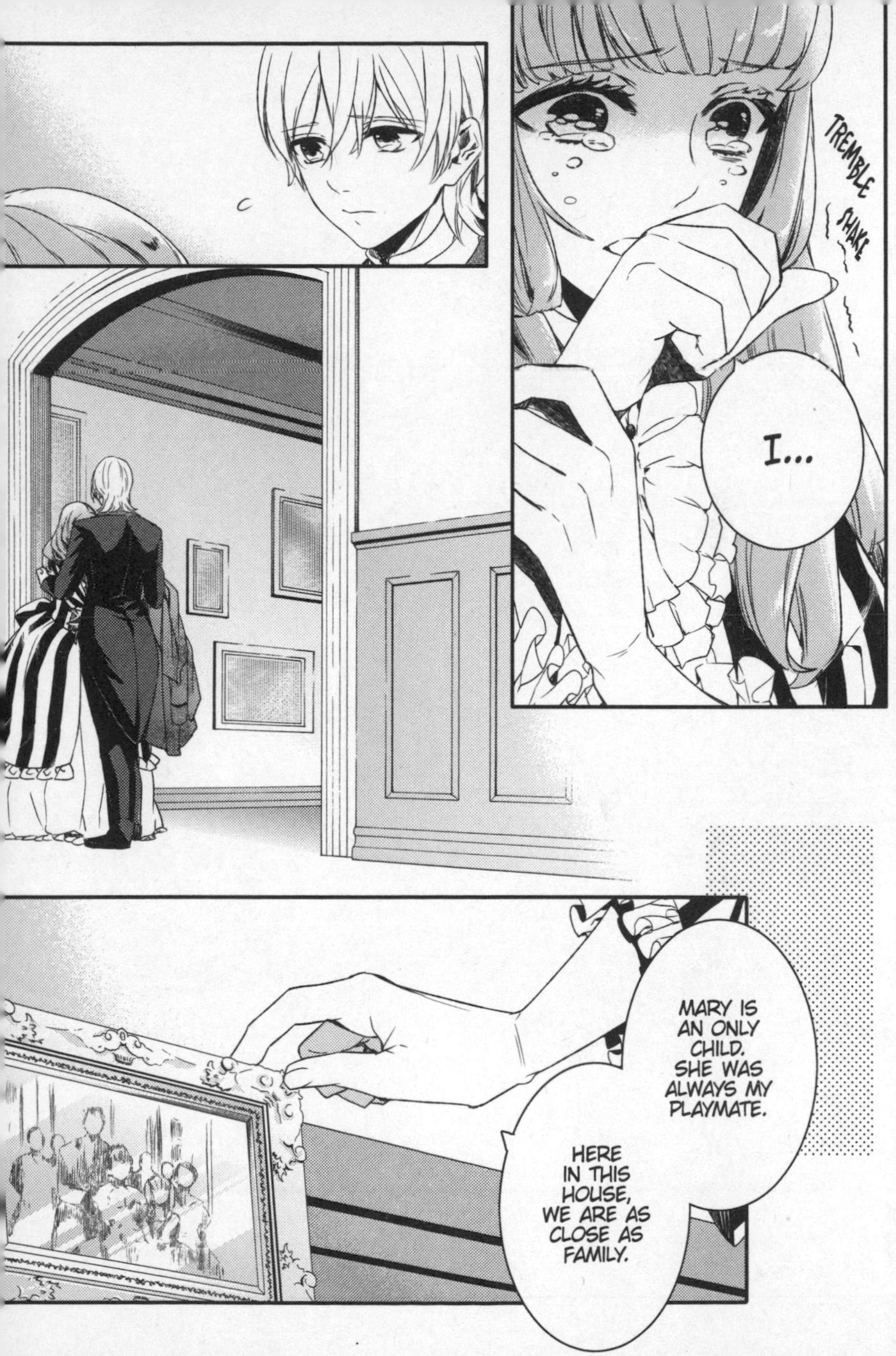
TREMBLE
SHAKE
I...
MARY IS AN ONLY CHILD. SHE WAS ALWAYS MY PLAYMATE.
HERE IN THIS HOUSE, WE ARE AS CLOSE AS FAMILY.

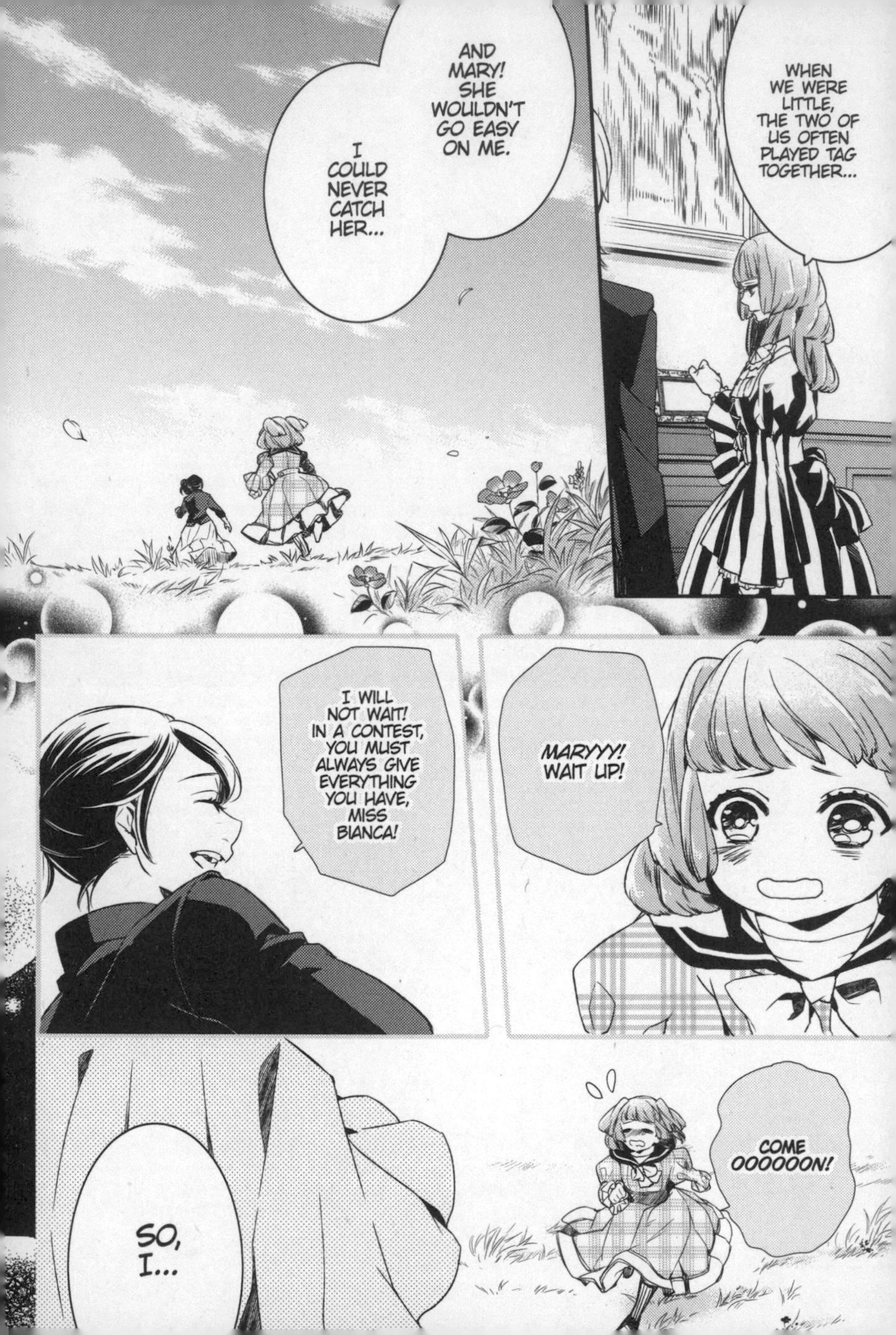
WHEN WE WERE LITTLE, THE TWO OF US OFTEN PLAYED TAG TOGETHER...
AND MARY! SHE WOULDN'T GO EASY ON ME.
I COULD NEVER CATCH HER...
MARYYY! WAIT UP!
I WILL NOT WAIT! IN A CONTEST, YOU MUST ALWAYS GIVE EVERYTHING YOU HAVE, MISS BIANCA!
COME OOOOOON!
SO, I...

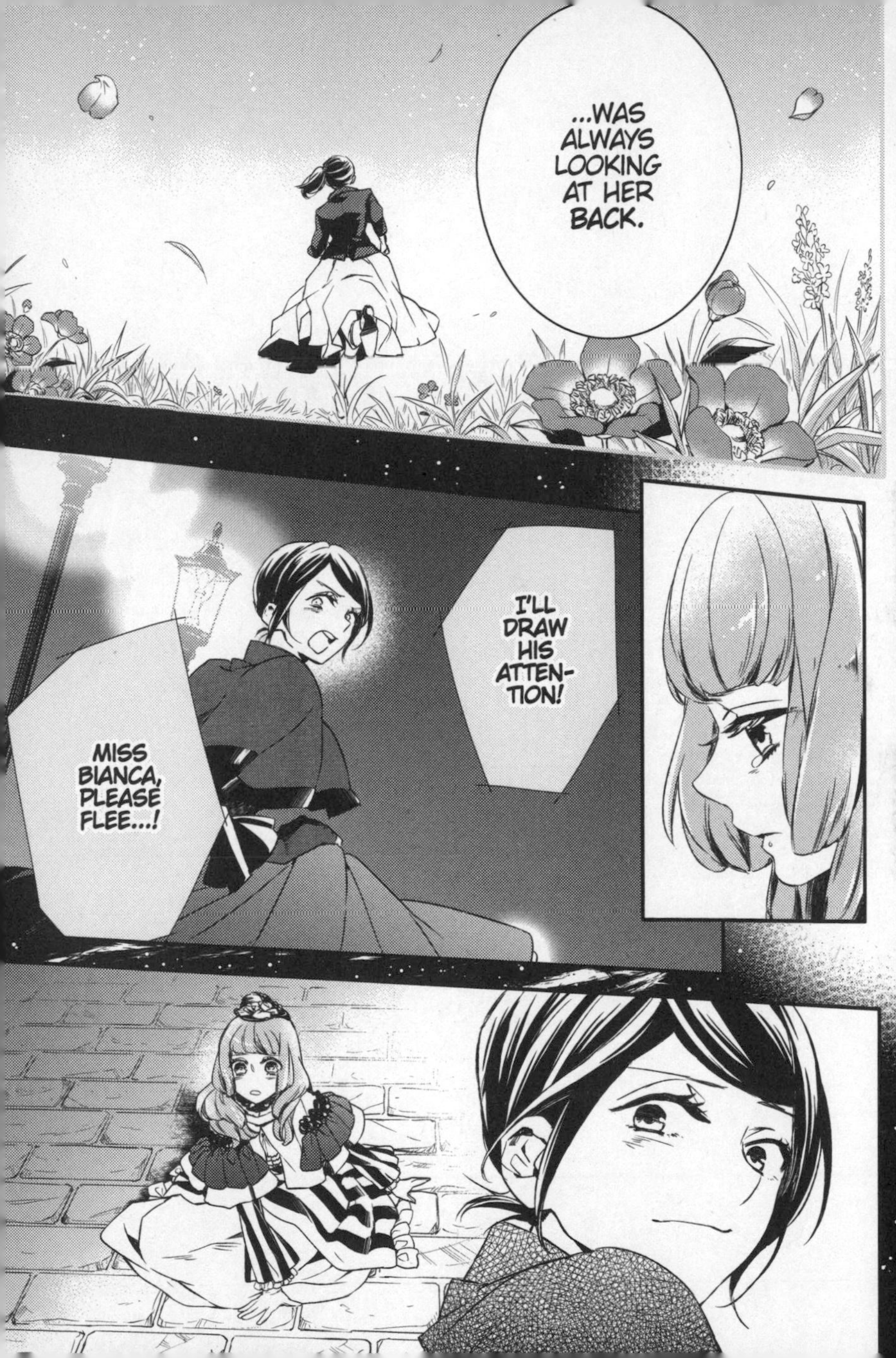
...WAS ALWAYS LOOKING AT HER BACK.
I'LL DRAW HIS ATTEN-TION!
MISS BIANCA, PLEASE FLEE...!

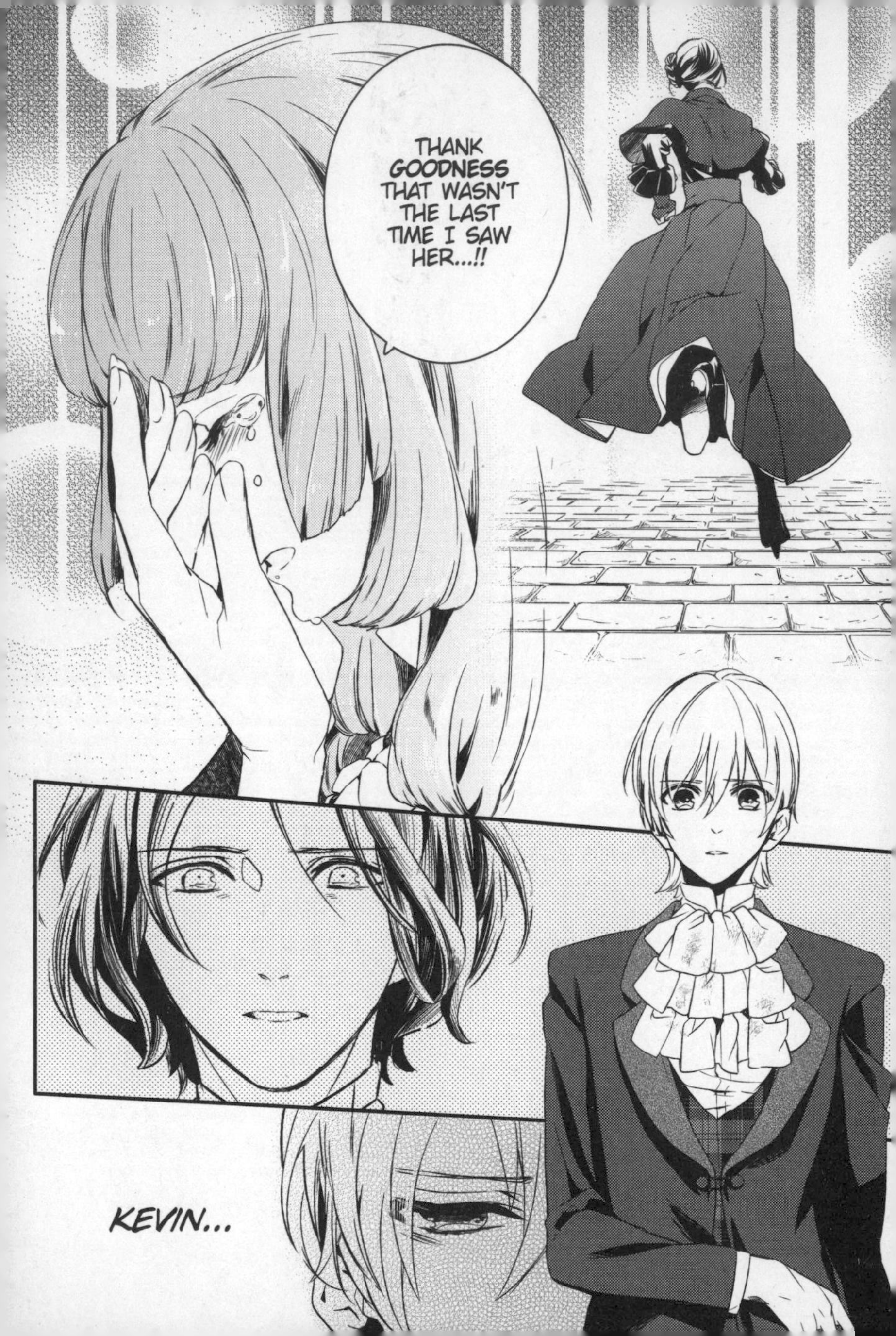
THANK GOODNESS THAT WASN'T THE LAST TIME I SAW HER...!!
KEVIN...

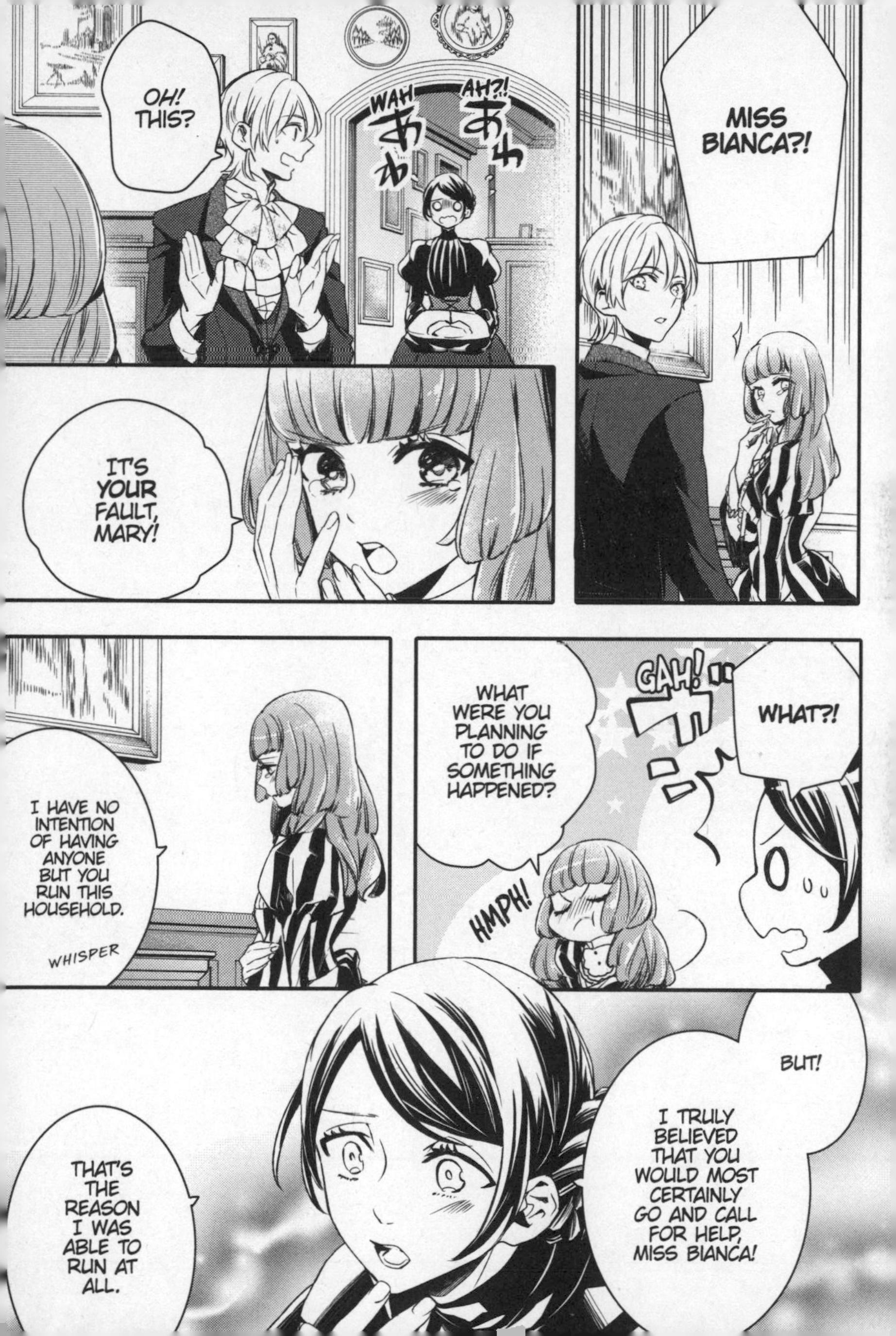
MISS BIANCA?!
AH?!
WAH
OH! THIS?
IT'S YOUR FAULT, MARY!
WHAT?!
GAH!
WHAT WERE YOU PLANNING TO DO IF SOMETHING HAPPENED?
HMPH!
I HAVE NO INTENTION OF HAVING ANYONE BUT YOU RUN THIS HOUSEHOLD.
WHISPER
BUT!
I TRULY BELIEVED THAT YOU WOULD MOST CERTAINLY GO AND CALL FOR HELP, MISS BIANCA!
THAT'S THE REASON I WAS ABLE TO RUN AT ALL.

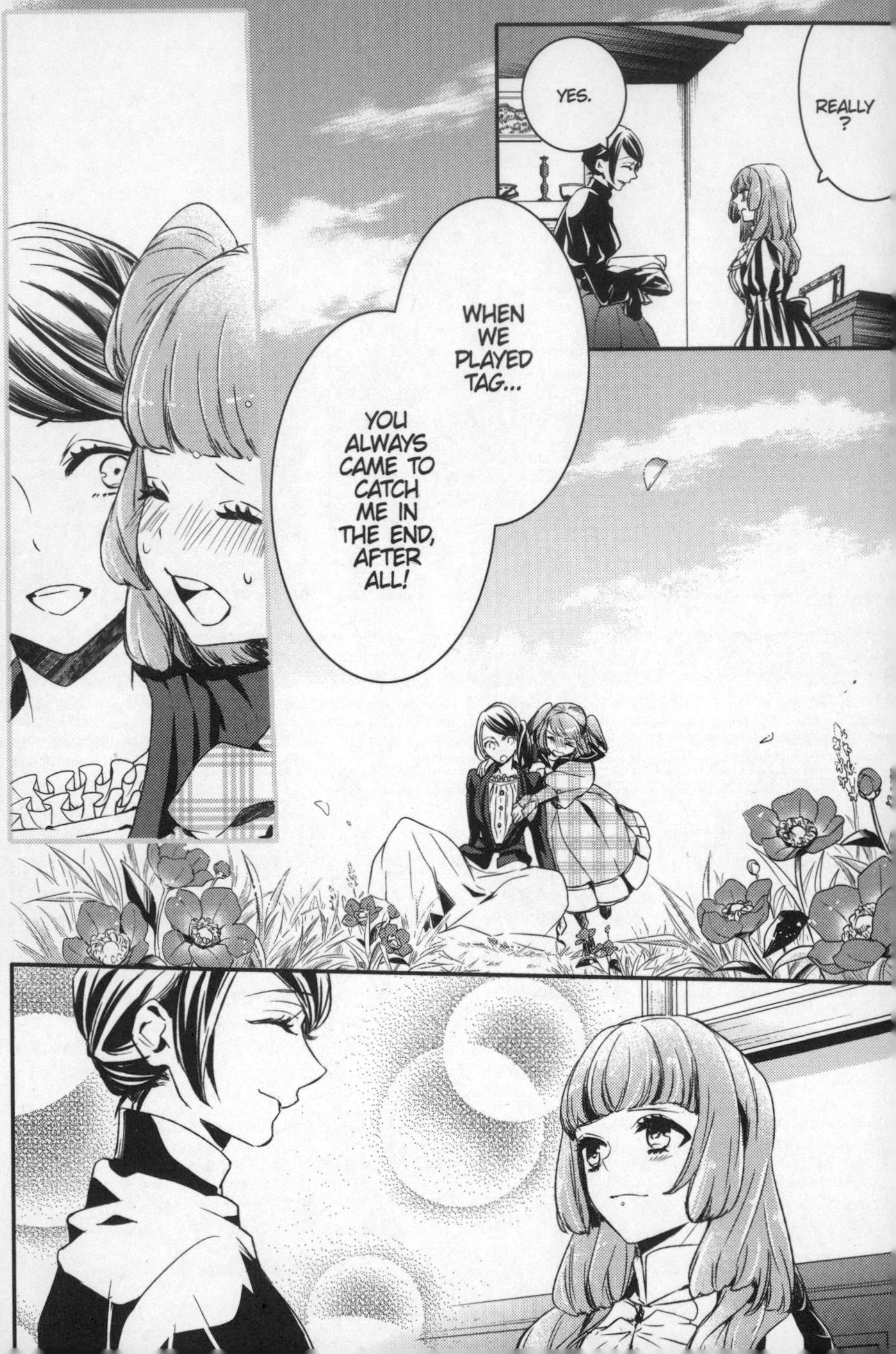
REALLY?
YES.
WHEN WE PLAYED TAG...
YOU ALWAYS CAME TO CATCH ME IN THE END, AFTER ALL!

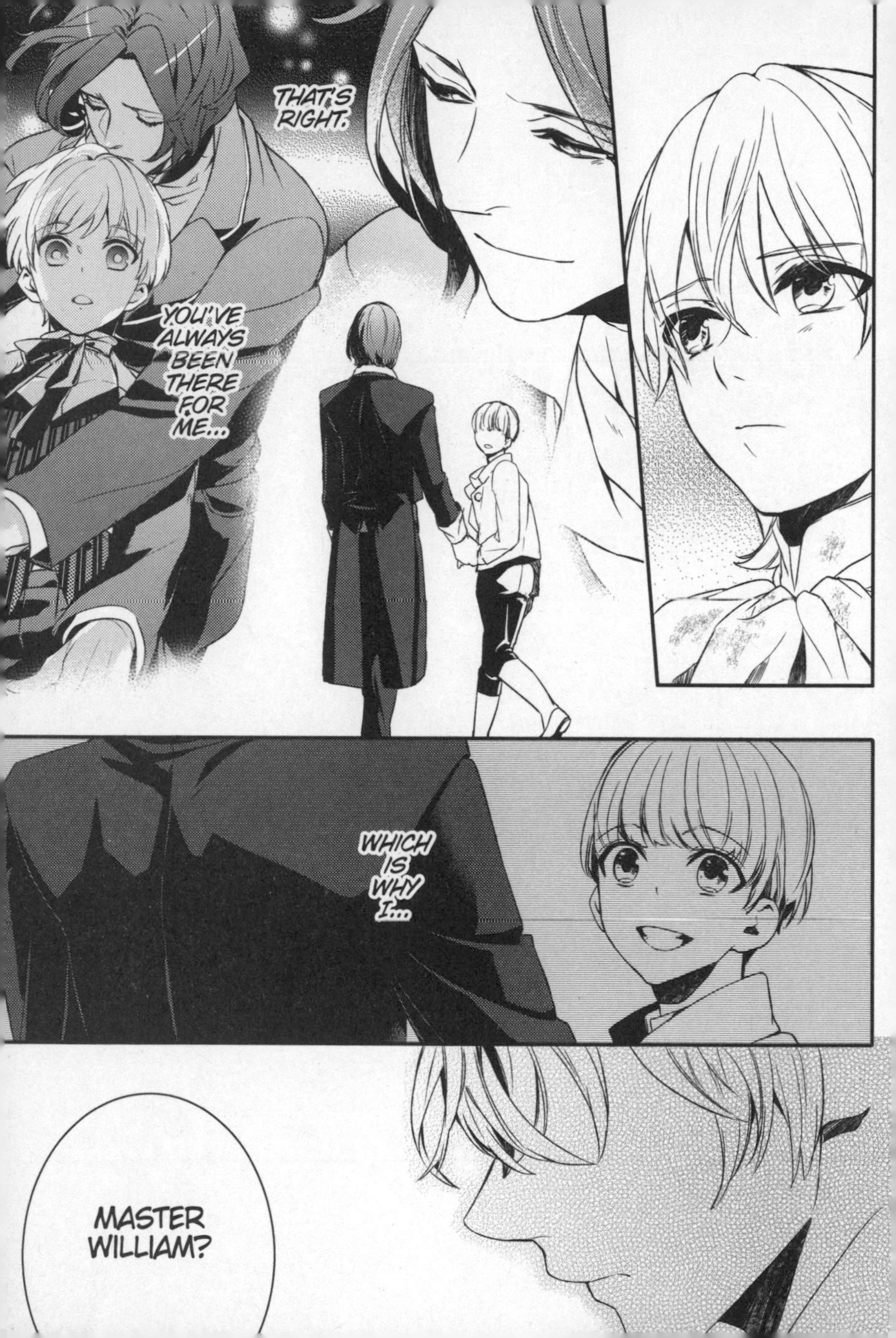
THAT'S RIGHT.
YOU'VE ALWAYS BEEN THERE FOR ME...
WHICH IS WHY I...
MASTER WILLIAM?

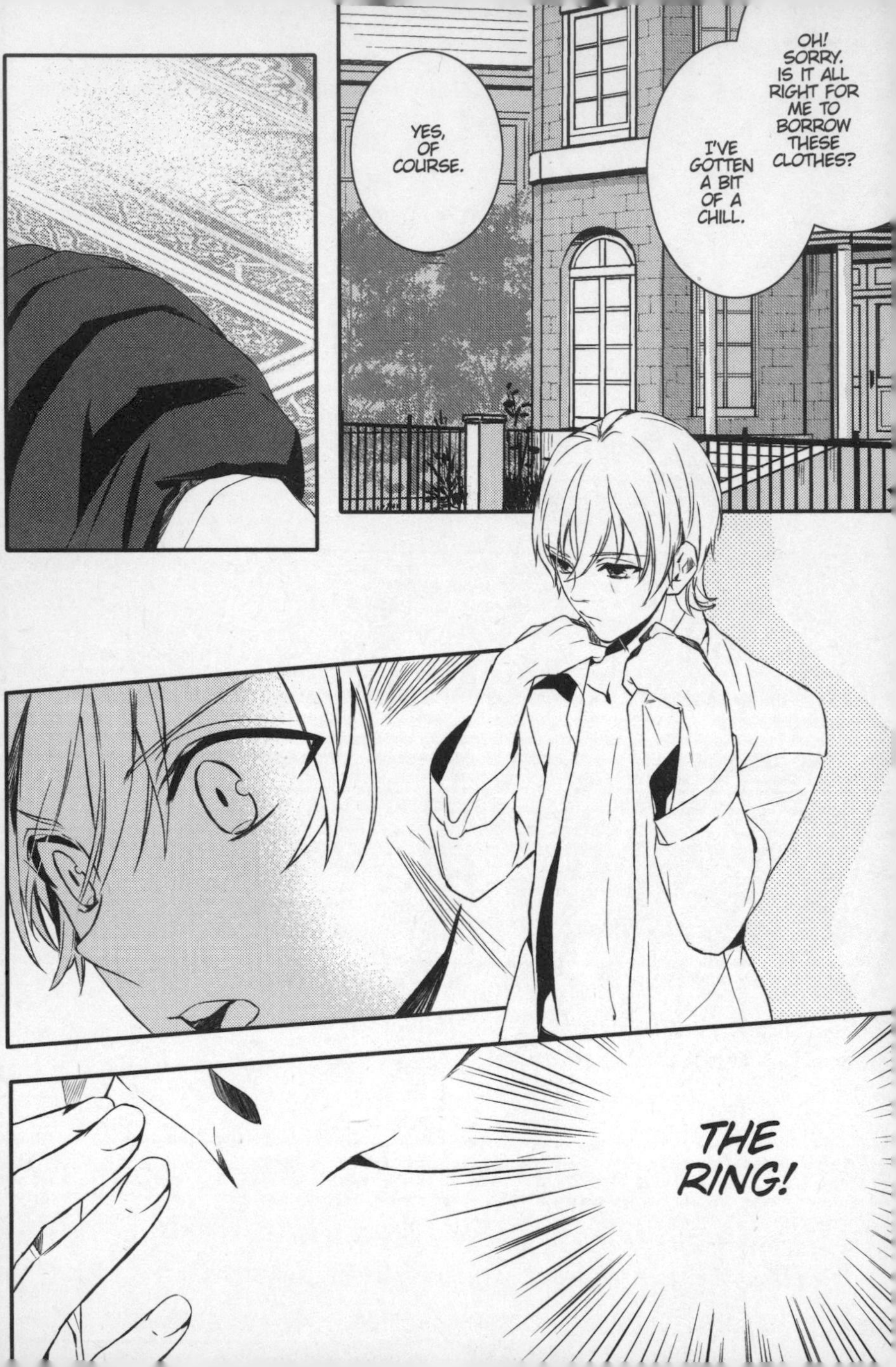
OH! SORRY. IS IT ALL RIGHT FOR ME TO BORROW THESE CLOTHES?
I'VE GOTTEN A BIT OF A CHILL.
YES, OF COURSE.
THE RING!

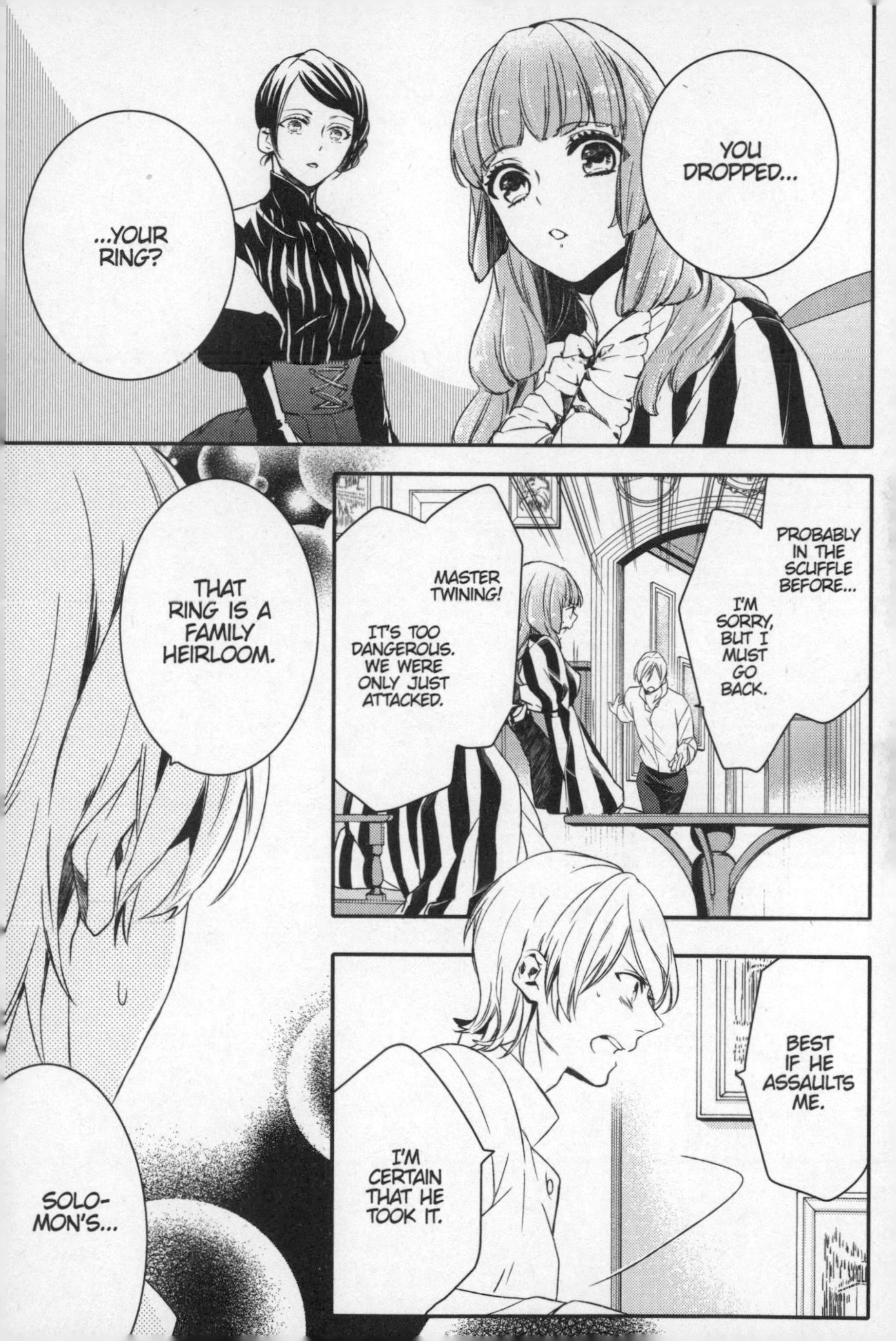
YOU DROPPED...
...YOUR RING?
PROBABLY IN THE SCUFFLE BEFORE...
I'M SORRY, BUT I MUST GO BACK.
MASTER TWINING!
IT'S TOO DANGEROUS. WE WERE ONLY JUST ATTACKED.
BEST IF HE ASSAULTS ME.
I'M CERTAIN THAT HE TOOK IT.
THAT RING IS A FAMILY HEIRLOOM.
SOLO-MON'S...

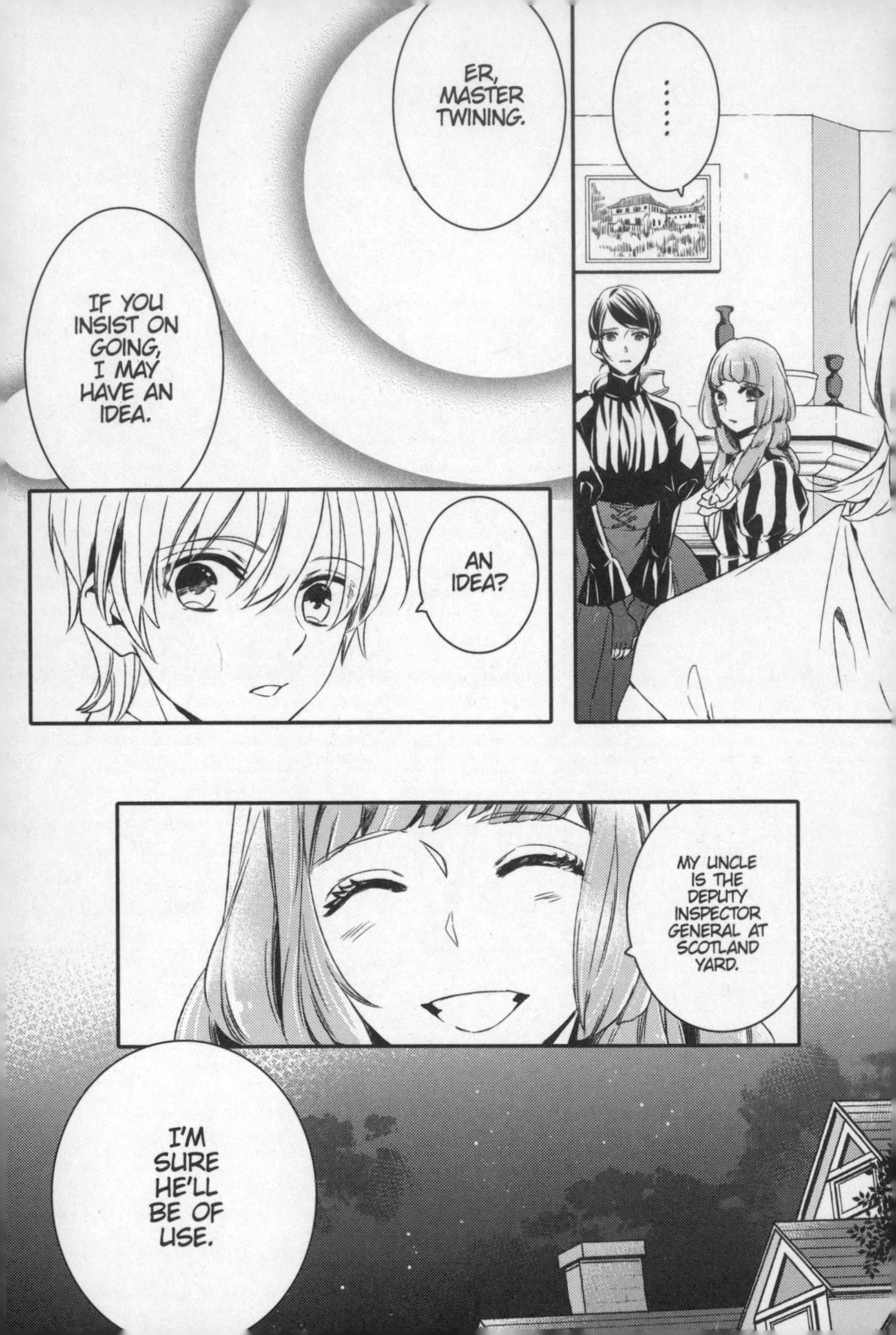
......
ER, MASTER TWINING.
IF YOU INSIST ON GOING, I MAY HAVE AN IDEA.
AN IDEA?
MY UNCLE IS THE DEPUTY INSPECTOR GENERAL AT SCOTLAND YARD.
I'M SURE HE'LL BE OF USE.

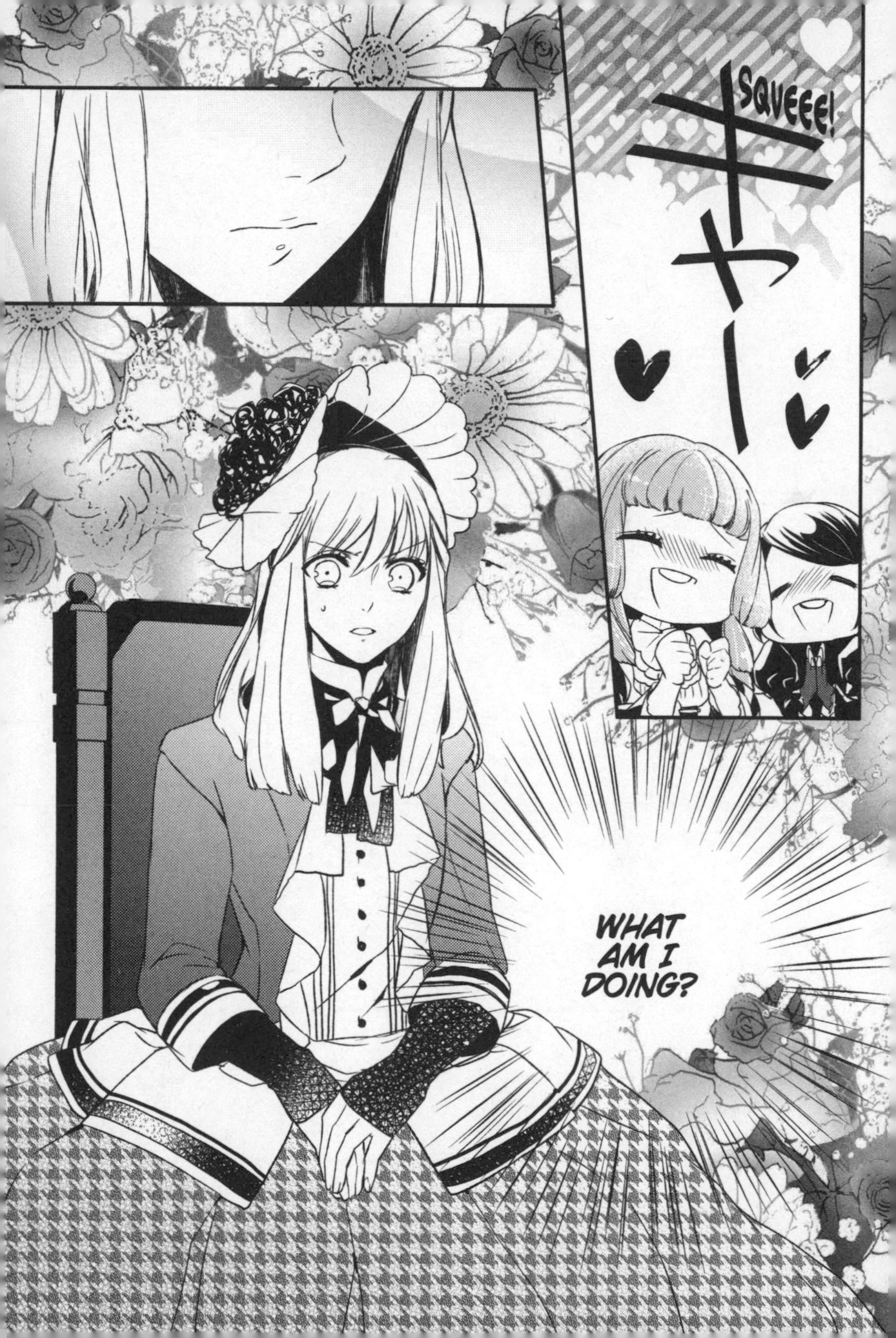
ギャー
SQUEEE!
WHAT AM I DOING?

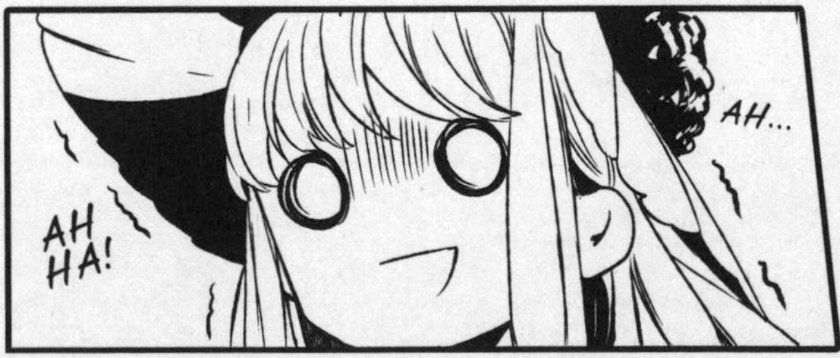
AH...
AH HA!

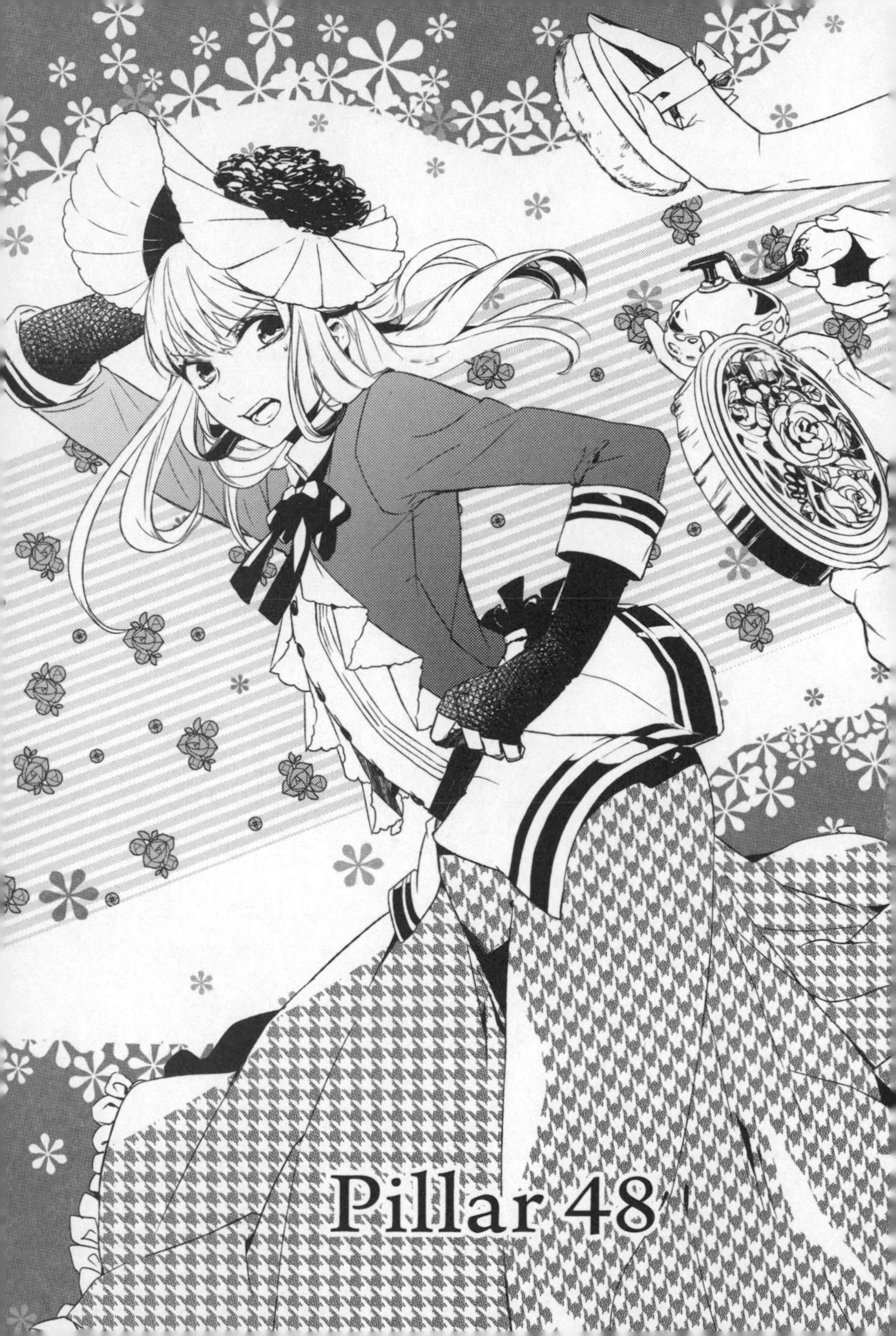
Pillar 48

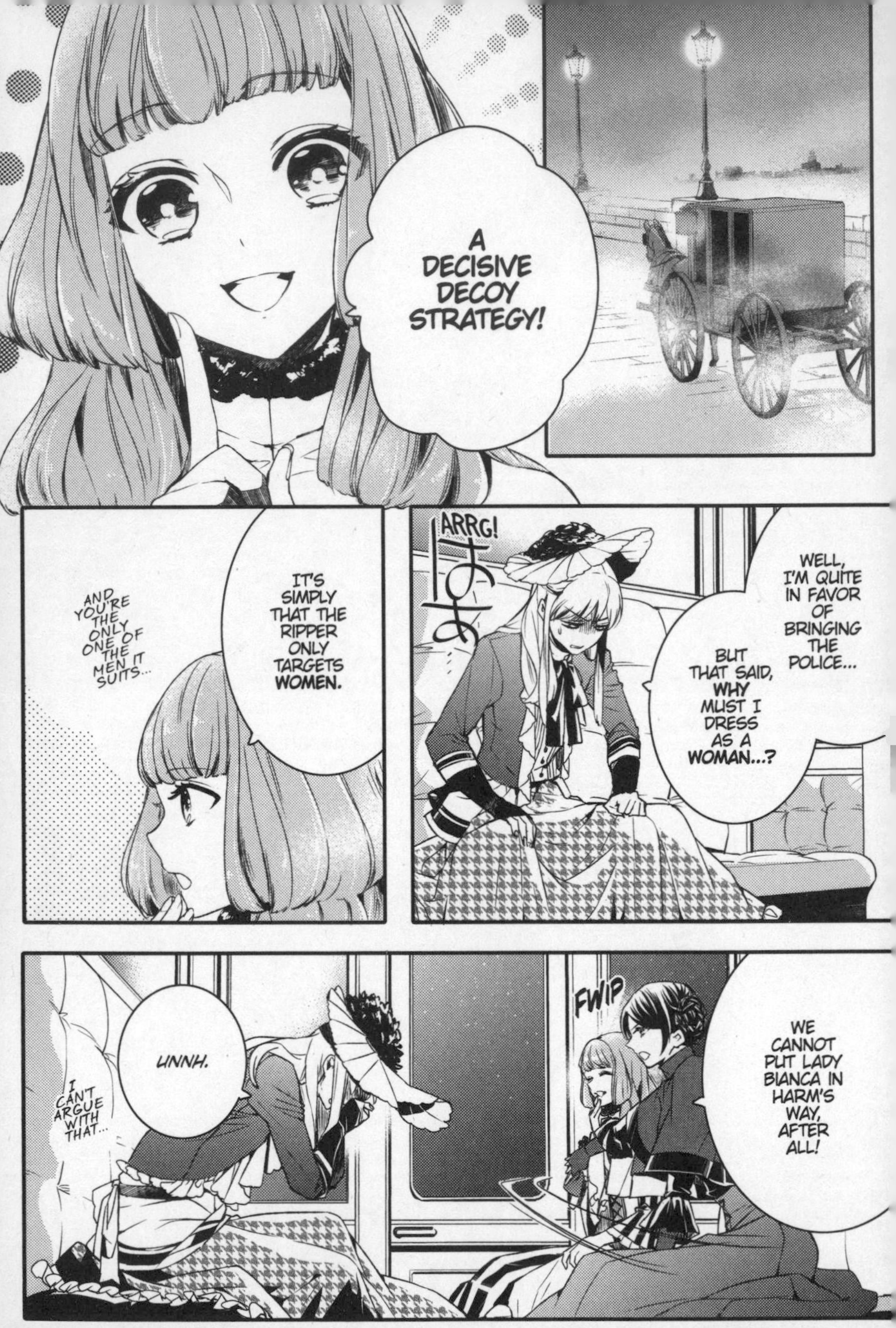
A DECISIVE DECOY STRATEGY!
ARRG!
WELL, I'M QUITE IN FAVOR OF BRINGING THE POLICE...
BUT THAT SAID, WHY MUST I DRESS AS A WOMAN...?
IT'S SIMPLY THAT THE RIPPER ONLY TARGETS WOMEN.
AND YOU'RE THE ONLY ONE OF THE MEN IT SUITS...
FWIP
WE CANNOT PUT LADY BIANCA IN HARM'S WAY, AFTER ALL!
UNNH.
I CAN'T ARGUE WITH THAT...

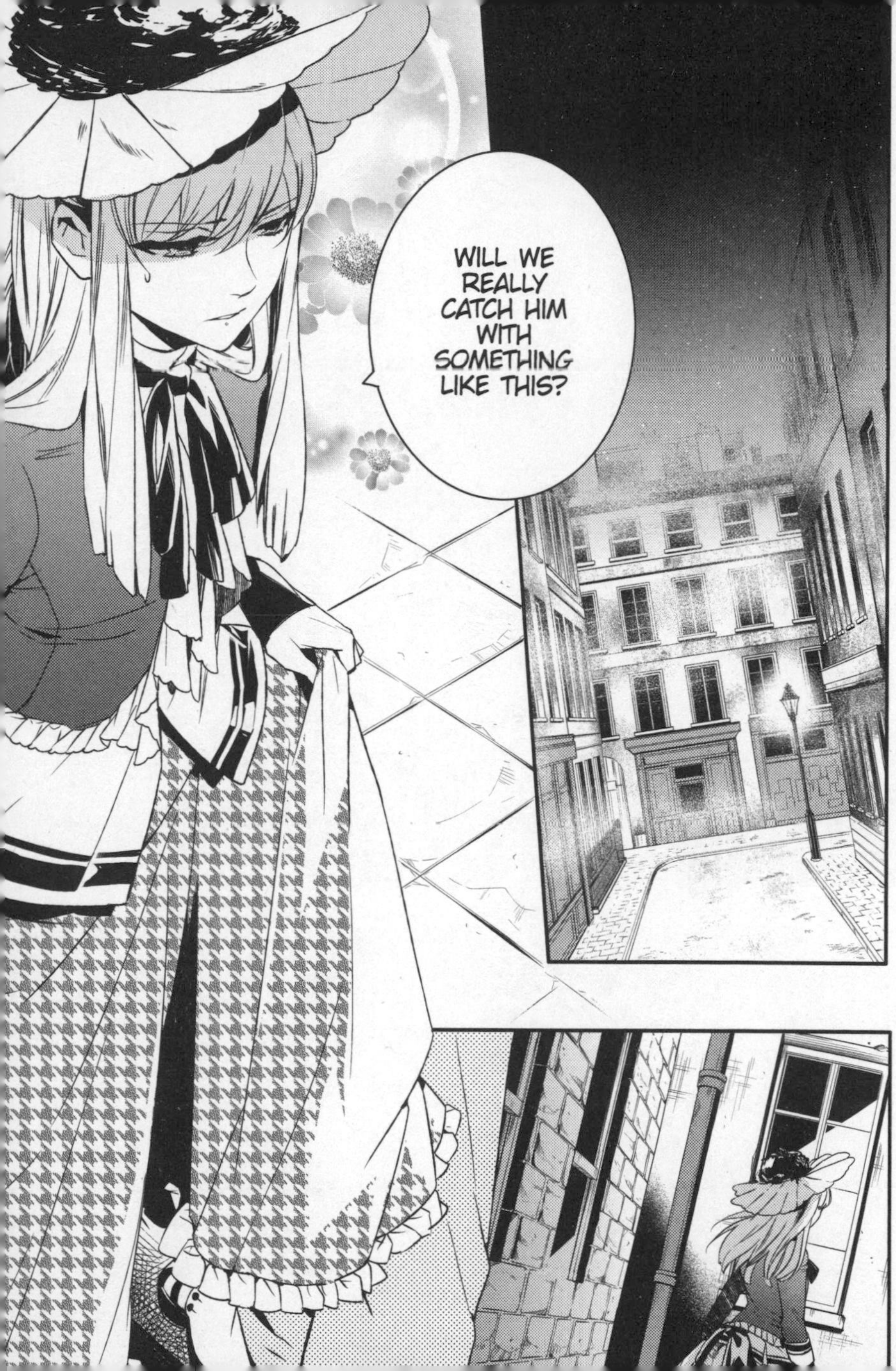
WILL WE REALLY CATCH HIM WITH SOMETHING LIKE THIS?

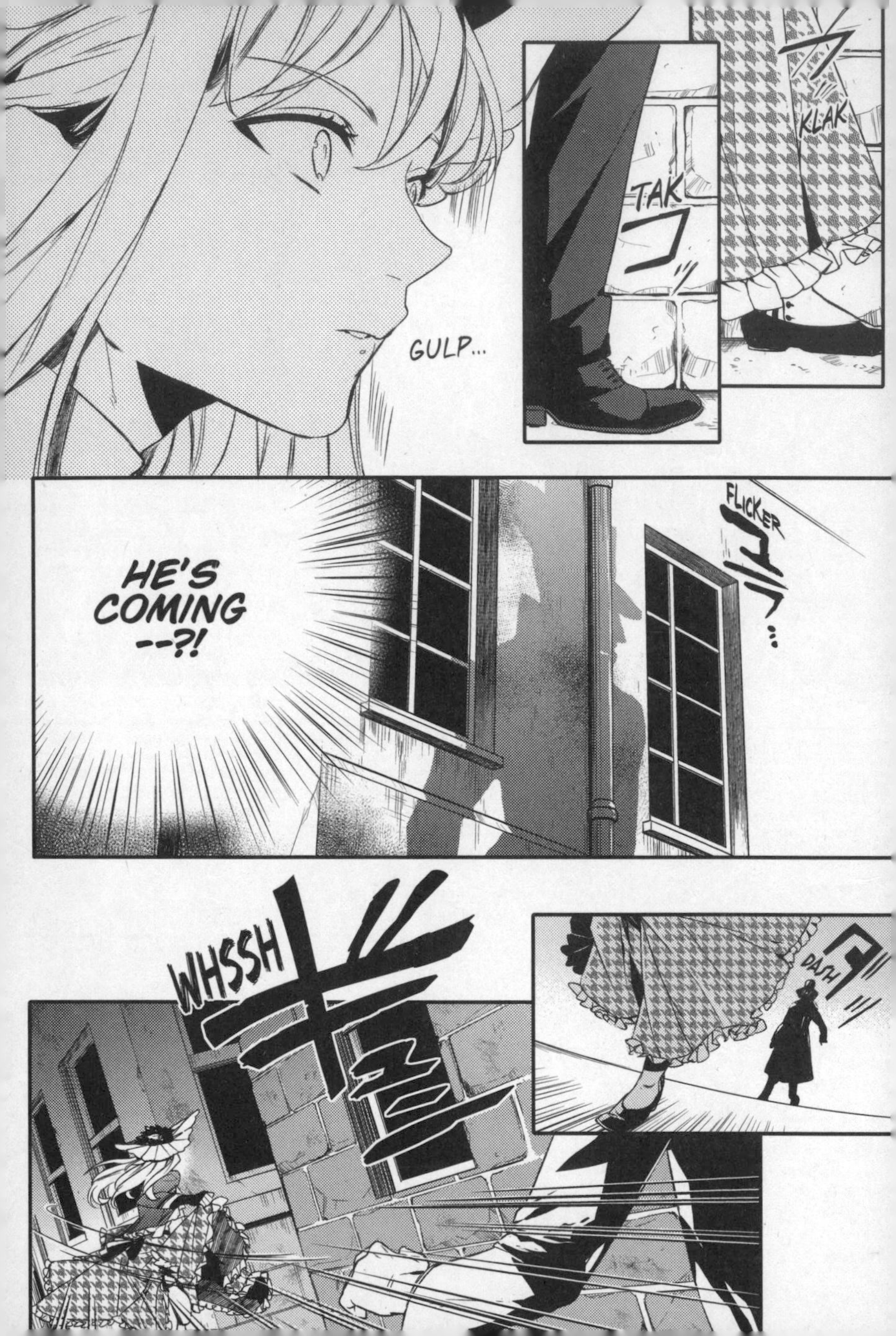
KLAK
TAK
GULP...
FLICKER
HE'S COMING --?!
DASH
WHSSH

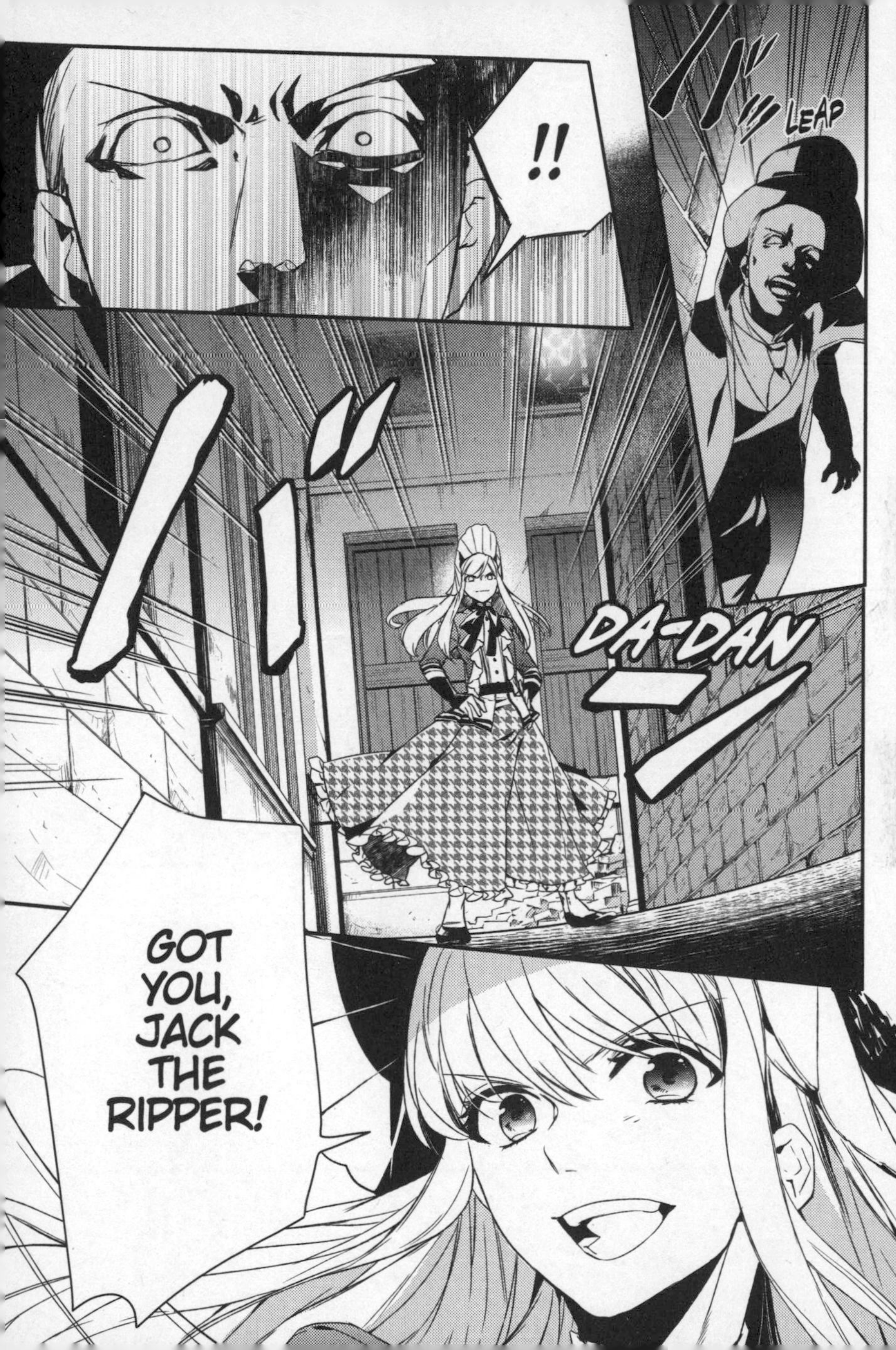
LEAP
!!
DA-DAN
GOT YOU, JACK THE RIPPER!

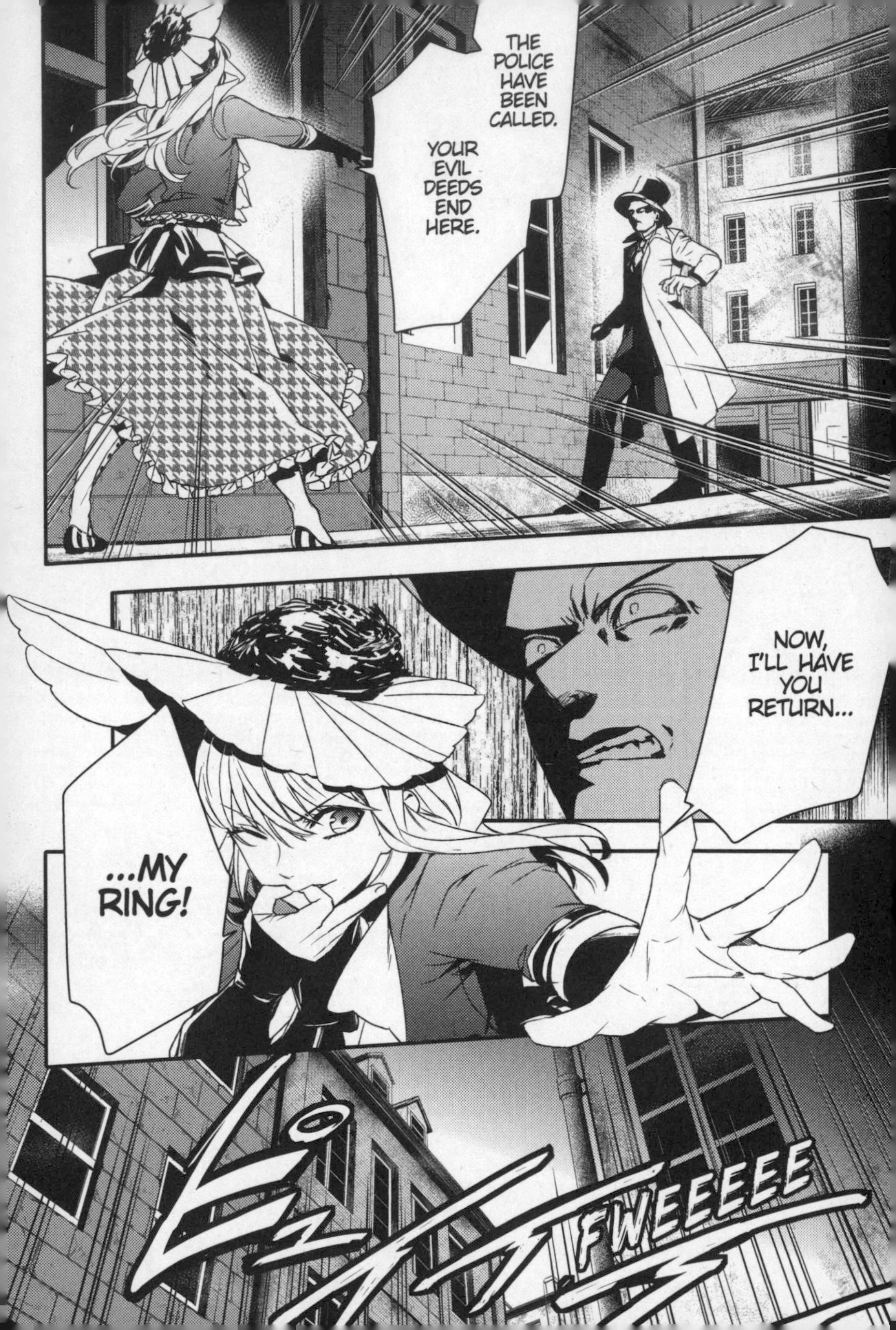
THE POLICE HAVE BEEN CALLED.
YOUR EVIL DEEDS END HERE.
NOW, I'LL HAVE YOU RETURN...
...MY RING!
FWEEEEEE

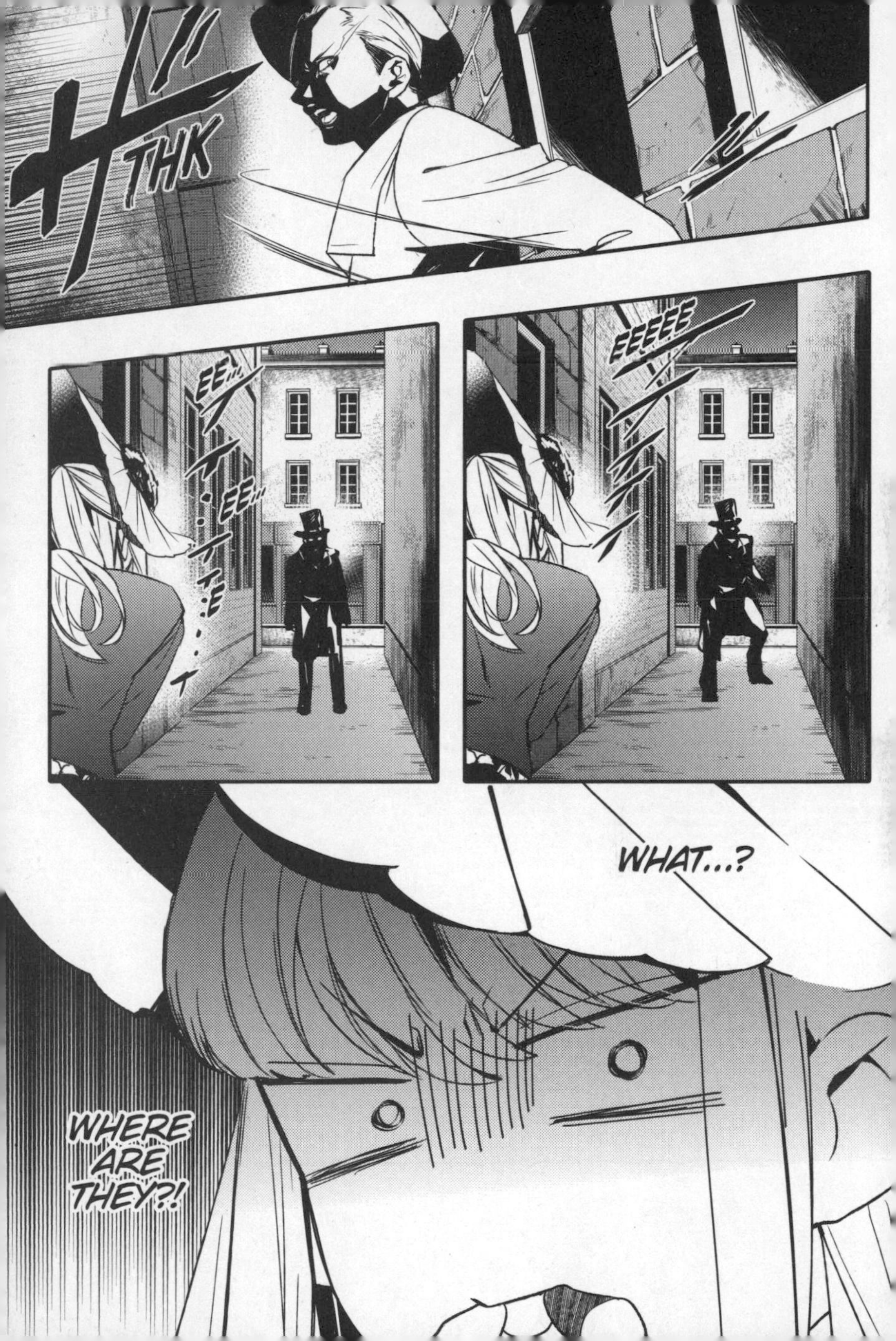
THK
EEEEE
EE...
EE...
WHAT...?
WHERE ARE THEY?!

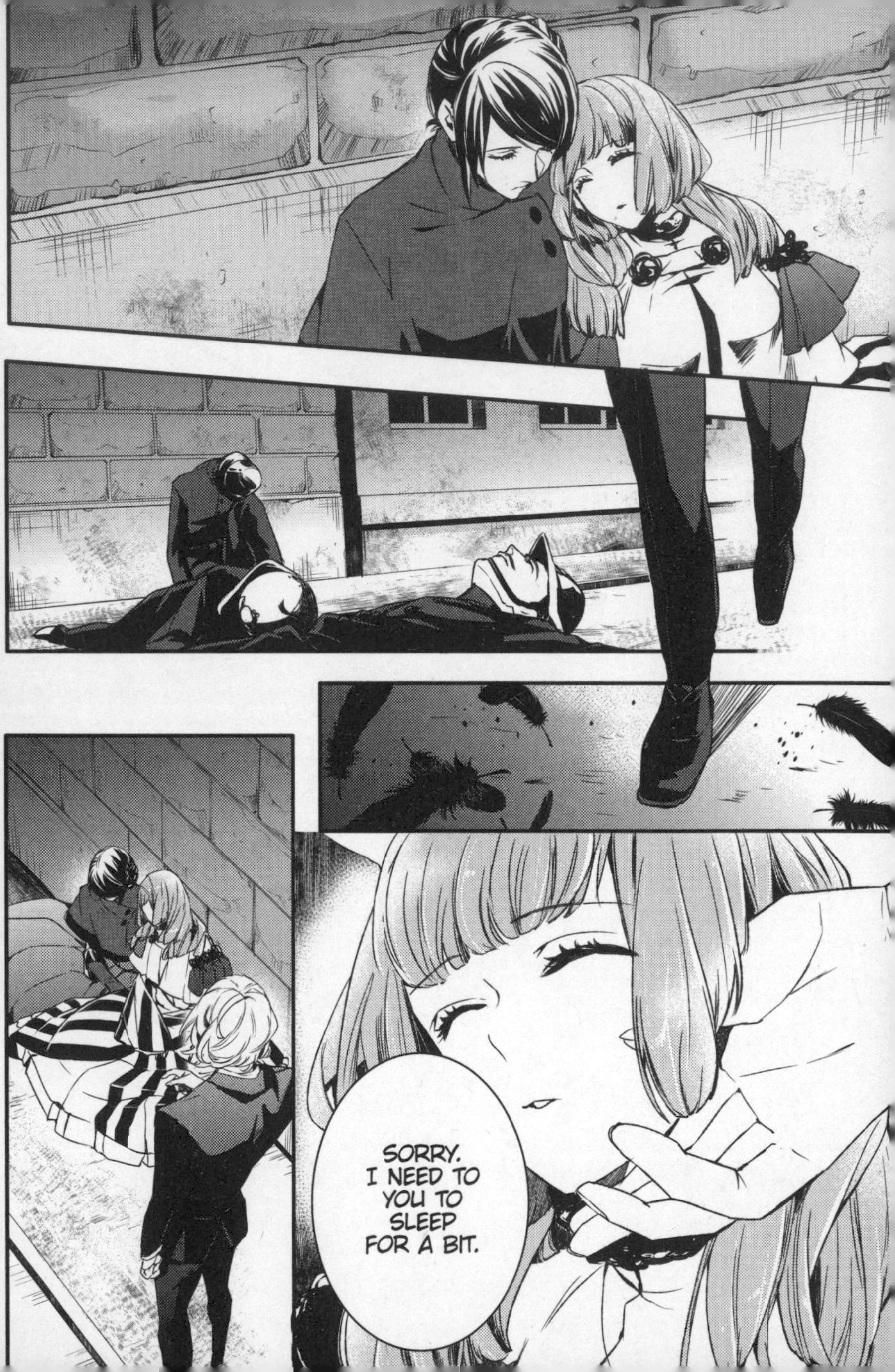
SORRY. I NEED TO YOU TO SLEEP FOR A BIT.

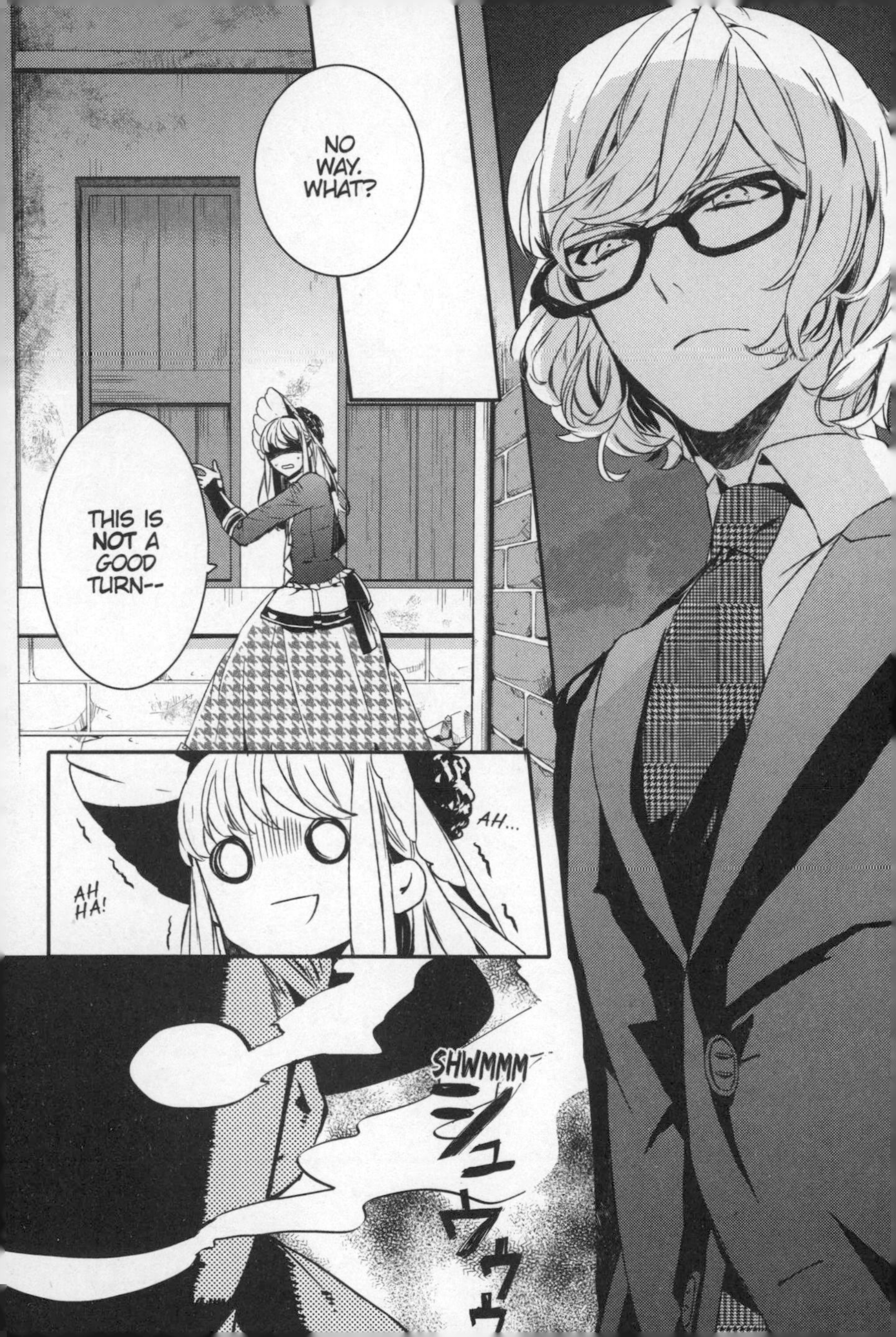
NO WAY. WHAT?
THIS IS NOT A GOOD TURN--
AH...
AH HA!
SHWMMM

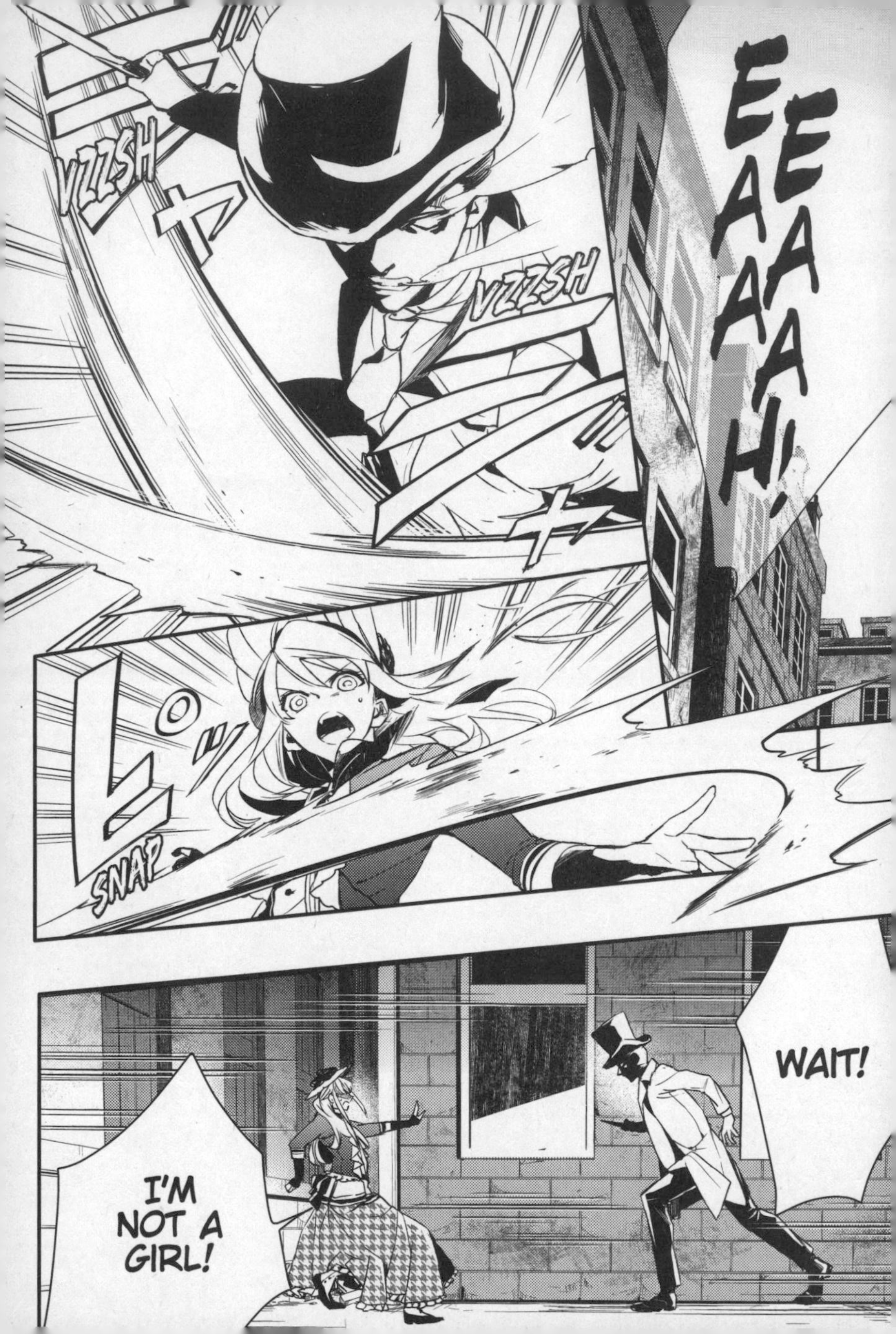
EEAAAAH!
VZZSH
VZZSH
SNAP
WAIT!
I'M NOT A GIRL!

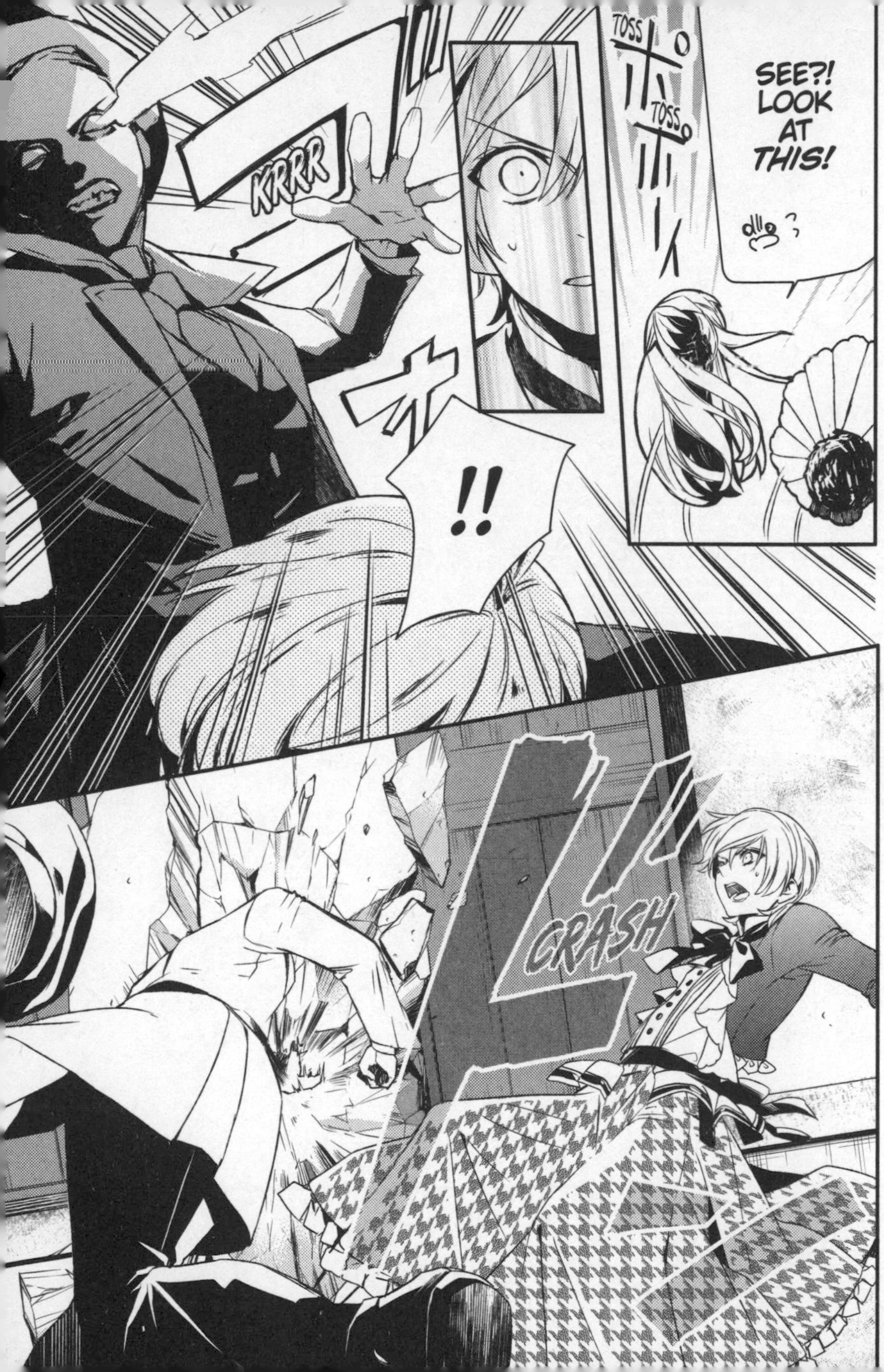
SEE?! LOOK AT THIS!
TOSS
TOSS
KRRR
!!
CRASH

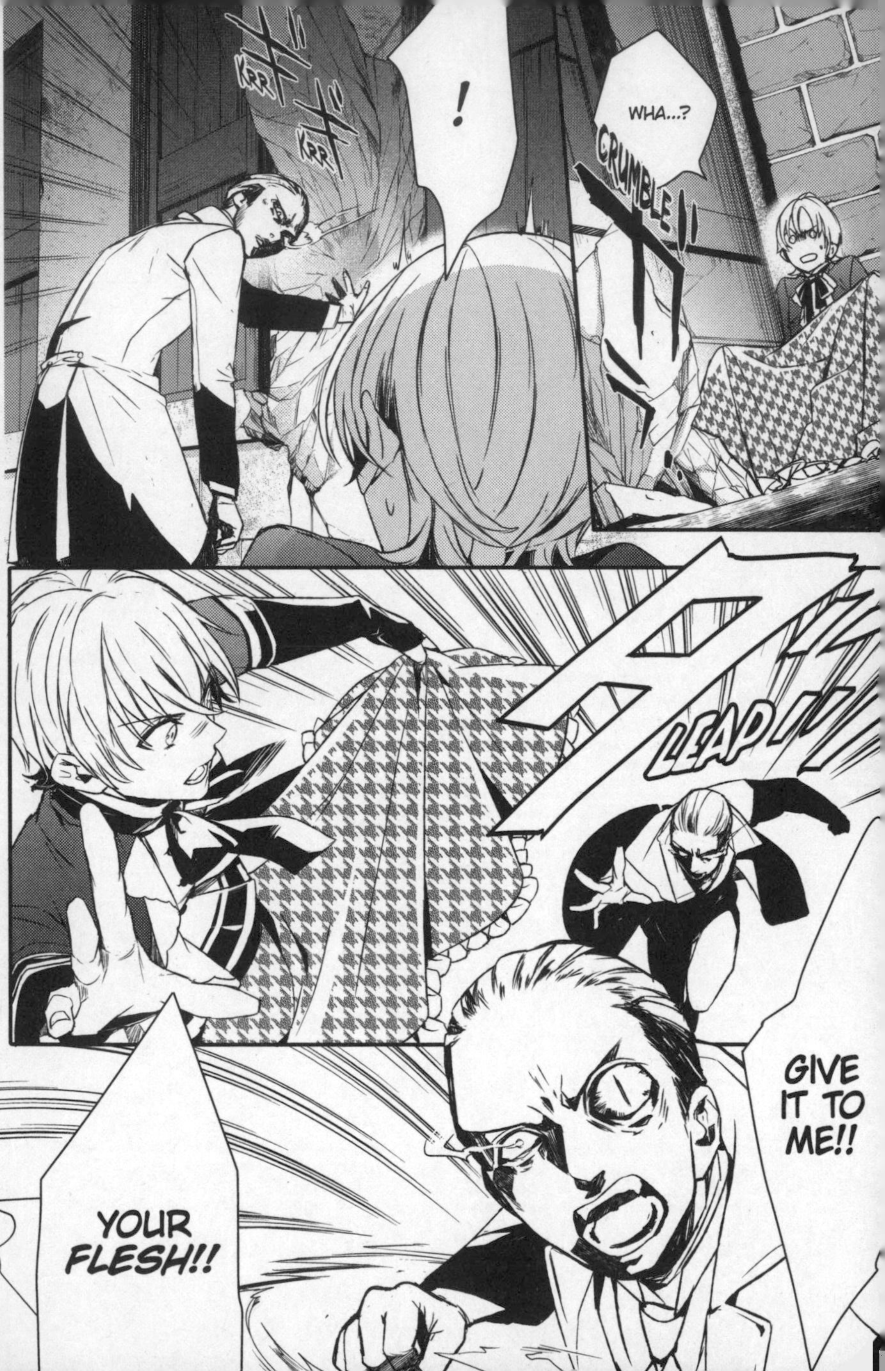
WHA...?
CRUMBLE!!
KRR
KRR
!
LEAP!!
GIVE IT TO ME!!
YOUR FLESH!!

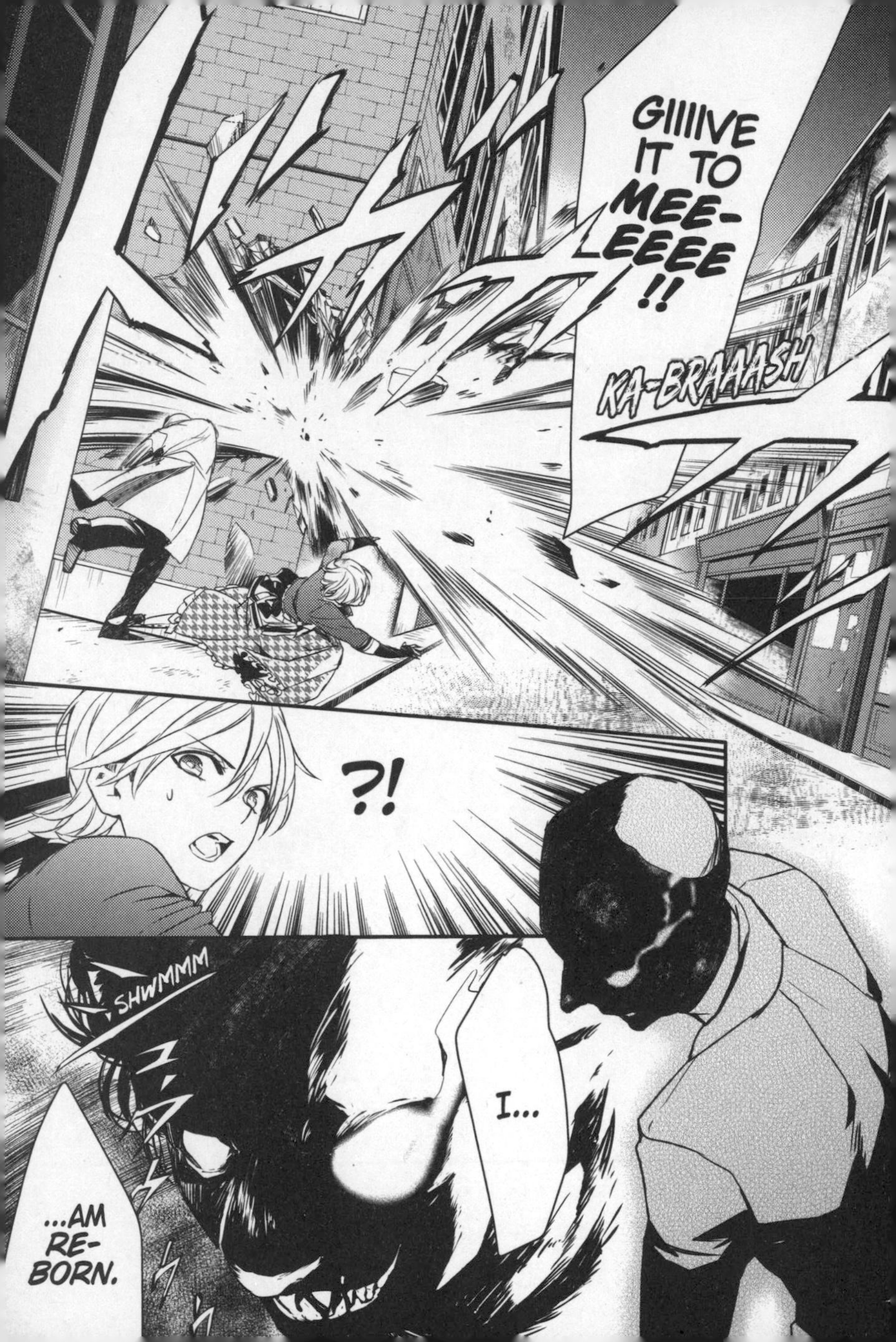
GIIIIVE IT TO MEEE-LEEEE!!
KA-BRAAASH
?!
SHWMMM
I...
...AM RE-BORN.

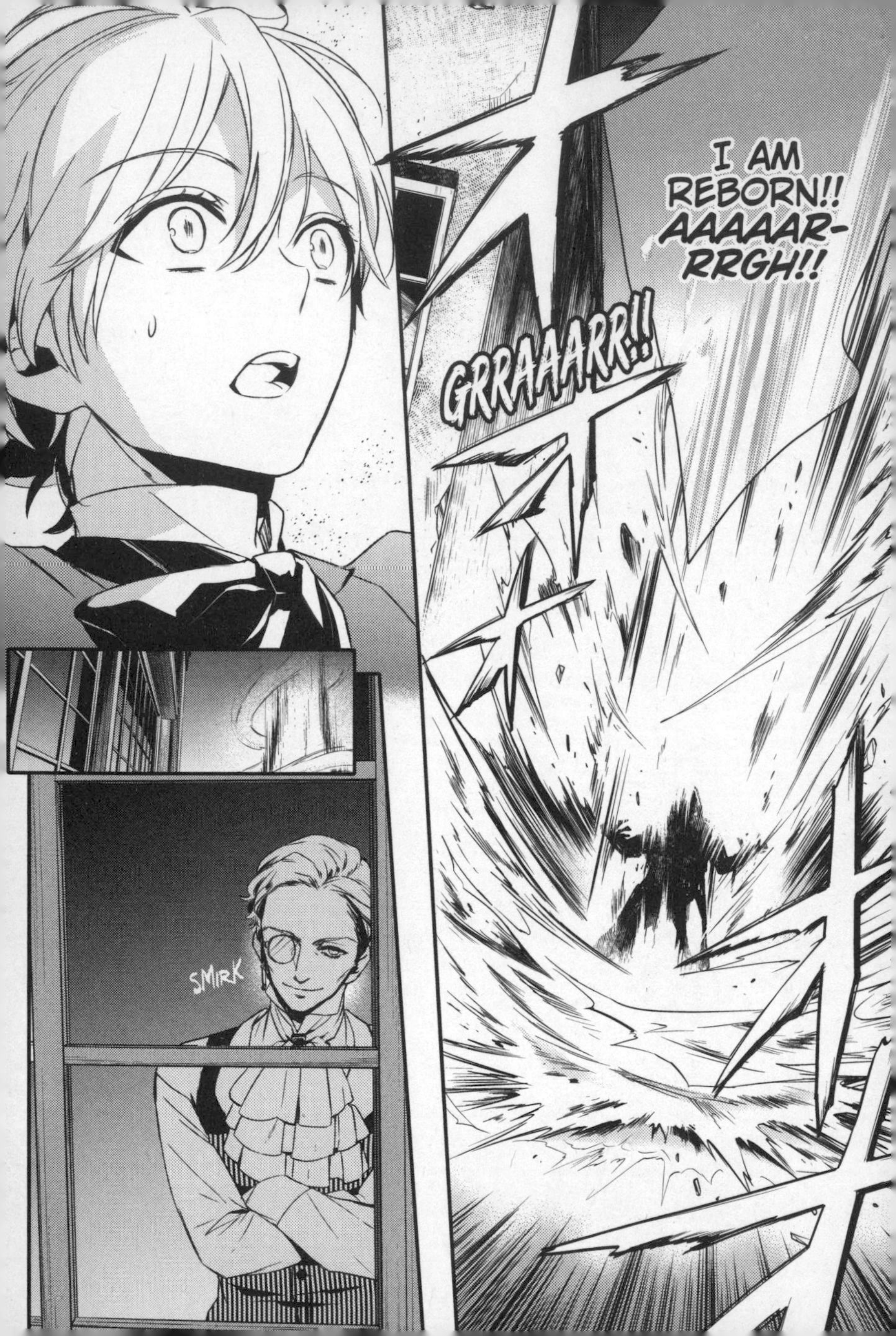
I AM REBORN!! AAAAAR-RRGH!!
GRRAAARR!!
SMIRK

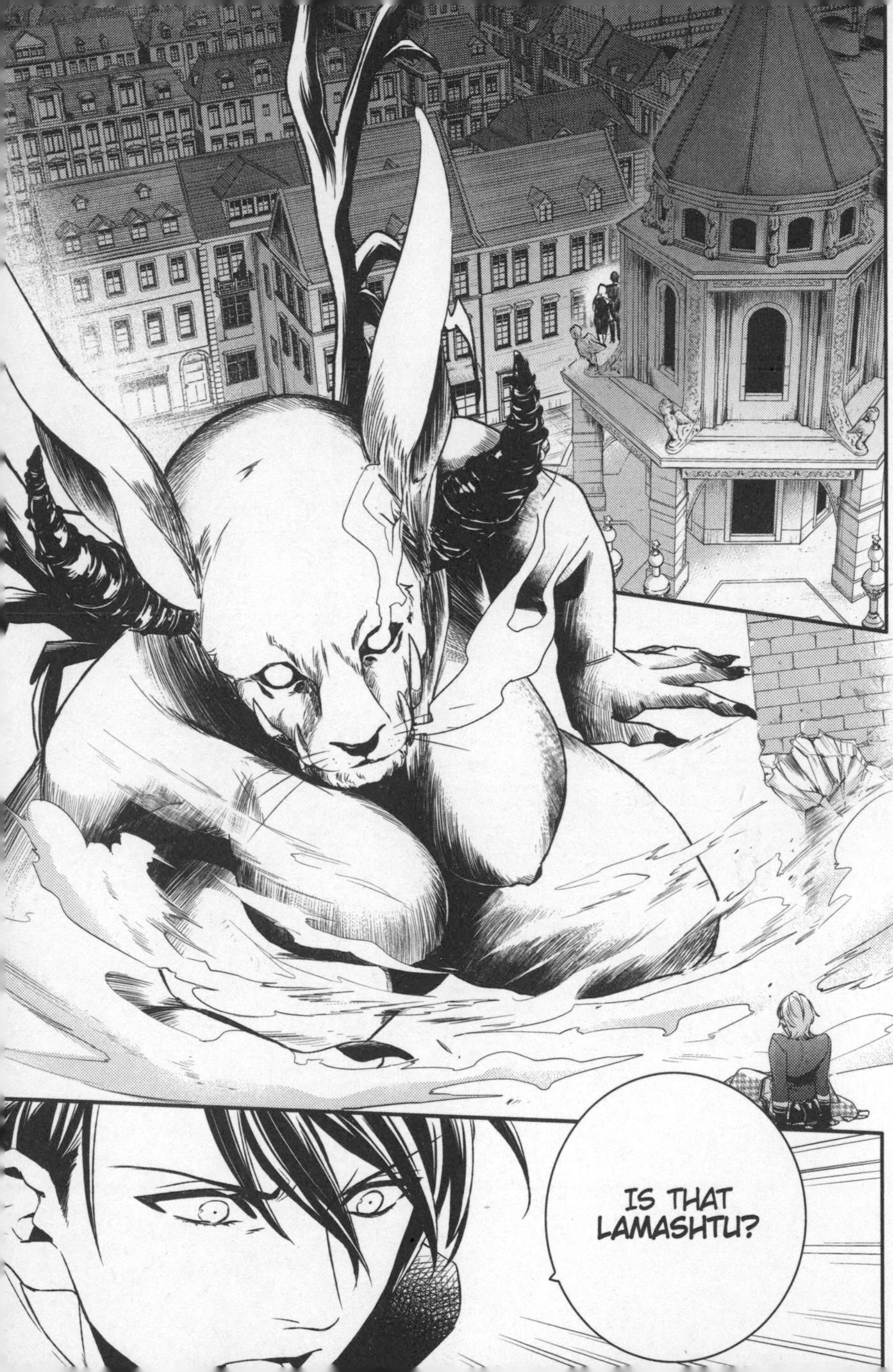
IS THAT LAMASHTU?

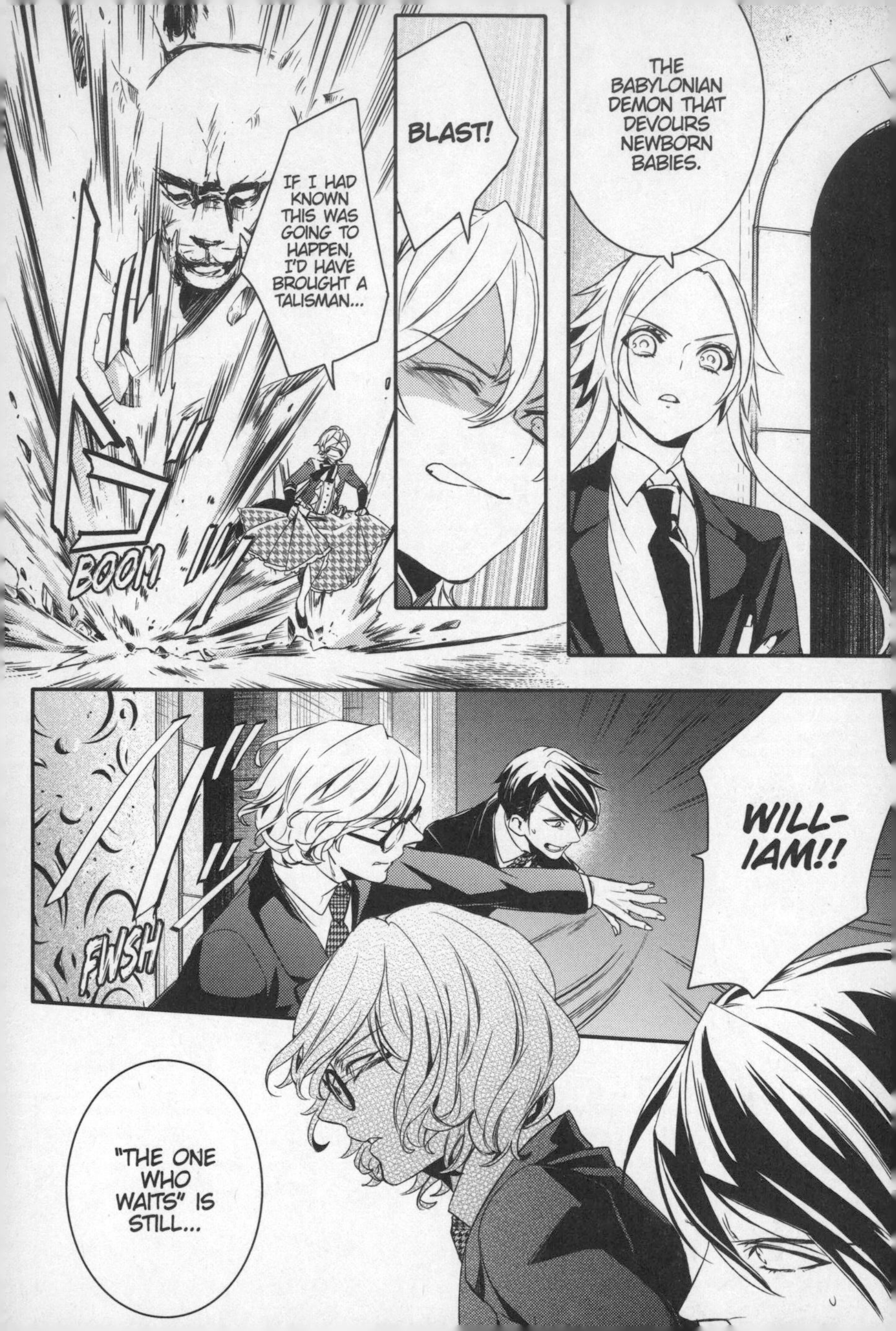
THE BABYLONIAN DEMON THAT DEVOURS NEWBORN BABIES.
BLAST!
IF I HAD KNOWN THIS WAS GOING TO HAPPEN, I'D HAVE BROUGHT A TALISMAN...
BOOM
WILL-IAM!!
FWSH
"THE ONE WHO WAITS" IS STILL...

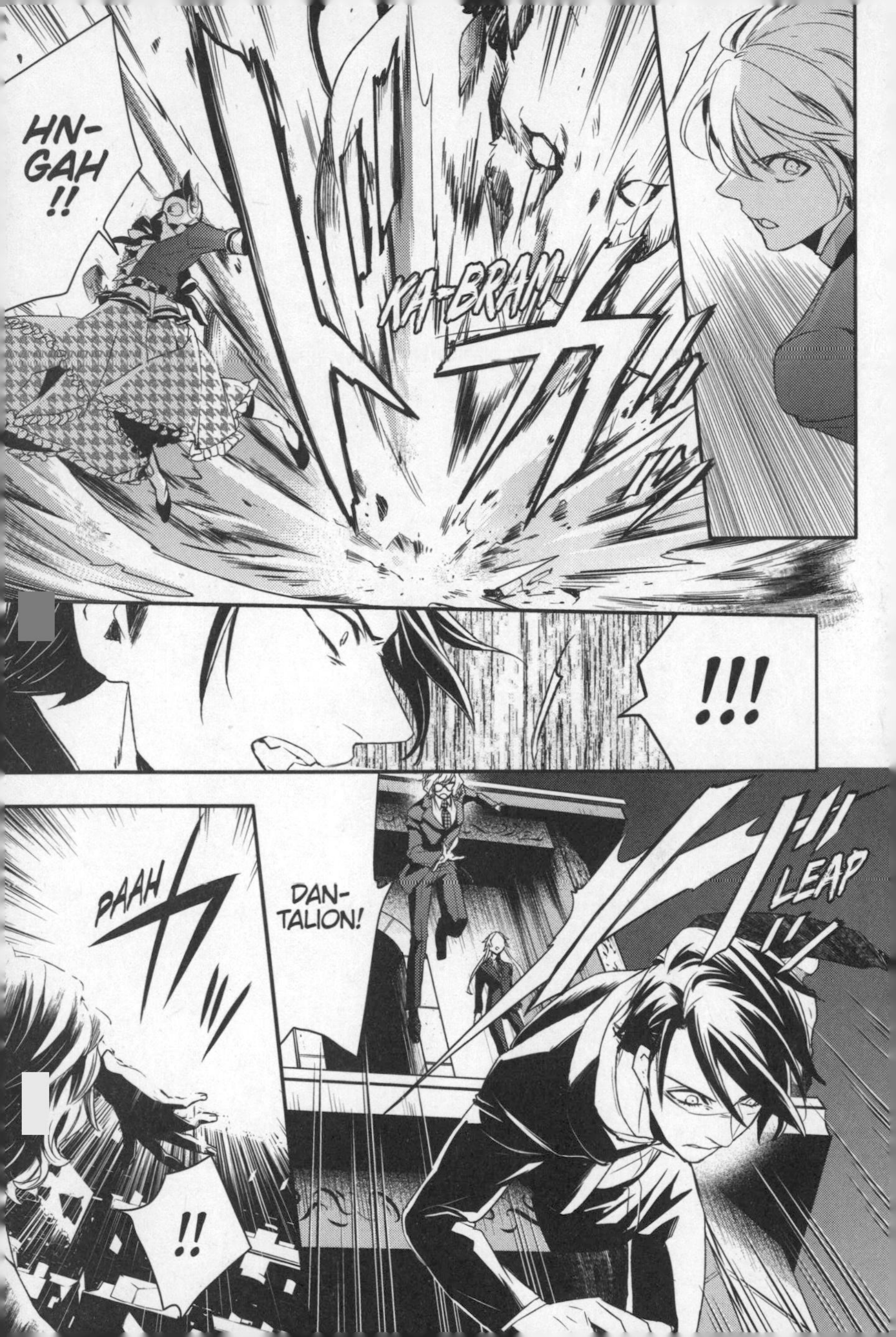
KA-BRAM
HN-GAH!!
!!!
LEAP
DAN-TALION!
PAAH
!!

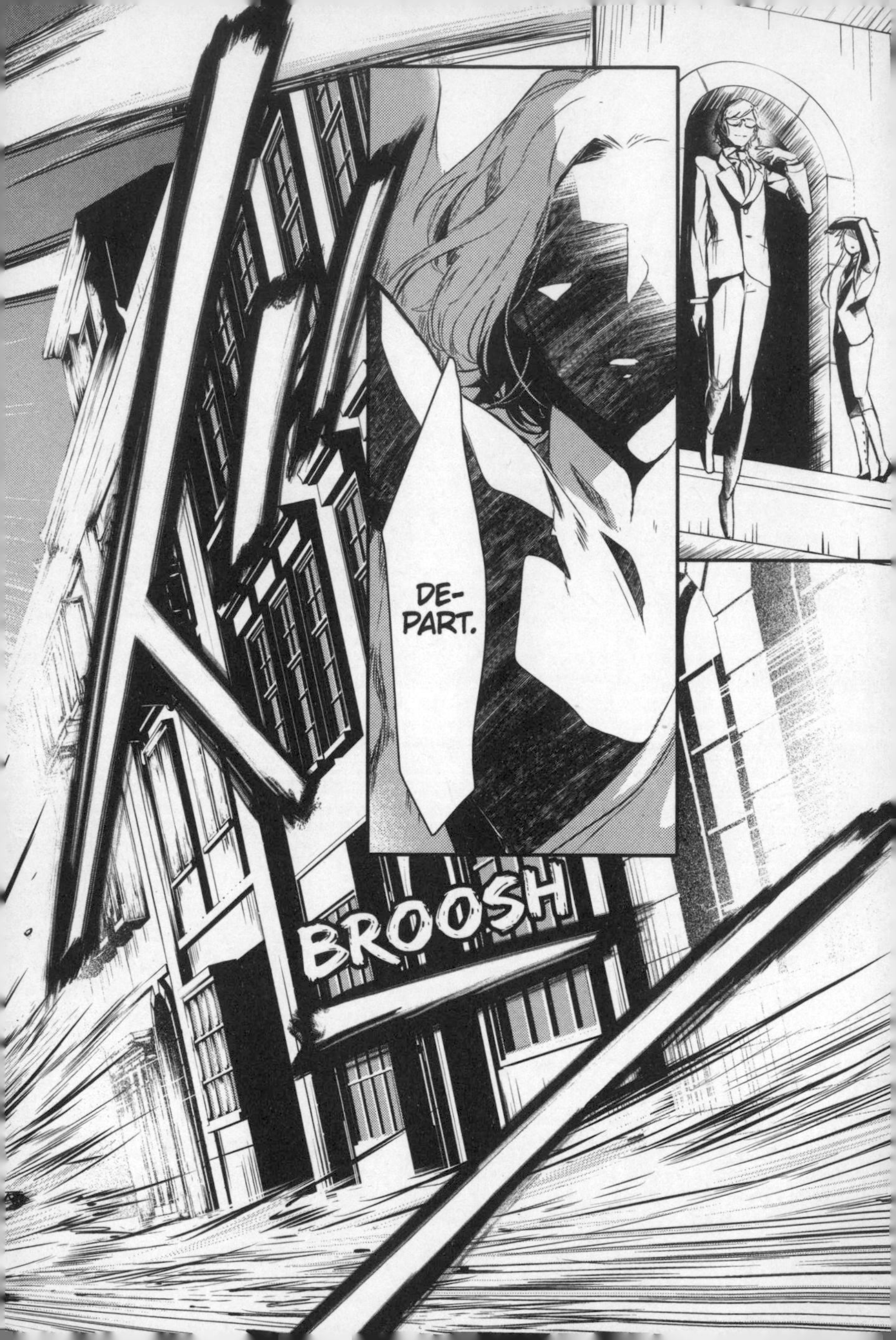
DE-
PART.
BROOSH

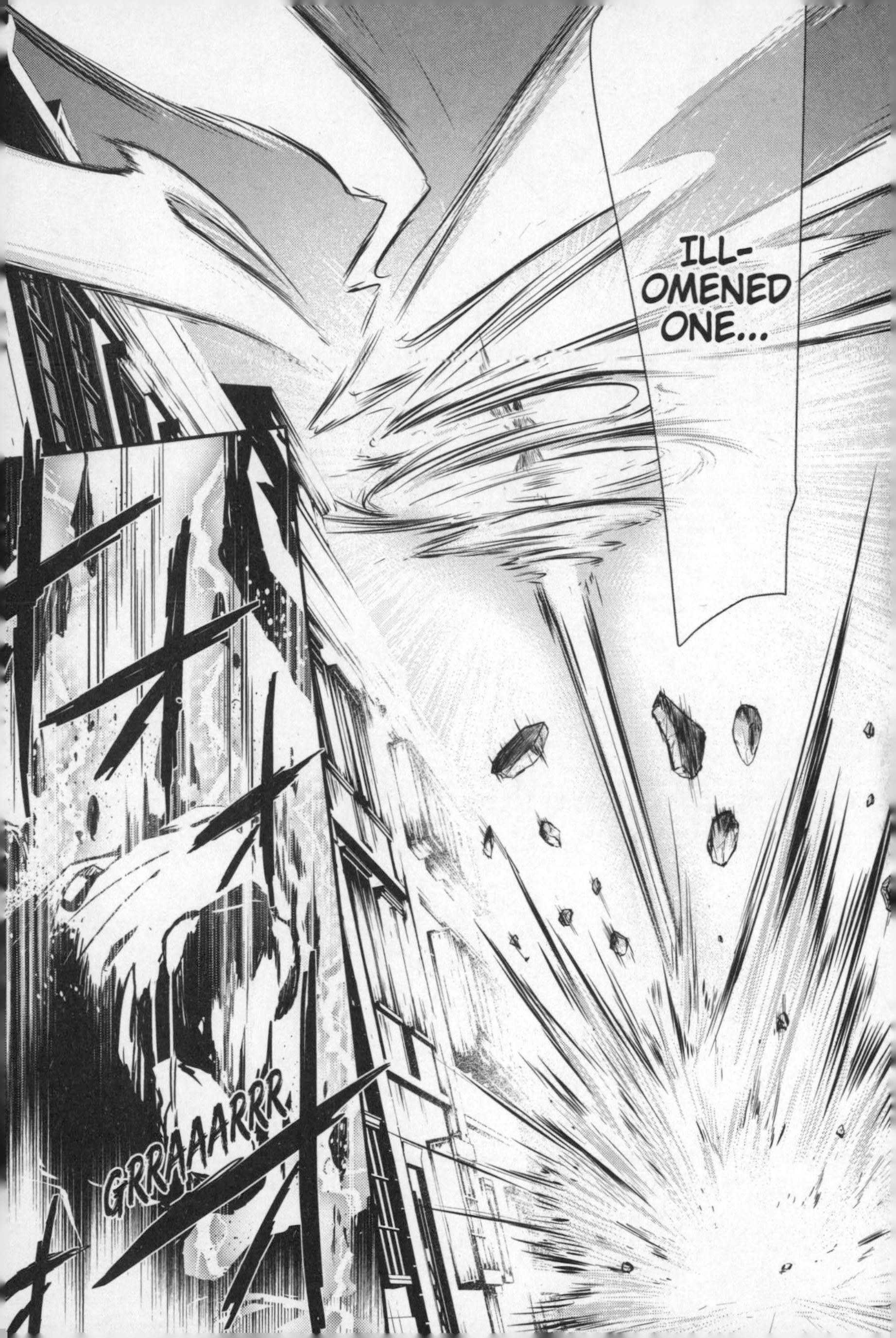
ILL-OMENED ONE...
GRRAAARRR

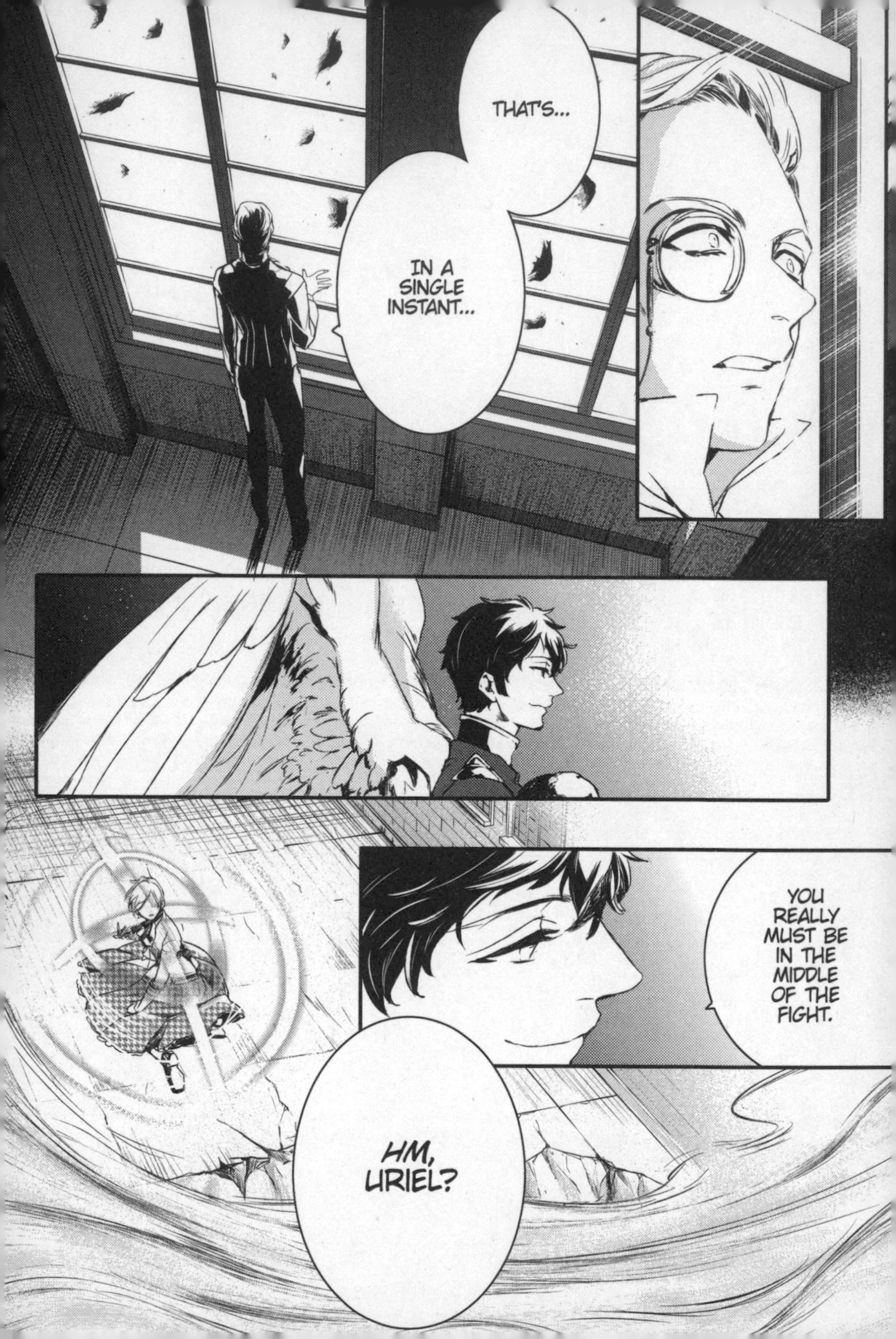
THAT'S...
IN A SINGLE INSTANT...
YOU REALLY MUST BE IN THE MIDDLE OF THE FIGHT.
HM, URIEL?

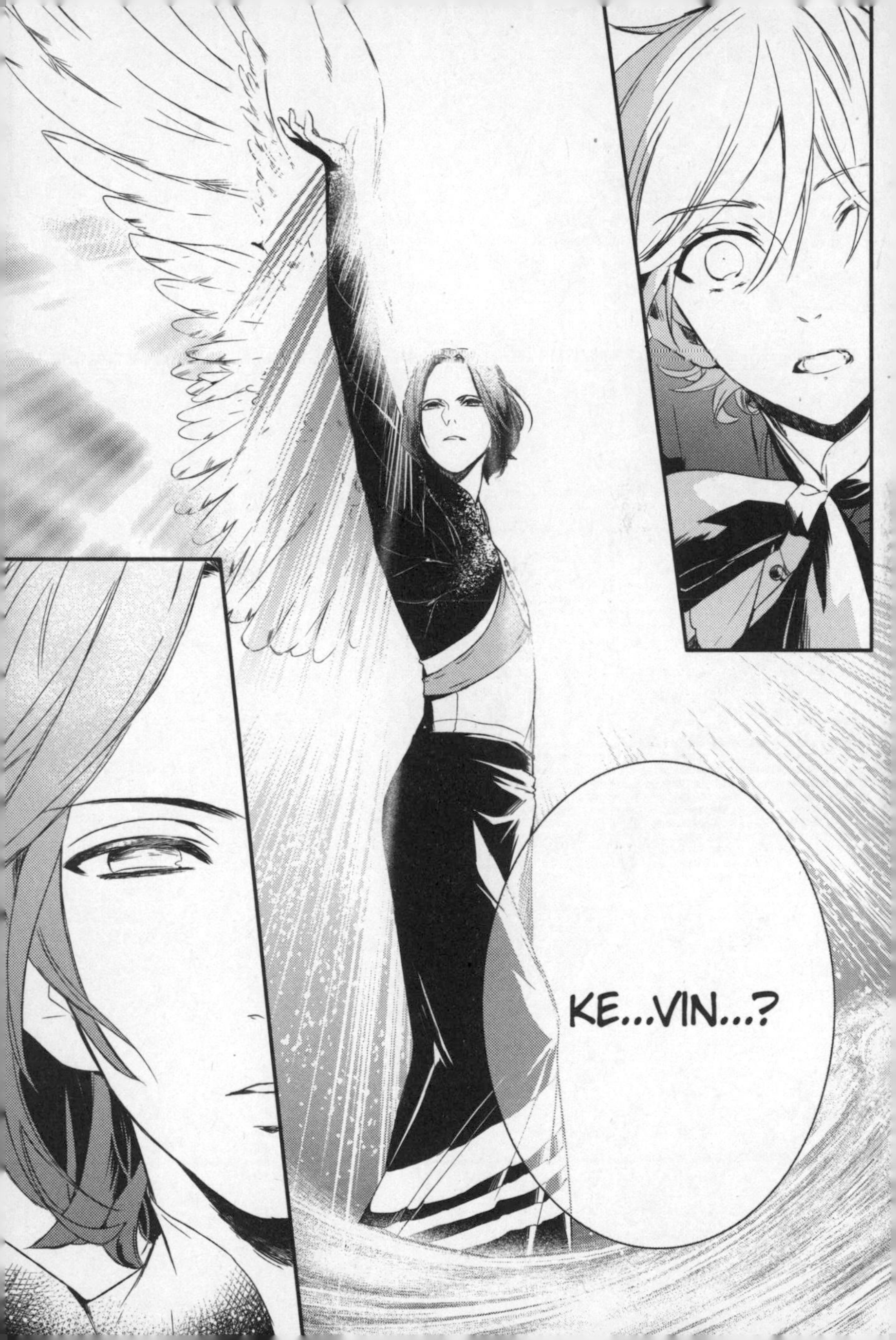
KE...VIN...?

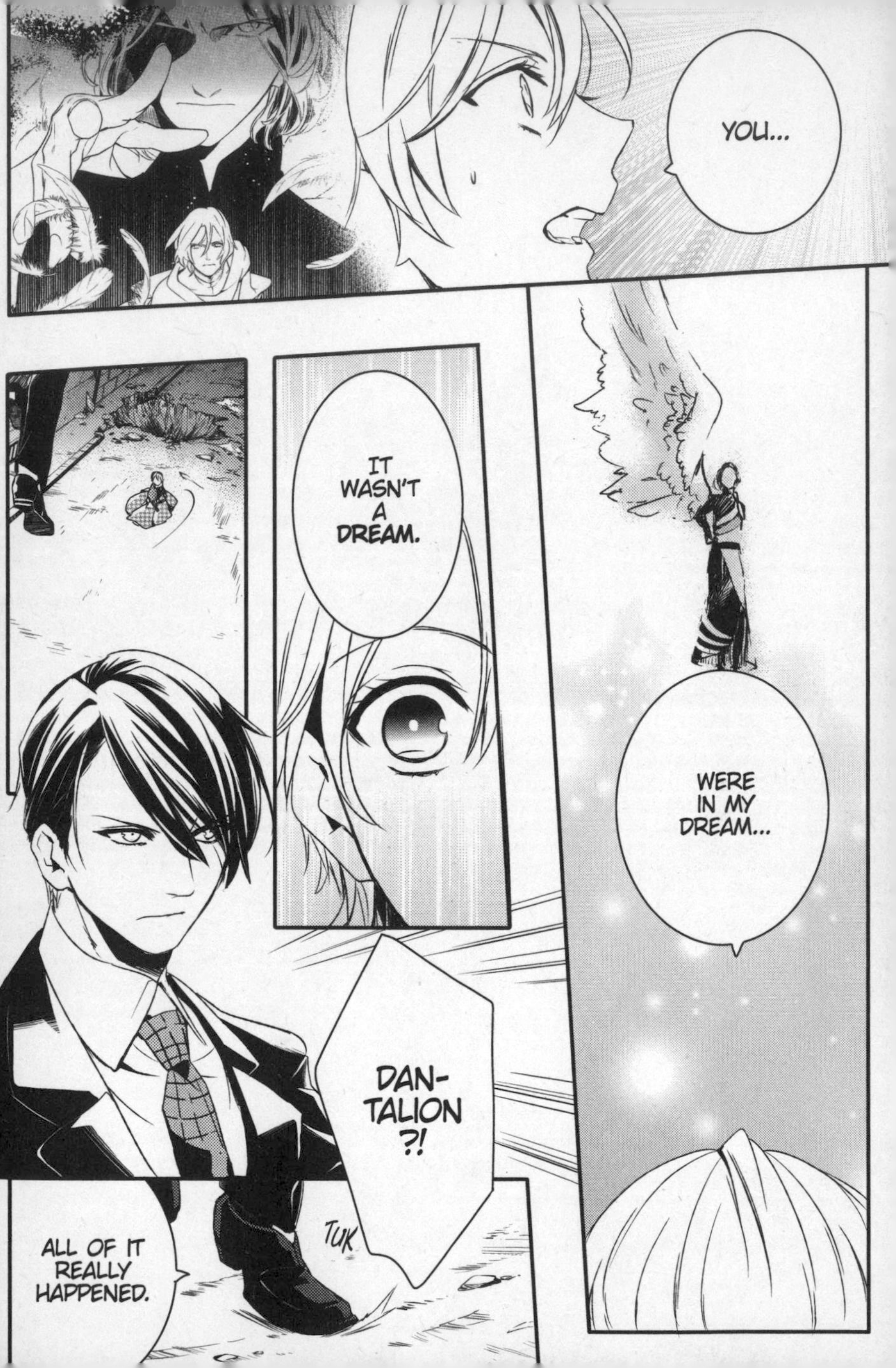
YOU...
WERE IN MY DREAM...
IT WASN'T A DREAM.
DAN-TALION ?!
TUK
ALL OF IT REALLY HAPPENED.

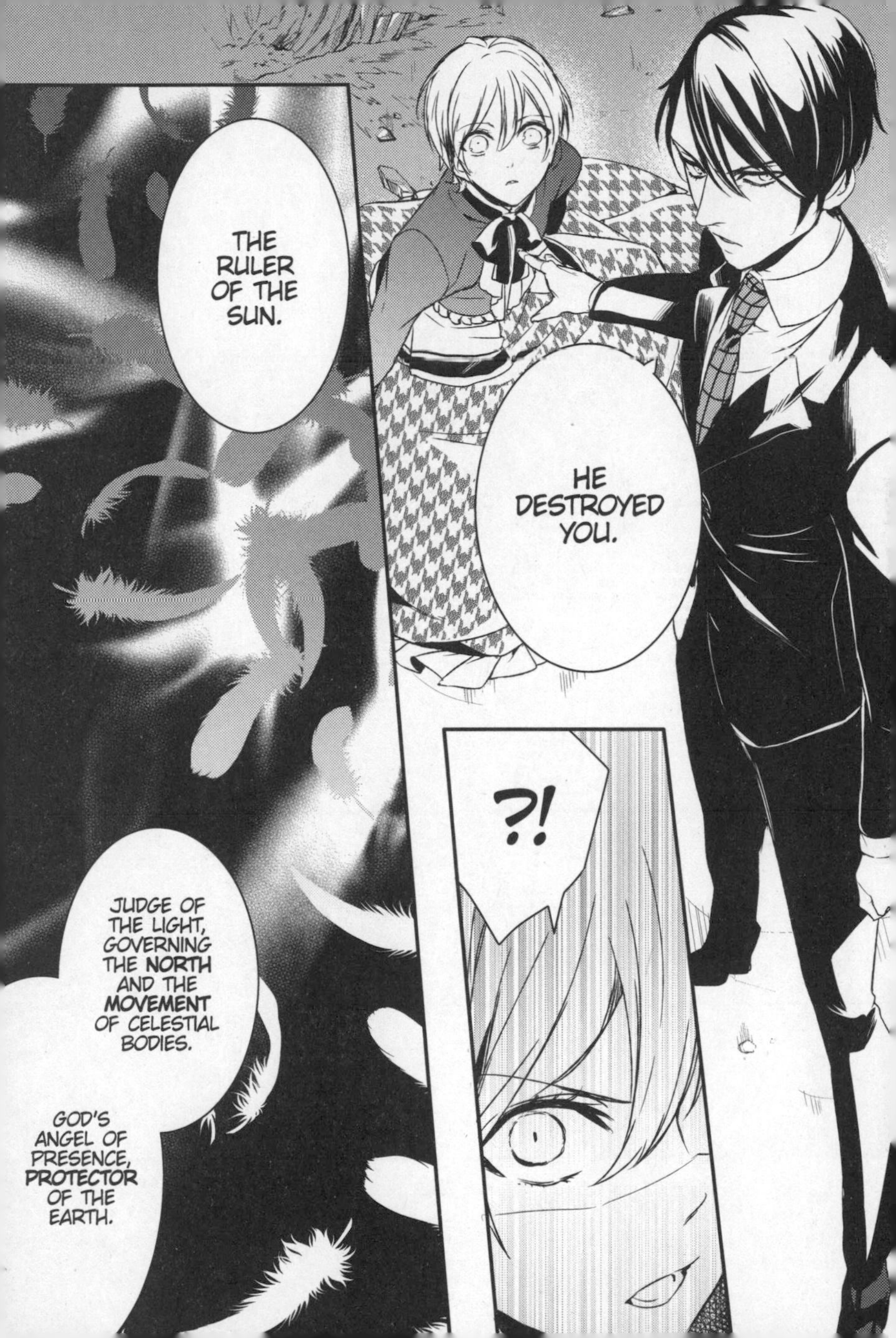
HE DESTROYED YOU.
?!
THE RULER OF THE SUN.
JUDGE OF THE LIGHT, GOVERNING THE **NORTH** AND THE **MOVEMENT** OF CELESTIAL BODIES.
GOD'S ANGEL OF PRESENCE, **PROTECTOR** OF THE EARTH.

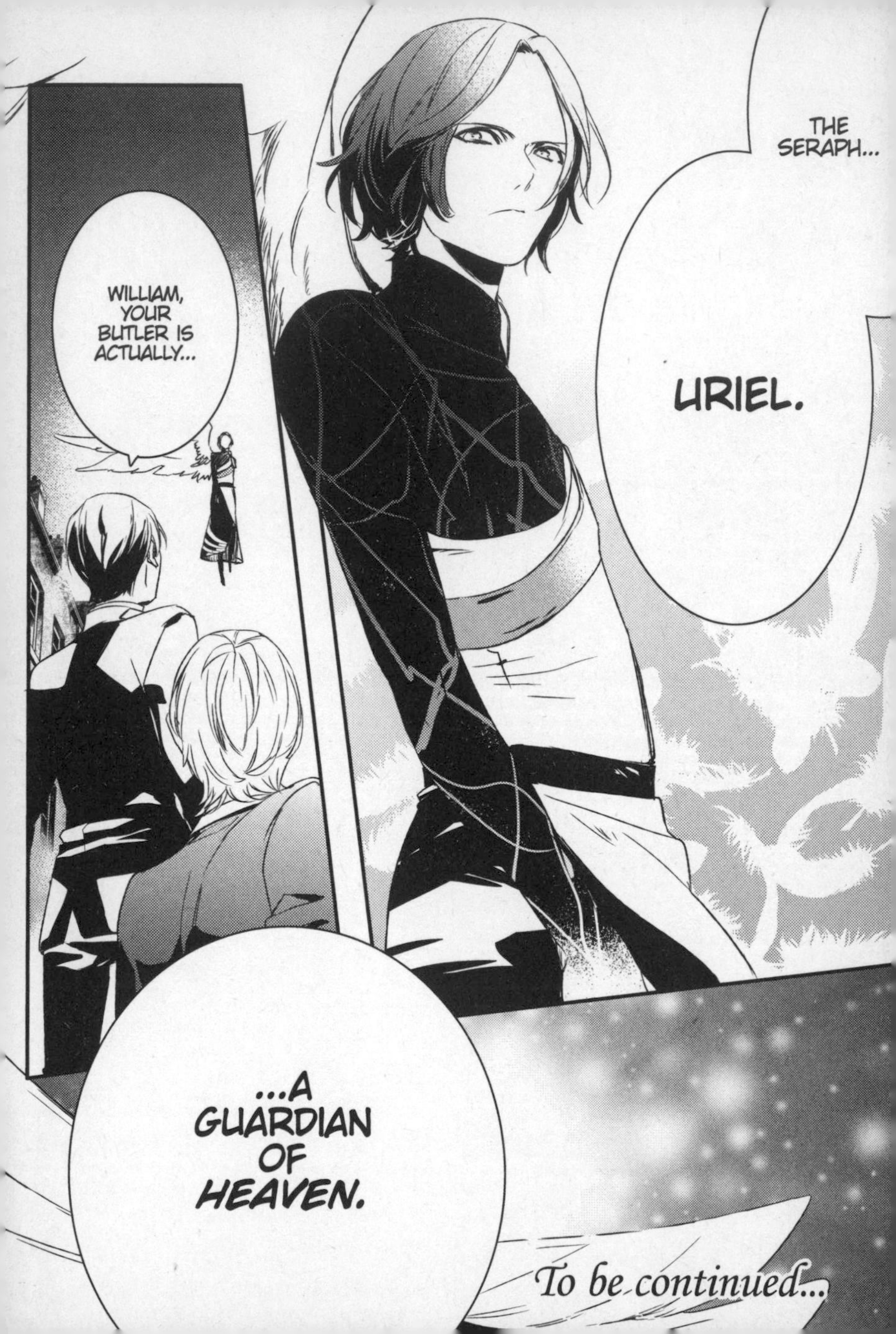
THE SERAPH...
URIEL.
WILLIAM, YOUR BUTLER IS ACTUALLY...
...A GUARDIAN OF HEAVEN.
To be continued...

魔界王子

devils and realist

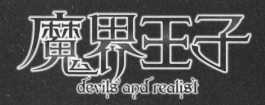

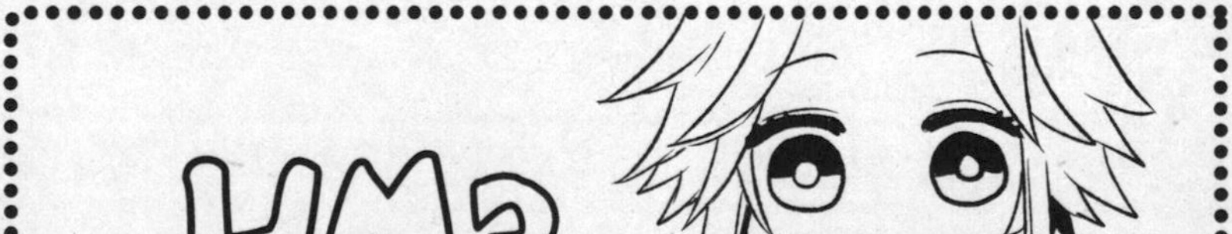
HM?

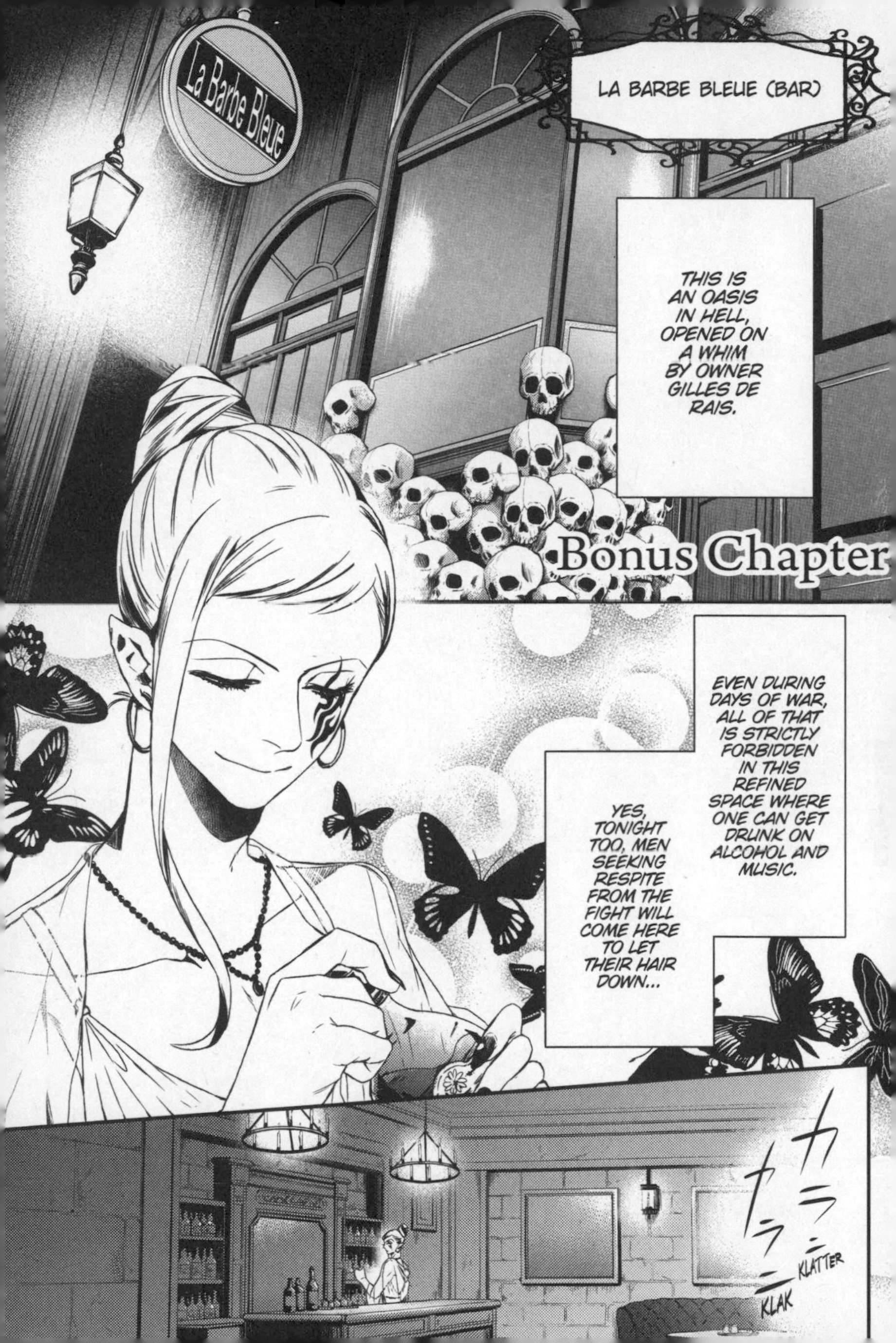
LA BARBE BLEUE (BAR)
La Barbe Bleue
THIS IS AN OASIS IN HELL, OPENED ON A WHIM BY OWNER GILLES DE RAIS.
Bonus Chapter
EVEN DURING DAYS OF WAR, ALL OF THAT IS STRICTLY FORBIDDEN IN THIS REFINED SPACE WHERE ONE CAN GET DRUNK ON ALCOHOL AND MUSIC.
YES, TONIGHT TOO, MEN SEEKING RESPITE FROM THE FIGHT WILL COME HERE TO LET THEIR HAIR DOWN...
KLATTER
KLAK

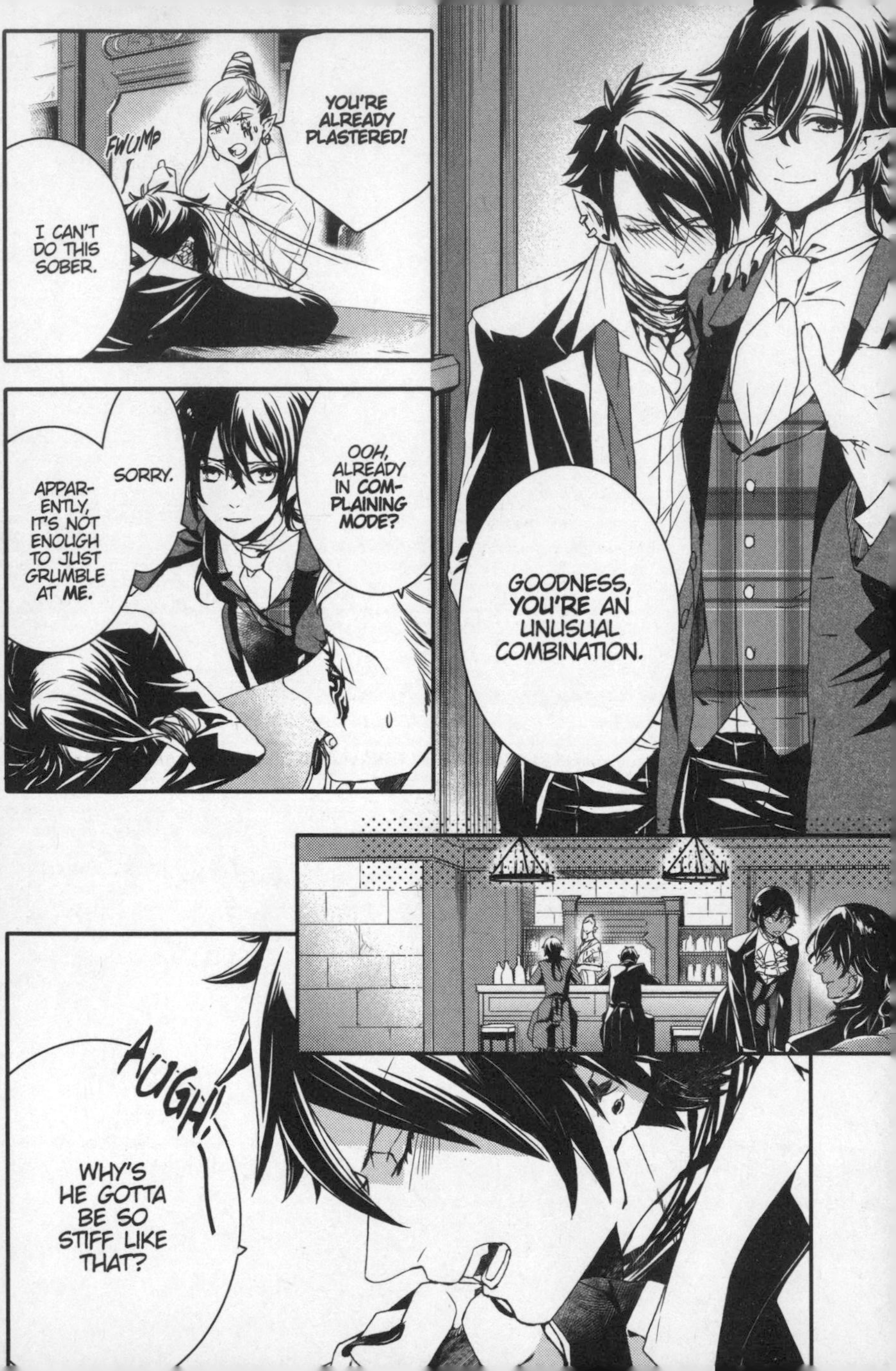
GOODNESS, YOU'RE AN UNUSUAL COMBINATION.
YOU'RE ALREADY PLASTERED!
FWUMP
I CAN'T DO THIS SOBER.
OOH, ALREADY IN COM-PLAINING MODE?
SORRY.
APPAR-ENTLY, IT'S NOT ENOUGH TO JUST GRUMBLE AT ME.
AUGH!
WHY'S HE GOTTA BE SO STIFF LIKE THAT?

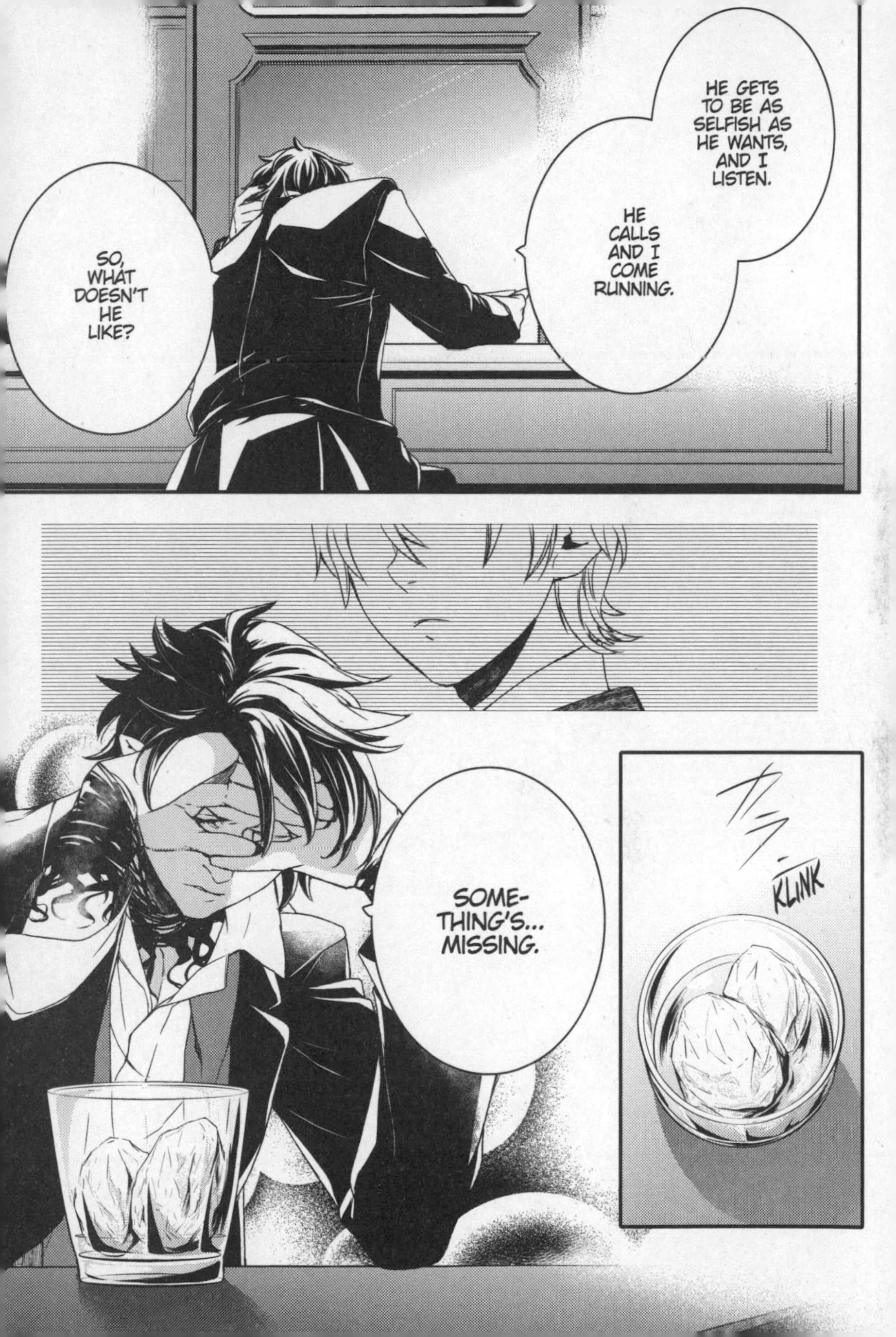
HE GETS TO BE AS SELFISH AS HE WANTS, AND I LISTEN.
HE CALLS AND I COME RUNNING.
SO, WHAT DOESN'T HE LIKE?
KLINK
SOME-THING'S... MISSING.

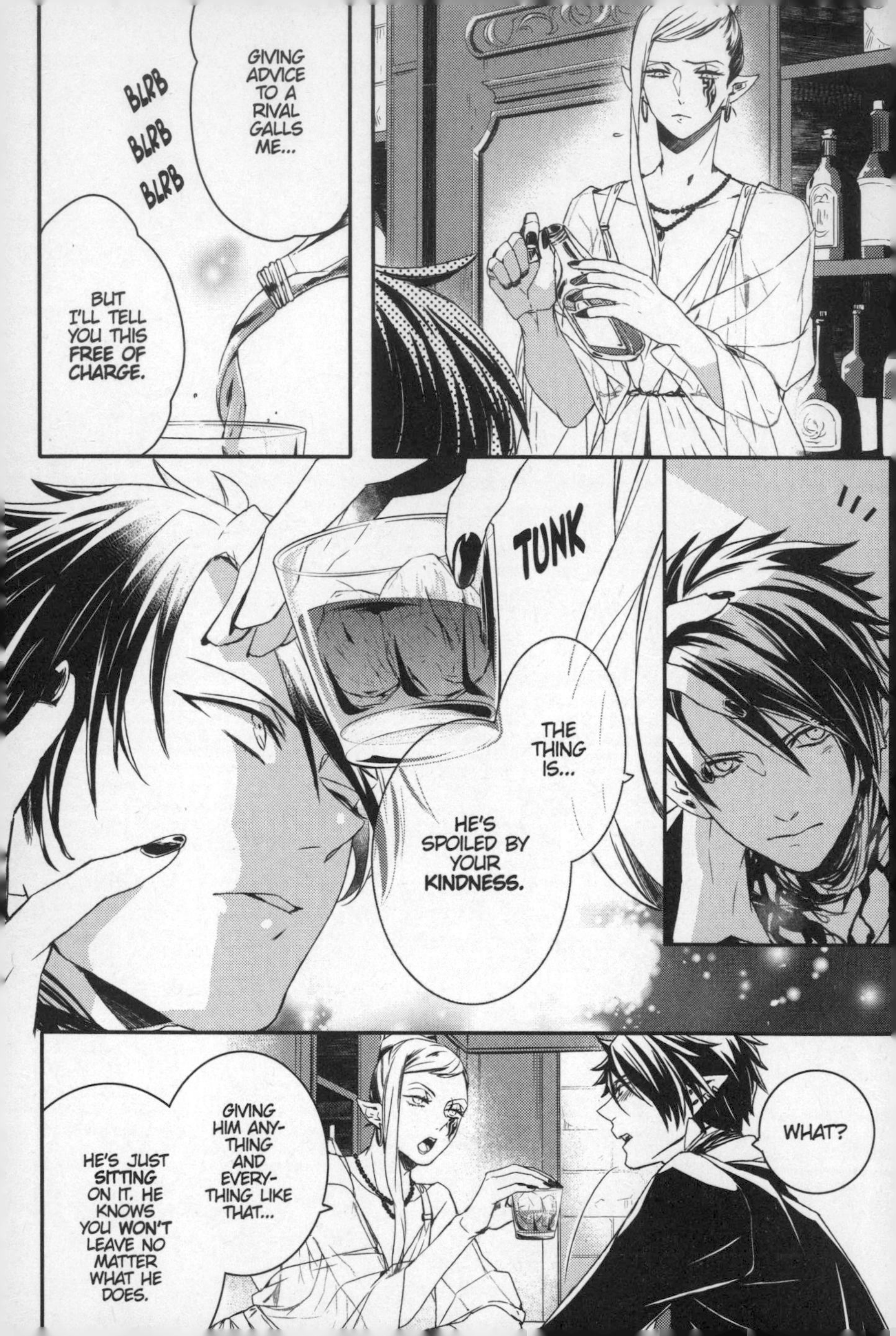
GIVING ADVICE TO A RIVAL GALLS ME...
BLRB BLRB BLRB
BUT I'LL TELL YOU THIS FREE OF CHARGE.
TUNK
THE THING IS...
HE'S SPOILED BY YOUR KINDNESS.
WHAT?
GIVING HIM ANY-THING AND EVERY-THING LIKE THAT...
HE'S JUST SITTING ON IT. HE KNOWS YOU WON'T LEAVE NO MATTER WHAT HE DOES.

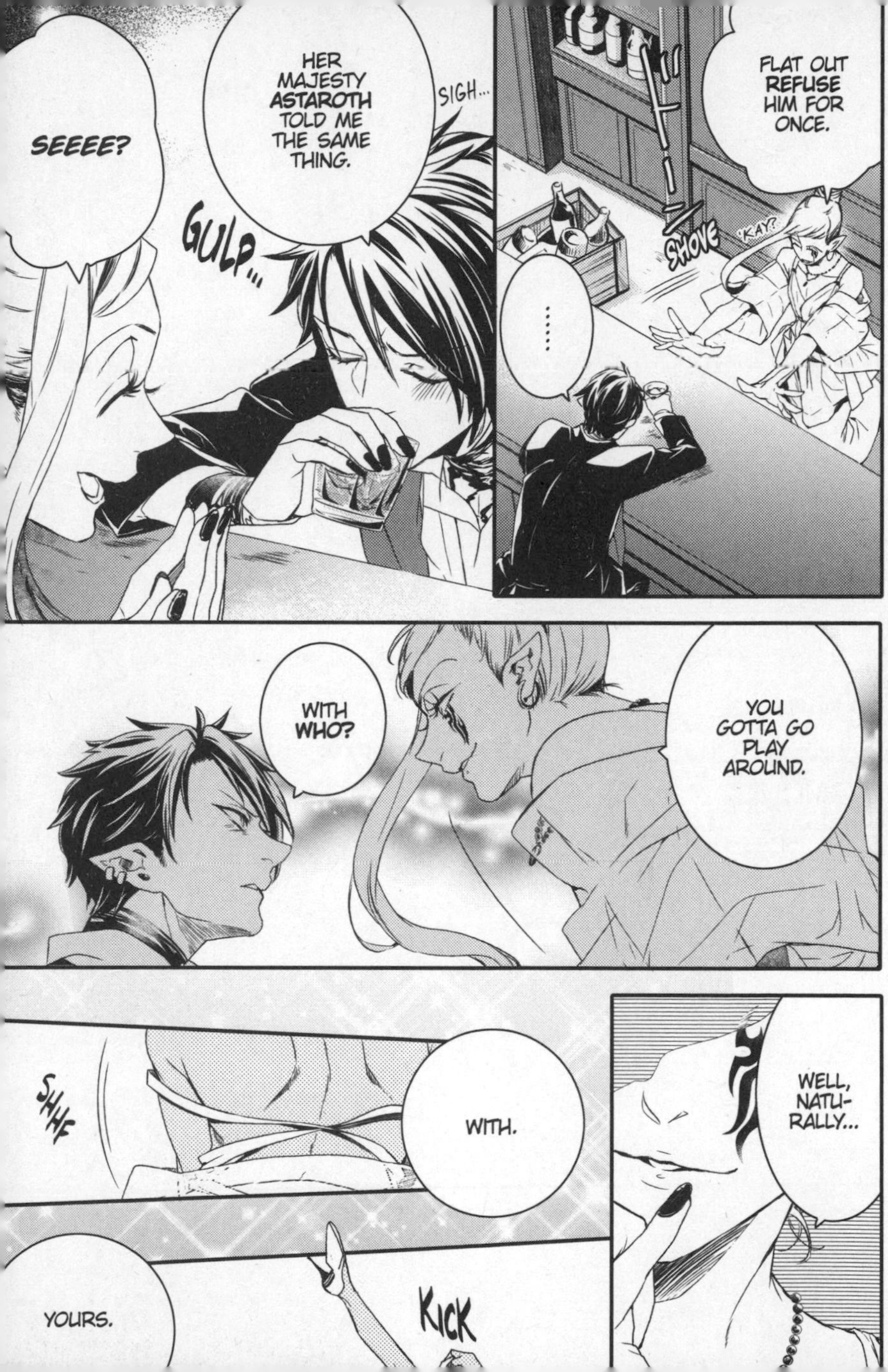
FLAT OUT REFUSE HIM FOR ONCE.
SHOVE
'KAY?
......
SIGH...
HER MAJESTY ASTAROTH TOLD ME THE SAME THING.
SEEEE?
GULP...
YOU GOTTA GO PLAY AROUND.
WITH WHO?
WELL, NATU-RALLY...
WITH.
SHHF
KICK
YOURS.

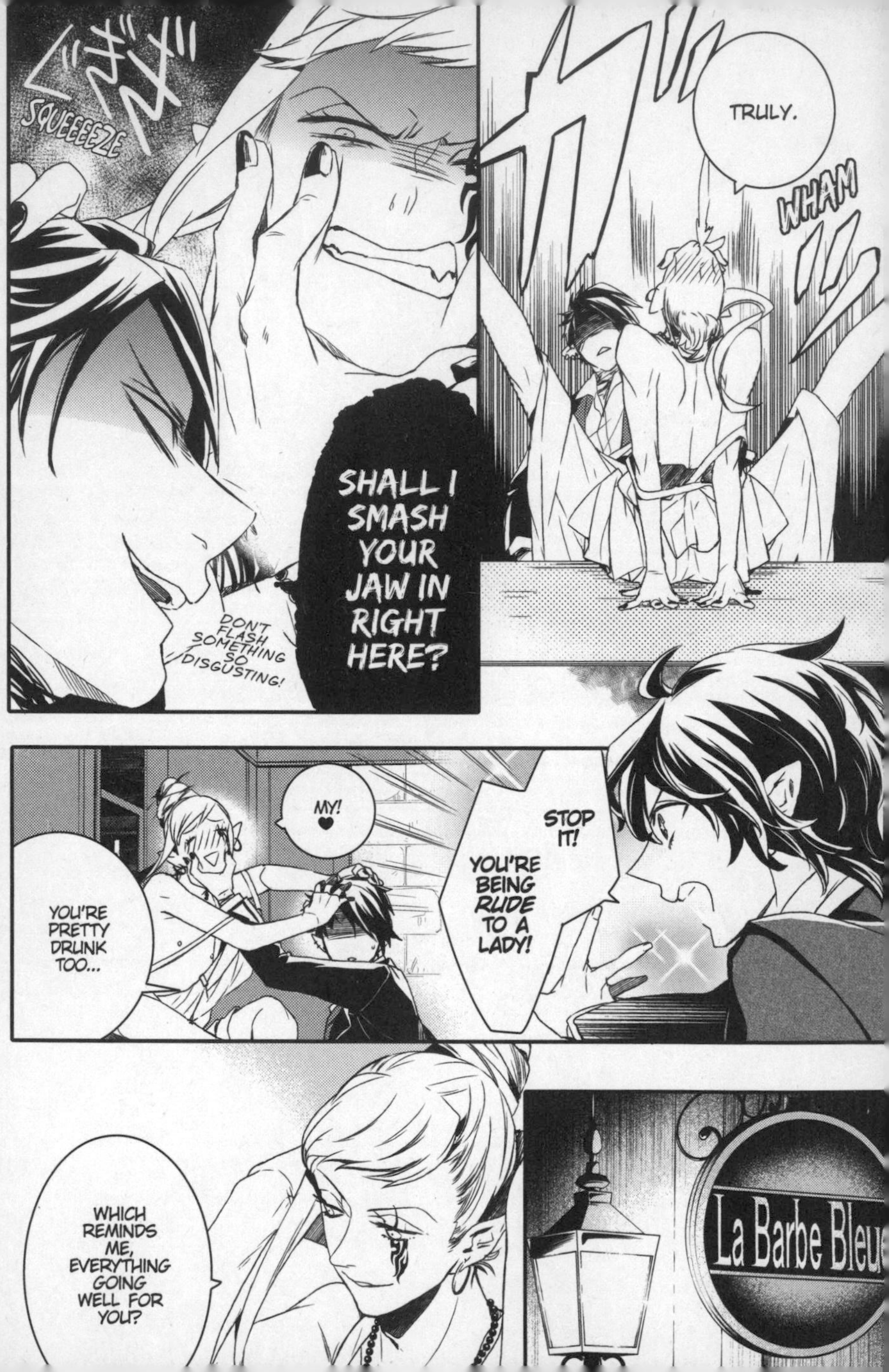
TRULY.
WHAM
SQUEEEEZE
SHALL I SMASH YOUR JAW IN RIGHT HERE?
DON'T FLASH SOMETHING SO DISGUSTING!
STOP IT!
YOU'RE BEING RUDE TO A LADY!
MY! ♥
YOU'RE PRETTY DRUNK TOO...
La Barbe Bleu
WHICH REMINDS ME, EVERYTHING GOING WELL FOR YOU?

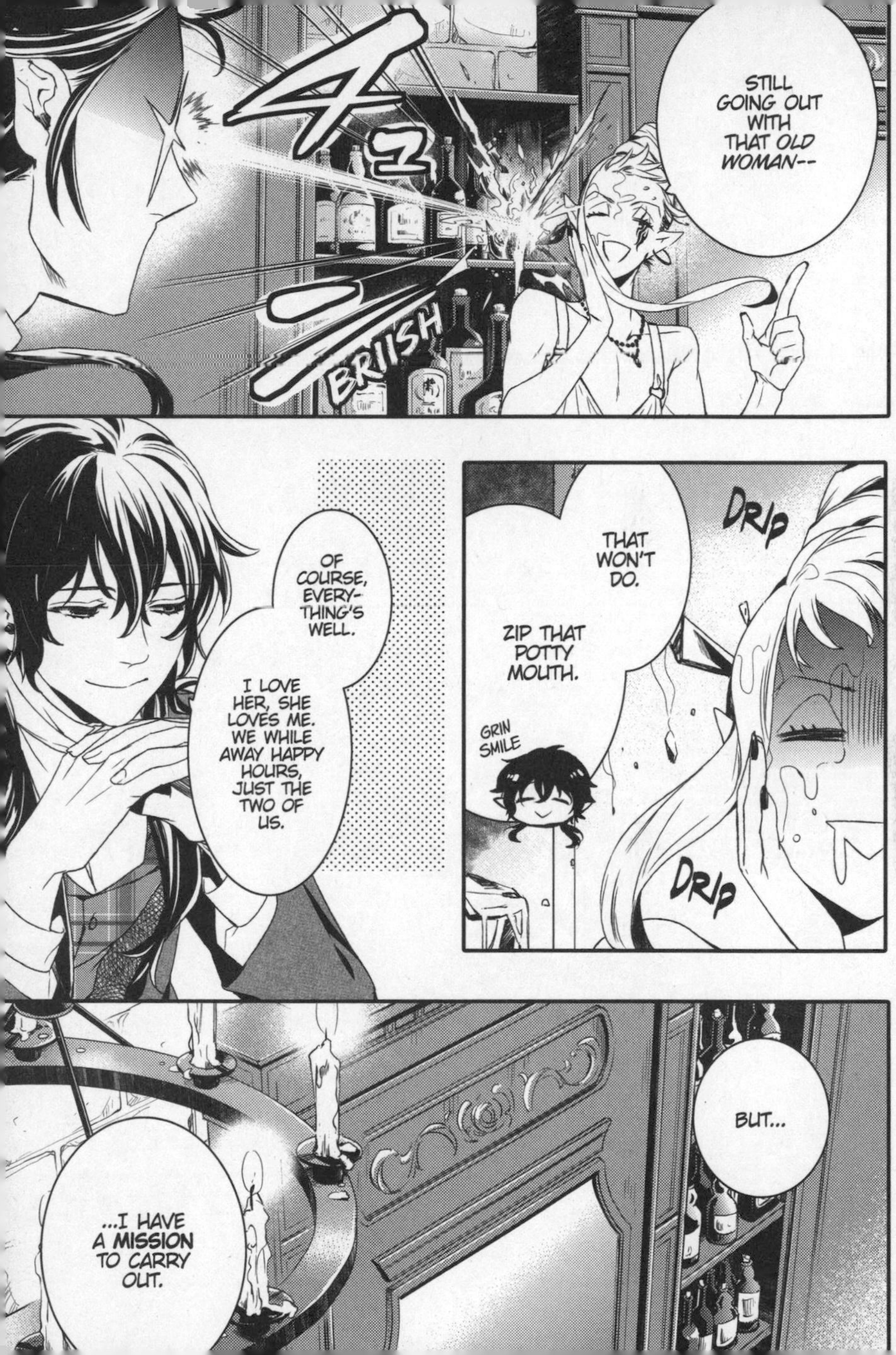
STILL GOING OUT WITH THAT OLD WOMAN--
BRIISH
DRIP
THAT WON'T DO.
ZIP THAT POTTY MOUTH.
GRIN SMILE
DRIP
OF COURSE, EVERY-THING'S WELL.
I LOVE HER, SHE LOVES ME. WE WHILE AWAY HAPPY HOURS, JUST THE TWO OF US.
BUT...
...I HAVE A MISSION TO CARRY OUT.

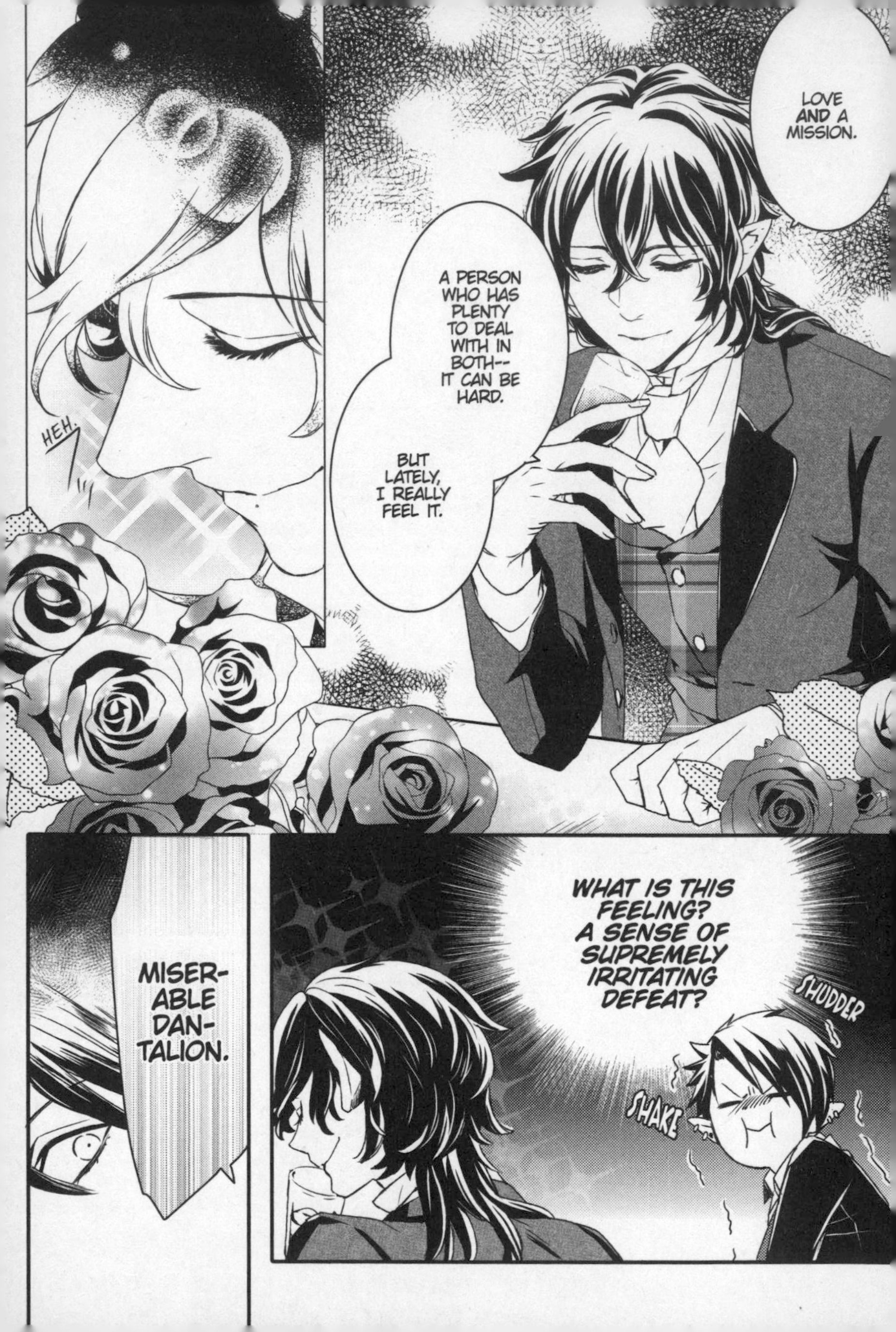
LOVE AND A MISSION.
A PERSON WHO HAS PLENTY TO DEAL WITH IN BOTH-- IT CAN BE HARD.
BUT LATELY, I REALLY FEEL IT.
HEH.
WHAT IS THIS FEELING? A SENSE OF SUPREMELY IRRITATING DEFEAT?
SHUDDER
SHAKE
MISER-ABLE DAN-TALION.

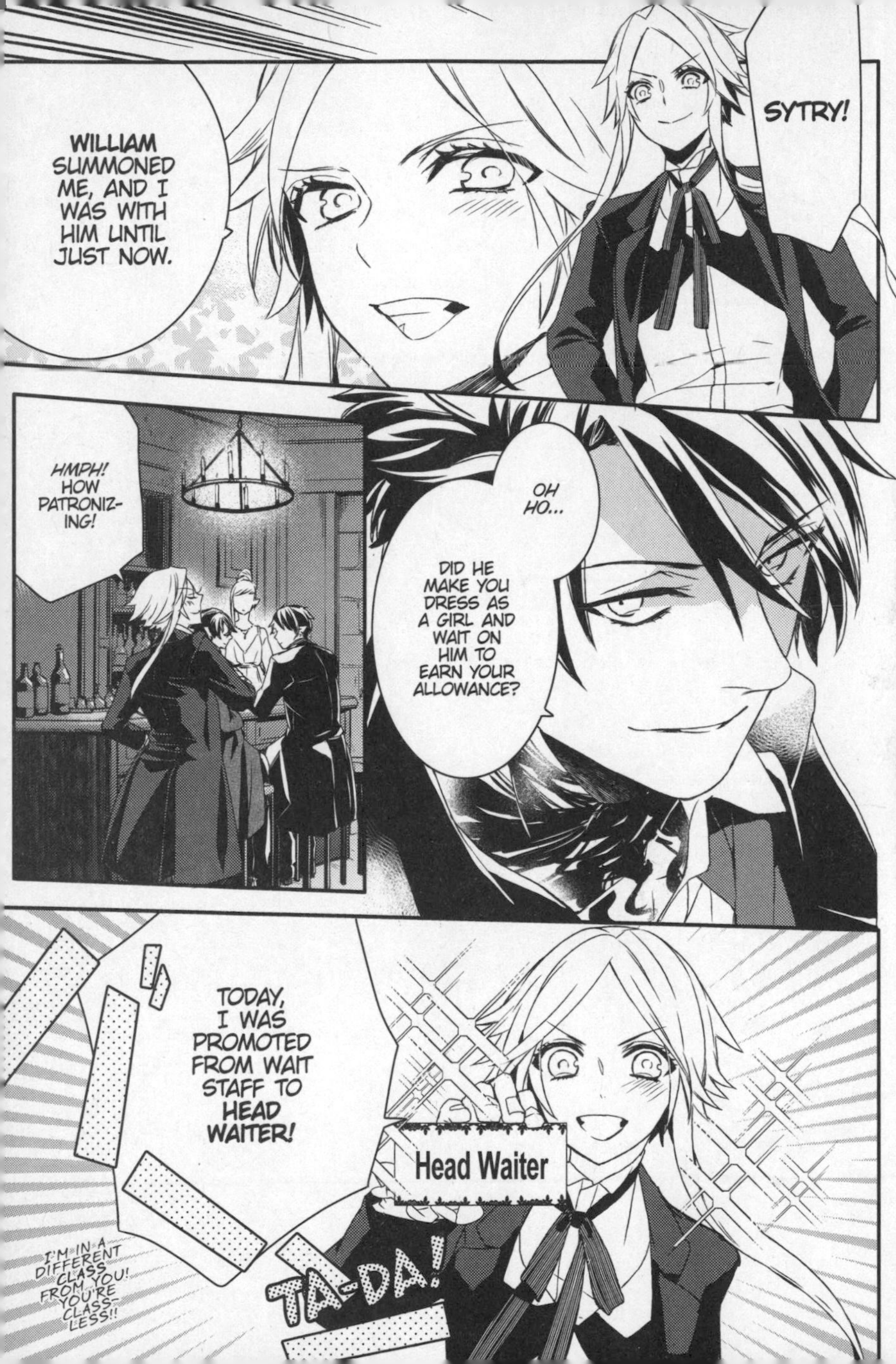
SYTRY!
WILLIAM SUMMONED ME, AND I WAS WITH HIM UNTIL JUST NOW.
OH HO...
DID HE MAKE YOU DRESS AS A GIRL AND WAIT ON HIM TO EARN YOUR ALLOWANCE?
HMPH! HOW PATRONIZ-ING!
TODAY, I WAS PROMOTED FROM WAIT STAFF TO HEAD WAITER!
Head Waiter
TA-DA!
I'M IN A DIFFERENT CLASS FROM YOU! YOU'RE CLASS-LESS!!

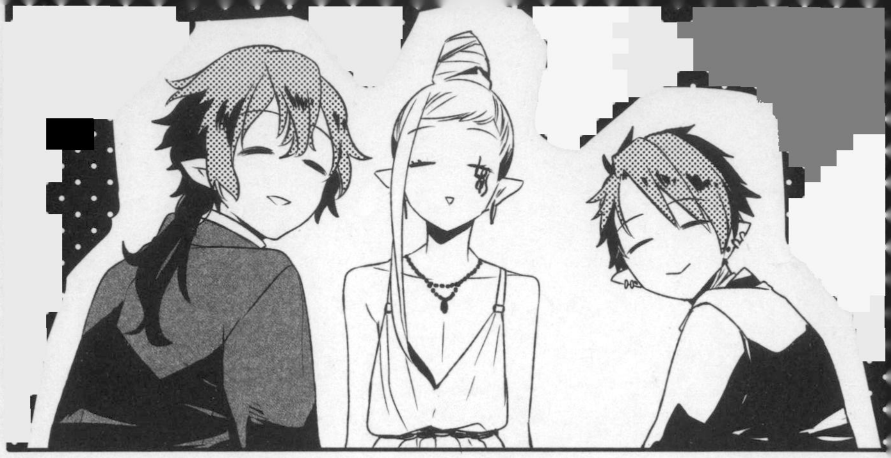

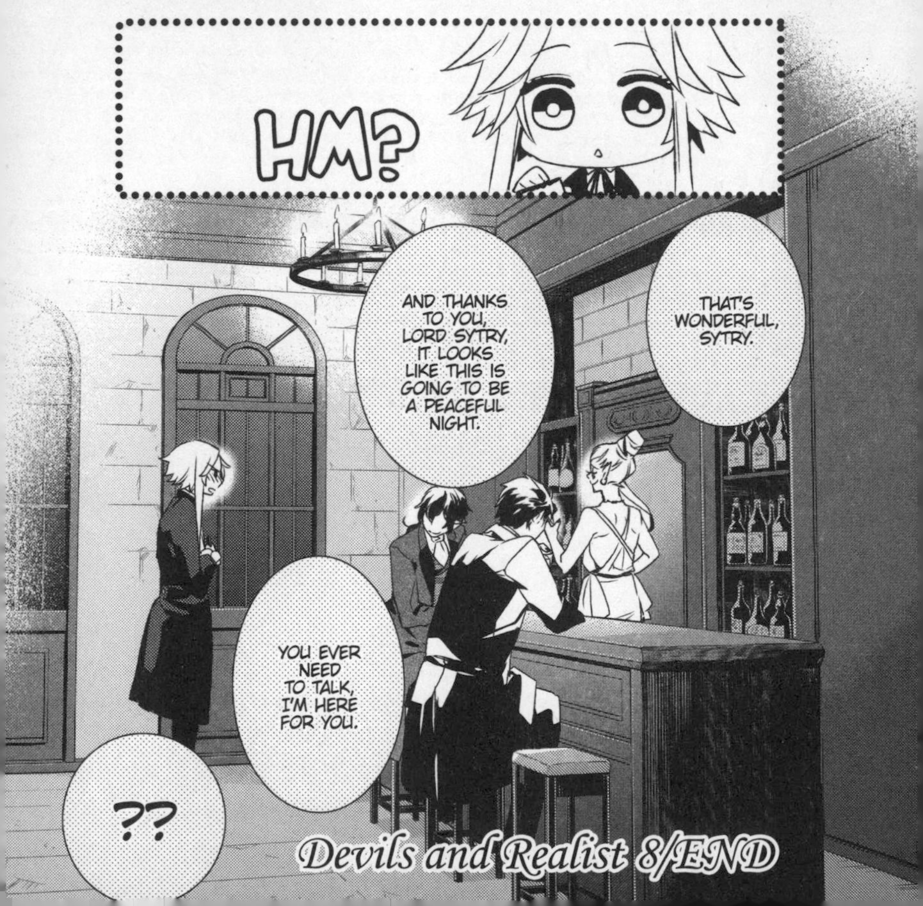
HM?
THAT'S WONDERFUL, SYTRY.
AND THANKS TO YOU, LORD SYTRY, IT LOOKS LIKE THIS IS GOING TO BE A PEACEFUL NIGHT.
YOU EVER NEED TO TALK, I'M HERE FOR YOU.
??
Devils and Realist 8/END

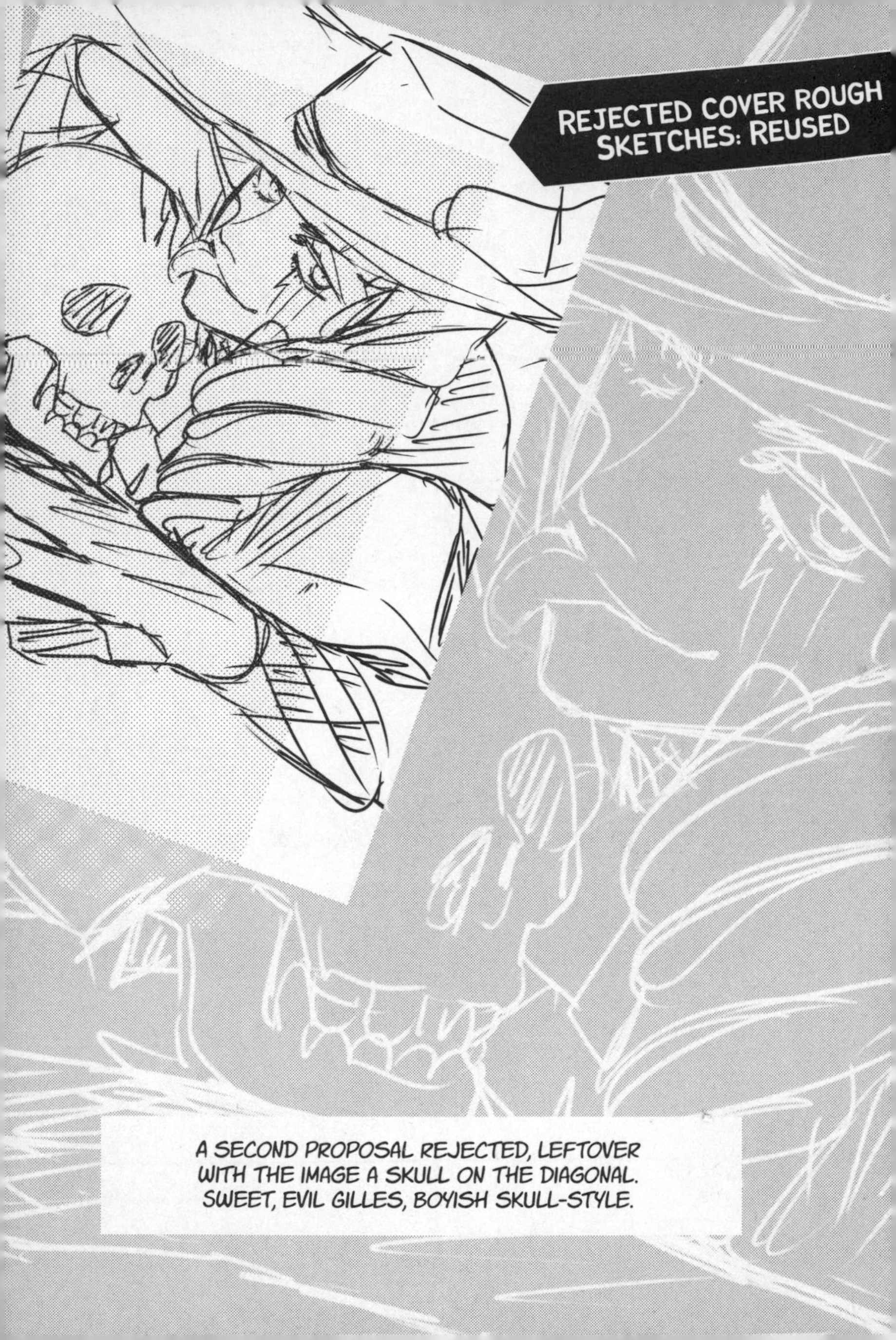
REJECTED COVER ROUGH SKETCHES: REUSED
A SECOND PROPOSAL REJECTED, LEFTOVER WITH THE IMAGE A SKULL ON THE DIAGONAL. SWEET, EVIL GILLES, BOYISH SKULL-STYLE.

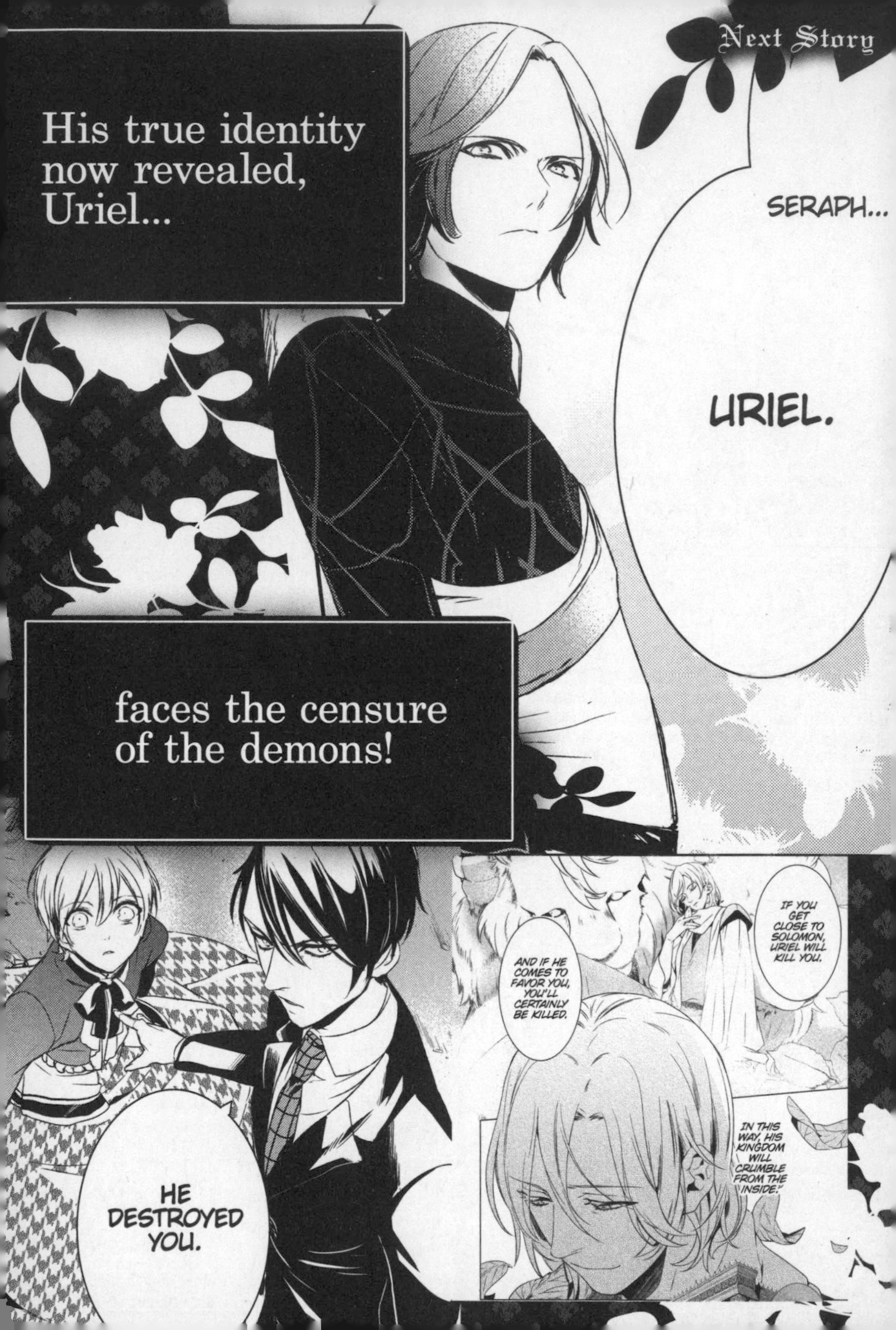
Next Story
SERAPH...
URIEL.
His true identity now revealed, Uriel...
faces the censure of the demons!
IF YOU GET CLOSE TO SOLOMON, URIEL WILL KILL YOU.
AND IF HE COMES TO FAVOR YOU, YOU'LL CERTAINLY BE KILLED.
IN THIS WAY, HIS KINGDOM WILL CRUMBLE FROM THE INSIDE."
HE DESTROYED YOU.

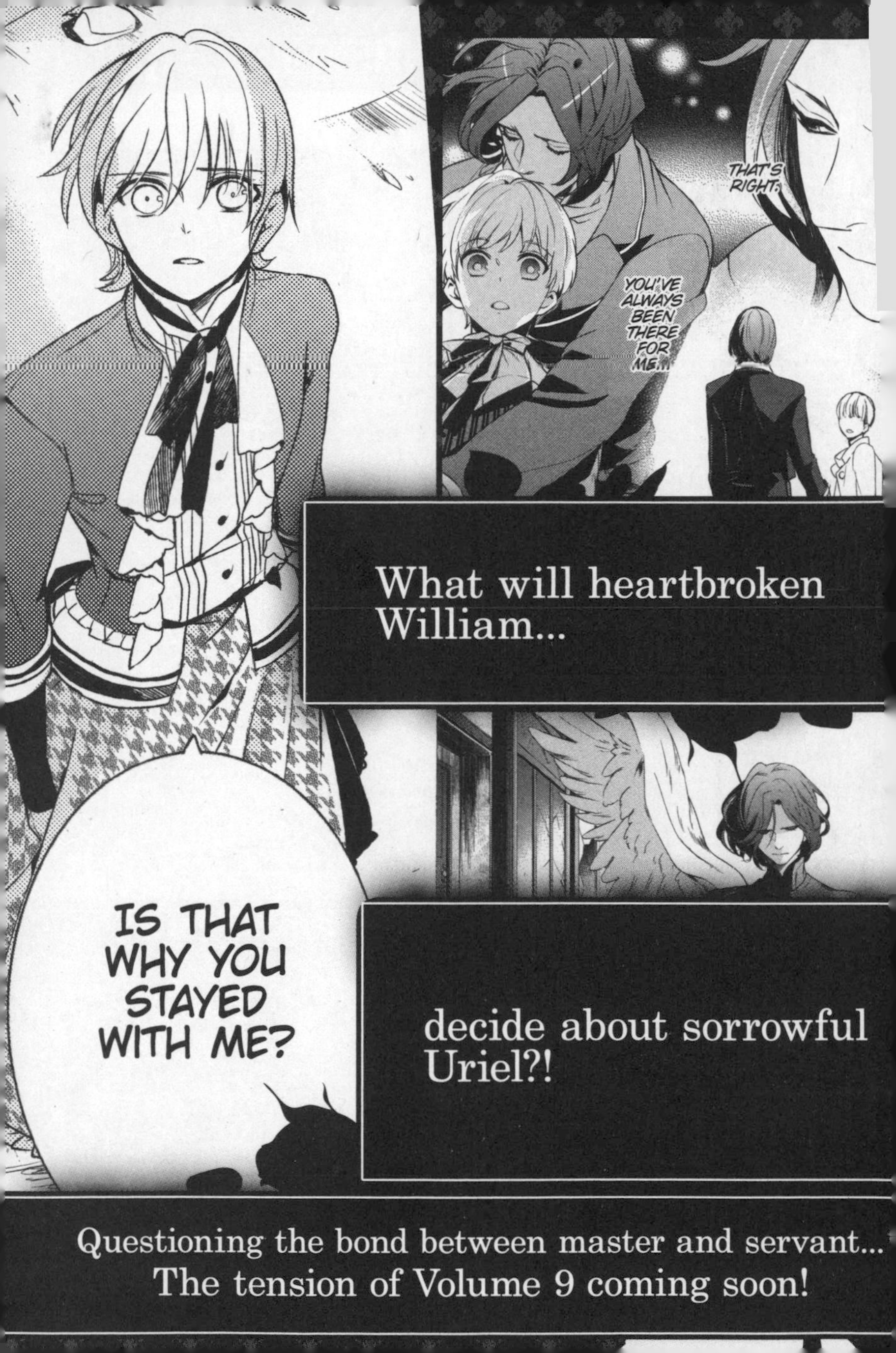
THAT'S RIGHT.
YOU'VE ALWAYS BEEN THERE FOR ME.
What will heartbroken William...
decide about sorrowful Uriel?!
IS THAT WHY YOU STAYED WITH ME?
Questioning the bond between master and servant...
The tension of Volume 9 coming soon!

SEVEN SEAS ENTERTA

Devils and Realist

art by UTAKO YUKIHIRO / story by MADOKA TAKADONO   VOLUME 8

TRANSLATION
Jocelyne Allen

ADAPTATION
Danielle King

LETTERING
Roland Amago

LAYOUT
Bambi Eloriaga-Amago

COVER DESIGN
Nicky Lim

PROOFREADER
Lee Otter

PRODUCTION MANAGER
Lissa Pattillo

EDITOR-IN-CHIEF
Adam Arnold

PUBLISHER
Jason DeAngelis

MAKAI OUJI: DEVILS AND REALIST VOL. 8
© Utako Yukihiro/Madoka Takadono 2014
First published in Japan in 2014 by ICHIJINSHA Inc., Tokyo.
English translation rights arranged with ICHIJINSHA Inc., Tokyo, Japan.

Seven Seas books may be purchased in bulk for educational, business, or
promotional use. For information on bulk purchases, please contact Macmillan
Corporate & Premium Sales Department at 1-800-221-7945 (ext 5442)
or write specialmarkets@macmillan.com.

Seven Seas and the Seven Seas logo are trademarks of
Seven Seas Entertainment, LLC. All rights reserved.

ISBN: 978-1-626921-81-8

Printed in Canada

First Printing: February 2016

10 9 8 7 6 5 4 3 2 1

FOLLOW US ONLINE: *www.gomanga.com*

READING DIRECTIONS

This book reads from *right to left*, Japanese style. If
this is your first time reading manga, you start
reading from the top right panel on each page and
take it from there. If you get lost, just follow the
numbered diagram here. It may seem backwards at
first, but you'll get the hang of it! Have fun!!

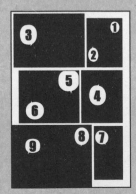